Communities in Cyberspace

In cyberspace, communication and co-ordination is cheap, fast, and global. With powerful new tools for interacting and organizing in the hands of millions of people worldwide, what kinds of social spaces and groups are people creating? How is the Internet changing our basic concepts of identity, self-governance and community?

This wide-ranging book looks at virtual communities in cyberspace and their relationship to communities in the physical world. The roles of race, gender, power, economics, and ethics in cyberspace are discussed by leading experts on the subject, and are grouped into four main sections:

- identity
- social order and control
- community structure and dynamics
- collective action

Communities in Cyberspace investigates how the idea of community is being challenged and rewritten by the widespread use of online interaction. This edited volume is an essential introduction to the landscape of social life in cyberspace. It will appeal to academics, students and professionals, and to those concerned about the changing relationship between information technology and society.

Contributors: Byron Burkhalter, Judith S. Donath, Milena Gulia, Laura J. Gurak, Peter Kollock, Christopher Mele, Jodi O'Brien, Elizabeth Reid, Anna DuVal Smith, Marc A. Smith, Willard Uncapher and Barry Wellman.

Marc A. Smith is a doctoral student in sociology at the University of California, Los Angeles. **Peter Kollock** is Associate Professor of Sociology at the University of California, Los Angeles. Both have lectured widely on the history and development of cyberspace.

LONDON AND NEW YORK

Communities in Cyberspace

Edited by

- Marc A. Smith and
- Peter Kollock

First published 1999
by Routledge
11 New Fetter Lane, London EC4P 4EE

Simultaneously published in the USA and
Canada
by Routledge
29 West 35th Street, New York, NY 10001

Reprinted 2000

Routledge is an imprint of the Taylor & Francis Group

© 1999 Selection and editorial Marc A. Smith
and Peter Kollock; individual chapters, the
contributors

Typeset in Perpetua by Keystroke, Jacaranda
Lodge, Wolverhampton
Printed and bound in Great Britain by TJ
International Ltd, Padstow, Cornwall

British Library Cataloguing in Publication Data
A catalogue record for this book is available
from the British Library

Library of Congress Cataloging in Publication Data
Communities in cyberspace / [edited by]
Marc A. Smith and Peter Kollock.
    p.   cm.
Includes bibliographical references and
index.
1. Computer networks – Social aspects.
2. Internet (Computer network) – Social
aspects.   3. Interpersonal relations.
4. Social problems.   5. Social control.
6. Technology and civilization.
    I. Smith, Marc A.   II. Kollock, Peter.
HQ1178.C65   1999
303.48'33–dc21   98–2657
                                    CIP

ISBN 0–415–19139–4 (hbk)
ISBN 0–415–19140–8 (pbk)

Contents

Part one

INTRODUCTION

Part two

IDENTITY

Part five

COLLECTIVE ACTION

Figures and tables

Figures

Tables

Contributors

Byron Burkhalter is completing his dissertation in sociology at the University of California, Los Angeles; he is also an assistant professor of Social Science at Santa Monica College where he teaches race and ethnic relations.

Judith S. Donath is an assistant professor at the MIT Media Laboratory, where she directs the sociable media research group, which builds innovative interfaces for the online communities.

Milena Gulia is completing her doctorate in sociology at the University of Toronto; her interests include immigration, housing and sociology of community.

Laura J. Gurak is an associate professor in the Scientific and Technical Communication Program, University of Minnesota and is a rhetorical critic who specializes in the relationship between language and technology.

Peter Kollock is associate professor of sociology at the University of California, Los Angeles; his research focuses on cooperation and collective action, online communities and markets, and economic sociology.

Christopher Mele is assistant professor of sociology at the State University of New York at Buffalo where his speciality is urban and community sociology.

Jodi O'Brien is associate professor of sociology at Seattle University; her research interests include communities, inequalities, sexual politics and social psychology.

Elizabeth Reid is a doctoral student at Royal Melbourne Institute of Technology and a postgraduate fellow of Telstra Research Laboratories. Her research interest is the development of graphical virtual worlds.

CONTRIBUTORS

Anna DuVal Smith is a labour mediator and arbitrator in private practice; she is a member of the adjunct faculty of the Weatherhead School of Management, Case Western Reserve University.

Marc A. Smith studies sociology at the University of California, Los Angeles, specializing in the structure, dynamics and life cycles of social cyberspaces and online communities.

Willard Uncapher is a doctoral candidate at the University of Texas at Austin, College of Communication, where he has concentrated on issues of globalization, media history, cultural complexity and critical studies.

Barry Wellman is professor of sociology at the University of Toronto and has been studying communities as non-local social networks since 1967.

Acknowledgments

We would like to thank our editor, Mari Shullaw, and the staff at Routledge for their help and support at every step of the publication process. We also greatly appreciate the comments of the reviewers of this book. As always, such projects exact an unreasonable cost on one's family. Marc would like to thank Christine Morton and Eli Smith-Morton for their enduring support; Peter is ever grateful to his partner, Jennifer Lowe, for offline support and understanding. We contributed equally to the production of this volume; our names appear in random order.

Part one

Introduction

Chapter 1

Communities in cyberspace

Peter Kollock and Marc A. Smith

> The sociologists are going to love the next 100 years.
>
> John C. Dvorak (1996)

Since 1993, computer networks have grabbed enormous public attention. The major news and entertainment media have been filled with stories about the "information superhighway" and of the financial and political fortunes to be made on it. Computer sales continue to rise and more and more people are getting connected to "the Net."[1] Computer networks, once an obscure and arcane set of technologies used by a small elite, are now widely used and the subject of political debate, public interest, and popular culture. The "information superhighway" competes with a collection of metaphors that attempt to label and define these technologies. Others, like "cyberspace," "the Net," "online," and "the Web," highlight different aspects of network technology and its meaning, role, and impact. Whichever term is used, it is clear that computer networks allow people to create a range of new social spaces in which to meet and interact with one another.

Instead of people talking to machines, computer networks are being used to connect people to people (Wellman *et al.* 1996).[2] In cyberspace the economies of interaction, communication, and coordination are different than when people meet face-to-face. These shifts make the creation of thousands of spaces to house conversations and exchanges between far-flung groups of people practical and convenient. Using network interaction media like email, chat, and conferencing systems like the Usenet, people have formed thousands of groups to discuss a range of topics, play games, entertain one another, and even work on a range of complex collective projects. These are not only communication media – they are group media, sustaining and supporting many-to-many interactions (Licklider *et al.* 1978; Harasim 1993).

What kinds of social spaces do people create with networks? Two opposing visions are popular. One highlights the positive effects of networks and their benefits for democracy and prosperity. A prominent proponent is Al Gore (1993), who captures this vision by saying, "Our new ways of communicating will entertain as well as inform. More importantly, they will educate, promote democracy, and save lives. And in the process they will also create a lot of new jobs. In fact, they're already doing it." The promise is that networks will create new places of assembly that will generate opportunities for employment, political participation, social contact, and entertainment. At their best, networks are said to renew community by strengthening the bonds that connect us to the wider social world while simultaneously increasing our power in that world.

An alternative view notes that this glowing vision is in part driven by significant investments in public relations, advertising, and political rhetoric.[3] Critics see a darker outcome in which individuals are trapped and ensnared in a "net" that predominantly offers new opportunities for surveillance and social control. For Theodore Roszak (1986: xii), "information technology has the obvious capacity to concentrate political power, to create new forms of social obfuscation and domination." While these critics do not rule out the idea that computers and networks increase the power of individuals, they believe that networks will disproportionately increase the strength of existing concentrations of power.

The chapters in this volume share a common understanding that the kinds of interactions and institutions that are emerging in cyberspace are more complicated than can be captured in one-sided utopian or dystopian terms. These chapters do not ask whether online interaction is "good" or "bad." Our focus is on describing and analyzing patterns of online social interaction and organization as they exist.

The Internet is a strategic research site in which to study fundamental social processes. It provides a level of access to the details of social life and a durability of the traces of social interaction that is unprecedented.[4] We use this research site to investigate how social action and organization change as they are refracted through online inter-action. How do the economies (taking that term very broadly) of social life shift? What becomes easier to do? What becomes more difficult? And what are the aggregate consequences of these changes? The outcomes are not uniformly positive or negative. The new opportunities and constraints online interaction creates are doubled-edged, leading to results that can amplify both beneficial and noxious social processes.

Technology has its most profound effect when it alters the ways in which people come together and communicate. In this volume, we focus on computer network systems that directly support the interaction of people with other people. Before we turn to a discussion of the chapters in this volume, we review the types of systems discussed here and offer some technical background.

The landscape of cyberspace

Each online communication system structures interaction in a particular way, in some cases with dramatic effect on the types of social organizations that emerge from people using them. We examine in turn email and discussion lists, Usenet and BBSs, text chat, MUDs, World Wide Web (WWW) sites, and graphical worlds.

Email and discussion lists

Email and discussion lists are the oldest and most popular form of interaction on the Internet.[5] Email allows an individual to send a message directly to another person. However, email is often used to go beyond a one-to-one interaction. In an email discussion list a message sent to a group address is then copied and sent to all the email addresses on a list. When people direct a series of messages and responses to the list, a group discussion can develop. As of 1998, there are tens of millions of email users and thousands of public mailing lists as well as hundreds of thousands of less formal discussion lists in existence.[6] These lists are maintained for the discussion and distribution of information on thousands of topics. This may be the most common form of group interaction on the Internet, and a number of lists contain thousands or tens of thousands of members.

Email discussion lists have some important qualities that distinguish them from other Internet communication tools. Email lists are typically owned by a single individual or small group. Since all messages sent to the list must pass through a single point, email lists offer their owners significant control over who can contribute to their group. List owners can personally review all requests to be added to a list, can forbid anyone from contributing to the list if they are not on the list themselves, and even censor specific messages that they do not want broadcast to the list as a whole. Because active review requires significant time and effort, most email lists are run as open spaces, allowing anyone to join the list and anyone to contribute to it. Still, even open lists can be selectively closed or controlled by their owners when faced with disruption. Most email lists operate as benign dictatorships sustained by the monopoly power that the list owner wields over the boundaries and content of their group. As a result, email lists are often distinguished by their relatively more ordered and focused activity.

Usenet and BBSs

Email discussion lists are asynchronous media. Interaction is structured into turns, but a reply may occur minutes or months after the prior turn. There are a number of benefits to asynchronous interaction. A group can interact without everyone gathering at a particular time. As a result people on very different schedules or in distant time zones can still exchange messages and sustain discussions.

Bulletin board systems (BBSs – also known as conferencing systems) are another form of asynchronous communication that refine email discussion lists in a number of ways. Most BBSs allow participants to create topical groups in which a series of messages, similar to email messages, can be strung together one after another. There are a number of conferencing systems. Well-known ones include the Usenet, the WELL (picospan),

ECHO (caucus), and the bulletin board discussion groups run on the commercial online services such as America Online and the Microsoft Network. Each sustains a wide collection of topics of discussion and an ongoing give-and-take between participants. BBSs differ from email discussion lists in another way. Email is a "push" media – messages are sent to people without them necessarily doing anything. In contrast, conferencing systems are "pull" media – people must select groups and messages they want to read and actively request them.

The Usenet is the largest conferencing system and has a unique form of social organization. The Usenet is composed of a distributed database of messages that is passed through an informal global network of systems that agree to a standard message format. As of 1998, tens of thousands of "newsgroups" are carried over the Usenet, each containing from a few dozen to tens of thousands of messages. On an average day tens of thousands of different people contribute hundreds of thousands of messages to the Usenet. A new site "joins" the Usenet simply by finding any existing site that is willing to pass along a copy of the daily "feed" (the collection of messages it receives). As a result, the Usenet has no central authority, no single source of power that can enforce boundaries and police behavior. No one owns most Usenet newsgroups; most newsgroups are anarchic in the technical sense of the term – they have no central authority though they do have an order and structure. Almost anyone can read the contents of a Usenet newsgroup, create entirely new newsgroups, or contribute to one.[7] This makes the Usenet a more interesting and challenging social space than systems that are ruled by central authorities. Whatever order exists in the Usenet is the product of a delicate balance between individual freedom and collective good. Many newsgroups are wild, unordered places, but what is startling is how many are well organized and productive.

Text chat

Text chat differs from email lists and BBSs in that it supports synchronous communication – a number of people can chat in real time by sending lines of text to one another. Chat is one of the most popular forms of interaction on the Internet, and accounts for a sizeable proportion of the revenue of the commercial online providers such as America Online. Text chat is often organized around the idea of channels on a text-based "Citizens' Band (CB) radio" system. Most chat systems support a great number of "channels" dedicated to a vast array of subjects and interests.

Text chat also uses a centralized server that grants the server owner a great deal of power over access to the system and to individual channels. In the commercial chat services, chat channels frequently are policed by the provider's staff or by appointed volunteers. In the largest non-commercial system – Internet Relay Chat (IRC) – each channel has an owner who can eject people from the channel, control who enters the channel, and decide how many people can enter.

MUDs

Email discussion lists and conferencing systems are based on the models of postal mail and bulletin boards. Text chat is based on the model of CB radio. In contrast, Multi-User Domains or Dungeons (MUDs) attempt to model physical places as well as face-to-face interaction.[8] MUDs are text-based virtual realities that maintain a sense of space by linking different "rooms" together. MUDs grew out of interest in adventure-style games that presented a textual description of different rooms and the objects in them and allowed the player to move from room to room, take and drop objects, and do things such as fight dragons and solve puzzles. With the growing availability of networked computers on university campuses in the late 1970s, MUDs were developed to allow people to play Adventure games with other people instead of against computers.

Since the early 1980s MUDs have become increasingly sophisticated and complex. Modern social MUDs allow users to build new spaces, create objects, and to use powerful programming languages to automate their behavior. While many MUDs continue to focus on combat role-playing, many "social" MUDs have become a means for widely dispersed groups to maintain personal contact. MUDs incorporate a range of other modes of communication like email and discussion groups to link users with other users. But like text chat, their key quality is that they support synchronous communication – people interact with each other in real time. MUDs allow a number of people in the same "room" to meet and talk by sending lines of text to one another. MUDs often support simulations of the multi-channel quality and nuances of face-to-face interaction by framing the lines of text users send to one another as "say," "think," or "emote" messages. This allows users to provide meta-commentary on their turns of talk and to create "gestures" or make parenthetical comments.

Like email lists, MUDs are typically owned by the individual or group that provides the hardware and software and the technical skill needed to maintain the system. Because these skills and resources have until very recently been rare, owners of MUD servers have had nearly complete control over the system. MUD owners are often referred to as "Gods." Gods can delegate their power in whole or in part to selected participants, who commonly take on the status of "Wizards." Other users can be granted more access to the computer's memory and network capacity, allowing them to build larger and more elaborate virtual spaces and objects. Users can be granted or denied the right to enter the MUD, be given the power to build new objects or enter specific rooms, and can have limited abilities to communicate with other users. MUDs can contain sophisticated forms of social stratification and elaborate hierarchies.

World Wide Web sites

While the World Wide Web has been hugely popular for some time, it is only more recently that it has become a site for interaction. In its original incarnation, the Web served as a powerful way of accessing and linking documents. Web sites can now support both asynchronous and synchronous communication. Through the use of various software tools, Web sites can host asynchronous discussion groups as well as real-time text chat.

Because of its graphical user interface and the ability to integrate images and sounds, Web sites can create a more intuitive and richer context for text chat. As navigating through a Web site is a familiar experience for most online users, entering into a discussion can be easier than learning a propriety system on a BBS. In addition, Web sites can increase the channels of communication, setting the mood or style of the interaction through layout design, images, and sounds.

Web sites can also serve as a separate supplement to text-based communities. For example, a number of MUDs have elaborate Web sites that are used to collect images and documents related to the MUD, as well as links to the personal Web pages of its members. While text communication can be a very powerful form of interaction, the fact that MUDs establish Web sites suggests that the Web's interface and graphical design provide important benefits.

Graphical worlds

As computing power and network bandwidth increase, the kind of media that people can use to interact with one another expands to include images, sound, and two- or three-dimensional models of spaces. Real-time video and audio interaction tools have developed, as have online interaction systems that integrate text chat with a visual representation of each participant (often called "avatars") and some representation of a place. Some of these graphical worlds allow people to engage in a real-time audio conversation, a high-tech return to the low-tech telephone party line.

As these systems become more sophisticated they have taken on some of the characteristics of other older media. For example, WorldsAway (www.worldsaway.com) – a descendant of the earliest graphical interaction system, Habitat – has developed a social structure similar to that found in MUDs. In WorldsAway, some users become "acolytes" who serve as helpers in the community and have a higher status than regular members. For other users a token economy adds another form of social stratification, creating virtual millionaires as well as beggars.

While these new graphical spaces present interesting research possibilities, the case studies in this volume all concentrate on text-based social systems. This was done because text-based systems have been in existence much longer than graphical systems. Hence, social interaction and groups in text-based systems have a longer history, are often more developed and elaborated, and there is a greater variety of textual online social spaces to compare and contrast. Most of the lessons drawn in these case studies of text-based interaction are also applicable to the emerging graphical worlds.

Each of the parts in this volume explores the implications of online interaction in terms of a key concept, and each part builds on the previous one. The chapters are organized into four major groups. We treat in turn issues of identity, social order and control, community structure and dynamics, and collective action.

Identity

We begin with a consideration of identity, the basic building block of social interaction. All of our interactions, even those with strangers, are shaped by our sense of with whom we are interacting. In face-to-face and telephone interactions there are a wealth of cues of varying reliability to indicate our identity and our intentions. Our clothes, voices, bodies, and gestures signal messages about status, power, and group membership. We rely on our ability to recognize fellow group members in order to know who we can turn to and what we can expect. Our ability to identify others also allows us to hold individuals accountable for their actions.

Online interaction strips away many of the cues and signs that are part of face-to-face interaction. This poverty of signals is both a limitation and a resource, making certain kinds of interaction more difficult but also providing room to play with one's identity. The resulting ambiguity over identity has been a source of inspiration to many who believe that because people's physical appearance is not manifest online (yet), individuals will be judged by the merit of their ideas, rather than by their gender, race, class, or age. But others (including authors in this volume) argue that traditional status hierarchies and inequalities are reproduced in online interaction and perhaps are even magnified. In Part 2 we examine how identity is established online as well as the durability of the institutions of race and gender in online interaction.

Honesty and deception

How is identity – true or counterfeit – established in online communities? This question is at the heart of Judith Donath's chapter on "Identity and deception in the virtual community." Deception can bring great benefits, but deception is useful only if some members of a community honestly signal what sort of person they are. A signal that is used deceptively by an entire population carries no information. Donath thus asks what maintains the balance between honest and deceptive signaling, and makes the point that some signals are inherently difficult to mimic.

A signal is inherently reliable to the extent that it is more costly for mimics to emit than it is for those who actually possess the quality. A classic example is conspicuous consumption as a signal of wealth. A person of limited financial means will find it very difficult to display the chauffeur-driven limousine, mansion, and other signals of wealth.[9] To take an example from the Internet, one's proficiency as a programmer can be signaled by including an example of one's work in a Usenet posting. Indeed, there is a convention in the Usenet newsgroup alt.hackers of including a clever hack in each post to establish one's identity as a skilled hacker and to keep out impostors. Signals that are to some degree inherently reliable are called assessment signals. This is in contrast to conventional signals, which have no necessary connection to the trait they advertise (e.g. simply stating one is wealthy or a skilled programmer).

With these issues as a background, Donath then goes on to dissect the anatomy of a Usenet post in order to examine how identity is established or concealed. The first source of clues is the account name itself. Although a seemingly sparse source of information, Donath demonstrates how much can be squeezed out of this basic ID. Knowledgeable members of the Internet realize that each domain name has its own reputation and recognize the different implications of commercial versus institutional accounts. The content of the post contains its own set of signals about the identity of the author. The writing style, the facts that are brought forth, the proper use of abbreviations and argot that are specific to the group, all help establish or challenge the user's identity. At the end of each post is a signature which has also become an important element in establishing an identity. Signatures are a combination of business cards and bumper stickers that members use to display their interests, opinions, and occupation. By providing the address of one's company and position, the signature can help establish one's credentials and create the possibility of accountability (one can check the company to verify the information). Donath also provides a number of fascinating examples of the use of codes or esoteric knowledge as a way of establishing one's identity. Another common element that is now seen in signatures is the address to the author's Web page. The simple link to a Web page is significant in a number of ways. By providing a link to a detailed document, the author is able to establish his or her identity in a very elaborate way. The fact that an elaborate set of Web pages represent a substantial investment of time and effort may also have the effect of encouraging identity persistence – throwing away an alias used in previous postings may be a trivial act, but dismantling a set of Web pages and constructing a new set may involve costs that the author is not willing to bear.

There is yet another source of identity information: the author's history of previous posts on the Internet. Interaction on the Net leaves a trace of varying durability. Posts to Usenet discussion groups can usually be accessed for a few weeks and some groups maintain archives of past discussion. The search for the traces of someone's past interactions has changed radically in recent years with the development of extremely powerful search engines and durable, extensive databases.

Donath raises two extremely important issues at the end of her chapter: to what extent can online interaction and communities be structured so as to encourage honest signaling and identity persistence? And to what extent is a known, stable identity a desirable thing for the person and for the community?

The persistence of race

An early promise of online interaction was that it would render irrelevant such markers as race, gender, status, and age. Because online interaction strips away physical markers, the assumption was that social categories assumed to rest on physical characteristics would wither away. The next two chapters argue against this view, taking as their focus race and gender respectively.

As Byron Burkhalter points out in "Reading race online: discovering racial identity in Usenet discussions," the connection between racial identity and the physical body has been so strong that it is simply taken for granted in most settings. Yet racial identity can be an ambiguous thing even in face-to-face interaction. Indeed, Burkhalter argues provocatively that race does not disappear online and that "racial identity is no more ambiguous online than offline. . . . Certainty of racial identity offline or online is always contingent – absolute proof is not available and rarely necessary."

At the same time, Burkhalter believes that online interaction does change the dynamics of racial identity, shifting how racial identification is achieved and how stereotypes operate. In online interaction racial identity springs from a participant's perspective on racial issues rather than from physical cues. The reliance on a participant's written words as a source of racial identity also reverses the usual sequence in stereotyping. Burkhalter argues that in online interaction, an individual's beliefs and attitudes are used to make inferences about the individual's race, rather than the more familiar route of inferring attitudes based on physical racial cues.

Burkhalter goes on to examine how racial identity is achieved, maintained, questioned, and reestablished in Usenet discussion groups. Using the soc.culture.african. american discussion group as his case study, he examines how any topic can potentially be framed as race-relevant and how this link to racial identity can ebb and flow during the course of a discussion.

While any racial identity might be claimed in this textual world, this does not guarantee that others in the group will acknowledge or support the claimed identity. Racial identity, Burkhalter argues, is interactionally negotiated – people do not create racial identities by themselves and the identity portrayed in a posting might be accepted or vigorously contested by other members in the group. Sometimes a group member will attempt to cast the poster in another identity as a way of challenging the poster's arguments. Burkhalter reports that this is a common method of challenging a person, and that arguments often center around what identity a poster can reasonably claim rather than directly challenging a poster's arguments and views.

The structure of the Usenet also makes it a useful research site for studying the dynamics of group boundaries. Because messages can easily be crossposted to other groups, the audience for a discussion can rapidly expand or contract, drawing in other groups with different identities at stake. Burkhalter points out that a discussion that remains within soc.culture.african.american can make use of fine-grained racial distinctions that are a meaningful framework for members within the group. However, once another newsgroup becomes involved in the discussion, such distinctions tend to collapse as each group orients itself in a monolithic manner toward the other group. Within-group variation is attenuated while across-group differences are accentuated.

The conservatism of cyberspace

The most optimistic proponents of the Internet have argued that gender, race, and age become unimportant in online interaction. At the very least, many assume that the absence of these markers will provide the opportunity to explore and invent alternate identities.

Jodi O'Brien sharply contests this view in her chapter on "Writing in the body: gender (re)production in online interaction." O'Brien argues that gender is such a central feature for organizing interpersonal relations that persons go to great pains to reproduce gender in online interaction. "Are you male or female?" is such a commonly asked question that it was long ago abbreviated to "RUMorF?" Significantly, no such abbreviations are in widespread use for questions concerning age, height, weight, socio-economic status, etc. Gender is the one characteristic of our embodied lives that is a central feature in interaction throughout the Internet.

And it is not simply that gender is reintroduced in a world without physical markers. O'Brien makes the striking point that gender is reintroduced in a more limited and stereotypical manner than exists in embodied interaction. There are no limitations to how one might describe oneself in cyberspace. Yet the gender descriptions one encounters on the Internet show far less variation and imagination than occurs in face-to-face interaction. People recreate themselves as stereotypical ideals, and O'Brien points out that this "hyper-gendering" is especially prevalent among those who attempt to "cross-dress" (i.e. males presenting themselves as females). The implication is that a world without constraints has led to greater homogeneity rather than new forms of identity.

The attention given to the possibility that someone might be gender-switching points out the crucial importance of gender identity in cyberspace. The fear is that a close friend or the object of one's seduction is not "really" the gender they present themselves as. The debate as to whether and when gender-switching is appropriate has led to a vocabulary of motives (Mills 1940) that makes crossing acceptable as a way of avoiding harassment or experimenting with a new perspective, but inappropriate if there is an intent to "deceive." This is hardly a clear line, and one person's experimentation is another person's deceit.

There is a deeper tension. O'Brien points out that there is strain between those who view online interaction as an opportunity to "perform" a variety of perhaps fabricated roles versus those who see cyberspace as a new communication medium between "real people." O'Brien argues that the distinction between the intent to "be" and the intent to "perform" may be much more useful than discussions about what is real versus non-real, or honest versus deceitful. She concludes that "the most contested issue at the moment in the history of online communication may be how to establish ways of underscoring real versus fictitious sites so that users can reliably distinguish 'real authenticity' from 'authentic fantasy'." Thus, the issue is clearly signaling the frame of the interaction so that individuals know whether this is a site having more to do with theater (and therefore authentic and consistent fabrication, as is true in many role-playing MUDs), versus a site where identity is tied in some reliable way to one's "real-world" embodied self (as would be necessary for legal and financial transactions).

Social order and control

Social organizations vary in terms of the amount of control, coordination, and ultimately the coercion they can exercise over themselves. Social control rests in large part on a group's ability to identify individuals in order to hold them responsible. Building on identity, we look at the nascent institutions of self-regulation and governance in online groups. We examine the ways in which cyberspace enhances or erodes the methods of social order and control that already exist in human societies.

In Part 3 we examine a range of power structures that have emerged in cyberspace. It is widely believed and hoped the ease of communicating and interacting online will lead to a flourishing of democratic institutions, heralding a new and vital arena of public discourse. But to date, most online groups have the structure of either an anarchy or a dictatorship. Some notable experiments with democratic electoral politics have failed dramatically, raising questions about what sort of governance is possible and what the prerequisites are for democratic institutions. These chapters highlight the fact that cyberspace is often a domain of vast power imbalances. Several different approaches to social order are examined, including public punishment, ostracism, and mediation.

The first age of social control

Despite the utopian hopes of early settlers, it became clear very quickly that some form of monitoring and sanctioning would be necessary in online groups. "The failure of the ideal of complete freedom in cyberspace was an early phenomenon." So begins the chapter by Elizabeth Reid on "Hierarchy and power: social control in cyberspace."

Reid examines the dynamics of power and methods of social control in two kinds of MUDs: adventure MUDs and social MUDs. In adventure MUDs, users participate in role-playing games which involve scoring and strict hierarchies. The structure of the games requires a serious commitment to the community for the reason that one must play the game frequently in order to collect the resources necessary to keep one's character "alive." Social MUDs, in contrast, involve more free-form interaction and the ability to build new objects in the world. It is possible to participate in social MUDs much less frequently than in adventure MUDs because one's character continues to exist over time without the need to explicitly find food, shelter, etc., as is the case in the role-playing adventure MUDs.

In common with many other forms of online interaction, the relative anonymity and lack of physical contact that is a feature of MUDs encourages users to become less inhibited. This is not to say that members of MUDs exist in an anomic state. Reid rightly points out that there is "no moment on a MUD in which users are not enmeshed within a web of social rules and expectations."

The disinhibition that is common in MUDs can encourage the formation of intimate relationships and deep feelings of attachment to other users. The other edge of this dynamic, however, is that members of MUDs can act out in a hostile and violent way without the usual fears of retribution. While it is true that threats of physical violence in online interaction are almost always empty threats, there is the possibility to do great symbolic violence. Tales of online harassment and "rape" are already well known, and Reid adds a particularly striking example of virtual violence involving a MUD dedicated to the support of persons who have experienced sexual assault.

Reid uses the community's response to this crisis as well as examples from other social and adventure MUDs to describe a variety of methods for social control. Some forms of social control require the intervention of the owner of the MUD or one of the high-ranking "Wizards" who can control and rewrite the software that underlies the MUD. Other methods come from the members themselves, acting either singly or in concert with others. Among the possible forms of social control that are brought up in Reid's discussion (and in the subsequent chapter by A. Smith) are the following:

- Eliminating commands in the system that chronically lead to objectionable behavior. An example is the decision by the owner of the MUD mentioned above to eliminate the "shout" command in that community.

- Providing commands that allow members to filter out objectionable behavior. "Gag" commands, which are available in many communities, allow users to ignore what a particular person is saying and doing. However, as Reid discusses, there are important limitations to this technique. Some communities also allow its members to intentionally select what actions they wish to expose themselves to. In some adventure MUDs, one can choose to open oneself up to the risk of having one's character killed, or alternately to prohibit this kind of attack on oneself.

- Temporarily restricting the rights of transgressors. A member might have their movements restricted or lose the right to use certain commands for a period of time.

- Shaming and humiliating a transgressor in public rituals. The owner or Wizard of a MUD can force a transgressor into a public space, strip away their abilities and perhaps allow other members to shame and ridicule the person.

- Banishing a transgressor from the community. A Wizard can also force a transgressor out of a community, although the ease with which one can acquire another account and identity on the Internet means that a determined person might find a way back into the community.

- Instituting stricter criteria for admission to the community. To try to avoid problems to begin with, some communities restrict membership, imposing a limit on the total number of users, for example, or requiring that new members be sponsored by existing members. Other communities prohibit guest visitors or severely restrict their abilities.

- Increasing accountability by registering identities. Some communities require that members have one persistent identity as a way of increasing accountability. Other communities also require members to register their legal names and phone numbers with the head of the community.

- Regulatory committees. Some MUDs have experimented with regulatory boards composed of members to oversee, for example, the construction projects of the community's members.

- Moral entrepreneurs and vigilante groups. Of course, individual members can take it upon themselves to express their dissatisfaction with the behavior of another. In some cases, groups of members can even band together in order to try to right some perceived wrong. In some adventure MUDs, for example, posses are formed to hunt down and punish users who have killed other users. There have also been incidents in which groups have brought in a "hired gun" to punish another member.

Reid makes the provocative point that the emphasis in many MUDs on public punishment, humiliation, and ostracism marks a return to the medieval in terms of the technology of punishment. The body of the users – albeit a virtual body – is once again the site for punishment.

Institutionalized mediation

If Reid documents the return to medieval forms of punishment in online communities, Anna DuVal Smith discusses a very different source of social control. In her chapter on "Problems of conflict management in virtual communities," she documents the emergence of institutionalized mediation in one community.

Online communities, Smith observes, are distinguished from many face-to-face communities by their open boundaries (users can enter and leave the MUD with much lower costs than physically moving to a new community), the relative anonymity of computer-mediated interaction, and the possibility of great social diversity (members may come from many different countries or ethnic groups, and may have very different expectations about what the goals of the community are). Each of these features can encourage conflict. Smith argues this means that methods of conflict resolution may be both more important and more of a challenge than in many face-to-face settings.

Research in dispute resolution has identified three basic routes for conflict resolution: exercising power, reconciling interests, and adjudicating rights. Many of the examples in the previous chapter by Reid fall into the first category – Wizards in a MUD will use their control over the software that is the infrastructure of the community in order to force a member to be shamed, humiliated, or banished. But a resort to raw power has many limitations, both in terms of the technical capacity to carry out decrees and the threat that is posed to the legitimacy of the rulers because of their capricious use of power. Another response is adjudication, though this carries its own costs and requires the establishment of a system of rights and judicial processes.

Between the raw exercise of power and a formal judicial system lies mediation. Drawing on her experience in dispute resolution in face-to-face communities, Smith introduced mediation and factfinding procedures into the MUD in which she was a member. The catalyst for these reforms was an episode in which the Wizards of this MUD intervened to punish a member by using the technical powers at their command to banish the member and destroy the objects he had created in the MUD. Their response was widely seen as inappropriate and illegitimate by many members and led to a series of reforms aimed at trying to better manage conflict. The community decided to severely limit the abilities of visitors to the community, to require sponsorship by two mentors and a period of socialization prior to full membership, and to provide a dispute resolution process (which was carried out by Smith).

Among the important lessons she reports is the double-edged effects of online interaction on the conflict resolution process. On the one hand, the mediator's role was made more difficult by the fact that users connecting from different time zones made it difficult to schedule meetings. Lag in the network, and the fact that some members had to deal with much more severe lag than others, also meant that it was very difficult for some users to participate. There was also the problem that evidence (such as email logs) could be falsified. On the other hand, the same disinhibition that may have provoked the conflict to begin with also encouraged members to be forthcoming with facts and details about an episode. The absence of physical cues also had some positive consequences, making it easier, for example, to overcome the barriers of socio-economic differences. Even network lag had a positive side in that it provided time for thought and reflection before reacting.

Smith concludes that the conflict resolution methods that were introduced to the community were useful. The Advisory Board of the community agreed and institution-alized the mediation procedures. Nevertheless, she cautions that there are significant challenges to establishing and maintaining a system of mediation. Members must be aware that a mediation procedure exists and believe it is a fair and legitimate process. A second challenge is that cases can take quite a long time to resolve. Finally, there is the simple fact that members of the community who are both skilled and willing to invest substantial time and effort must staff the process. A system for resolving disputes is a public good, and there is the temptation to free ride on the efforts of others.

Community structure and dynamics

Cyberspace is already the home of thousands of groups of people who meet to share information, discuss mutual interests, play games, and carry out business. Some of these groups are both large and well developed, but critics argue that these groups do not constitute *real* communities. Something is missing, they argue, that makes these online groups pale substitutes for more traditional face-to-face communities. Others respond that not only are online communities real communities, but also that they have the potential to support face-to-face communities and help hold local communities together.[10] Opinion rather than analysis and evidence characterizes much of this debate, and surprising little is known about the actual structure and dynamics of online groups.

In Part 4 we consider questions of community structure and processes, beginning with a detailed comparison of online and "real-life" communities. We then examine the structure of online groups, and the surprising amount of cooperation in cyberspace.

Online communities as "real" communities

Online communities surely differ in important ways from face-to-face communities — that is a premise of this volume. But when contrasts between online and face-to-face communities are made, especially if these contrasts have a moral character, it is imperative that we be clear what the comparison point is. When, for example, critics describe online communities as more isolated than "real-life" groups, their comparison seems to be to an ideal of community rather than to face-to-face communities as they are actually lived. There is a great deal of loneliness in the lives of many city dwellers.

What is needed is a detailed comparison of online and "real-life" communities by someone who has studied both. Barry Wellman and Milena Gulia provide this in their chapter, "Virtual communities as communities: Net surfers don't ride alone." In asking what kinds of communities exist online, they chastise many participants of this debate on several grounds. Most commentators have fallen on one extreme end of opinion or the other, painting pictures of unrelenting hope or despair. Critics and enthusiasts alike also speak as if they were unaware that there is a long history of thinking and research on the topic of community. Finally, Wellman and Gulia make the point that most analysts of online interaction and community treat the subject as if it had no connection to the other facets of a person's life.

The authors begin their analysis by pointing out that even before research on online groups had begun, researchers on community had gone through a very important shift. Community is now conceptualized not in terms of physical proximity but in terms of social networks. Telephones, automobiles, and airplanes have long meant that it was possible to establish and sustain important social relationships outside of one's immediate physical neighborhood.

Wellman and Gulia frame their discussion around several key questions: (1) Are online relationships narrowly specialized or broadly supportive? (2) In what ways are the many weak, less intimate relationships on the Net useful? (3) Is there reciprocity online and attachment to online communities? (4) Are strong, intimate relationships possible online? (5) How does online community affect "real-life" community? (6) Does the Net increase community diversity? (7) Are online communities "real" communities? Their conclusion is that online communities meet any reasonable definition of community, that they are not a pale, artificial substitute for more traditional forms of community. At the same time, there are many distinguishing features of online communities that change the economies of social action and organization in important ways.

Visualizing social cyberspaces

In William Gibson's now famous vision, cyberspace is

> A consensual hallucination experienced daily by billions of legitimate operators, in every nation. . . . A graphic representation of data abstracted from the banks of every computer in the human system. Unthinkable complexity. Lines of light ranged in the nonspace of the mind, clusters and constellations of data. Like city lights, receding.
>
> (Gibson 1984: 51)

In practice, however, the landscape of the Net has been difficult to see. There is no single unified representation of cyberspace or even of its major components. The tools used to connect to social cyberspaces leave us blind to a range of information that is otherwise visible in face-to-face interaction – information such as who is in the room, where they are located and clustered together, what the room is like and what expectations for behavior it signals. In online interaction the experience is something like attending a cocktail party and being able to see only people who are actively speaking, while the room and all the listeners are invisible.

But what if we could see the landscape of specific parts of the Net? In "Invisible crowds in cyberspace: mapping the social structure of the Usenet," Marc Smith explores a method for generating maps of the social networks created in the Usenet. Smith proposes a research agenda in which long-term historical studies of large-scale social networks can be carried out. His goal is to create a series of maps showing what different regions of social activity look like.

Smith discusses a range of measurements that can be generated from a collection of data from the Usenet news feed. Relationships between groups – in particular through a practice called crossposting that links groups together through shared messages – can be visualized as networks and then contrasted with other groups. The Usenet is examined in terms of the distribution of activity and diversity of participants. Smith proposes to use these measures to develop a classification system for online groups. What his research makes clear is that cyberspace is not homogeneous. The Usenet newsgroups he studies are as varied as any set of face-to-face social groups and spaces.

Smith highlights the range of methodological and ethical issues raised by research conducted in this manner. The maps created by this project reveal in great detail a social space that had previously been cloaked by the unwieldy nature of the data. Many people have a high expectation of privacy in computer-mediated interaction despite the fact that they interact in what can be seen as a public space. But new technical tools change and shift the nature of this space. Smith explores the implications of these tools and data for researchers interested in developing further studies based on records of interactions in cyberspace. He concludes that while online records are remarkable sources of data, they are also ambiguous and limited and require that researchers handle them with care.

The possibilities and limits of online cooperation

Anyone who has spent time online has probably experienced aggressive, flaming responses from someone. The hostility that exists on the Internet is a common and oft-repeated complaint. But Peter Kollock, in his chapter on "The economies of online cooperation: gifts and public goods in cyberspace," argues that the puzzle to be explained is not the prevalence of hostility in online interaction, but rather how it is that there is any significant cooperation at all.

In fact, it is common to find individuals who are remarkably generous with their time and expertise. Howard Rheingold (1993) has even described the interactions within one online community as a gift economy. Kollock takes this metaphor as his starting point and examines the structure of gift-giving and whether that is an appropriate model for online interaction. He argues that much online interaction is characterized by a form of exchange that is both more generous and riskier than gift-giving. Many of the favors and benefits provided in online communities are public goods, i.e. a good from which all may benefit, regardless of whether one has helped create the good. In such a situation there is a temptation to free-ride on the efforts of others, but if all do so, everyone is worse off.

Kollock argues that the economies involved in producing many public goods change radically as one moves to an online environment. The costs of communicating and coordinating the actions of a group, for example, are often much lower than in face-to-face interaction. And the value of a piece of information or advice that is offered to a group can be amplified because of the fact that this is a realm of digital information in which an unlimited number of people might use or make copies of the information provided. It is also the case that the size of the group necessary to produce many public goods is often reduced to one. This is to say that single individuals are capable of producing and distributing valuable goods or services to a huge audience on the Internet. As he states: "Shifts in the economies of production mean that individuals are *able* to produce many public goods on their own. And the decrease in contribution and coordination costs as well as the potential amplification in the value of the contribution (because of the huge audience) makes it more likely that an individual will experience a net benefit from providing the good."

He goes on to discuss the various motivations that might encourage individuals to produce public goods. Kollock then examines two provocative case studies: the production of a new computer operating system, known as Linux, through the use of voluntary labor, and the 1996 effort to wire California's elementary schools for Internet access. The success of these two projects illustrates the potential of online interaction in facilitating the production of public goods that would otherwise be much more difficult or even impossible to produce.

However, this is not to say that online cooperation is inevitable or expanding. Kollock ends his chapter with a caution on the limits of online cooperation, arguing that while shifting costs make the provision of some public goods much more likely, there are also a number of requisites for online cooperation that limit the extent to which many other kinds of goods will be produced. Kollock also makes the point that successful collective action will not always be in the interest of the larger society – the changing economies of online cooperation benefit all groups regardless of their aims and goals.

Collective action

Communities rarely exist exclusively in cyberspace. It is important to investigate the ways in which social groups in cyberspace spill out into the "real" world and vice versa. Can the social relations created or supported in cyberspace alter the fabric of our physical communities? We look at the concrete uses of networks to build or enhance communities and the ways online networks can be used for collective action. Social protest, the linking together of rural communities, and collective action by a disadvantaged community are examined in Part 5.

The dynamics of online social protest

The effectiveness of the Internet as a tool for coordination and communication can be seen in the success of social protests that were carried out online. Particularly striking was the critical response to MarketPlace – a CD-ROM that was to contain information about 120 million American consumers – and the Clipper chip, an encryption technology that provided a "backdoor" to be used by the government as a form of wiretapping.

These are the two case studies that Laura Gurak analyzes in her chapter on "The promise and the peril of social action in cyberspace: *ethos*, delivery, and the protests over MarketPlace and the Clipper chip." Her interest is in examining how online interaction either enhances or complicates traditional rhetorical activities such as speeches and debates. In particular, she focuses on two rhetorical features: *ethos* and delivery.

Ethos is classically used to refer to the character or tone of a speaker. Gurak makes the case that *ethos* can also be a group quality, referring to the cultural and moral tone of a community. This is the sense in which she uses the term in her examination of social protest on the Internet. The second rhetorical feature she examines – delivery – traditionally refers to a speaker's gestures and expressions. However, the delivery of messages online differs in many significant ways from face-to-face communication. Gurak discusses a number of features of online communication, including the speed, reach, and durability of messages.

Picking up on a theme woven throughout this volume, the effects of online interaction on rhetorical activity are neither simple nor unitary; rather the outcome is double-edged. On the one hand, online interaction permits individuals to mobilize far more quickly, cheaply, and efficiently than is usually possible. Relevant information can be posted publicly or forwarded to particular individuals or groups at little or no cost. Significantly, it is also relatively easy for individuals to find other individuals with similar concerns and interests. In both the cases Gurak examined, specialized discussion groups quickly formed and served as a locus for debate and the exchange of information. Gurak argues that the protests were effective not simply because of these reductions in time and costs, but also because of a strong community *ethos* that focused participants. The fact that specialized discussion groups brought people of similar interests together meant that participants were likely to share many assumptions and concerns, which would facilitate communication within the group.

Yet these same features can also be problematic. The speed and range of communication can encourage the spread of inaccurate information, and the common *ethos* shared by many of the participants can discourage challenges to the information and conclusions of the group. The specialized nature of the discussion groups can become too insular and force out dissenting voices. Gurak documents a number of examples in which inaccurate information was widely spread without being seriously challenged or questioned by the participating protesters.

Thus, her conclusion sounds more than one note. While Gurak applauds the ability of online interaction to "provide space for many more voices," she also cautions that "speed may supersede accuracy and that the beliefs of the community may preside over the responsibility of citizens to make informed decisions."

Bringing rural communities online

While space can be rendered nearly irrelevant by online interaction, there have been many online networks that have been organized around specific physical communities. Willard Uncapher discusses one of the earliest community networks in his chapter on "Electronic homesteading on the rural frontier: Big Sky Telegraph and its community." In the late 1980s a computer network was set up to serve the needs of an entire physical community. The location was Montana, which is a huge and sparsely populated state. Social and business communication is often difficult and expensive across such a vast place and the hope was that a computer network would make it easier for people to share resources and socialize. This case study is valuable both for its historical significance and because it illuminates many of the issues surrounding the adoption of new technology, as well as how physical and online communities mutually affect each other.

The community network, called Big Sky Telegraph (BST), was the idea of Frank Odasz. While his hope was that the network would serve many needs and constituencies in Montana, he initially started with the idea of linking teachers together online. Montana still has a number of "one-room" schools run by single teachers, and it was felt there was a real need and desire for isolated teachers across the state to come together and help each other. Odasz also believed strongly that technology should be deployed to serve clear, demonstrated needs, rather than being implemented for its own sake.

Odasz approached Dave Hughes, a well-known computer network activist, to help set up the network, and in January 1988 Big Sky Telegraph went online. There was immediate interest in the network and teachers learned about Big Sky Telegraph through the mail and through the face-to-face conferences that teachers had twice a year in Montana. The network made use of outdated but still serviceable Apple II/e computers that many schools had. Once teachers had connected to Big Sky Telegraph, they could take a variety of classes through the network to improve their online skills.

The network had a number of important benefits for teachers. For example, people made themselves available online to answer questions, lesson plans were shared, and the circulation of library materials was organized online. New areas on Big Sky Telegraph were also set up for other groups and activities including business, Internet access, tourist information, and community services.

As Uncapher reports, despite the many benefits of the network, the adoption rate stalled after a time. Only 30 out of 114 one-room schools were active on the network two years into its existence. This leads to the crucial question of what was keeping teachers offline. While it was true that money, modems, and the information to make it all work were sometimes in short supply, Uncapher asserts that the factors driving adoption rates were more complex than simple structural constraints.

The ascension of the Internet has also created questions and tensions about the future of Big Sky Telegraph itself. Moving to a model based on the World Wide Web, for example, risked leaving behind those users with outdated equipment. Big Sky Telegraph is attempting to adopt to these changes, and whatever the outcome, it remains an important model for community-based computer networks. Uncapher lists the key lessons Frank Odasz learned in running the system, and they serve as valuable principles for other community networks. Uncapher also makes the point that although technology continues to advance, the simple, text-only system used for Big Sky Telegraph is a useful model for those areas of the world where the most current technology remains out of reach.

Online interaction and social change

We end this volume with an optimistic story. In "Cyberspace and disadvantaged communities: the Internet as a tool for collective action," Christopher Mele illustrates how online networks can be used as a tool for collective action and empowerment. His case study is Robert S. Jervay Place, a low-income public housing development in Wilmington, North Carolina.

As part of a major downtown redevelopment program, the city of Wilmington wished to renovate Jervay Place. This brought the residents, all African-American women, into contact with the local housing authority. Residents were encouraged to take part in the planning process as decisions were made about how to modernize and rebuild the public housing project. Although the residents had some early success in working with the housing authority, the relationship soon fell apart.

The residents and the local housing authority jockeyed back and forth, and in the end a Jervay Place Task Force was created to plan and implement the reconstruction of Jervay Place. While the Task Force provided a formal means by which the residents could make their views known, they felt they could not rely on the housing authority to provide them with the information and technical knowledge they needed to participate effectively. If the residents' organization could not bring to the Task Force detailed plans, the housing authority would have an easy time pressing forward with its own development ideas. To make matters worse, there was no local organization in Wilmington that could provide the residents with the kind of specialized information and assistance they needed.

This encouraged the residents to strike out in another direction. Some Jervay Place residents had become familiar with personal computers through courses at a community college. With this background, the resident leaders began to search the Internet, at first through public terminals at a university library, and then through their own computer, purchased with a public service grant from a local university.

Their first action was to search for discussion groups devoted to urban planning and architecture. They sent out a plea for help to three such groups and within two weeks the residents received responses from twenty-three individuals and organizations, including architects and lawyers specializing in low-income housing. Working back and forth with three architectural firms, the residents were able to design a housing community that they felt would best meet their needs. As a result of this collaboration, the residents' organization was able to dominate the discussion at the Task Force meetings, making use of their sophisticated and carefully prepared plans and graphics.

The residents also used the Internet in another important way by establishing a Web site devoted to Jervay Place. The Web site allowed the residents to publicly post status reports on the redevelopment project. They also included historical and cultural information about Jervay Place as well as providing a set of links to other relevant sites on the World Wide Web.

Thus, we have a story that seems to confirm the optimists' hope that the Internet will bring new power and reach to traditionally disadvantaged communities. While these possibilities are exciting, Mele points out that the implications for social change are unclear. The success of the Jervay Place residents rested on their access to knowledge, technology, and financial resources. The ability to export the organizational lessons of Jervay Place will therefore be limited to the extent that other communities lack these resources.

Nevertheless, the Jervay Place residents have at least demonstrated the potential of online networks to decrease the costs of communicating and organizing. As one resident said, "On that machine in the center, there are people who are listening."

The lessons from these studies are many. Online interaction creates new forms of deceit and new ways to establish identities. And despite the new freedoms of online interaction, old institutions and stereotypes are reproduced, sometimes in exaggerated forms.

Social control is a necessary component of online communities. The forms examined here – the exercise of power and reconciling interests via mediation – are all still evolving, and the latter form is still in its infancy. As the number of people interacting online continues to increase, and as the interactions online become more important, developing forms of mediation, and eventually adjudication, will be a necessary though difficult task.

One can find online groups that meet any reasonable definition of community, but this is not to say that online and face-to-face communities are identical. The economies of cooperation and collective action, as one example, shift significantly as one moves to online interaction. We also need better tools and models for studying online communities, and we see here new tools for mapping social structure and new models for exploring the ecology of online groups.

We also see the interplay between online communities and the "real" world. The Internet has been used as an extremely effective tool for carrying out social protest, but many of the same features that make the Net effective for coordination and communication also encourage the spread of inaccurate information and force out dissenting voices. Online networks are used to link dispersed rural communities, but the effort also brings up complex issues about the adoption of new technology. The Internet is used as a tool for change in a disadvantaged community, demonstrating a way to route around unhelpful government agencies to find people with information and expertise that they are willing to share. But the ability to take these lessons to other disadvantaged communities may be limited by the lack of equipment and the information to make it work.

We return again to the double-edge of online interaction. These chapters avoid the extremes of utopian and dystopian visions to examine the details and sometimes conflicting processes within online communities. Assessing the meaning and impact of new technology is always a challenge. Many predictions about the ways new technologies will transform society fade quickly – the telegraph, radio, movies, and television did create revolutions, but not the ones that were expected. Hence, it is especially important that we turn from opinions and predictions to the serious analysis and description of online groups.

Notes

1   The subscription base of the commercial online providers and Internet service providers has risen dramatically over the past few years. However, there are recent signs of slowing and there are real limits to the continuation of the current growth curve. At its current rate, everyone on earth will be on the Net by 2018, which is unlikely since it is estimated that more than half the world's population has never made a phone call. Still, it is likely that network access will be as widespread as the telephone and television within a few years. The estimated number of people on the Net is widely debated and ranges from a low of millions or tens of millions to as high as 100 million people. Most people who get connected to the Net stay connected. A 1996 Neilson study shows that only about 11 percent of people who used the Internet last year no longer use it at all this year (*Los Angeles Times* September 1, 1996).

2   Email, while relatively primitive in contrast to more recent network interaction media, is said to continue to be the "killer app" that drives the rapid growth in the population of users of computer networks. This is a powerful indication that much of the attraction of cyberspace for many people is its ability to help them access other people. Newer media like the World Wide Web are increasingly integrating more social interaction components to provide people with access to one another. But even static Web pages sustain social relationships (Blythe and McGrath 1997).

3   In the United States, both Democrats and Republicans cite the role of the Internet as justification for a range of policies. Republicans highlight networks as the source of renewed employment and competitive advantage and justification for a decentralization of political power. Democrats are equally enthused but draw different conclusions about the implications of networks, highlighting increased government efficiency and access.

4   The opening quote from John Dvorak is the conclusion to an essay discussing how the World Wide Web makes visible interests and activities that were previous hidden or restricted to narrow audiences. These new research opportunities also raise new ethical issues. See Marc Smith (Chapter 8 in this volume) for a discussion of these issues.

5   In its 1995 study of the use of electronic communication, the Rand Corporation found that email was the most popular use of networks (www.rand.org).

6   Public mailing lists are recorded at www.rtfm.mit.edu.

7   As of November 1997, about 10 percent of all newsgroups were moderated. In moderated groups, similar to email discussion lists, contributions are restricted to those selected by the moderator. Unlike email lists, moderated groups can not limit access to the messages that are in the group. In many cases moderated newsgroups are intended as "read-only" groups that are used to distribute announcements but not contain follow up discussions. It takes significant work to convert an open group to a moderated one.

8   Other acronyms for these real-time textual environments are also used, including: MUSH, MUCK, MUSE, and MOO.

9 Difficult, though not impossible, as a variety of clever con artists have shown. In this sense, con artists can be seen as specialists in deceptive signaling.

10 The fear complementing this hope is that local communities will become increasingly irrelevant and wither in the face of global cyberspace.

References

Blythe, James and Cathleen McGrath. 1997. "Web Linkages as Social Networks," Paper presented at Sunbelt 1997 International Network for Social Network Analysis Annual Meeting.

Dvorak, John C. 1996. "Understanding Bizarre and Kinky Web Sites," *PC Magazine Online* July 1: http://www.zdnet.com/pcmag/dvorak/jd960701.htm.

Gibson, William. 1984. *Neuromancer*. New York: Ace.

Gore, Al. 1993. Speech at the Superhighway Summit Royce Hall, January 11, 1993, UCLA, Los Angeles, CA (www.eff.org/pub/GII_NII/Govt_docs/gore_shs.speech).

Harasim, Linda M. 1993. "Networlds: Networks as Social Spaces," in *Global Networks: Computers and International Communication*, ed. L.M. Harasim. Cambridge, MA: MIT Press.

Licklider, J.C.R., Robert Taylor, and E. Herbert. 1978. "The Computer as a Communication Device," *International Science and Technology* April.

Mills, C. Wright. 1940. "Situated Actions and Vocabularies of Motives," *American Sociological Review* 5: 904–13.

Rheingold, Howard. 1993. *The Virtual Community: Homesteading on the Electronic Frontier*. New York: Addison-Wesley.

Roszak, Theodore. 1986. *The Cult of Information: The Folklore of Computers and the True Art of Thinking*. New York: Pantheon.

Wellman, Barry, Janet Salaff, Dimitrina Dimitrova, Laura Garton, Milena Gulia and Caroline Haythornthwaite. 1996. "Computer Networks as Social Networks," *Annual Review of Sociology* 22: 211–38.

Part two

Identity

Chapter 2

Identity and deception in the virtual community

Judith S. Donath

Identity and the virtual community

Identity plays a key role in virtual communities. In communication, which is the primary activity, knowing the identity of those with whom you communicate is essential for understanding and evaluating an interaction. Yet in the disembodied world of the virtual community, identity is also ambiguous. Many of the basic cues about personality and social role we are accustomed to in the physical world are absent. The goal of this chapter is to understand how identity is established in an online community and to examine the effects of identity deception and the conditions that give rise to it.

In the physical world there is an inherent unity to the self, for the body provides a compelling and convenient definition of identity. The norm is: one body, one identity. Though the self may be complex and mutable over time and circumstance, the body provides a stabilizing anchor. Said Sartre in *Being and Nothingness*, "I *am* my body to the extent that I *am*." The virtual world is different. It is composed of information rather than matter. Information spreads and diffuses; there is no law of the conservation of information. The inhabitants of this impalpable space are also diffuse, free from the body's unifying anchor. One can have, some claim, as many electronic personae as one has time and energy to create.

"One can have . . . ?" Who is this "one"? It is, of course, the embodied self, the body that is synonymous with identity, the body at the keyboard. The two worlds are not really disjoint. While it is true that a single person can create multiple electronic identities that are linked only by their common progenitor, that link, though invisible in the virtual world, is of great significance. What is the relationship among multiple personae sharing a single progenitor? Do virtual personae inherit the qualities – and responsibilities – of their creators? Such questions bring a fresh approach to ancient inquiries into the relationship between the self and the body – and a fresh urgency. Online communities are growing rapidly and their participants face these questions, not as hypothetical thought experiments, but as basic issues in their daily existence. A man creates a female identity; a high school student claims to be an expert on viruses. Other explorers in virtual space develop relationships with the ostensible female, relationships based on deep-seated assumptions about gender and their own sexuality; patients desperate for a cure read the virtual virologist's pronouncements on new AIDS treatments, believing them to be backed by real-world knowledge. For assessing the reliability of information and the trustworthiness of a confidant, identity is essential. And care of one's own identity, one's reputation, is fundamental to the formation of community.

Identity cues are sparse in the virtual world, but not non-existent. People become attuned to the nuances of email addresses and signature styles. New phrases evolve that mark their users as members of a chosen subculture. Virtual reputations are established and impugned. By looking closely at these cues, at how they work and when they fail, we can learn a great deal about how to build vibrant online environments.

The Usenet environment

This chapter examines identity and deception in the context of the Usenet newsgroups. Although technically simple – they are essentially structured bulletin boards – a complex social structure has evolved within them. Unlike many MUDs, which are intended as fantasy worlds, most of Usenet is meant to be non-fiction; the basic premise is that the users are who they claim to be. There is, however, a significant variance between newsgroups as to what constitutes a real or legitimate identity. And there are numerous cases of identity deception, from the pseudo-naive trolls to the name-switching spammers.

People participate in Usenet newsgroups for a variety of reasons. They may be seeking information or companionship, advocating an operating system or a religion. As in the real world, their motivations may be complex: both the desire to be helpful and the desire to be noticed may prompt the writing of a lengthy exposition. For most participants, identity – both the establishment of their own reputation and the recognition of others – plays a vital role.

Information exchange is a basic function of Usenet. Requests for information are very common and answers, both right and wrong, are usually forthcoming. In the real world we may believe a story if it was published in *The Wall Street Journal* and dismiss it if it appeared in *The National Enquirer*. With Usenet, there is no editorial board ensuring standards of reliability; each posting comes direct from the writer. Thus, the writer's identity – in particular, claims of real-world expertise or history of accurate online contributions – plays an important role in judging the veracity of an article. Similarly, knowing the writer's motivation – e.g. political beliefs, professional affiliations, personal relationships – can greatly affect how we interpret his or her statements. Is the persuasive posting about the virtues of a new compiler coming from a programmer who has evaluated its code output or from a marketer of the product? The reader who knows that the author stands to gain from promoting a product or an idea is likely to doubt the veracity of the claims (Aronson 1995).

The cost of identity deception to the information-seeking reader is potentially high. Misinformation, from poor nutritional advice to erroneous interpretations of drug-smuggling law, is easy to find on the Net – and it is more likely to be believed when offered by one who is perceived to be an expert (Aronson 1995). The limited identity cues may make people accept at face value a writer's claims of credibility: it may take a long time – and a history of dubious postings – until people start to wonder about the actual knowledge of a self-proclaimed expert.

Providing affiliation and support is another important function of Usenet (Sproull and Kiesler 1991; Wellman and Gulia, Chapter 7 in this volume). Here, too, identity is central. The sense of shared community requires that the participants be sympathetic to the ideas around which the group is based; even if they disagree, there needs to be some fundamental common ground. Trust in the shared motivations and beliefs of the other participants – in other words, their social identity – is essential to the sense of community (Beniger 1987).

Identity also plays a key role in motivating people to actively participate in newsgroup discussions. It is easy to imagine why people may seek information on the Net: they have a problem and would like a solution. What prompts someone to answer? Why take the effort to help an unknown and distant person? Altruism is often cited; people feel a desire or obligation to help individuals and to contribute to the group (Constant et al. 1995). Yet selfless goodwill alone does not sustain the thousands of discussions; building reputation and establishing one's online identity provides a great deal of motivation. There are people who expend enormous amounts of energy on a newsgroup: answering questions, quelling arguments, maintaining Frequently Asked Questions (FAQs).[1] Their names – and reputations – are well known to the readers of the group; other writers may defer to their judgment, or recommend that their ideas be sought in an argument. In most newsgroups, reputation is enhanced by posting intelligent and interesting comments, while in some others it is enhanced by posting rude flames or snide and cutting observations. Though the rules of conduct are different, the ultimate effect is the same: reputation is enhanced by contributing remarks of the type admired by the group. To the writer seeking to be better known, a clearly recognizable display of identity is especially important. No matter how brilliant the posting, there is no gain in reputation if the readers are oblivious to who the author is.

Models of honesty and deception

The approach of this chapter is ethnographic – an interpretation of closely examined social discourse (Geertz 1973). As a framework for the examination I will look at the virtual community as a communication system, its inhabitants as signalers and receivers.

Examples of identity deception abound in the animal world.[2] The deception is quite harmful to those deceived, whose costs range from a lost meal to loss of life. However, it is beneficial to the deceivers, who gain food, free child care, or their own safety. What maintains the balance between honest and deceptive signaling and why, since it can be so beneficial to the deceiver, isn't deception more common? Why don't more harmless butterflies mimic the bad-tasting monarch? And why don't weak, undesirable mates just pretend to be strong, desirable ones?

There is not a simple answer to this question; there is not even agreement among biologists as to how common, or effective, is deception. If a signal becomes very unreliable due to excessive cheating it ceases to convey information – it stops being a signal. Yet there are stable systems of deception, where the percentage of deceivers does not overwhelm the population, and the signal remains information-bearing, however imperfectly. And there are signals that are inherently reliable: signals that are difficult, or impossible, to cheat.

Biologists and game theorists have developed an analytical framework for modeling the interplay between honesty and deception in a communication system. Of especial interest to us is the work done by Amotz Zahavi and others in examining what makes a signal reliable. Zahavi proposed the "handicap principle," which states that

> for every message there is an optimal signal, which best amplifies the asymmetry between an honest signaler and a cheater. For example, wasting money is a reliable signal for wealth because a cheater, a poor individual claiming to be rich, does not have money to throw away; the message of strength may be displayed reliable by bearing heavy loads; and confidence may be displayed by providing an advantage to a rival.
>
> (Zahavi 1993)

Signals that follow the handicap principle are called assessment signals. They are costly and the cost is directly related to the trait being advertised. Big horns on a stag are an assessment signal for strength, for the animal must be quite strong and healthy to support these massive growths. The horns are a signal: potential rivals or mates need not directly test the stag's strength; they can simply look at the size of the horns. The thick neck of a brawny bouncer in a bar sends a similar signal in the human world and few patrons demand a personal exhibition of strength. Assessment signals are reliable, since sending an assessment signal requires that the sender possess the relevant trait.

Signals that do not follow the handicap principle are called conventional signals. Here, the signal is correlated with a trait by custom or convention: the sender need not possess the trait in order to make the signal. Wearing a T-shirt that says "Gold's Gym Powerlifter" or signing "Mr. Deadlift" in your letters to a weightlifting newsgroup is a signal of strength, but not a reliable one. Anyone can wear the shirt or type the signature: no feats of strength are involved in the signal's production. Conventional signals are open to deception. If being thought of as strong is highly desirable, it seems reasonable that many people, weak or strong, would choose to wear "Powerlifter" T-shirts. Yet, if

T-shirt wearing by the weak becomes prevalent, the signal loses its meaning as an indicator of strength. Conventional signals can thus be unstable: due to excessive deception, a once meaningful signal can become noise.

Since assessment signals are so reliable, and conventional ones not, why use the latter at all? One reason is that conventional signals are often less costly, for both the signaler and the receiver (Dawkins and Guilford 1991). If the costs associated with deception are relatively low, then a conventional signal may be more suitable than a more reliable, but costly, assessment signal. Think of a job applicant. The text in a résumé is a conventional signal, for one can write down an impressive job history without having actually experienced it. Statements made during an extensive interview are more like assessment signals, for one must have actually acquired the knowledge in order to display it. It is much quicker and easier (that is, less costly) for the employer to just look at the résumé, but the chances of being deceived are much higher. If the costs of deception are high – say, the job is a responsible one and an inexperienced employee may cause a great deal of harm – then it will be worth making the effort to make the costlier evaluation.

The spread of deception can be limited. In particular, imposing a cost to being caught deceiving – that is, punishing deception – is a deterrent (Hauser 1992). Going back to our résumé example, there is usually little penalty for being caught padding one's employment history when seeking, say, a job waiting at tables, whereas the punishment for being caught amplifying one's medical qualifications may be quite severe. By imposing high costs on deception a social system can make conventional signals more reliable.

There are costs to imposing the punishment. For a deceptive signaler to be caught, someone must make the effort to assess the honesty of the signal (termed the cost of probing among biologists). In addition to the time and energy thus expended, probing may itself have high costs if the probe turns out to be honest (Dawkins and Guilford 1991). For instance, imagine probing the strength of our "Powerlifter" T-shirt wearers by challenging them to a fight. If the wearer is "deceptive" he or she will lose the challenge – and quite likely be dissuaded from misleading T-shirt practices. If, however, the wearer is "honest," it is the prober who loses.

Applying the model is an interpretive process. Even in the relatively simple world of biological signaling, there is often disagreement about whether a particular signal is inherently or conventionally tied to a trait (see Dawkins and Guilford 1991 and Zahavi 1993 for opposing views). Interpreting the social world of cyberspace is a far more subjective process. The purpose of the model is to help articulate the arguments: it is a framework on which to begin sorting out the intricate and often murky discussion about identity in cyberspace.

The anatomy of a Usenet letter

Usenet news is accessible by millions of people all over the world. Subscribers range from the highly technical to the computer illiterate, from young children playing with their parents' account to homebound elderly people using the Net for social contact, from young American urban professionals to radical Afghani Muslims. Some are posting from work accounts, knowing their boss monitors online exchanges; others are posting from a recreational service, entertaining themselves by playing an imaginary character.

There are several thousand discussion groups, covering topics ranging from computer networking protocols to gun-control and vegetarian cooking. Some newsgroups encourage anonymous postings; in others such postings are coldly ignored. Some newsgroups are close-knit communities, in which people refer to each other by name and ask after each other's friends and family members. Others are primarily places to exchange information, repositories of knowledge where one can submit a question and receive a (possibly correct) answer. Some groups provide a warm, trusting, and supportive atmosphere, while others promote a raw and angry free-for-all.

This range of styles, topics, and participants makes Usenet an especially interesting focus for this study. Although the groups share a common technology and interface, the social mores – writing style, personal interactions, and clues about identity – vary greatly from forum to forum.

In the mediated world of the Usenet newsgroups, the letter is not only the basic form of communication, but also one's primary means for self-presentation. In the following section, we will take a close look at the anatomy of a Usenet letter and at how identity is established or concealed within it.

Example 2.1 is a typical Usenet letter. In this example, the writer is offering advice in response to a request for information. What does the reader of this posting know about Mr. Koslov?[3] Clues can be found in each part of the letter: the header provides the writer's name and email address, the body of the letter reveals voice and something of the history of the exchange, the signature shows the writer as he or she chooses to be identified.

Header	Owen@netcom.com (Owen Koslov)
	Re: Brine Shrimp
	Mon, 24 Jan 1994 09:38:23 GMT
	Newsgroups: sci.aquaria,rec.aquaria
Message body: extract from original question	In article llawrence@aol.com (Leo Lawrence) writes: >I tried to hatch some brine shrimp for my fish. I could >only get the shrimp to live for 2 days. Could someone tell >me what to feed them and give me details on hatching >them.
Message body: response	You are not supposed to keep them alive for longer than a day or so. They should be fed to the fish as soon as they hatch. Otherwise, you need the type of set up you'd expect in a regular saltwater tank: low bio-load, plenty of water circulation, and adequate filtration. You can feed the shrimp OSI's APR or other commercial invert foods, or use green

water. In all cases, unless you are doing it on a large scale,
buying live brine shrimp at a shop is simpler, faster and easier.
--

Signature   Owen Koslov at home (owen@netcom.com) or work
(okoslov@veritas.com)

Example 2.1 *A Usenet letter*

The account name: basic ID

The most straightforward form of identification is the writer's account name (i.e. email address). This information is automatically included in the header by the posting software. It appears in the article lists that Usenet readers skim to find postings of interest and it is the data used in killfiles to identify writers one finds onerous.[4] The automatically inserted account name may be the only overt identifier in the posting; while people do not always sign their letters, all postings must have the sender's account name in the header.

A close look at the account name, a seemingly simple identification signal, proves to be quite interesting for it touches on issues ranging from the reputations of various virtual neighborhoods to techniques for detecting identity deception. There may be a clear and straightforward mapping from an account name to a real-world individual – or it may be deliberately opaque. The domain (account names are in the form name@domain, where domain is the organization that provides the account) yields contextual clues about the writer – and about the reliability of the header information.

While the name of the individual writer may be unfamiliar, often the name of the domain is not. Like notes written on letterhead, a posting submitted from a well-known site shares in its reputation: a posting about oceanography has added authority if it came from whoi.edu (Woods Hole Oceanographic Institute) and a question about security breaches may seem more intriguing if it came from .mil (the US military).

The domain is a virtual neighborhood and, as with real-world neighborhoods, some names bring to mind a wealth of demographic data. The domain may correspond to a real-world place, indicating that the writer is in, say, Thailand or Israel or working at Raytheon or Greenpeace. Even some of the commercial services have distinctive reputations: San Francisco's The WELL is tie-dyed and politically active while New York City's ECHO is black-clad and arts-oriented. There are "poor" neighborhoods, addresses that reveal a limited budget:

>> jake@cleveland.freenet.edu
>> Hacker wanted to disassemble commercial program and rewrite to our specs. This is not a B.S.
>> post, we will pay BIG $$$ to have this service performed. Email for details

Nobody with "BIG $$$" to spend is going to be writing that message from Cleveland Freenet. :-)

And, while there are not yet any recognized "wealthy" virtual neighborhoods, it is probably only a matter of time until exclusive online addresses become symbols of status.

To understand the significance of the domain it is useful to distinguish between institutional and commercial accounts. Institutional accounts are online addresses from universities, research labs, and corporations; they are given to people because of an association with the institute. Commercial accounts are available for a fee from various service providers. Unlike the institutional accounts, these commercial accounts do not imply any affiliation; they simply mean that the user has signed up for the service.

In the early days of the Net, all accounts were institutional. Most sites were big universities and laboratories and the users were academics and researchers at these institutes. In the mid-1990s, the situation is more complex and not all postings are from recognizable institutes. Some are from small businesses unknown to the reader; others are accounts from commercial service providers –somewhat like electronic post office boxes. Furthermore, as Net access becomes widespread, a posting from a research lab domain no longer necessarily means a researcher sent it. Support staff as well as scientists have computers: the posting from Woods Hole may be from a prominent oceanographer – or a temporary receptionist. There is a great deal of contextual and other information to be found in the domain name, but it needs to be evaluated within the culture of the Net and of the organizations that provide access.

The opening up of the online world to anyone with a computer and modem has met with quite a bit of resistance from the original residents. Most maligned are newcomers who have accounts with the consumer-oriented commercial services such as Prodigy and America Online (AOL). Postings with aol.com addresses are sometimes greeted with derision; newsgroups such as alt.aol-sucks exist solely to spurn America Online subscribers. This resistance is partly a reaction to the loss of exclusivity – access to online communication no longer means one is at the forefront of technology – but there are also substantive differences between the postings of the old guard and the newcomers.

> I have to admit, i do have an account on prodigy, becasue my mom has had it for a few years, and it was free for me, i never use it though, it's embarassing.. I think i'd be the same way if i had AOL, i would be embarassed to post or reply or just be seen anywhere with a loser@aol.com address. I guess it just seems that they are so stupid..
> – alt.2600

Some of the differences are stylistic. The consumer-oriented services offer their own communication forums in which the conversational conventions are quite different than within Usenet. For instance, in an AOL chat room, it is fine to simply respond "yes" to a statement. On Usenet, where each statement is a stand-alone posting, it is considered poor manners to post a response with no added content and with no indication of the original statement. Newcomers to Usenet from AOL, accustomed to chat room style interactions, frequently post one word rejoinders, infuriating other Usenet users and adding to the image of AOL-based participants as thoughtless and ignorant of local customs.

There are also differences in accountability. The holder of an institutional account – a student or employee – has reasons, such as a job or degree, for remaining in good standing with the account provider. A user who engages in malicious or illegal activity online stands to lose more than just the account: a number of students have been disciplined – and some expelled – for violations of institutional policy. The relationship of a subscriber to a commercial service is much less consequential. While most services have policies about what constitutes acceptable behavior, the repercussions for infractions are limited to termination of service – an inconvenience, certainly, but not the equivalent of demotion or firing. In other words, higher punishment costs can be imposed on the institutional account.

Institutional accounts are also less private than commercial accounts. A work- or school-based account name is known within the organization and there are many people who can make a direct connection between the name on a posting and the real-world person. For the writer using an institutional account, the online world is a public forum in which he or she can be seen by numerous colleagues and acquaintances. With a commercial account, it is up to the user to decide who should know the link between physical self and virtual appellation. Some services allow subscribers only a single account name and the user thus has some concern about the reputation that attaches to that name. Some consumer-oriented commercial services make it easy for subscribers to create multiple, fictitious names and to keep their real names from appearing on their postings. The anonymity of these accounts makes them popular for disruptive and harassing posting.

Truly anonymous postings can be sent using anonymous remailers. These are forwarding services which will strip all identifying information from a letter and then forward it, anonymously or under a pseudonym, to the intended recipient or newsgroup. The pseudonymous address added by many, though not all, remailers clearly indicates that the posting is anonymous: an12321@anon.penet.fi and anon-remailer@utopia. hacktic.nl are typical. While remailers can be used maliciously, their primary use is to provide privacy. Anonymous posts are common in groups where the participants reveal highly personal information and many of the support groups (e.g. alt.support. depression) periodically provide instructions on how to use an anonymous remailer. Use of a remailer can also be a political statement, an affirmation that one supports the citizen's right to privacy (which includes anonymity, access to strong encryption tools, etc.) and opposes government and corporate surveillance.

Many Usenet participants frown upon anonymous postings:

> I don't like dealing with anyone that uses an anonymous remailer! I will, however, assume you are doing this for 'legitimate' reasons and try to render assistance.
>
> –comp.unix.security

> The anonymous address and excessive crossposting were a bit much don't you think? I'll humour you this time . . .
>
> – alt.2600

These writers felt compelled to point out their disapproval of anonymous posting before answering the question. And the stigma of writing anonymously was clearly felt by an451494@anon.penet.fi, the writer of an innocuous request for reviews of a human interface, who signed his posting with his real name and the note "sorry; my employer doesn't like seeing me posting to news-groups."

The account name is thus an important, but limited, form of online identification. It is important because it is ubiquitous: all postings must have the account name in the header. It is a key marker of individual identity: although there is not always a one-to-one mapping between an account name and a real-world person (accounts may be shared, some people have several accounts), the account name is generally perceived to refer to a single person (or persona). And it may provide some contextual information about the writer, information that, while quite sketchy, may be the only such cues in the posting.

Identity in voice and language

The contents of the posting can reveal a great deal more about the writer. It may include overtly identity-related data: name, age, etc. More importantly, it provides a chance to get a sense of the writer's "voice" and to see how he or she interacts with others in the online social environment.

Erving Goffman (1959), in his classic work *The Presentation of Self in Everyday Life*, distinguished between the "expressions given" and the "expressions given off." The former are the deliberately stated messages indicating how the one wishes to be perceived; the latter are the much more subtle – and sometimes unintentional – messages communicated via action and nuance (Goffman 1959). Both forms of expression are subject to deliberate manipulation, but the "expression given off" may be much harder to control. One can write "I am female," but sustaining a voice and reactions that are convincingly a woman's may prove to be quite difficult for a man.

Is the "expression given off" an assessment or conventional signal? Even in the real world, with its far richer array of social nuance, impostors exist. Drag queens, confidence men, undercover spies – all are adept at mimicking subtle social codes. Yet, although nuance is not an infallible indication of a social role, the experience of living the part greatly influences one's ability to play it: years of socialization make most women adept at playing the role of woman in their culture.[5] One can argue that the cost in time that it takes to fully attain the role makes it an assessment signal. Is the same true in the virtual world – is there sufficient complexity to the nuances in a Usenet exchange for one's experience in living a role to be revealed in the "expression given off"?

Looking again at Example 2.1, from the header and signature we know the writer's name (Owen Koslov), we know that he writes both from home (as owen@netcom.com) and from work (okoslov@veritas.com). Neither location tells us a great deal about the author – netcom is a commercial service provider and veritas.com is not a well-known company. The writer's history on the Net reveals much more. A look at recent articles shows that he is a fairly frequent writer, not only on sci.aquaria, but also on the closely related groups rec.aquaria and alt.aquaria. Indoor aquaria seem to be his passion. He provides a fellow killifish fancier with the address of a mailing-list devoted solely to killifish. He writes several letters a day on aquaria-related topics. We learn that he has perhaps too many fish: "I wish I had your discipline in keeping the number of species down. I have 9 species of lampeyes alone." His letters are usually answers to questions posed by others, his voice is usually authoritative, pedantic, occasionally dryly humorous. Here are selections (ellipses mine) from his response to someone who said to avoid charcoal in tanks with plants.

> While activated carbon does adsorb more than just organic carbons, a categorical statement like that is inaccurate. Carbon may remove some trace minerals, but I challenge you to substantiate the statement that it is a "bad thing" for live plants. . . . Further more, Dick Boyd's Chemi-Pure uses activated carbon as one of its ingredients and I am yet to hear one credible report of it negatively affecting live plants. The late Dr. Bridge had used a mix of activated carbon and peatmoss as a filtration medium for his planted show tank and reported excellent results.

Over time, the frequent contributors to a newsgroup creates a strong impression. The reader of rec.aquaria is likely to be familiar with these postings and has come to some conclusion about both Mr. Koslov's reliability and his personality. Although this writer says little about himself, there is a great deal of expression given off.

Writing style can identify the author of a posting. A known and notorious Net personality hoping to appear online under a fresh name may have an easier time disguising his or her header ID than the identity revealed in the text. The introduction to the cypherpunks newsgroup includes this warning:

> The cypherpunks list has its very own net.loon, a fellow named L. Detweiler. The history is too long for here, but he thinks that cypherpunks are evil incarnate. If you see a densely worded rant featuring characteristic words such as "medusa", "pseudospoofing", "treachery", "poison", or "black lies", it's probably him, no matter what the From: line says.
> "About Cypherpunks", ftp://ftp.csua.berkeley.edu/pub/cypherpunks/mailing_list/list.html

In this case, where the usual assessment signal – the name in the header – is believed to be false, language is used as a more reliable signal of individual identity.

Language is also an important indication of group identity: "regarding group membership, language is a key factor – an identification badge – for both self and outside perception" (Saville-Troike 1982). Language patterns evolve within the newsgroups as the participants develop idiosyncratic styles of interaction – especially phrases and abbreviations. Some are common to all groups: BTW, IMHO, YMMV (By The Way, In My Humble Opinion, Your Mileage May Vary). Others are of limited extent: MOB, ONNA (Mother Of the Bride, Oh No Not Again – used in misc.kids.pregnancy by women who were trying to get pregnant to report the monthly disappointment). New words are coined and ordinary words gain new meaning: flame, spam, troll, newbie. Using these phrases expresses one's identification with the online community – it is akin to moving to a new region and picking up the local accent.

Participants interpret these language cues according to their own position within the social group. A newsgroup can be home to two or more factional groups, each of which tries to establish its style and views as the rightful culture of the group. Alt.2600 is a newsgroup devoted to computer hacking and related topics. Being a hacker – or appearing to be one – has recently gained mass popularity, and would-be hackers and trend-conscious teens have adopted a style of writing that features alternative spellings (such as "kewl" for "cool") and random capitalization. Older or more experienced hackers felt compelled to separate themselves from the crowd. In a thread called "Attn LaMerZ and Wana-B's," one wrote:

> ATTENTION you are not a hacker if you have seen the movie HACKERS. ATTENTION you are not a hacker if you post here looking for AOLHELL, free AOL, Unix passwords, crackerjack, or virus creation lab. ATTENTION you are not a hacker if you HaVE A PrOOBLEM WiTh YOuR CaPS LOckS KeY.
>
> –alt.2600

Here, the language markers that one group developed to distinguish themselves are a sign of scorn for the other.

The signature

Language markers such as the above are an important element in signatures, which are the online world's most deliberate identity signals. The signature is added at the discretion of the user, though once designed, it is usually appended automatically to postings. It may be an electronic business card, an elaborate work of self-expression, a cryptic remark, or simply a name. Not everyone uses one, and they are far more prevalent in certain forums than others. Although the signature itself is an easy to copy conventional signal, it is often used as a means to link to more robust and reliable indicators of identity and to show the writer's affiliation with a subgroup.

Signatures can be used to anchor the virtual persona to the real-world person. The Net is a great leveler: no one knows if you are male or female, boss or underling, gray-haired or adolescent; "on the Internet, nobody knows you're a dog." This is not to your advantage if in the real world you hold some authority: no one can see that you are a respected professional at work in your office, not a teenager logging in from a bedroom. One use of the signature is to present real-world credentials: your full name, title, department, office phone number; enough information so that someone could, if they were curious, check to see that you were really who you claimed to be. Such business card signatures are common in the technical newsgroups. Advice from someone whose job title is "Unix System Specialist" or "Director, Software Development" has added weight, particularly if it is in a known and respected company (for the important sounding "Director of Software Development" at unknown "ABC Software Co." may also be the founder and sole employee). These signatures imply that the writer is posting in his or her official, employed capacity – willing to publicly stand behind the statements.

One newsgroup that contains many business card signatures is comp.security.unix. The discussion here is about how to make Unix systems secure – and about known system flaws. While many of the participants are system administrators of major institutions, others are just learning how to set up a system in a fledgling company and some, of course, are hoping to learn how to break into systems. Someone posting a question may wish to include credentials to assure potential responders that the question is legitimate, not a disguised dig for information from a would-be hacker. A posting suggesting that administrators improve their sites by changing this or that line of code in the system software could be a furtive attempt to get novice administrators to introduce security holes; a signature verifying the legitimacy of the writer alleviates this suspicion. Identity deception is a big concern of the participants in this group, and they are very aware of signatures and their implications.

An important new use of the signature is to refer to the writer's home page on the World Wide Web. Like the business card signature, the Web address may contain credentials – and much more. A home page may provide a detailed portrayal of its subject: people include everything from résumés and papers to photographs and lists of favorite foods. A person's presence on the Web has depth and nuance not found in the ephemeral Usenet environment and a writer's self-presentation on the Web can provide a very enlightening context for understanding his or her postings.

Signatures often include a disclaimer, saying something to the effect that "These are my opinions and not those of my employers." For many people, participating in Usenet newsgroups occupies a sometimes awkward position between work and private life. The newsgroups may be an important resource for one's work; they may also be a purely recreational pasttime. Whether a posting is about signal processing or Argentine culture, if sent from one's work account it will show up under the company's electronic letterhead. The disclaimer proclaims that the writer is appearing as an individual, not as an official company spokesperson.

Signatures are also used to establish one's ties to online groups. Many signatures contain computer jokes and phrases, showing that the writer is a programmer – a member of the old guard of the Net (see Example 2.2).

(a)   #include <stddisclmer.h>
(b)   Write failed on /dev/brain: file system full
(c)   Doom: 5% Health, 0 % Armor, 59 cent Tacos, Lets Go!
(d)   Dave Mescher dmescher@csugrad.cs.vt.edu
GCS d H>+ s+:- g+ p3 au a - w+ v, - ->! C++++,++ UU++++,A$ P - L-
3- E - - N++ K- W - - M V - po Y+ t - - 5 jx R G+ !tv b++ D- B - -
e+,* u+ h- f+ r(+,++)@ !n, - - y?

Example 2.2 *Programmer signatures*

In (a), the phrase #include<stddisclmer.h> uses a C language construct to make a reference to the disclaimer signature. It has both the effect of being a disclaimer (the writer is not speaking officially) and of proclaiming the writer's affinity to the C programming world; (b) uses the format of a common Unix error message. For the

Unix-literate reader, the phrase is familiar and the joke obvious; for others it is simply obscure. Similarly, (c) plays off the scoring style of the popular computer game Doom. Signatures such as these are often individual creations, meant to be used only by their author. Since one needs to be familiar with a subculture in order to make a joke in its vocabulary, these signatures, when original, show their author's familiarity with the programming world. Furthermore, the world in which they are used is small. A writer who simply copies the clever phrase of another is likely to quickly come to the attention of the potentially irate creator. The possible cost of copying – public humiliation through accusations of plagiarism – is quite high. (Smitten by a phrase too witty not to use, some writers have taken to using others' signatures – with attribution.)

These signatures are what Fiske calls "producerly" writings, easily accessible yet playing with complex mixes of vocabularies and codes (Fiske 1989). Such puns, he says, entertain both through the process of discovering the layers of meaning and in their juxtaposition of social contexts. "Write failed on /dev/brain: file system full" not only is a play on Unix error messages, but also can be read as a comment on information overload – or as a subtle jab at those who post, but seem not to absorb anyone else's comments. "#include <stddisclmr.h>" in addition to mixing the culture of Usenet with the code of C programmers, also refers to the numbing ubiquity of disclaimers.

The signature in (d), which includes the writer's "Geek Code," is a bit different. Proclaiming one' s "geek identity" – both one's identification with geeks as a group and one's particular and individual type of geekiness – is the purpose of this code:

> How to tell the world you are a geek, you ask? Use the universal Geek code. By joining the geek organization, you have license to use this special code that will allow you to let other un-closeted geeks know who you are in a simple, codified statement.[6]

The code consists of a series of descriptive categories and modifiers. The first category is G, Geek type. GCS stands for Computer Science Geek (GSS would be Social Science Geek). The second category, d, is for dress style. In the example above (d) is without modifiers, meaning: "I dress a lot like those found in catalog ads. Bland, boring, without life or meaning." There are many possibilities, ranging from "d++: I tend to wear conservative dress such as a business suit" to "!d: No clothing. Quite a fashion statement, don't you think?" The Geek Code can become quite complex. For instance, the modifier ">" means moving towards. Thus, the symbol H>+ above is interpreted as someone whose hair (H) is striving to achieve (>) shoulder length (+). The code is full of inside jokes, e.g. !H, the code for baldness, refers to the computer language convention of ! meaning negation. It is also full of cultural references: to operating systems, to Internet personalities, to TV shows and to various games. One has to be quite dedicated to decipher a Geek Code, but its primary message – identification with the online "geek" world – is easily perceived by anyone who knows what a Geek Code looks like.

The Geek Code has inspired a number of other identity codes. The Goth Code has categories for dress style, body piercings, musical taste; the Magic Code provides the means to express one's opinions of the Kabbala, Aleister Crowley, and one's own supernatural powers; the Cat Code has categories ranging from breed to purr volume. The codes seem to have originated in the gay and lesbian online community, inspired both by the handkerchief codes of the gay bar scene and (according to the introduction to the progenitor of all the codes, the Bear Code) by the astronomical classification schemes for stars and galaxies. Until recently, seeing these codes in a signature would be a puzzle to all but the initiated. The Web has now made finding esoteric information – such as the decoding scheme for the Muffdiva Code – simply a matter of a quick Net search. The codes still function as subcultural membership markers, though their meaning is now open. They can function as a tourist's introduction to the subculture, enumerating the features of greatest interest to the group.

Some signature styles are unique to particular newsgroups. Often they refer to the writer's role within that group. For example, soc.couples.wedding is a newsgroup devoted to planning weddings from the fine points of invitation-writing protocols to advice about how to deal with hostile in-laws. The participants include people who are engaged to be married, people who would like to be engaged to be married, and people who like giving advice. The brides-to-be are the central group: they ask questions, they share their experiences, they write to complain about their caterers, bridesmaids and future mothers-in-law. And they have developed their own signature pattern:

> Joan (and Mike, May 27, 1995)
> Amy (& Chris Sept. 7, 1996)

A similar signature pattern is found on misc.kids.pregnancy, where the expectant mothers sign with the baby's due date. These signatures show the special status of the writer: as bride- or mother-to-be, her real-world situation is the focus of the group's interest. The signatures also highlight the temporal nature of this identity. The readers know the stages of wedding preparation and pregnancy. Responses to letters often include references to the signature ("June 10th – I'm getting married the next day! Are you nervous yet?") even if the body of the letter was unrelated to the writer's wedding.

An especially well-defined community has emerged in the group rec.motorcycles, where an online club, called the Denizens of Doom (DoD), has formed. The DoD began as a satire of the newsgroup and of real motorcycle clubs, but is now a real club, with membership lists and real-world badges. Members get DoD numbers, which they use in their signatures. One must apply for membership, and, while the procedure is not terribly secret, it does take a bit of knowing who's who in the group to apply: a DoD number in a signature means that the writer is not a newcomer to the group. Here is a signature from rec.motorcycles:

> whiteb1@aol.com (Ben White)
> AMA # 580866 COG # 1844
> DoD # 1747 Better watch out, He turned me loose!
> '95 VFR 750 5 bucks more, I coulda got a red one
> '85 Shadow
> No more Connie

In addition to the DoD number, it features the writer's membership in the American Motorcycle Association plus the motorcycles he owns (or used to own); this signature is a virtual world substitute for the colors and badges of real-world biking.

Finally, signatures make it easier to quickly identify the writer. In the uniform environment of ASCII text, there is little to visually distinguish one letter from another and it is easy to confuse two writers with similar names, or to simply not notice the attribution at all. Signatures are easily recognized, identifying the writer at a glance.

Individual recognition is important in many newsgroups. Participants in arguments often call each other by name – both heated flames and supportive letters are often written as person-to-person missives. Online status is recognized and there is deferral to respected members. This writer, himself an aerobics instructor, described a modification he had made to a move, and then asked:

> Bill Whedon and Larry DeLuca, Are you There? You guys have seemed to be the most vocal AND concientious . . . By turning lunges into squats, have Lori and I traded one problem for another?
>
> – misc.fitness.aerobics

High status participants get special treatment. A bridal consultant who contributes frequently to soc.couples.wedding asked the newsgroup to help her plan a vacation. Such a request is quite outside the group's domain, and would normally result in a sharp request to keep the postings on topic; instead, several people enthusiastically wrote in with advice and suggestions. The signature is an important technique for insuring that one's postings are accredited to one's name.

From the header to the signature, identity cues are scattered throughout the Usenet letter, from declarations of one's name, age, sexual orientation, to the subtler "expressions given off" through voice and vocabulary. The virtual world's subcultures have developed their own patois, with codes and linguistic patterns that identify affiliated participants. And people have found ways to control the degree of personal identity they wish to expose online, from authentication through business card signatures to the private cloak of anonymous remailers.

Deceptions and manipulations

Yet these identity cues are not always reliable. The account name in the header can be faked, identity claims can be false, social cues can be deliberately misleading.

Many varieties of identity deception can be found within the Usenet newsgroup. Some are quite harmful to individuals or to the community; others are innocuous, benefiting the performer without injuring the group. Some are clearly deceptions, meant to provide a false impression; others are more subtle identity manipulations, similar to the adjustments in self-presentation we make in many real-world situations.

Trolls

In the spring of 1995 a new user appeared in the wedding newsgroups. She signed her letters Cheryl, the name on her account was ultimatego@aol.com and her letters espoused a rigid interpretation of formal etiquette. The discussion in these groups is often about how to have a wedding on a limited budget. When the women would talk about using balloons for decorations, Ultimatego would post that balloons were vulgar; when the discussion turned to do-it-yourself laser-printing she would interject that only engraving is acceptable to people with taste. Some readers were intimidated by her intimations of upper-crust social knowledge; others were infuriated by her condescending remarks. When she wrote that people who could not get married in full formal splendor should not have a wedding at all but should simply go to the city hall, an intense and angry exchange ensued. At this point, someone said that Ultimatego was probably a troll.

> Are you familiar with fishing? Trolling is where you set your fishing lines in the water and then slowly go back and forth dragging the bait and hoping for a bite. Trolling on the Net is the same concept – someone baits a post and then waits for the bite on the line and then enjoys the ensuing fight.

Trolling is a game about identity deception, albeit one that is played without the consent of most of the players. The troll attempts to pass as a legitimate participant, sharing the group's common interests and concerns; the newsgroup members, if they are cognizant of trolls and other identity deceptions, attempt to both distinguish real from trolling postings and, upon judging a poster to be a troll, make the offending poster leave the group. Their success at the former depends on how well they – and the troll – understand identity cues; their success at the latter depends on whether the troll's enjoyment is sufficiently diminished or outweighed by the costs imposed by the group.

Trolls can be costly in several ways. A troll can disrupt the discussion on a newsgroup, disseminate bad advice, and damage the feeling of trust in the newsgroup community. Furthermore, in a group that has become sensitized to trolling – where the rate of deception is high – many honestly naive questions may be quickly rejected as trollings. This can be quite off-putting to the new user who upon venturing a first posting is immediately bombarded with angry accusations. Even if the accusation is unfounded, being branded a troll is quite damaging to one's online reputation.

Rec.motorcycles is a free-wheeling group where tough-guy banter mixes with advice about riding techniques and equipment. Being able to ride on a challenging bike in difficult conditions is respected – but attempting feats beyond one's capabilities is greatly disapproved of. Beginners who want to start out on a powerful bike are likely to be severely lectured. Provoking this response is the goal of flame-seeking trolls.

> Subject: New Rider; what bike? Is ZX11 good to start with?
> From: crystllthr@aol.com (CrystlLthr)
> Organization: America Online, Inc. (1-800-827-6364)

> Hi. I am a college junior and am interested in buying my first motorcycle. I've seen the Kawasaki ZX11 and think it looks pretty hot. Would this be a good bike to buy. Money is no problem. My dad will buy me anything I want. Also, I've heard that you should get a turbo kit from Mr. Turbo in Houston, because the bike needs more power. Any other modifications suggested? Also, where should I go to learn to ride?
> Derick Nichols
> Tulane University

A few took this posting seriously. Some responded angrily:

> Cool Derick. Great bike! The turbo kit will make it awesome. Don't worry about learning to ride, just go pick it up and ride it home. Good idea though to have your dad buy a coffin and funeral plot at the same time. I think they offer a deal on those when you get a zx-11 as your first bike. Oh yeah. Don't worry about hitting any manhole covers on your way home – if you warp the wheel you can always sue the city.

Others tried to be helpful:

> Well, I agree with Sherry [quoted above].though i problby wouldnt have put in quite like that. Derick, if you have never ridden before maybe you can start with something a bit smaller. You dont hae to buy your first bike nwe.,that way, when you otgrow it, you wont have put a lot of money into it (if you bought it cash), or if you financed, you can get out ot it easier.

Most readers, however, decided it was a troll:

> This has got to be bait, right?????

> Sounds like extreme flamebait to me..
> Yes, get the ZX, (a used '91.) I'll buy the resulting wreck for parts for $100.00 :-)

Several pointed out the discrepancy between the signature and the domain:

> >> This has got to be bait, right?????
> Since the "college junior" is not coming from an .edu address, then I would guess yes it does. :-)

> College junior @ aol.com? Bad bait, too obvious.

Still, as with many issues of online identity, the question of Derick's intentions remained unresolved:

> >> >>I worry about people like this on motorcycles.
> >>I worry about people like this behind on computers. No matter how lame the bait someone will bite.
> What scares me even more is teh possibility that it isn't bait.

In a group such as rec.motorcycles an occasional troll is not too harmful. The troll's game of testing the participants' astuteness is not too far in spirit from the newsgroup's normal banter and remarks such as "Bad bait, too obvious" imply the testing goes both way. A better troll would be admired for cleverness; the offense here was not trolling *per se*, but doing it so poorly.

In other groups the presence of a troll can inflict quite a bit of harm by undermining the trust of the community. The wedding newsgroups that Ultimatego frequented consist of women (and a few men) from very disparate backgrounds discussing the planning of a highly emotional event fraught with concerns about family, tradition, money, and status. The culture that has evolved frowns upon any authoritative statement of the "right" way to do things and writers frame their advice with phrases such as "in my opinion" or "it is often done this way." Ultimatego's early posts were not overtly offensive, but their formal and imperative voice was at odds with the conversational tone of the other participants.

One woman wrote:

Hi Everyone, Some of my coworkers and I were wondering if it is still considered a faux pas to wear white to someone else's wedding. One of the girls just got married and said she noticed that about 20 women (400 guests) wore white outfits. It didn't bug her, but another guest commented about it later. thanks, Jaime (and Jet) 03-09-96

Ultimatego responded:

Dear Jaime,

It is consider improper to wear white at a whedding, since it appears to compete with the bride. The guests were improperly dressed. It is taboo to wear black...even as a fashion statement since it is associated traditionally with mourning.

Kindly,
Cheryl.

Had Ultimatego maintained this persona, it is quite possible that she would have been accepted as the wedding groups' duenna, uninvited but not entirely unwelcome. However, Ultimatego's facade kept slipping. She went from chilly to rude, her proper grammar sliding into vicious name calling. Participants who could otherwise count on a generally supportive reaction from the group found themselves subject to Ultimatego's attacks. To someone seeking advice about a painful issue, such as a parent who is refusing to come to the wedding, the feeling that part of the audience was motivated by hostility or perverse humor was inhibiting.

Some trolls post deliberately misleading information. In rec.pets.cats a writer named keffo suggested deterring cats from clawing furniture and chewing on wires by spraying hydrogen peroxide at them. Again, the readers' reactions were mixed. Rec.pets.cats has had a great deal of experience with Usenet pranks and many readers immediately cried "troll!" Others believed that she was well-meaning and simply did not know that such a technique would be extremely painful to the cat; the fact that she claimed to be a girl in eighth grade helped to explain her naiveté. And some readers thought it was a reasonable suggestion, at least until a number of more knowledgeable ones explained the danger to the cat's eyes. Although past experience had taught the readers of rec.pets.cats that ignoring hostile posts was the best approach, this case was a bit different:

> Personally I find her type of marginal sadism towards cats as disturbing as the more overt alt.t*steless stuff, in that she could actually convince people that her suggestions are harmless. Do people who don't wear contacts know how painful it is to get the wrong solution in their eyes? I think this type of insidious troll needs stamping on as much as any other, with the proviso that in this case it is important that other people quickly point out the cruelty of her suggestions; other trolls, I think, should be ignored completely.

Responding to a troll is very tempting, especially since these posts are designed to incite. Yet this is where the troll can cause the most harm, by diverting the discussion off the newsgroup topic and into a heated argument. Instead, most groups advise ignoring such posts, both to keep the discussion topical and in the hope that, if ignored, the troll will go away. Several point newcomers to FAQs that explain how to use a killfile, which is a filter that allows one to avoid seeing any postings by a particular person or on a given topic. (Indeed, an extensive description of killfile techniques in a group's FAQ is a kind of virtual scar-tissue, an indication that they have had previous trouble with trolls or flame-wars.)

Rebuking the offending writer privately through email is also often recommended, for it does not derail the group's discussion. Such a response can be quite effective in stopping someone whose goal was not primarily to annoy others:

> I would like to apologize, to any and all of you who downloaded the junk I posted . . . Again I am sorry and will be more carefull in the future. Oh and I would like to thank the hundreds of you sent me E-Mail bringing it to my attention.
>
> – comp.cad.autocad

though it may encourage the troll whose intent was to inflame. If, however, the writer uses a false name and address, such contact is not possible.

Responding to a troll can be costly. One may be unpleasantly insulted, as happened to this person who tried to explain to keffo (who, it later transpired, was actually a male university student) the error of her ways:

> I have tried twice to communicate with Kristen (Keffo) (by e-mail). I have found that she is nothing but a foul mouthed, uneducated, little girl who lacks respect for anything Adults;Education; Culture; Life; etc. I have received nothing but insulting profanity from this child. I explained that IF she wanted to be accepted by this group that she should issue a **Blanket Apology** to the group - I was told what to do with my "Blanket Apology."

Others who have responded in person to newsgroup harassers have been mail-bombed or have had their own system administrator – or boss – contacted and told that they were making trouble online.

Contacting the offender's system administrator is usually done as a last resort, when it is clear that the rules of Usenet etiquette have been transgressed. Mail to keffo's postmaster complaining about the increasingly hostile postings resulted in the account being closed:

> Actually, keffo is a male university student. I've had enough of these complaints though, so don't expect to hear from him again. This is the last straw.

How seriously the system administrators or other authorities take such complaints varies greatly from provider to provider. Some may do nothing; others may be very quick to expel a user based on even a spurious complaint.

Category deception

Our perception of others is not one of wholly unique individuals, but of patterns of social categories. Our first impressions, based on brief observation, determine the basic social categories in which we place the new acquaintance, and which shape our subsequent and more detailed interpretations of their motives and behaviors (Simmel 1971). It can take significant evidence to change this initial categorization – we are more likely to reinterpret the events than to re-evaluate the basic classification (Aronson 1995).

The troll is engaging in category deception. By giving the impression of being a particular type – a conservative etiquette zealot helping brides avoid errors in taste, a young girl sharing her discoveries about cat care, an earnest college junior shopping for his first motorcycle – the troll manipulates the readers' initial interpretations of his or her postings. Only when the contradictions between the troll's actions and the expectations raised by the category assessment strongly conflict does the deception begin to unravel; when, in Goffman's (1959) performance metaphor, the troll speaks out of character. Still, many readers attempt to reinterpret the actions rather than disbelieve the identification. The decisive moment in the group's realization that the postings are coming from a troll is when someone offers evidence that the real person behind the virtual identity is at odds with the one presented.

There are many other varieties of online category deception. Gender deception (O'Brien, Chapter 4 in this volume; Turkle 1995) is the classic one, especially in the MUDs and in chat rooms where sex is a predominant topic of conversation (or at least, a very significant subtext to the discussion). In the Usenet newsgroups, gender deception appears to be much less common, except in forums where sex and gender are the main conversational topics. Similar category deceptions, e.g. age deception, do occur in Usenet; however, since many cases are not obvious, it is impossible to know how often or to what degree this occurs.

What does seem to be quite common here is status enhancement. Many news-groups have some exemplary model: the consummate hacker in alt.2600, the cool biker in rec.motorcycles, the well-built body in misc.fitness.weights. The participant who tries to pass as an incarnation of the ideal is closely examined by the others in the group. Status in these groups is prized and, for those whose claim on it is legitimate (or who have quite thoroughly deceived the others), accepting claims of dubious provenance would lessen the value and exclusiveness of their own position.

> WE all know Barry is a pathetic puppy, but his recent freaking out about my posting a picture of me has really set him off. I have many times told him to post a picture of himself so he can put up or shut up about "how ripped an huge" he claims to be.
> — misc.fitness.weights

The verbal claim of being muscular is a conventional signal. A change in the environment (the advent of the Web) has made it possible to send a more reliable signal of muscularity – a photograph. A prominent member of the group (the author of the above quote) put his photograph online, thus strengthening his claim to status (the photo is very impressive). Most participants applauded this effort, saying that they found it helpful to see what another participant looked like and reassuring to know that this writer's claims of expertise were indeed backed by his appearance. "Barry," however, greeted it with a great deal of hostility and renewed claims of his own strength; he was then challenged by many others to prove his words – to back up the conventional verbal signal with the assessment signal of a photograph.

In some groups the postings themselves are assessment signals for a salient trait. In rec.arts.poetry, aspiring poets submit their verses for critique by their peers; in comp.lang.perl programmers provide elegantly coded solutions in response to requests for help. An interesting example is alt.hackers. This is a moderated group, meaning that postings cannot be submitted directly to the newsgroup, but must be sent to the moderator, who (in ordinary moderated groups) filters out irrelevant or otherwise unacceptable material and posts the rest. Alt.hackers uses this mechanism, but without any actual moderator: to post to the group one must be able to figure out how to hack the news system. In such groups status claims and posturing are far less pervasive. This is especially noticeable in the contrast between alt.hackers and its non-assessment analogue alt.2600. Posts to the former tend to be on topic and informative; those to the latter are often (when they are not completely off topic) escalating boasts about petty criminal prowess.

> Why is it that everyone keeps posting that they can do amazing things, yet no proof has surfaced? Making up all this is easy because no one can rebute it, yet no one has confirmed these either. Don't post this crap unless you have some way of confirming it.
> —alt.2600

Impersonation

Not all online deception involves categories. Individual identity – one's claim to be a particular individual, either in the physical or the real world – can also be challenged. A particularly costly form of identity deception is impersonation. If I can pass as you, I can wreck havoc on your reputation, either online or off.

Compared to the physical world, it is relatively easy to pass as someone else online since there are relatively few identity cues.[7] A surprising number of impersonated postings are made simply by signing the target's name, without copying the writing style or forging the header information. Even more surprising is how successful such crude imitations can be. Readers may pay little attention to the header information – or they may encounter the forgery in a subsequent posting, quoted without the header.

How harmful are such impersonations depends upon how defamatory the faked postings are and whether readers believe the false attribution. When impersonations are made in a newsgroup in order to discredit one of the group's participants, the target is likely to notice and post a denial:

> I am very disturbed to find that after only two weeks of Internet use, I am already being "impersonated" by another user . . . Is this really so easy to do? Or did this person have to work at it? I discovered postings to a Newsgroup that appeared to come from me . . . but which in fact did not.
>
> - alt.alien.visitors

Since Usenet postings are not necessarily read in sequence some readers may read the forgery and miss the one that reveals the deception. This is especially likely if the faked posting set off an acrimonious flame-war: many readers will simply skip the rest of the thread and any subsequent postings made by the apparent participants.

Some of the most harmful impersonations are done without deliberate malice toward the victim, who may simply have inadvertently provided a useful identity for the impersonator to hide behind. New computer users are warned to guard their passwords carefully and to be sure to log off from public terminals. It can be very difficult to prove that one did not actually write the words that are clearly traceable to one's account.

> I would like to think everyone for bringing to our attention the outrageous message that was posted to this group several days ago . . . After talking with the owner of the account that generated this post. It has become clear that this is a case of a new user leaving the terminal before logging off. I ask that you please refrain from sending mail to this user (ST40L) regarding the post. He is shaken from the incident and has learned a valuable lesson the hard way.
>
> - soc.culture.jewish

In this case, the user convinced the administrators that the posting (an anti-Semitic letter) was forged. Still, he must deal with the fact that a message that he finds abhorrent went out under his name. (This is particularly unfortunate since the debut of searchable Usenet archives. A search for letters written by this user will turn up the forgery, but not clarifications written by others, such as the one above.)

Identity concealment

Many individual identity deceptions are acts of omission, rather than commission; they involve hiding one's identity. Sometimes identity is hidden to circumvent killfiles. Killfiles are filters that allow you to skip unwanted postings: if you put someone in your killfile, you will see no more of their postings. While killfiles may sound like the electronic version of the ostrich putting its head in the sand, they are said to be very effective in keeping a newsgroup readable. Those using a killfile no longer see the offending posts and are not tempted to respond, thus lowering the number of angry, off-topic postings. To the person who has been killfiled, Usenet becomes a corridor of frustratingly shut doors: one can shout, but cannot be heard. Some writers, determined to have their say, continuously switch the name under which their postings appear.

> I gave up trying to killfile Grubor and his myriad aliases when my filter file exceeded 10k. I am not joking about this. Admittedly only half was Johnny-boy; the other half was phone-sex spams. Still, 4–5k just on one person is a little ridiculous.
>
> - news.groups

The killfile program looks for the account name in the header, which is usually inserted automatically by the posting software. The reason someone can create "myriad aliases" has to do with the transformation of the header from an assessment to a conventional signal.

Until recently, header information was quite reliable. Most people accessed Usenet with software that inserted the account name automatically – one had to be quite knowledgeable to change the default data. Many programs now simply let the writer fill in the name and address to be used, making posting with a false name and site much easier. The astute observer may detect suspicious anomalies in the routing data (the record of how the letter passed through the net) that can expose a posting from a falsified location.[8] Yet few people are likely to look that closely at a posting unless they have reason to be suspicious about its provenance.

With the header data becoming a conventional signal, such deception may be quite widespread. There are many benefits to using a pseudonym online and, unless the writer is imposing a cost on the group (i.e. being a nuisance or impersonating another participant), there is little reason to pay the costs of verifying each posting.

People have many reasons for not wanting their real names to be revealed online:

> As far as letting you know my name or giving you my fingerprints or whatever else you demand, no I don't think so. There is more going on in this net than just misc.fitness.weights. I'm involved in the net war in alt.religion.scientology. Those cultists have so far raided 4 of their net critics on bogus copyright violation charges, and in one

case they placed a large amount of LSD on the toothbrush of a person who was raided, a couple of days before he was to undergo a video deposition. In my city they have been convicted of several crimes, including infiltrating the municipal, provincial, and federal police forces. No, I will not give out my name just to satify your curiousity. Deal with it.
                                                                        - misc.fitness.weights

There can be real harm in being "seen" online. One Usenet troublemaker forwards postings to their authors' supervisors, claiming that they were inappropriate uses of the Net and that the author is a troll, etc. Although the original posts are completely legitimate (questions about integer precision in database packages and the like) many managers know little about Usenet culture and will assume that the employee must have been doing something wrong – and doing it on company time and under the company name. In an online discussion about this case, several people mentioned that, although they had free Internet access through work, they subscribed to a commercial service for their personal use, particularly for Usenet discussion: "I'd rather pay an ISP [Internet service provider] to maintain a home account than risk getting some nut-case harassing my employers."

Privacy is a common reason for using a pseudonym, for Usenet is an exposed public forum in which the writers have no control over who reads their posts. People who are embarrassed use pseudonyms, such as system administrators who are asking how to fix something with which they ought to be familiar. People who are revealing extremely personal data (as in alt.support.depression) or who are discussing matters of dubious legality (as in rec.drugs.psychedelic) often use anonymous remailers. Finally, some people may simply not want their participation in Usenet, no matter how innocuous, to be public knowledge.

It is useful to distinguish between pseudonymity and pure anonymity. In the virtual world, many degrees of identification are possible. Full anonymity is one extreme of a continuum that runs from the totally anonymous to the thoroughly named. A pseudonym, though it may be untraceable to a real-world person, may have a well-established reputation in the virtual domain; a pseudonymous message may thus come with a wealth of contextual information about the sender. A purely anonymous message, on the other hand, stands alone.

Anonymity (including pseudonymity) is very controversial in the online world. On one side, anonymity is touted as the savior of personal freedom, necessary to ensure liberty in an era of increasingly sophisticated surveillance. It "allows people to develop reputations based on the quality of their ideas, rather than their job, wealth, age, or status" (May 1994). On the other side, it is condemned as an invitation to anarchy, providing cover for criminals from tax-evaders to terrorists. The "very purpose of anonymity," said Supreme Court Justice Scalia, is to "facilitate wrong by eliminating accountability" (quoted in Froomkin 1995).

There is merit to both sides of the argument, much of it contingent on the distinction between anonymity and pseudonymity. Many of the strongest proponents of cryptographic privacy would agree that "anonymous community" is an oxymoron; their ideal is a pseudonymous world with merit-based reputations (May 1994). Purely anonymous individuals are capable of communicating with each other, but there is no accretion of personal histories in their interactions: reputation of any kind is impossible in a purely anonymous environment. The motivation for many of the qualities we associate with community, from cooperative behavior to creative endeavor, depends on the existence of distinct and persistent personae.

An interesting question is the accountability of a pseudonymous persona. The sanctions to offensive online behavior can be roughly divided into two main categories: those that involve making a connection to a real-world person and those that do not. Complaints to a system administrator or other real-world authority are in the former category; killfiles and public castigation are in the latter. Email flames are somewhere in-between – one must know an electronic address that the offender accesses in order for them to be seen at all, but that address may be quite securely pseudonymous in relation to the real-world identity. In an electronic environment in which pseudonyms are prevalent, only the sanctions that do not require a connection to the real world are practical. While these mechanisms can only discourage, and not eliminate, outlawed behavior, they can have a significant effect (Kollock and Smith 1996).

The evolving virtual world

In the world of biology, changes in signaling behavior may occur quite slowly, over evolutionary time. In the world of human interaction, changes can occur quite quickly. If excessive deception makes a signal lose its meaning, it can be replaced by a more reliable assessment signal or the community may begin to punish deception. In the virtual world, both the participants and the environment itself change: the participants establish new styles of interaction and the environment evolves as it is further designed and developed.

Killfiles are a good example of a social action that is poorly supported by the existing technology. One of the basic features (or drawbacks) of Usenet is that the readers are invisible. On the positive side, this lends it an aura of intimacy that would quite possibly be lacking if each writer were viscerally aware of the enormous number of people who follow the newsgroup. On the negative side, it makes the fact that one is ignoring someone very hard to indicate. The need to publicly turn away from someone can be seen in the custom of sending a posting that says "Plonk!," in response to that last-straw posting that caused one to killfile someone – "plonk" is the sound of dropping the offender into the killfile.

> Why do people feel the need to announce to the whole world that they have
> justplonked someone? Big deal. It happens all the time. Plonk 'em and get
> n with your life.

"On the Internet, no one can hear your killfile." Sometimes it is not only neccisary to regard someone as an idoit, you have to make them aware of it as well. I just wonder where they got the idea that killfiles have sound effects.

-alt.cypherpunks

The counterpart of "plonk" is the posting that simply says "yes, I agree!" These affirmations show that a particular opinion has enthusiastic backers and they provide a way to indicate an affiliation to an idea or person. These are frowned upon in Usenet etiquette because as a full-scale posting, they require too much time and effort to download, given the minimal information they include.

The online world is a wholly built environment. The architects of a virtual space – from the software designers to the site administrators – shape the community in a more profound way than do their real-world counterpart. People eat, sleep, and work in buildings; the buildings affect how happily they do these things. But the buildings do not completely control their perception of the world. In the electronic domain, the design of the environment is everything. Whether or not you know that other people are present or privy to a conversation, whether you can connect an online identity to a real-world person, whether you have only a faint notion of the personalities of those around you or a vibrant and detailed impression – this is all determined by the design of the environment.

How can Usenet – or other discussion-based systems – be redesigned to allow for better communication of social cues? Systems that are able to show participants or participant behavior – how other readers have navigated a newsgroup or how close or far other readers place themselves from an idea or person – are technically feasible. The real question is how they would affect the Usenet community. My prediction is that making the social patterns more visible would increase the strength of social pressures, making the community both more orderly and less spontaneous. But predicting the social ramifications of technology is difficult, especially when the whole environment is in constant flux.

For example, Usenet postings used to be ephemera, remaining available for only days or weeks before they disappeared from the Net. Starting in 1995, several news archives have become available. These archives extend the lifetime of a posting indefinitely and, more significantly, they are searchable. One can request a listing of someone's entire Usenet oeuvre. Without such a search mechanism, finding all of someone's postings was nearly impossible: you might know that they were a frequent contributor to, say, the nutrition and medical groups, but have no idea that they spent their evenings as a verbal warrior in the ethnic disputes on soc.culture.turkey or writing baby-talk "meow-chat" postings to rec.pets.cats. The archives bring forth all of one's contributions for public examination, removed from the social context for which they were written. It involves a paradigm shift, from perceiving Usenet as a series of effectively private areas, bounded not by technical means but by their sheer numbers and parochial focus, to seeing it as a public repository of neatly cross-referenced postings.

This is not necessarily a harmful development for the Usenet community. One of the drawbacks of the virtual world has been that one's view of others is sketchy and one-sided. Being able to gather a more complex image of one's fellow participants can deepen the social ties as the users see each other as more fully-rounded individuals (Sproull and Kiesler 1991). Again, prediction is tricky. As awareness of the new paradigm increases, people may become far more concerned with managing their online reputation, resulting in widespread use of multiple pseudonyms – and an even murkier view of who's who online.

The Usenet reader's picture of the other participants is also being filled in by the Web. Whereas the archives present a documentary recording, the Web-based home page presents a crafted self-presentation (Donath and Robertson 1994), showing how one wishes to appear – which can, of course, be quite inadvertently revealing (Goffman 1959). As home pages grow increasingly elaborate, their value to their creator grows. While it may not be terribly costly to discard, say, a name on AOL in order to escape from the consequences of actions done under it, one is far less inclined to abandon an online presence that has taken great effort to create. With an increasing number of articles signed with the writer's Web page, the Usenet readers gain both a deeper context for understanding an author's view, and a greater commitment by participants in the virtual environment.

Here again, the social ramifications may be unexpected. In a forum where a link to one's Web page is the norm, the opportunity to explore multiple personae may be greatly curtailed (though perhaps given greater depth, if one was then motivated to create an elaborate series of pseudonymous portraits). For most people, one Web presence suffices – and it is often an official one, created for one's employer, one with a picture revealing age, race, gender, etc. The cost of deception would certainly be higher – the question remains whether that is necessarily a good thing.

New ways of establishing and of hiding identity are evolving in the virtual world. There is no formula that works best in all forums: balancing privacy and accountability, reliability and self-expression, security and accessibility requires a series of compromises and trade-offs whose value is very dependent on the goals of the group and of the individuals that comprise it. The role of this chapter has been to examine closely the approaches – the signals – that have developed in a very diverse yet technically simple environment. What we have seen is a world of complex interactions, one that intermingles people from disparate real-world cultures and disparate virtual-world cultures; a world in which the boundaries exist only as social mechanisms and are both fluid and surprisingly durable. It is a world in which a technology built for the exchange of scientific data among a small class of academics and professionals has evolved into a communications forum in which information is still exchanged, but so is support and affiliation and adolescent bonding and outbursts of anger. It is a world that has evolved an intricate system of signals and behaviors that aid in establishing identity and in controlling identity deception.

Notes

1 A FAQ is a document that contains many of the facts and anecdotes relevant to a group; their purpose is to answer these questions before they are asked – yet again – in the newsgroup. A FAQ may be quite long and require much effort to create and keep up to date.

2 Examples include "femme fatale" fireflies, brood parasites such as the cuckoo and the cowbird, and Batesian mimics such as the burrowing owl and the viceroy butterfly. "Femme fatale" fireflies are predatory females of the species Photuris who are able to mimic the flash pattern of females of the species Photinus. The deceptive Photuris female signals, the

unsuspecting Photinus male approaches, and the predatory female attacks and eats him. Brood parasites lay their eggs in the nest of another bird. The unwitting adoptive parent hatches the egg and raises the parasite, often at the expense of its own offspring. Batesian mimics are harmless species which imitate species that are repellent to predators or competitors: the Viceroy butterfly resembles the bad-tasting Monarch; the hissing call of the burrowing owl sounds like a rattlesnake's rattle.

3 Names and other identifying features have been changed.

4 Killfiles are used to filter out postings by people or about topics one does not wish to read. For more about killfiles see p. 52.

5 This is not to say that these "parts" are necessarily straightforward. See O'Brien (Chapter 4 in this volume) for a discussion of the complexity of gender roles – and the added intricacy of their virtual manifestation.

6 Robert Hayden, "The Code of the Geeks", http://krypton.mankato.msus.edu/~hayden/geek.html, 1995.

7 There exists a technological solution to this problem. A digital signature can ensure that a message has not been altered since it was signed and, given various levels of certification, it can guarantee that a particular person was the signer. Interestingly, the certification of identity is personal trust. Individuals vouch for individuals and their personal guarantees become a part of one's digital signature. If I know nothing about the people who vouched for you, the guarantee is meaningless. They are currently rather difficult to use, though this is a problem more of interface than underlying technology. As encryption and decryption become an integrated part of the virtual environment, the appearance of a real, vouched-for persona may begin to differ markedly from other, more ephemeral beings (see Garfinkel 1995 for a full technical exposition).

8 A letter posted to Usenet is distributed through the Net by being passed from the sender's machine through a series of Usenet sites, each of which distributes it to a number of other sites. When it finally reaches a particular reader's machine, it may have passed through twenty or more sites or "hops," each of which records its name on the header of the posting. While the exact route a posting from A to B will take is not predictable (one of the distinctive technological features of the Internet is its ability to re-route itself around a down machine and clogged regions), obvious peculiarities in the route are signs of a forged message.

References and further reading

On identity, society, virtual community

Aronson, E. 1995. *The Social Animal* (7th edn). New York: W.H. Freeman.

Beniger, J.R. 1987. "The personalization of mass media and the growth of pseudo community," *Communication Research* 14(3): 252–371.

Constant, D., Kiesler, S. and Sproull, L. 1995. "The kindness of strangers: the usefulness of weak ties for technical advice," *Organization Science* 7(2): 119–135.

Curtis, P. 1992. "Mudding: social phenomena in text-based virtual realities," *Proceedings of the 1992 Conference on Directions and Implications of Advanced Computing*. Berkeley, CA, May.

Davis, F. 1992. *Fashion, Culture and Identity*. Chicago, IL: University of Chicago Press.

Dibbell, J. 1993. "A rape in cyberspace," *The Village Voice* December 21.

Donath, J. 1995. "Sociable information spaces," *Proceedings of the Second IEEE International Workshop on Community Networking*. Princeton, NJ, June.

Donath, J. and Robertson, N. 1994. "The sociable Web," *Proceedings of the Second International WWW Conference*. Chicago, IL, October.

Fiske, J. 1989. *Understanding Popular Culture*. London and New York: Routledge.

Froomkin, A.M. 1995. "Anonymity and its enemies," *Journal of Online Law* art. 4.

Garfinkel, S. 1995. *PGP: Pretty Good Privacy*. Sebastopol, CA: O'Reilly & Associates.

Geertz, C. 1973. *The Interpretation of Cultures*. New York: Basic Books.

Goffman, E. 1959. *The Presentation of Self in Everyday Life*. New York: Doubleday.

Goffman, E. 1967. *Interaction Ritual*. New York: Pantheon.

Kollock, P. 1994. "The emergence of exchange structures: an experimental study of uncertainty, commitment and trust," *American Journal of Sociology* 100: 313–45.

Kollock, Peter, and Marc Smith. 1996. "Managing the virtual commons: cooperation and conflict in computer communities," in Susan Herring (ed.) *Computer-Mediated Communication: Linguistic, Social, and Cross-Cultural Perspectives*. Amsterdam: John Benjamins.

May, T. 1994. The cyphernomicon: cypherpunks FAQ and more. http://www.oberlin.edu/%7Ebrchkind/cyphernomicon/

McCracken, G. 1988. *Culture and Consumption: New Approaches to the Symbolic Character of Consumer Goods and Activities*. Bloomington, IN: Indiana University Press.

Milgram, S. 1977. *The Individual in a Social World*. Reading, MA: Addison-Wesley.

Reid, E. 1991. "Electropolis: Communication and Community on Internet Relay Chat," thesis, Department of History, University of Melbourne.

Rheingold, H. 1993. *The Virtual Community: Homesteading on the Electronic Frontier*. Reading, MA: Addison-Wesley.

Saville-Troike, M. 1982. *The Ethnography of Communication*. London: Basil Blackwell.

Simmel, G. 1971. *On Individuality and Social Forms*, edited by D. Levine. Chicago: University of Chicago Press.

Sproull, L. and Kiesler, S. 1991. *Connections: New Ways of Working in the Networked Organization*. Cambridge, MA: MIT Press.

Sproull, L. and Faraj, S. 1995. "Atheism, sex, and databases: the Net as a social technology," in B. Kahin and J. Keller (eds) *Public Access to the Internet*. Cambridge, MA: MIT Press.

Stone, A.R. 1992. "Will the real body please stand up? Boundary stories about virtual cultures," in M. Benedikt (ed.) *Cyberspace: First Steps*. Cambridge, MA: MIT Press.

Synnott, A. 1993. *The Body Social: Symbolism, Self, and Society*. London: Routledge.

Turkle, S. 1995. *Life on the Screen: Identity in the Age of the Internet*. New York: Simon & Schuster.

On signals and modeling deception

Alcock, John. 1989. *Animal Behavior: An Evolutionary Approach* (4th edn). Sunderland, MA: Sinauer.

Dawkins, M.S. and Guilford, T. 1991. "The corruption of honest signalling," *Animal Behavior* 41: 865–73.

Dawkins, R. and Krebs, J.R. 1978. "Animal signals: information or manipulation?" in J.R.

Krebs and N.B. Davies (eds) *Behavioural Ecology: An Evolutionary Approach*. Oxford: Blackwell Scientific.

Grafen, A. 1990. "Biological signals as handicaps," *Journal of Theoretical Biology* 144: 517–46.

Hauser, M. 1992. "Costs of deception: cheaters are punished in rhesus monkeys," *Proceedings of the National Academy of Sciences of the USA* 89: 12137–9.

Hauser, M. 1996. *The Evolution of Communication*. Cambridge, MA: MIT Press.

Johnstone, R.A. and Grafen, A. 1991. "Error-prone signalling," *Proceedings of the Royal Society of London* B 248: 229–33.

Krebs, J.R. and Davies, N.B. 1993. *An Introduction to Behavioural Ecology* (3rd edn). Oxford: Blackwell Scientific.

Maynard Smith, J. 1974. "The theory of games and the evolution of animal conflicts," *Journal of Theoretical Biology* 47: 209–21.

Zahavi, A. 1977. "The cost of honesty (further remarks on the handicap principle)," *Journal of Theoretical Biology* 67: 603–5.

Zahavi, A. 1993. "The fallacy of conventional signalling," *The Royal Society Philosophical Transaction* B 340: 227–30.

Chapter 3

Reading race online

Discovering racial identity in Usenet discussions[1]

Byron Burkhalter

In both academic studies and in common understandings, the connection between the body and racial identity is strong. From the sixteenth century, race has been used to denote common descent and was seen as carried by blood (Banton 1987; Gossett 1965). In the nineteenth century, genes replaced blood but still race was contained by the body. This connection still holds. Van Den Berghe (1993: 240) distinguishes race as a bodily feature from ethnicity, which is a cultural feature: "Ethnicity is based upon cultural markers of membership, such as language, religion, and countless symbols such as clothing, holidays, music, literature, tattooing, and so on, whereas race is marked by heritable phenotypes." Being a member of a racial group is now fundamentally a claim about physical features such as skin color, hair texture, facial features, and musculature.

Even when scholars conceive of race as a status, a class, or a social construction, still race is described as a biological phenomenon in which societies invest social meaning (for example, Lyman and Douglass 1973). When psychologists test children to find out if they correctly label themselves racially or ethnically, the body is the independent variable. That is, if children label themselves white but they are phenotypically black, the former basis of identification is brought into question not the latter (Phinney and Rotheram 1987). When sociologists study the phenomenon called "passing" they do not find that just because a person is living socially as a Latino that they are in fact Latino. Instead, the social circumstances are seen as hiding the actuality of the inherited lineage. The body's phenotype, and when that fails its genotype, is the anchor of racial identity.

As with gender and age, establishing racial identity in face-to-face interaction relies heavily on physical cues provided by the body. Physical characteristics like skin color and vocal patterns are pivotal clues to racial identity that can eliminate the need for an explicit claim to racial membership. People expect others to take their race into consideration on "appropriate" occasions, and interactants may take offense when their race or gender or age is misidentified. Even if the offended party has not specified his or her race, there is an expectation that race should have been gleaned from embodied physical signals alone. In Goffman's terms, race is a sign "given off" (1959: 2). This makes race useful in interaction because it provides for stereotypical understandings based upon a racially immutable body. Once established, racial identity is a reliable social resource that organizes the behaviors that one anticipates, allows, and accepts from another. Knowing another's racial identity provides ways of understanding and acting toward the other. For example, Spaights and Dixon (1984) use racial and gender identity to understand the pathological motivations of Blacks and Whites entering into inter-racial romantic "alliances." White males are understood as having a set of potential motives for being romantically involved with a black female because of their racial identity:

> He may view her as the "earth mother," a source of spontaneous sexual play that he has not found among white women. . . . He may view black lifestyle as having a richness lacking in a more inhibiting white social group. A liberal upbringing may lead him to identify with the underdog. . . . He may take the pleasure from offending his friends or relatives. He may respond to a black woman out of guilt, to expiate the sins of his race against black people.
>
> (Spaights and Dixon 1984: 135)

More than a novel approach to the absolution of sin, this motive explains the action of interracial coupling through the racial identities of the participants. This is how racial stereotyping works, action is explained by reference to racial identity which is in turn based upon physical characteristics. However, the physical characteristics that indicate racial identity offline are lacking in online communication. Indeed, this textual medium would seem to render race an unreliable resource for understanding the other. Some social commentators are seeing racial identity as capricious or obsolete in online interaction. If that is true then the basis of stereotyping would seem to be in a precarious position.[2]

While physical cues are lacking online, for better or worse racial identification is not lacking. Racial identity is a feature of many online interactions. There are, in fact, many online discussion groups specifically dedicated to the discussion of racial and cultural issues. These groups, known as soc.culture newsgroups, are perspicuous settings for exploring the organization of online racial identity. My focus was on a particular soc.culture group, soc.culture.african.american (SCAA), and to a lesser degree on two similar groups, soc.culture.jewish (SCJ) and soc.culture.mexican.american (SCMA). As participants in these groups describe and debate racial issues, they categorize themselves and others in racial terms that range from general racial categories (African-American, Chinese, European-American, White, Latino, etc.) to vernacular expressions (sell-out, banana, brother).[3] Racial identity is a feature of these discussions, without the presence of the body. Because of the technological environment these online discussions allow the study of race in interaction in a way that removes the body and the propensity to see the body as the site of actual racial identity.[4]

Race and racial identity are not capricious features of online interaction. The participants in these groups do not racially identify themselves or others randomly but in an orderly fashion as part of their ongoing discussions. In private conversations some observers have suggested that online interaction creates an ambiguous social space. My argument is that such claims are not the experience of the participants. Ambiguity implies that reading the Usenet gives participants a doubt-ridden, hesitant, and uncertain feeling. Reading a thread titled "All niggers must die" brought with it no ambiguous social space. I felt that I recognized the racially salient features of the interaction and the racial identities of the participants were unproblematic. Reading Usenet messages suggests that people are quite certain of the other's identities, far from showing the hesitancy that ambiguity would predict, participants label, preach, advise, agree and disagree without equivocation. Racial identity is no more ambiguous online than offline. The resources of the medium are sufficient for participants' determinations of racial identity. Offline, of course, people do not present themselves with their lineage documentation or DNA analysis attached. Certainty of racial identity offline or online is always contingent – absolute proof is not available and rarely necessary.

While the certainty of racial identification is not significantly affected by the medium, the achievement, maintenance, and use of racial identity is changed. The fixed reference of the body is online transformed into the largely immutable text of the message. Most software allows one to quote but not otherwise alter the messages of others. As authors in soc.culture groups write on racial topics for particular audiences, their messages serve as an important source of racial cues. These messages offer the author's understandings of self, audience, and topic. Responses quote parts of the author's own message to join or invalidate the previous author's claims and their words serve the discernment of identity as much as hair texture or skin color does in offline discussions. As discussions unfold, the most reliable foundation for categorizing an author is in the author's message. It is the perspectives in those messages that reveal the participants' actual racial identities. Without physical cues, racial identification is anchored to the perspectives on racial issues offered in authors' messages.

The change from a reliance on a physical body to reliance on an author's perspective has consequences for the usefulness of racial identity and for the way in which stereotyping proceeds. One consequence is that any discrepancy between author's perspective and author's stated identity may be resolved by adjusting the identity to fit the perspective. In offline interaction, individuals may use another's racial identity to make assumptions about their perspectives, beliefs or attitudes. Online interaction uses an individual's perspectives, beliefs and attitudes to make assumptions about the individual's racial identity.

Online interaction does not create a confused social situation, nor does it give racial identity a chimerical quality. Racial identity is consequential in online interactions. This chapter, after introducing the Usenet environment, uses observational data to look first at how racial identity is achieved, maintained, questioned, and reestablished. Next the consequences of online racial identity for stereotyping are considered. In fact, stereotypical notions of particular racial identities may be more immutable in online interaction than offline. Far from eliminating race as a salient characteristic, online inter-actants employ the limited resources available in a textual medium to establish a racial world online that resembles the offline world.

Usenet newsgroups

The Usenet, a global electronic bulletin board, comprises a set of "newsgroups" on the Internet. There are several thousand different newsgroups, each devoted to a specific topic or interest. Newsgroups are named in a hierarchical scheme: general categories like "comp" (computers), "rec" (recreation) and "soc" (social) identify the generic topic of the group. More specific terms are added until a complete newsgroup name is created. For example, a group that discusses a computer programming language called "Perl" (Practical Extraction and Report Language) is named "comp.lang.perl," a group devoted to producing plays is named "rec.arts.theatre.stagecraft."

A Usenet newsgroup is a site for the collection of messages. Participants send messages to a newsgroup where others can read and download them. About 125 Usenet groups have a particular culture as their primary topic. "Soc.culture" groups vary in size from apparently empty groups (soc.culture.welsh) to groups that contain thousands of messages (SCJ, SCAA). Large Usenet groups receive between 200 and 1,000 messages per day.

A group like SCAA may contain thousands of messages. Most readers have neither the time nor the inclination to read all the messages in a large newsgroup. Messages are often linked in "threads" – chains of responses and counter-responses on a particular topic. Threaded messages are located under a "subject line" that allows participants to view only messages of interest.

The display of threads on the screen gives an illusion of orderliness that is not present in the posts themselves. Usenet discussion groups are not like conversations in which participants are present from the beginning and have heard everything the other participants have said, thus forming a single temporally unfolding discussion. Instead, threads are conversations in which individuals constantly enter and exit, speak on the basis of the last few exchanges, and go off to other conversations. In other words, the Usenet resembles a large cocktail party.

Racial identity

In face-to-face interaction an individual's physical characteristics, from skin color to vocal patterns, help convey racial identity. Lacking such physical cues on computer networks, one might predict that discrimination on the basis of race, age, gender, sexuality, class, status, and group membership would disappear. Indeed, some participants use the lack of physical cues to claim any identity they want. An SCAA message suggests: "You are welcome here! Come on in. Would you like a beer or something? The only true color here is the monitor screen. Here I can be Black, White or Green."

The sense of freedom when establishing an online racial identity derives from a persistent belief that racial categorization is determined exclusively by corporeal traits. Although much sociological and anecdotal evidence has challenged this belief, race is still popularly seen as a characteristic of bodies (Spickard 1992). The body does not reveal race irrefutably. Multiracial individuals chronicle incidents in which their physical attributes were variously interpreted. The question multiracial individuals are so often asked – "what are you?" – displays the problematic relationship between physical characteristics and racial identity. The possibility of passing or being mistaken for a different race in face-to-face interaction is also evidence of the fallible relationship between observable traits and identity (Bradshaw 1992). Of course, answers to the question "what are you?" must be appropriate to the individual's observable character-istics. Physical characteristics are a resource that permit and limit a range of interpretations, but they are only one medium among a variety of resources.

In online interactions, participants are reduced to textual resources, but these resources can be just as determinant as physical indicators are offline. The posts show that racial identity, although fixed differently than it is offline, is firmly established online. Racial characterizations of others are done with little hesitancy. For example, in an SCAA discussion concerning Supreme Court Justice Clarence Thomas's race, the responder does not hesitate to "identify" the author of the quote:

> >What? Clarence Thomas is not Black? I don't know, he sure
> > looks Black to me. What's a "real Black" in this case?
>
> Spoken like a true White boy.

Online communication, at first glance, intensifies the problem of verifying other people's racial identities because it obscures many of the cues that people use in identifying self and others racially. This has led some researchers to focus on the possibility for deception in online discussions (Donath, Chapter 2 in this volume). However, participants in Internet newsgroups seem more concerned with being known than remaining anony-mous – they seem more interested in reception than deception. Many people put their names and workplaces at the end of their messages; other messages include home phone and office fax numbers. As interesting as the possibilities for deception may be, of equal interest are the ways individuals make themselves known, understood, and characterized in online interactions. The following sections sketch the way individuals come to know each other's racial identity.

Racial frames and racial relevance

Each soc.culture newsgroup concerns a particular racial or cultural group around which members organize their participation. One aspect of participation are the subject lines in soc.culture groups which quite often mention a cultural, racial, or ethnic term in bringing a topic up for discussion. Even potentially race-neutral topics are made race-relevant in subject lines. For example, an SCAA discussion about women not properly appreciating "men who treat them right" was titled "Sisters please explain," "Sisters" here being an idiomatic reference to African-American women. In this way, the topic is framed as a question to African-Americans. Through the use of such "cultural frames" discussions start with an explicit connection to a specific racial topic.[5]

However, subsequent postings may or may not pick up on the original post's explicitly racial elements. This falls in line with Okamura's (1981) discussion of the subjective or cognitive dimension of "situational ethnicity." This aspect "pertains to the actor's subjective perception of the situation in which he finds himself and to the salience he attributes to ethnicity as a relevant factor in that situation" (1981: 454). The way in which race is made relevant in any posting is at the discretion of the author. The following responses are from a thread which concerned a report of the Nation of Islam caning two black youths whom they caught shoplifting. The initial post framed the issue as a racial topic concerning an African-American group punishing African-American youths. In looking to the cause of the youth problem the first author sees community and parenting as causes without mentioning race:

> I grew up in a household where everyone had carte blanche to whup my butt. Neighbors, teachers, older siblings etc.. The only rule was let my mother know what happened so she could get some later!!!... I've seen most of my friends children hit them more often than I've seen the parents hit the kids. In my house, that was a good way to get your teeth knocked out. Don't get me wrong I wasn't abused in the least bit, but it seems that somewhere along the line parents have substituted being a good parent with buying all the Power Rangers or doing what the kids want.

Another response characterizes the cause as parenting and the community but with race featured prominently. The problem is not community in general but the black community in particular:

> It is not easy putting up with many members of the black community. Without knowledge and understanding of the black condition, Black people will make you hate them. I know for a fact that the Muslims are trained not to be the aggressors. There had to be some kind of provocation for those youngsters to be physically disciplined. Too many people rush to the defense of the wrongdoer when authority is involved. If the children were wrong, they were wrong.
>
> A woman by the name of _____ stated that the [Nation of Islam] was not the law enforcer of her choice. When our people are arrested by local or state police agencies and disciplined within the prison system little opposition is expressed. White discipline: Yes!; Black discipline: No!

Responses can variously describe the salience of race. Over the course of a long thread, a discussion of residential segregation can shift to a conversation on "being a good neighbor" before ending as an exchange of ideas on home landscaping. Despite the newsgroup's name or subject line heading, the relevance of race is not assured through the thread's course.

Identity as a consequence of racial relevance

While taking a position is at the discretion of the author, these positions are not without consequence. There is choice but not free choice. What can be missed in conceiving of identity as subjective and cognitive is the empirical dimension of identity as an inter-subjective and interactional phenomenon. Identity is interactionally negotiated. The description of the relevance of race an author puts forth has consequences for how their identity is established. As a result of particular positions and ways of describing racial issues, authors are racially identified, as in the next example of responses to an initial letter on affirmative action from SCAA:

>> I wouldn't hire a minority just out of principal. I would hire a woman but because
>> of the fact that there are people out there trying to force me to hire minorities just
>> because they're black or Hispanic or whatever else I would refuse to hire a minority
>> out of principal. If you want a job then earn it or just live your life in poverty but
>> don't expect white America to hire you just because your not white.

> And there you have it. A stupid white bigot. . . .

I thought the same thing, but this person is probably one of those Black people that got IN under affirmative action, and doesn't realize it! One must not assume he's white. There are so many Black people that are AGAINST affirmative action because they are brainwashed into believing that the "color of his skin is no more important than the color of his eyes!"

Recognition of this interactional dimension to racial identity goes against the popular sense that online racial identity is exclusively the crafted product of the author. If the reader cannot see the author, the reader cannot assert the author's race with any certainty – the author seemingly has total control. Without disconfirming physical evidence, online authors may feel free of the usual constraints when establishing a racial identity. While many talk about the power of authors' claims in online interaction, few have discussed the power of audience reception. Although any identity may be asserted online, such assertions can be disputed or differently received. Having concentrated on physical characteristics as disconfirming evidence for authors, it is possible to overlook the confirming evidence those physical signals provide. An author may claim to be "green" but getting others in a newsgroup to accept the claimed identity, without recourse to physical signals, is another matter.

As evidence of the limits of authors' identification choice, online authors cannot simply dispense with identity. A service known as an anonymous mailer sends Usenet messages that are virtually untraceable – readers cannot tell where anonymous messages originated or gather clues about the author's identity from the heading. The removal of these identifiers does not undermine identification but instead offers the respondents a myriad of options to discredit the author. Anonymous messages serve to undercut the credibility of an author's identity and argument. For example, as participants in SCAA debated forming a moderated newsgroup in which a central authority determines which messages are appropriate to post to the newsgroup, an anonymous response weighed in:

> Who is to say what the purpose of the ng [newsgroup] is? It can be a place where
> people of all races come to discuss the effect of african american culture, as
> interpreted from the nobody actions of african americans, on school educational
> standards, violent crime rates, etc.

Anyone that's too cowardly to post under a name has no input anywhere except down in the slime with the rest of their ilk.

Anonymity, which might be considered an asset for authors, can instantly disqualify them.

The recognition of the interactional character of identity can offer some insight into the reason that racial identity comes up in particular situations and not in others. Authors offer perspectives, descriptions, and arguments on racial issues, with race depicted as an essential or incidental feature. As authors position the relevance of race, they also potentially reveal for others their own "true" racial identity. Thus, as a consequence of messages posted concerning racial topics, SCAA becomes populated by sell-outs, white supremacists, pro-Black-overkill Blacks, liberal-well-meaning Whites, in-cog-Negroes, brothers-who-are-down-with-their-people, religious conservatives, and other racial identities.[6]

Identity disputes

Over the course of a single message, authors may racially identify themselves in several ways. In the following message sent to SCAA, which generated a small thread over a few days, the author employs a hodgepodge of identity cues:

Hi. I find that many African-Americans where I live (northern California) tend to act in a way they think they should act, rather than just be themselves. I'm acknowledging this because the reality is, the behavior of the minority completely stands out, as opposed to the behavior of the majority. I must say, that I am part African-American. I don't feel ashamed of this in any way, but I am ashamed of the African-American behavior of many citizens in my area. I am proud of all the ethnicities my gene pool possesses, while at the same time, I am proud of the ethnicities I don't possess. I ACCEPT those who are different from me. Different is good: it is new. it is unique. it is you. it is me. Let me explain more of what hits home for me. I must say that I am extremely proud of my mom. She is African-American and she is an individual. She speaks proper english because she chose to get an education, no matter how difficult that path would be. She's had a tough life; she grew up poor in Michigan; her mother died when she was five; she lived in foster homes her whole life; she was looked down upon because of status and her pigmentation. She is a very beautiful person. There are many more hardships to tell about her, but my point is, she's African-American and she is an individual. I want to let African-Americans know that they don't have to act "black." It doesn't make you more of an "African-American" to do things you think "black" people should do. I've had friends who felt that acting "black" was cool, both black and white ones. Did you know much of what many people refer to as being "black" resulted from their overseers who were know as "poor white trash"? It's true. They were the ones the slaves learned English from, yet many people don't realize this. Please let me know that the majority of African-Americans are not like the ones I see on Ricki Lake. They don't have attitudes, move their necks from side to side, wave their hands in people's faces, speak loud and improper English, don't listen to what people are saying, don't speak out vulgarly, don't resort to violence because they can articulate how they feel. I'm not trying to put down African-Americans, I want to recognize a problem in the United States. The more people group themselves in simplistic categories, based on skin color, the harder it will be for ALL of us to get along, live as the HUMANS we are ... Ask me what my culture is and I'll tell you "I'm American."

This post offers explicit self-identifications in racial terms, for example, part African-American, as well as more general identities like human and American. Descriptions of heritage, parents, hometown, and contacts with other racial groups imply specific features of the author's racial identity.

The variety of cues leaves readers with many options for interpreting an author's racial identity. One option is an "identity challenge." If all multivalent self-identifications brought challenges there would be little room left on SCAA for substantive discussion. Indeed, identity challenges do not occur often. However, when participants dispute an author's perspective they often challenge the author's identity. Though disagreements come in a variety of forms, one recurrent practice for disputing an author's arguments involves challenges to author's identity. In the following section I explore how such challenges are pursued.

Racial identity and disagreement

What are authors doing by including cues to their racial identification in their messages? The above author's goal is to inform African-Americans that they need not act "Black," a potentially controversial claim in SCAA. Perhaps, the author assumed that such advice to African-Americans would engender strong disagreement, especially if it came from someone other than an African-American. The author of the post makes numerous identifying remarks (e.g., "part African-American," etc.) and offers a short biography of the author's mother.[7] These self-revelations formulate the post as offering advice from within the African-American community. Thus, I submit that the author uses these identity cues to guard against anticipated attacks, especially attacks claiming the author is an outsider. In general, racial self-identification is used by authors to establish a social position. These include positions from which to safely make potentially controversial comments.

Conversely, respondents' challenges to an author's identity dispute the social position from which the author makes his/her claim. Instead of arguing with the author's view of the world by presenting a contrasting view, respondents attempt to invalidate the argument by invalidating the author's claimed social position. The first reply to the above post mentions little on the issue of Africans-Americans acting Black, instead focusing on the author's identity:

> I'm acknowledging this because the reality is, the behavior of the minority completely
> stands out, as opposed to the behavior of the majority. I must say, that I am part
> African-American. I don't feel ashamed of this in anyway, but I am ashamed of the
> African-American behavior of many citizens in my area.

emphasis on the "part African-American"? why are you ashamed of people you don't personally know? (unless of course, you are referring to the [African-American] folks from your personal lineage?) do you bear the burden for speaking for the race you "partially" belong to?

> I am proud of all the ethnicities my gene pool possesses, while at the same time, I
> am proud of the ethnicities I don't possess. I ACCEPT those who are different from
> me. Different is good: it is new. it is unique. it is you. it is me.

ummm, excuse me but this little Pollyanna statement just negated the part where you wept tears over the behavior of total strangers. If different is good, you should absolutely love those [African-Americans] that are causing you such embarrassment, doncha think? me thinks you bear more pride for the paler side of your life. perhaps that is who is speaking in this message?

This reply does not directly disagree with the description of African-Americans acting as Black or dispute whether moving one's "neck from side to side" is an accurate or positive treatment of Black culture. Instead, when the reader cites the author's "emphasis on the 'part African-American' " and accuses the author of having "pride for the paler side," the reader is using the very identifying resources the author offered defensively to dismiss the author's perspective. By modifying the author's original identity from "part African-American" to "part African-American who has pride in her paler side," the respondent challenges the position from which the advice is offered and consequently questions its acceptability by the community at large. Thus, racial identity is employed here to dispute various formulations of the world in racial terms.

To the extent that these challenges are taken up they determine the course of the discussion. Challenging an author's racial identity diverts attention away from the author's ideas. In effect, challenging an author's identity attempts to shift the other reader's engagement with the thread's original topic.

Collaboration and racial identity

If a respondent gets others to join in challenging an author's identity, or if the author feels sufficiently challenged to defend his/her identity, then the author's argument may become sidetracked. Challenges may be ignored or other readers may join in to support the author's stated identity. Clearly, no single reader determines the fate of a claimed racial identity any more than any particular author does.

In the following example, Sam challenges Lee's claim that he is a pro-Black African-American by suggesting he is a "white racist troll." Toni's contribution rebuts Sam's recharacterization and defends Lee's racial identity without defending Lee's opinions.

> Lee: > If you don't like my dialog, then put me in your killfile rather than subject blacks who care about blacks to your pro-white agenda. Everybody here ain't Toms.

> Sam: Please post your non-Tom list, so we know who's OK and who isn't. Why do I get the feeling that this is another white racist troll?

> Toni: You must have not been here, last time. [Lee] just got back. He's got *lots* of problems, and when he airs them directly or not in this newsgroup, grab some popcorn and sit back- it's *Showtime*! No cheaper entertainment can be found elsewhere.

Sam's characterization of Lee as a white racist troll is diametrically opposed to Lee's self-identification as a pro-Black African-American. By characterizing Lee as a white racist troll, Sam invites other participants on SCAA to reinterpret Lee's perspective in light of a new racial identity. This recharacterization of Lee's racial identity is an attempt to undermine the seriousness with which Lee's comments should be taken.

The challenged author, Lee, has a long history and is known to others through his prior postings to the group. Lee's identity for this group is solid enough to resist such a recharacterization. Although Toni's reply dismisses Sam's recharacterization of Lee's identity, it leaves intact Sam's claim that Lee's comments should not be taken seriously. In short, Toni's reply implies that Lee's posts, formulated as entertainment, are pursuable in ways other than by challenging his identity.

In sum, racial identity does not necessarily change with each participant's new claim. A participant's history in the newsgroup counts and collaboration among participants is important for sustaining online racial identities. Just as authors cannot choose any racial identity (including a green identity), a respondent cannot recast the racial identity of another at will. Here we find that online racial identity is no more chimerical or fluid than its offline counterpart. Group history matters and recharacterizations of identity that are not grounded in an author's present and past posts are typically ignored or dismissed, as in the case above.[8]

Racial identity across newsgroups

Newsgroups are an important aspect of the online interactional situation. The technology that organizes newsgroups allows participants to post their comments or to repost others' comments to more than one newsgroup. This practice is called crossposting. Through crossposting, other newsgroups can be brought into a discussion taking place in a cultural newsgroup. Crossposting can greatly increase the volume of messages posted and the number of newsgroups receiving the posts. For example, a discussion among three participants on a marriage between an Asian-American woman and a Caucasian man was going for a few days in the soc.culture.couples.intercultural newsgroup. A message concerning the relevance of race in the couple's relationship was reposted to soc.culture.asian.american where thirty posters joined the discussion. A comment concerning the relative merits of Asian/Caucasian unions versus Asian/Black unions was then reposted to SCAA, where another forty-four posters joined the discussion over a week's time. Thus through crossposting, the audience reading a thread can expand from a few people in a single newsgroup to many people and then quickly shrink to a two-person correspondence. In a medium in which the audience changes quickly and without warning, how is the construction of racial identity affected? One initial observation is that group history can be definitive only in those instances where a single newsgroup is concerned. If a number of groups are participating this can change the appropriateness and relevance of particular racial frames, categorizations, and established identities.

Crossposting and changing audiences

By crossposting a message, a participant can bring other newsgroups into a thread. When this occurs, an ongoing discussion that may have had a relatively stable and identifiable audience can be radically transformed. There is a palpable change between a single "other" in a conversation and a new newsgroup joining a discussion – one white supremacist can be an annoyance, but a hundred white supremacists constitute an altogether different racial environment.

Crossposting also can change the set of meanings attached to particular racial terms. For example, consider a discussion in soc.culture.mexican.american (SCMA) that gets crossposted to a thread in SCAA. An important distinction between Salvadorans, Mexicans, and Nicaraguans in SCMA may seem an unimportant geographical distinction in SCAA. The distinction between "Black" and "African-American," which can be a vital distinction in SCAA, may not be similarly understood in soc.culture.russian. Individuals who normally post in one newsgroup may be inexperienced with another group's terms. Yet when groups are brought together they must work out enough common ground to carry out a discussion. Lack of familiarity with in-group racial distinctions can alter groups' orientations to each other – the resources available for racial identification are limited. What resources do participants fall back on and how are their discussions transformed?

Crossposting and inter-group discussions

In a thread within a single newsgroup, fine racial distinctions are made, but such distinctions can be problematic in crossposted threads. For example, a thread in SCJ concerning lyrics from a Michael Jackson song that could be interpreted as anti-Semitic ("Jew me, sue me, kick me, kike me") was crossposted to SCAA where Michael Jackson's racial status was a current topic of discussion. In SCAA, the discussion included many racial terms familiar to the newsgroup, such as "toms," "role models," and "sell-outs." In SCJ discussion concerned the ways in which Jews respond to anti-Semitism, with some participants characterized as too sensitive while others were chastised as "Jews without proper vigilance." Such in-group distinctions are lost on the newsgroups to which the discussions are crossposted.

Discussions not possible within a particular newsgroup become possible in discussions among newsgroups. In discussions within SCAA, participants posted as individuals, whereas in discussions with other newsgroups many participants framed their messages as emanating from the racial group as a whole:

> Speaking for African Americans. . . .

> We have always felt . . .

One consequence of these generalizing practices is that messages in crossposted discussions are generated between those holding expected positions. In other words, responses are made to those authors whose identity and perspective match the stereotype expected by the respondent. For example, although many African-Americans and Jews agreed on both sides of the Michael Jackson issue, their messages did not generate responses. The messages responded to were mainly those from African-Americans who defended Michael Jackson and from Jews who denounced him. Even this is not specific enough. Jews who denounced Michael Jackson as anti-Semitic garnered responses; those who denounced his androgyny did not. African-Americans who supported Michael Jackson as an African-American being persecuted by Jews were responded to; African-Americans supporting artistic freedom were not. Reading this discussion gave the impression of an "African-American position" and a diametrically opposed "Jewish position," whereas the discussion within each newsgroup had allowed for more complexity. However, the complexity of within-group opinion atrophies in inter-group discussions leaving visible only the stereotypical positions. Discussion between groups, which progressive people might hope would alleviate racial stereotypes, instead is a site where previously held stereotypes are made into self-fulfilling prophecies.

Consequences for race online

In online discussions, readers treat racial identities as entailing particular perspectives. Offline interaction has a name for the imputation of a characteristic, attitude, belief, or practice based solely on someone's race – "stereotyping." An observer may use physical characteristics to impute a racial identity and from that impute a delimited set of beliefs and perspectives. For example, after I confirmed that I was Black in a recent conversation, the talk turned to professional basketball. My co-interactants assumed that a Black male would be interested in basketball. While this stereotyping is not surprising, imagine that, on hearing of their interest in basketball, I had assumed they were Black. This would also be stereotyping, but an unusual variety. Stereotyping in face-to-face interaction follows from an assumed racial identity. Online interaction differs in that the imputation tends to go in the other direction – from stereotype to racial identity.

A discrepancy arises when a person identified as a member of a particular racial group by his or her physical characteristics offers a perspective that is inconsistent with the stereotype of that group. In face-to-face interactions, such an inconsistency can be resolved by modifying the stereotype or seeing the person as an anomaly – rarely are the person's physical racial indicators disputed. In online interactions perspectives resist modification because participants confront an immutable text, whereas racial identifications can be challenged.

Thus, during online arguments, authors' perspectives are used to challenge their claimed racial identity. For example, the following post responds to the author who was troubled by Blacks she had seen on a talk show and finds a discrepancy between the author's identity as Black and the perspective she offers:

> [And] it is a shame that you even have to ask these questions because I would hope that you see more blacks than on Ricki Lake, whether you are black or white. But being black, I am truly amazed at what you have asked. I will just guess that you are still a teen, (as opposed to a hick that has never seen a black person) and haven't been out in the world and exposed to much; because many of us grew up like that. I will also say God made us all different.

The respondent states that "being black, I am truly amazed at what you have asked," revealing a belief that a "Black" racial identity corresponds with a particular set of experiences. This poses a puzzle for the reader. How can the racial identity and the perspective be reconciled? The respondent in this case resolves this puzzle by modifying the author's racial identity to *adolescent* Black. Because adolescents are inexperienced, they ask questions that more worldly adults would not ask. More generally, discrepancies between the perspective in the text and the author's racial identity can be resolved by modifying the author's identity so that his/her competence is consistent with the faulty perspective.

Resolving these puzzles by modifying the author's identity allows readers to maintain the connection between racial identities and perspectives, much as labeling discrepancies as anomalies does offline. Online, participants introduce these discrepancies as ways of pursuing disputes, but the discrepancies are rarely treated as innocuous anomalies – perspective and race are made to conform online. Far from being a site where race, racism, ethnocentrism, or stereotyping are banished, these phenomena flourish in newsgroups.

Conclusion

I have discussed some of the ways in which people's interactional organization responds to and uses the Usenet environment. The technological organization of the Usenet changes interaction because of the inaccessibility of physical cues as a resource in racial identification. Lacking physical cues that normally are taken as the source of racial identity offline, racial identification online relies on participants' perspectives as revealed in their posts.

Racial identification online occurs in a different context than that occurring offline. In face-to-face interaction, a situation can arise in which another individual's physical cues and his or her perspective do not agree with the observer's stereotypes. It is difficult to argue that the other didn't really offer that perspective or that the physical cues are not real. This creates space for anomalies and exceptions to a stereotype in offline interaction. In online interaction, readers are usually faced with explicit racial identifications and the person's textual perspective. If these do not agree with a reader's stereotypes, the person's racial identity can be read so that racial identity and perspective fit the stereotype.

Race is no less relevant in online interaction than it is in face-to-face interaction. Instead racial stereotypes may be more influential and resilient on the Usenet. At the same time, individuals participating in Usenet newsgroups can experience a variety of people, ideas, and cultures that could supplant stereotypes. Although the technology may be revolutionary and expectations utopian, newsgroups are made up of people neither revolutionary nor perfect, armed with ordinary ways of understanding each other. The medium that technologically constrains participants' interactions is also constrained by participants' methods of organizing interaction.

Notes

1 Direct correspondence to Byron Burkhalter, Department of Sociology, University of California, Los Angeles, CA 90095-1551 (burkhalt@ucla.edu). I would like to thank Geoff Raymond for his organizing talents and his careful eye for the details of human interaction. Thanks also to Peter Kollock and Marc Smith for their patience and their supportive editing. Finally, thanks to Genevieve Haldeman for encouragement and motivation.

2 One even gets the sense that all the talk about the impossibility of racial identity is driven by a frustration with race relations. Would it not be easier for racial stereotypes to be defeated by technological limitations rather than a missing political will?

3 See Nagel (1994) for a discussion of these labels as a "layering of ethnic identity."

4 It might be argued that online racial identity is virtual not actual. Goffman (1963: 2) distinguished between a "virtual social identity" and an "actual social identity" by reference to the latter being a proven identity. Since race has no biological or genetic essence and since race is not fundamentally a biological category but a social category (see Montagu 1964 for the classic treatment), no final proof is possible, online or offline.

5 Some subject lines in the screen displayed above are less culturally explicit. These are

usually posts from regulars with the group, individuals who are already known and have established an audience. The topics initiated by regulars need not be on cultural topics. SCAA maintains a sporadic but ongoing discussion on the benefits of different computer operating systems as well as a rivalry between East and West Coast participants. Some messages were intended for different newsgroups but have been crossposted to a soc.culture newsgroup. The crossposted message will be censured by participants for not being culturally relevant. However, regulars can post race neutral messages without reproach.

6 Some of these identities, especially religious conservative, may seem out of place as racial identities. However, these terms are ways in which authors understand each other's positions on racial issues and in that light are racial identities. In any case there was some scant evidence that the label "religious conservative" came with the inference that the author was white.

7 These stand in contrast to other self-characterizations, such as human and American, which are part of the advice she is offering rather than a defense against criticisms.

8 One topic of interest is with the success of such challenges. While a systematic treatment is not possible in this chapter, one clue is promising. A majority of successful challenges reused the exact terms of the previous post.

References

Banton, Michael. 1987. *Racial Theories*. Cambridge: Cambridge University Press.

Bradshaw, Carla K. 1992. "Beauty and the Beast: on racial ambiguity,' in Maria P.P. Root (ed.) *Racially Mixed People in America*. London: Sage.

Goffman, Erving. 1959. *The Presentation of Self in Everyday Life*. New York: Doubleday.

Goffman, Erving. 1963. *Stigma*. Englewood Cliffs, NJ: Prentice-Hall.

Gossett, Thomas. 1965. *Race: The History of an Idea in America*. New York: Schocken.

Lyman, Stanford M. and William A. Douglass. 1973. "Ethnicity: strategies of collective and individual impression management," *Social Research* 40(summer): 344–65.

Montagu, Ashley. 1964. *The Concept of Race*. New York: Collier.

Nagel, J. 1994. "Constructing ethnicity: creating and recreating ethnic identity and culture," *Social Problems* 41(1): 153–76.

Okamura, Jonathan Y. 1981. "Situational ethnicity," *Ethnic and Racial Studies* 4(4): 452–65.

Phinney, Jean S. and Mary Jane Rotheram (eds). 1987. *Children's Ethnic Socialization: Pluralism and Development*. Newbury Park, CA: Sage.

Spaights, Ernest and Harold E. Dixon. 1984. "Socio-psychological dynamics in pathological Black–White romantic alliances," *Journal of Instructional Psychology* 11(3): 132–8.

Spickard, P. 1992. "The illogic of American racial categories," in Maria P.P. Root (ed.) *Racially Mixed People in America*. London: Sage.

Van Den Berghe, Pierre. 1993. "Encountering American race relations," in John Stanfield II (ed.) *A History of Race Relations Research: First Generation Recollections*. London: Sage.

Chapter 4

Writing in the body

Gender (re)production in online interaction[1]

Jodi O'Brien

I'm thinking about subject position. My own. Wondering how you, the reader, are conjuring me in your mind. How do you imagine me to be? What characteristics concern you? Does it make a difference to you to know that as I write this I am wearing white cotton, button-fly briefs, a white cotton undershirt (European cut), hemp sandals and a purple cotton pullover dress? My straight brown hair is short by the standards of some and way too long by others (including the queen who cuts it). I have two pearl earrings in my left ear and a gold ring in my left nipple. I look young for my age, some say. Others think me too precocious for someone as young as I am. I'm not really tall or short. I have an athletic build. Do you assume I'm white? Are you reminding yourself that "jodi" spelled with an "i" must be a girl's name? Does it matter?

A well-known and highly reputable economist recently surprised his colleagues with the announcement that "he" was becoming "she." Deirdre McCloskey, formerly Donald, revealed the decision to colleagues in an article published in the *Eastern Economic Journal*. The piece was titled "Some News That at Least Will Not Bore You." According to a story in the *Chronicle of Higher Education* (Wilson 1996), reactions have ranged from positive enthusiasm as shown in a party thrown by female colleagues welcoming Deirdre as "one of us," to shocked silence. A pervasive theme in all the discussion of McCloskey's gender transition is how will it affect the authority and influence of the professor's work? Feminist supporters worry that they have "lost a powerful male ally." In the words of a Berkeley colleague: "Some people's reaction is that this is a real shame because we are going to lose a strong male voice standing up for female economists." World-class economists express concern that Donald's work, which was widely touted as "profound," will not be taken as seriously when it is attributed to Deirdre. One journal editor remarks, "Those who disagreed with Donald's criticisms of the field may now discount what Deirdre has to say. . . . You have somebody who has been a curmudgeon, and now people will say [he's] been a flake all along" (Wilson 1996). What I find noteworthy is the persistent assumption that the switch from "he" to "she" will (re)shape Professor McCloskey's interpersonal, professional and political relations.

Gender is a social institution (Lorber and Farrell 1991). Gender characteristics are a primary means by which we sort and define self and others. "Sex attributes" provide basic information about how to conduct interactions with others and how to organize social reality. People often act as if observable differences between the sexes reflect naturally occurring divisions that transcend the particulars of social convention. Gendered representations of self and other do not sort people "naturally" and benignly. This categorization scheme comprises ways of "naming" self and others that reflect cultural expectations and entrenched hierarchies. The observation that Professor McCloskey is perceived to be more influential as a male feminist economist than as a female indicates a hierarchy between the relative credibility of men and women who have otherwise similar professional achievements and political inclinations. The discomfort felt by people who have known Donald for decades, but who don't know how to "relate" to Deirdre, reflects the way in which gender is used to organize interpersonal communication. Gender categories evoke a deeply entrenched cognitive-emotive script for who we can be and how we should relate to others.

This real-life example contrasts sharply with science fiction stories in which gender is as mutable as a change of clothes. In one such acclaimed novel, *Steel Beach* by John Varley (1992), characters frequent the shops of artistic surgeons who deal in instant "make-overs" that routinely include sex changes. Throughout the novel characters cross back and forth between activities associated with both genders, including child-bearing. What is remarkable about Varley's characters is that their gender switching raises no more than an occasional eyebrow from fellow employees, family and friends. Varley's world maintains a conventional gender dichotomy as a recognizable classification scheme for biological reproduction and self-presentation, but he simultaneously attempts to render gender unremarkable as a basis for organizing interpersonal and social relations. In the case of McCloskey, we can imagine that communication among long-time acquaintances grinds to a confused halt as people reshuffle their scripts in the attempt to deal with Deirdre. In Varley's novel, showing up to work with a new gender has no more impact on interpersonal communication than a new haircut might.[2]

Current research, science fiction and wishful thinking suggest that cyberspace will be a realm in which physical markers such as sex, race, age, body type and size will eventually lose salience as a basis for the evaluative categorization of self/other. An implication in much of this writing is that these features will cease to be the basis of primary social systems of difference. They will lose their cognitive-emotive grip. This conclusion is based on the logic that because these features are not obviously discernible in cyberspace they will cease to be a primary means of structuring interaction; floating free of corporeal experience, the mind will generate new forms for rendering self and other and for organizing interpersonal communication. I am not convinced.

How elastic is the institution of gender? The proposition that gender is a social construction implies that, theoretically, the mind may be able to conceptualize variations along a "gender continuum," or perhaps do away with notions of gender as a line of distinction altogether. The weight of physical features as a source of symbolic information in everyday interaction makes it difficult to empirically separate gender as a social accomplishment from gender as the manifestation of embodied sex. When persons confront instances of gender stretching they tend to snap them back into the conventional physical sex dichotomy. "Is it really a man or a woman?" Depending on the researcher's intent, this behavior can be interpreted as either a case in point for the salience of a constructed gender institution or as evidence of the primacy of biological sex. Whether or not gender is "really" a social institution or a biological "fact" is a sort of truth trap that reflects the methodological and ontological assumptions of nineteenth-century natural science – there is a natural order of which human existence is a part and, using the appropriate methods, we can ascertain this "truth." The best logical positivists know that it is never possible to know, with certainty, whether or not "natural truth" has been "discovered." Thus, pursuits into the "truth" of nature versus nurture, essentialism versus constructionism, are misguided and subject to the trap of objectivism (Stein 1992). In their most distilled expression the two methodologies hold this in common: ontology is an assumption, not a testable hypothesis.

My ontology is this, the social significance of gender rests in the way in which we experience and understand our "selves" in relation to communication with other human beings. This experience is an act of subjective interpretation using available cultural scripts. The modern cultural script treats the self as being located in a single, fixed point of physicality, the body. Scholarly interest in the relationship between technology and the body not only is about how technology can enhance and alter physical presence in time and space – such as the telephone extending the presence of the voice across space – but also implies something much more pivotal, the potential dislocation of the self and the body. Locke reasoned that nature is transformed into "worth" by physical and mental labor. What differentiates person from beast, and gives us the "natural right to private property" is an awareness of what we are doing to nature. Thus, the mind and body were effectively split into awareness/action and reunited in the form of the "product" of one's conscious labor. The political authenticity of the modern self is grounded in the assumption that personhood is located in the physical body, which, in turn, is located in a state of nature as a single, classifiable object. What does this have to do with gender? The female/male dichotomy is the main line of classification, not only of bodies, but, by extension of the logic of a single, embodied self, the central distinction of "self." Based on what are generally taken to be naturally occurring distinctions in physical sex attributes, it is assumed that gender is the most natural, immutable aspect of "self." This illusion of immutability has become real in the cultural consequences of rules for who and what we can be.

Online interactions provide an excellent site for observing the dislocation of mind and body. In this interactional realm it is possible to observe how persons categorize self/other and structure interaction in the absence of embodied characteristics. Specifically in this case, "gender as performance" can be theoretically and empirically separated from corporeal sex markers. Cyberspace provides a site for studying the viability and implications of constructionist theories that emphasize "doing gender" as a social accomplishment (West and Zimmerman 1991). Sandy Stone (1992) frames such observations as:

> a venture into the heart of "technology" in search of nature – and not nature as object, place or originary situation, but in Donna Haraway's sense nature as Coyote, the Native American trickster – diversity, flexibility, irruption, danger, playfulness – put briefly, nature as actant, as process, a continual reinvention and encounter actively resisting representation.
>
> (Stone 1992: 610)

Interaction as we currently experience it and represent it in human cultural form is predicated on symbolic cues that derive from a lexicon based largely on face-to-face communication: gestures and voice. Whether someone is present or not, we conjure up and make sense of ourselves and others in terms of embodiment. The technology of online communications poses an occasion to explore the implications of interaction when the usual embodied cues for coding and responding to others are not present. Because she states the questions so well and because her words have cut the path that I intend to explore in this chapter, I quote Stone (1992) at length here:

> I am interested in the nets for what they make visible about the "real" world, things that might otherwise go unnoticed. I am interested because of their potential for emergent behavior, for new social forms that arise in circumstances in which "body" "meeting" "place" and even "space" mean things quite different from our accustomed understanding . . . how do groups of friends evolve when their meeting room exists in purely symbolic space? How does narrowing the bandwidth – that is, doing without the customary modes of symbolic exchange such as gesture and tone of voice – affect sharing and trust, how do inhabitants of virtual systems construct and maintain categories such as gender and race? How do people without bodies make love?
>
> (Stone 1992: 610)

In this chapter I explore the question, how likely is it that online communication will be a site/occasion for "complicating" the customary gender dichotomy? What is the potential that conventional gender boundaries will be erased, systematically altered or reproduced in their current form? This is a theoretical contemplation grounded in my own observations of online interactions and my interpretive reading of the current literature on the implications of disembodied social interaction. Cyberspace as an interactional medium is still an idea. As a working approach, I prefer Stone's definition of an interactional medium in which the bandwidth is narrowed to exclude usual modes of symbolic comprehension. In general I take a materialist-constructionist approach, according to which I assume that bodies, selves, technologies and cultures are mutually constitutive (Butler 1993; Stone 1992). In this case my focus is on the relationship between technology and culture in the (re)constitution of presentations of self when the body is not available as a source of information to others.[3] Explicitly, my interest in this chapter is what happens to gender as a primary cultural distinction when the narrow bandwidth of a technology precludes the common transmission of gender cues. My intent is to provoke thought among other researchers, particularly those interested in empirical studies of sex and gender online, regarding the conceptual orientations through which they design and interpret their research. I mean to complicate the working orientation considerably.

The hype: be everyone you've ever wanted to be

A friend phones to tell me that she has just been speaking with her mother, a 50+, working-class, twice married black woman who is, according to her daughter, "the ultimate femme." Her mother called to report that she had just been riding with the "Dykes on Bikes" in the Chicago Gay Pride Parade. My friend, a Black Indian who lives with her white boyfriend and says she loves women but doesn't relate to either the category "lesbian" or "bisexual," has often tried to explain to me that consideration of sexual preference is a luxury not affordable to working-class women of color who want to make a career for themselves. Now she is both taken aback and delighted at her mother's behavior.

"Who'd she ride with?" I ask.

"Her girlfriend, Myrna," my friend replies. "You remember, I told you about her. The butch that works in the pet store where my mom buys her cat food. My mom's been 'seeing' her, but they don't call it 'dating'."

"Is your mom into lesbians?" I inquire.

"She's comfortable with them but would never see herself as one. Myrna doesn't like being associated as a lesbian either."

"I thought you said she was a butch dyke?"

"She is. But she's not into the politics of it. She just likes sex with women. I think she sees herself as one of the guys."

"Is your mom having sex with Myrna?"

"She really wants to try it, but Myrna won't do it. Thinks my mom is too straight."

"Is she?"

" I don't know. I think she is just thrilled with the possibilities of trying out a new world and really doesn't care what anyone else thinks. She's obsessed with seducing Myrna as much for the experience of it as for the sex."

In a special to the *Chicago Tribune*, a journalist notes: "millions of Americans on networks are logging on . . . they're making friends and falling in love without the constraints and the protections that apply, as they say, IRL [in real life]" (Adams 1993). Rheingold (1993) notes that in cyberspace, "we're all thrown together without the cues of tone of voice, posture and facial expression." For many observers, this leads to the conclusion that physical features will no longer play a role in social interaction. Here is a typically hopeful expression of the potential of electronic interactions: "For me, words and thoughts and people's ideas are the most important thing about a person. Online reality gets to the core of things. In some ways there is so much less racism, sexism, lookism" (quoted in Adams 1993). Herring (1993/1996) in a critical survey of these ideals notes: "Part of the idealism surrounding the technology in the early decades of its development, and which still persists in many circles, was the belief that computer networks would neutralize gender and other status-related differences and empower traditionally underrepresented groups" (cf. Hiltz and Turoff 1993; Kiesler *et al.* 1984; Graddol and Swann 1989; Rheingold 1993).

At least two promises are implied about the "new frontier." One is that categories of difference that "constrain" everyday face-to-face (f2f) interaction will be erased because they will not be apparent online (e.g. Gearhart 1983). Another is that cyberspace will be a sort of Wild West in which one can cross over the boundaries imposed by physicality (e.g. Neutopia 1994). Not only can we interact almost instantaneously with persons who are geographically distant, but also we can experiment with the possibilities of traveling through electronic space as someone other than the person manifest through our bodies. Presumably this introduces a potential for creative interaction that is difficult to sustain with credibility in the corporeal realm. The characters that we author for ourselves and others are limited only by imagination. Or so the story goes. In the words of one sociologist:

> On the [bulletin boards] life reality is transformed into virtual reality. From the first moments of logging on, new users creatively craft ironically-intentioned or whimsically-concocted "handles" that replace everyday names. Newly generated personas – faceless, voiceless, bodiless – displace history with a time-less present and multiple selves easily co-exist with a flick of a finger. Fantasy is freed.

> (Wiley 1995: 9)

How likely is it that we can interact without differentiating characteristics to provide a guide for who to be and how to act? What is "reality" when one's emotions, future plans and recipes for interaction are considered? If I traverse the Net as a GWM named Lestat and you fall in love with me, are we content to linger and love forever in a text-based realm where our romantic energy is carried by standard electronic impulses across wires we will never see? Will we be living together in "a fiction" or an alternate reality? If most of my acquaintances/friends/lovers exist online, does it really matter whether or not my online characterizations of myself "match" my physical attributes? Does it matter that I have a penis between my corporeal brown, hairy legs if I am having fabulous online sex as Wanda the recent virgin who is blonde and buxom? Or, for that matter, does it matter that I don't have a penis between my black, lesbian legs while I am interacting as "myself" on a conference line in which it is presumed that all participants are male? Can I really expect to be treated just like everyone else? Does "just like everyone else" mean "just like one of the [white] guys"?

These sorts of questions illustrate the complications involved in breaking apart the assumed relationship between body/mind/self as a fixed, immutable unit. Much of the current hype implies that the body is a barrier to experiencing a wider range of interactions – in the absence of embodied symbolic cues to the contrary, one can be whomever one can imagine. Far from unraveling the helix of the Cartesian split, much of this hype simply twists the strands more tightly. Generating multiple personae begs the question, who/what becomes the site of interpretation and agency? Stone (1992) refers to this issue as the "metaphysics of presence." Cartesian reasoning posits "an individual social actor fixed with respect to geographical coordinates that determine physical locus . . . a body implies the presence within the body of a socially articulated self that is the true site of agency" (Stone 1992: 614). Her point, one that the hucksters of hype fail to discuss, but that governmental regulatory agencies have been quick to seize, is that the site of authentication of personhood is the body occupied by a self-aware mind. This is no small consideration in a political economy based on individual private property and agency. Governments are very concerned about the potential to generate multiple personae without a fixed location. Dislocated multiplicity makes it difficult to trace culpability.

There is another reason why the "metaphysics of presence" is more complicated than the "be anyone you want" hype conveys. What is the site and authenticating source of experience from which self-awareness is constructed? Social psychologists since James and Mead have wrestled with the idea of multiple selves and whether a "master consciousness" organizes these many experiential fragments of identity into a single core self. There is also the question of how we know what stimulates us: what "counts" and gets coded as "experience"? In accordance with classic Cartesian logic, the theories to date imply a master rank-ordering of experience and manifest identities according to some core self that is both anchored in, but also independent of, the body. For instance, I can readily determine the relative significance of my self presentation as a customer in the bank and my notion of myself as a college professor. As I understand and experience them, the former is much more temporary and fleeting than the latter. The idea of presenting multiple selves is not novel. The notion of multiple selves that have no awareness of one another, on the other hand, is a radical way to think about social interaction. In the current clinical terms, such a state marks a pathological disorder. I don't think that this is what the hypers have in mind when they suggest that one can be anyone. Underlying the hype the conventional foundation remains intact: there is a master consciousness that sorts and organizes our experiences, including various multiple self performances. How does the "master consciousness" sort and organize and determine what is memorable and in what form? In accordance with prevailing cultural scripts.

I'm looking at an ad in a recent issue of the *Advocate*. It's a full page color spread that announces:

There are no closets in Cyberspace.

The accompanying text reads,

They're called rooms, like America Online's packed Gay Member Rooms, or echoes, such as the say-anything Artlife echo, or groups, as in the sophisticated newsgroup soc.motss, or lists, like the sizzling Gay-LIBN list. They're meeting places are so free and open and wild and fun they make the Castro Street look Victorian.

How disembodied is the imagination? Can the mind stand alone? When we enter cyberspace do we really leave the physical behind and move into the realm of "words, thoughts and ideas" where the signs somehow float free from the signified? Can we be/come anything that the mind can conceive and author into text? How long will cyber users continue to differentiate between an IRL in which the physical equals the real and a transcendent space in which the imagined/authored equals pseudo reality or fantasy?

The text for the *Advocate* cyberspace ad is printed over a colorized photo of a bare male torso, arms raised above his head. It's a hot ad. Very physical. I want to caress it.

Male or female? Dichotomies we live and love by

I recently overheard this conversation in a sex toy shop:

CUSTOMER: What does it mean when someone looks at a woman and says, "she's packing"?

CLERK: Means she's wearing a dildo stuffed in her pants. To look like she has a cock.
[*Clerk takes a large brown, anatomically descriptive dildo from the shelf and stuffs it into the front of her khakis. She adjusts it a bit and then turns to show the customer.*]

CLERK: See, if you place it right you can even see the outline of the head.

CUSTOMER: What would you be trying to communicate? That you're a lesbian?

CLERK: Some women do it to signal they're ready for sex. Others just want to play at being boy-girls.

CUSTOMER: But it's still so obvious that you're a woman. [*She frowns in bewilderment.*] Do you have to wear one of these harnesses to hold it on?

CLERK: No. You don't wanna do that. Then it would be erect the whole time you were cruising around. You just wanna let it hang there.

CUSTOMER: But you can't fuck anyone with it like that. [*Shakes her head*] I don't get it.

CLERK: [*Removes the dildo from her pants, grasping it by the balls she points the head at the customer*] It's called "packing." From the term, packing a gun.

It's a question of identity. In an essay describing her experiences at her mother's funeral, transgendered author and performance artist, Kate Bornstein, writes:

"Who are you?" . . . It's my mother's funeral service and the little old ladies are taking inventory of the mourners. Me, I have to take inventory of my identities whenever someone asks me who I am, and the answer that tumbles out of my mouth is rarely predictable. I'm telling each of them the who of me I know they can deal with. "I'm Kate Bornstein," I answer her in this quiet-quiet voice of mine. "Mildred's daughter." "Daughter?!" She shoots back incredulously the same question each of her predecessors had asked, because everyone knew my mother had two sons. "Mildred never mentioned she had a daughter."

(Bornstein 1997: 70)

Bornstein, author of *Gender Outlaw* (1994) and the gender-bending cyberthriller novel, *Nearly Roadkill* (Sullivan and Bornstein 1996), notes that we pass through public space as if we are oblivious to gender – until we encounter someone whose sex is ambiguous. Then we do a double-take, even a triple-take. We scan for various categorical features – presence of facial hair, breasts, body size – in order to determine what the real sex is. A woman who is "packing" a dildo is neither male nor gender-ambiguous, she is a "woman wearing a dildo." Similarly, the allure of the drag queen is not that "he" has switched to "she," it is that someone who is "he" can perform so adroitly as "she." Cultural fascination with transgendering does not erase gender categorization, it underscores the dichotomy. The presence of gender "deviates" constitutes a boundary event (cf. Barthes) in which the collective norms for differentiating self and others are made visibly, viscerally apparent. Rather than being nullified or erased, boundary transgressions etch the boundaries deeper into the collective conscience.

When humans encounter one another the first act is an assessment of who/what the other is. We cycle through a mental checklist of queries: is this someone I should fear or trust? Is this person a potential mate? How much potential power do I have over this person? Can I "be myself" or do I need to maintain an armored stance? Social psychologists suggest one basic premise about interactional dynamics: we are unable to interact with someone else until we have been able to categorize them in a meaningful way. Before we can position ourselves, we must first "name" the other. Basic categorization schemes enable us to make gross assessments about whether and how to proceed with the interaction. There is general consensus among social psychologists that the primary categories of differentiation in the contemporary western world are gender, race and age. One explanation for the predominance of gender, race and age as categories of difference is the immediate (mostly) appearance of these features in social encounters.[4]

Basic categorization of others and the subsequent positioning of self in an interaction happens instantaneously. In general, we engage in these categorical assessments in a relatively mindless, or default manner (Hofstadter 1985; Langer 1989).[5] If we cannot determine, at a glance, how to position the other in accordance with these categories, we conduct a cognitive search for additional information; we do not abandon the intent to classify along these lines. Boundary events are occasions in which the stimulus that we encounter does not match our default categorical expectations. We are thus compelled to pay close attention, to "think twice" before arriving at a general assessment of who/what the other is. The success of the popular *Saturday Night Live* character, the gender-ambiguous "Pat," is based on the tease of whether or not Pat's "true gender" will be revealed in the various sketches. Watching Pat, we know that we are supposed to be confused. That's the joke. But most of us experience considerable discomfort when actually faced with the task of interacting with another whose gender is indeterminate (Bruckman 1993).

What happens in communication in which the bandwidth precludes symbolic cues of differentiation? How plausible is the assumption of the demise of any form of interactional categorization in cyberspace? Several observers note that because electronic communications with other individuals take place "without considerations that derive from the presence to the partner of their body, their voice, their sex, many of the markings of personal history, [c]onversationalists are in the position of fiction writers" (Poster 1990: 117). The result, they insist, is that cyberspace is a "Wonderland" in which "fantasy is freed" and conventional codes are fractured (Wiley 1995). The implied conclusion is that cyberspace is an amorphous realm in which identities are liquid; one can author oneself as any THING that one can imagine. Perhaps, but in doing so, can you compel others to carry on an interaction with you? Can you "realize" the projected identity, regardless of how momentary? Does successful enactment require interactional acknowledgment?

I suggest that even if it is possible for me to conceive and author characters that defy categorization along conventional lines, others cannot engage in meaningful interaction with me ("meaningful" being defined here as mutually comprehensible and generative) unless they too know something about the "script" through which I am representing myself and/or characterizing the situation. Categorization schemes provide scripts of interaction. They constitute a social grammar that enables generative interaction. Without some shared classification scheme, our individually authored characters, no matter how colorful and creative, would have only themselves to play with. A schizophrenic wonderland. A general cognitive implication of this is that all interactions would be suspended moments in time. We would not carry away with us any knowledge of who we had encountered; without "naming" the other or ourselves relative to them, we would not give the interaction any weight of reality. Theoretically, this suggests the ability to navigate a cognitive terrain that is in constant flux and the willingness/ability to interact with others in complete anonymity.

Neurologist Oliver Sacks relates the case of a man who suffers from a cognitive-language disorder in which he can no longer differentiate others according to basic social institutions of kinship. For this man, the distinctions between father, sister, brother are unknowable and, therefore, unimportant to his interactions. Imagine the consequences of his treating every woman as if she were his wife, and his sister, and his daughter. The subjectivity of human categorization schemes has both fascinated and troubled philosophers for centuries, but most agree that one idea is worthy of initial premise: we cannot apprehend our environments and behave with any consistency in an uncertain world, unless we render it meaningfully "fixed" through collective categories of representation. The way we do so is grounded in shared lines of distinction. These lines may or may not have physical referents. Regardless of the level of abstraction, they are understood in our heads and between one another as comprehensible forms of sociability. Thus, even when the body is anchored elsewhere and unavailable as a source of symbolic cueing, central distinctions that reference the body as connected to self will still be evoked as the basis of meaningful communication.

A related question is the durability of gender as a system of difference in an interactional realm in which the physical cues are not immediately available. Several observers have noted that when a conventional mode of symbolic interaction is not available, rather than dismiss it as irrelevant, interactants may become obsessive about determining the "missing information." This proposition raises the specific question of the extent to which gender is primarily an institution rooted in physical sex characteristics, or is a cognitive-emotional institution with extra-physical implications for (re)constructing meaningful realities. The probability of the perpetuation or demise of gender differentiation cannot be ascertained without first establishing, at least theoretically, whether gender is a feature of the flesh or a figment of the mind. Mapping how gender structures interaction, and the consequences, follow directly from this point.

This is indeed a research frontier. Thus far, there have been very few systematic studies of online gender interaction. At least two observations seem warranted at this point. One is that persons do "gender" online interactions. Another is that the dynamics of this gendering tend to reproduce conventional gender forms.

Gender is one of the first means by which persons introduce and represent themselves to others in electronic communications. In email communications gender is often discernible by name. Those with gender-ambiguous names generally provide additional cues that mark their sex. A frequently asked question on BBS is "are you male or female?" (Herring 1995; Kendall 1998). Individuals who evade this question are not considered to be creative mavericks, they are assumed to be hiding something. Interaction with those who are gender-ambiguous is generally not supported. If someone persists in maintaining a gender-neutral position, others online will inquire of one another about what the person's gender "really" is and why he or she is reluctant to reveal it. The failure to "reveal" gender is viewed with suspicion.

Kendall (1998) reports several interesting observations from her experiences as a participant on a MUD. MUDs were originally conceived as gaming sites. The development of whimsical characters is encouraged. Several choices for gender (which is coded as "sex") exist and include: neuter, male, female, either. Kendall notes that, "despite the inability to view physical attributes and the technical ability in most MUDs to designate a character by gender other than male or female, the view of gender as a strict polar binary persists" (1998: 137).

The questions that users must address when they sign on as new participants in MUDs and BBS underscore rather than erase the significance of gender. The system's operator (sysop) requires a real name, address and phone number. For many chat lines, where presumably individuals intend to cruise for friends and possible romance, users are required to specify sex and sexual orientation. These designations, which appear as biographical information available to other users, cannot be changed without going through the sysop. There are also reports that for some "spaces" the sysop attempts to verify aspects of user-identity, particularly gender, by making unannounced phone calls to the person's home and/or checking credit card information (Katz 1994; Wiley 1995). I do not have enough information to verify the veracity of these claims. But it does seem reasonable to conclude that gender, conventional binary gender, is being transported into online interactions as a significant, perhaps the significant, feature of identity.

I interpret this process of (re)gendering an otherwise gender-amorphous space as an attempt to reduce the uncertainty of interaction through ordering/structuring the possibilities of who/what roles persons can play *vis-à-vis* one another. The insistence that interactional partners have a gender is indicative of the primacy of this form of social categorization. We do not know how to behave in a gender-free environment. Once we travel beyond the frame of a gender-bound reality we are in an uncharted realm. The tendency in such a "space" is to (re)impose a meaningful order by mapping the space with known categories of distinction.

(Re)embodying the self in a disembodied realm is an exercise in textual production. Because physical cues are not available, online conversants must signal everything that they want others to know about them through a text-based medium. Transcribing a complex, nuanced range of physical gender attributes into text that can be typed out rapidly is a complex achievement.[6] The theoretical question is the potential of "gender mavericks" to stretch or alter our conceptions of gender forms. In physical/visual space gender performances are highly nuanced as conveyed through the variations in body types and the use of various props such as clothing. In contrast, I assume that a majority of persons engaged in online relations carry traditional stereotypes regarding gender; they have a limited repertoire for conceiving and writing about gender. In presenting self to others in electronic interactions it may be simpler to rely on stereotypes, especially those that are likely to elicit the desired response, than to author rich, complex composites of the gendered self. Thus, I expect the complexity of gender cues to be reduced rather than expanded in narrow bandwidth communications.

Stone (1992: 615) concludes that "the effect of narrowing the bandwidth is to engage more of the participants' interpretive faculties." She reports that in the instance of phone sex, another revealing site for observing interaction in narrowed bandwidth, "the most powerful attractor becomes the client's idealized fantasy . . . participants draw on cultural codes to construct a scenario that compresses large amounts of information into a very small space." She quotes one informant, a phone sex worker, as saying, "on the phone every sex worker is white, five foot four, and has red hair."

Interactions on the ubiquitous "chat" or "date" lines appear to be particularly likely to reproduce gender stereotypes. Far from being a wonderland of imaginative creativity, participants tend to "wear" gender features that replicate conventional gender stereotypes of sexuality and desirability. In other words, they reproduce themselves as Barbie and Ken (or Cindy Crawford and Richard Gere in the view of one cyberwatcher: Katz 1994). This "hypergendering" is especially prevalent among those who attempt to cross-gender themselves. Whether these individuals are successful or not at gender-switching, the point here is that in the attempt to portray themselves as one of two genders, they perpetuate common binary gender forms rather than stretch or alter these forms. Kendall (1998) notes that on MUDs, even when fictitious fantasy characters are introduced, they have the stereotypical gender features. For example, the female warrior is still buxom and blonde, i.e. evocative of a standard representational form.

Thus my summary considerations to this point. Gender, which is an embodied institution that requires interactional performance in order to be achieved and sustained, is not an easy thing to transport into the narrow bandwidth interactions that we call cyberspace. The proclivity for doing so, for lugging gender in where theoretically new forms of interactional categorization might emerge in its stead, suggests that gender is a dominant, shared social construction that constitutes a primary symbolic form around which we organize interaction. Despite the hype of cyberspace as "unmarked" territory, we are nonetheless mapping this frontier with the same social categories of distinction that we have used to chart modern reality — which we tend to code as based in a state of nature. Gender is foremost among these lines of distinction. Gender as a primary category for sorting self/other is not likely to be erased in the near future of cyberspace. Nor is there reason to assume that the constructed representation of a single physical body as the site of one true self is going to change anytime soon.

Gender switching: true deception[7]

We were in the sex shop because my lover wants a dildo so that we can have boy—boy sex. Or at least that's what I had in mind when I agreed to get the thing. But now that we have acquired the "purple penis" it turns out that she wants to perform "heterosexuality" with me positioned as the girl. "Take off your pants," she commands. "And bend over on your knees. I'm going to enter you from behind." "Do you want me to take off the rest of my clothes?" I ask. "No, this is just a quickie for me," she snaps. "And you are just a very bad girl who wants it more than she should." Girl?! I felt something in me shift. I really didn't know if I could do it; be a girl to her boy. In our repertoire this means letting her (playing as boy) control the sexual activity. But the experience was amazing. I've never "let go" like that before. Now I'm wondering why we don't just think of these acts as variations on submission-dominance sex. Why do we position ourselves as some combination of boy-girl? And what is it about the shifting that makes our sex so thrilling? Are we having sex in our heads or in our bodies I wonder?

In the early 1980s, a woman named Joan, who used the handle, "Talkin' Lady," was a popular online presence (Van Gelder 1991). A New York neuropsychologist in her late twenties, Joan had been severely disabled and disfigured in a car accident that had killed her boyfriend and damaged her own speech and motor coordination. Now, confined to a wheelchair, she had found in electronic communications an alternative community. Joan was described by the many who knew her online as generous, supportive, intelligent and a "very special person." She was so gregarious that many considered her a "telecommunications media star." Joan was especially close to her friend and mentor, Alex, a New York psychiatrist. Together Alex and Joan constituted the hub of an intense community of online friends and lovers. Although no one had met Joan in the flesh (she was reportedly very reluctant to show her disfigurement), she had several online affairs with women and was the confidante of many other women who were intimately involved with Alex. Alex often flew the women that he met online to New York for weekend frolics in the real flesh. Inevitably, these women, who were usually friends of Joan, would go online with her and share the details of their IRL encounters with Alex.

After a period of more than two years it was discovered that Joan was actually a character authored by Alex. Shock and outrage reverberated through this online community. The nearly uniform response was a sense of betrayal. Friends of Joan/Alex felt that they had been "victims" of the "ultimate deceit," that they had been "mind raped."

A cry went out for "regulation" against such "sick con games." Several former friends were reportedly so traumatized by the revelation that they stopped using their modems temporarily. The event caused enough of a furor that it was reported in several widely distributed publications and generated national debate regarding restrictions for and policing of the intentions and authenticity of online communicants. Van Gelder, who originally chronicled the story for *Ms. Magazine*, summarized the incident with the pat conclusion: "we have a long way to go before gender stops being a major, volatile organizing principle – even in a medium dedicated to the primacy of the spirit" (1991: 375).

The story of Joan/Alex raises two nested issues. One is the persistent belief that gendered differences result in expressly dichotomous distinctions between and among interactions of the two sexes. Women relate differently with one another than they do with men and vice versa. Alex reports that he originally conceived Joan when he was mistaken by an online client for a woman. He notes that he was astounded at how much more open she was when talking with someone she assumed was female. A whole new world of communication was revealed to him and he wanted to experience more of it. Thus Joan. Another issue that encompasses the gendered trait dichotomy is the notion that these features are "fixed" in a single biological body. Whether or not one thinks the traits to be biological in origin, the prevailing notion is that there is one fixed gender for each single body. Never mind that Alex did successfully interact as Joan for some time. Multiplicity confounds authenticity.

How prevalent is online gender switching? How acceptable is it? The prevalence of crossers is not a simple matter to sort out. Stone (1993) gives a ratio of physical men to women logging on to Tokyo's popular simulation site created by George Lucas, "Habitat," as 4:1, but points out that inside the Habitat simulation the ratio of men to women is 3:1. This means that a significant percentage of the users who are physically male are likely to be interacting online as females. The Habitat's simulation capacities are an advance over most of the spaces in the United States, where most users log on to "rooms" known as bulletin boards or participate in MUDs. Many users report that they have considered switching gender online, but that they are concerned about "deceiving" potential friends that might be made in these interactions.

Although the prevalence of gender switching is not readily knowable, it is the case that gender policing is considerable. The tacit agreement seems to be that crossing is acceptable – after all, this is a space in which one is supposed to "experiment" – but the motives for crossing must not involve an intent to "deceive." This introduces an interesting tension. What constitutes deception on a frontier yet to be ordered with social norms? Women who cross as men in order to avoid harassment or dismissal are "just being reasonable." Men who create female characters with the intent of understanding the "female experience" are acceptable it seems, so long as they provide this as an account when they discuss the experiences of their female characters. One reported theme among men who cross as women is statements about the discovery that "as soon as I log on as a woman, men swarm all over me with unwanted attention."

More problematic are those who appear to be using a gender switch as a means of eliciting behavior from another that would not be forthcoming if the person's "true" gender were revealed. For instance, in women-only chat spaces there is a constant vigilance against men posing as women in order to find out "how women think about men." Many of these user groups employ "gender authenticity tests." Questions that men presumably would not know the answers to, such as queries about the small print on tampon boxes, or lists of lesbian musicians, constitute the litmus tests of appropriate gender assignment (Herring 1993).

Consider the following exchange in which Kendall (as "hedgehog") is exploring the norms of gender probing in a MUDing encounter:

> Previous asks, "are you really female or is that just your char?"
> hedgehog [to Previous]: that question kind of surprises me.
>   Why do you want to know?
> Previous smiles at you.
> Previous says, "just checking"
> Previous says, "best to catch these things early . . . people here
>   tend to switch sexes almost as often as clothing"
> hedgehog is female in real life.
> Previous says, "good:)"
> hedgehog still isn't sure why you need to know my RL gender, though.
> Previous says, "I don't like being switched genders on, so I make sure
>   early on so I don't inadvertently use the wrong social mores with anyone"[8]
>   (Kendall 1995: 23)

Gender vigilance is especially keen on the date or chat lines. A common pattern when someone meets someone else with whom they would like to pursue further conversation or perhaps even "tinysex" is to ask additional questions about gender. A person who is coy or ambivalent in response to these questions is generally "dropped" from the interaction. Often, this character will be the subject of conversation among other users, all of whom are engaged in gender-sleuthing. It is often assumed that any "woman" who is cruising for sex and who is hypergendered is actually a guy trying to "trick" other men into having sex. Regarding the risks and morality of such encounters, one user sums it up thus: "I think the rule should be: if you are a homophobe don't have tinysex cuz that cute broad might be a guy in real life. If you aren't bothered by this, have fun" (Kendall 1995: 26).

One way to think about online gender-sleuthing is that gender is not just a cue about embodied characteristics, but a sign regarding the performance of very different interactional patterns. If, in fact, men and women generally employ different inter-actional approaches between members of the same sex than across sexes, then switches, once revealed, may indeed evoke a sense of betrayal, of having been "conned" into performing a role that was "inauthentic" and perhaps even compromising of the situation.

In an analysis of posting styles, Herring (1995) demonstrates not only that men and women have different styles, but also that these reflect traditional gender differences. Men tend to post in an adversarial, competitive voice; women seek consensus and are mutually supportive of one another. Interestingly, persons are often "miscast" as the wrong gender if they fail to present the presumed gender styles. Similarly, when gender is posted, persons may be suspected of "crossing" if their gendered "voice" doesn't seem to match the revealed gender. Herring relates the stories of women who, when seen as particularly aggressive, became the subject of much speculation regarding their "true" gender identity. In such cases a usual course of action is for other interactants to seek "gender verification" by locating someone who knows the person in question in "real" life. Interestingly, such sleuthing is not considered an invasion of privacy, but rather a search for information that people feel they "have a right to know with certainty."

Whether and when switching will alter/erode conventional gender lines is linked to the question of motivation. For many feminists and champions of cyberspace and utopia, the desirability of erasing gender as a form of interactional categorization is based on the premise that gender is a hierarchical form of differentiation. Male forms of interaction are associated with greater freedom and more power to determine the discourse. Based on the observation of a high ratio of male to female users, several researchers infer that the prevalence of men in online communications will result in the reproduction of male-dominant patterns of communication. Herring notes that the manuals on "netiquette" (e.g. Shapiro and Anderson 1985) perpetuate the "androcentric" biases of self-control, lack of emotion, assertiveness and rationality. She concludes that cyberspace is likely to be a site that perpetuates "oppressive power arrangements that disadvantage women and non-adversarial men" (Herring 1996: 17). Many women users report that they aim to keep their gender hidden on conference lines precisely so that they will not be disadvantaged in business transactions with male colleagues. To the extent that these women are successful in masking gender, they are likely to be performing patterns of interaction associated with male assertiveness.

Kendall (1998), among others, notes that those who log on as females can expect to be treated with a combination of excessive helpfulness and sexual advances. Many women users report that they attempt to pass as men so that they will be "taken seriously" or to avoid what many participants suggest is an unusually high level of sexual harassment. Rather than encourage alternative forms of interaction, the relative anonymity of online communication may be a site for the dismissal of the social norms that otherwise protect women from displays of outright predatory aggression and interpersonal hostility. Men, on the other hand, report that a common motivation for logging on as a female is because they are fascinated by the unusual amount of attention they receive from other men, when they are perceived as women. Whether the motivation is to gain respect or curiosity, reports to date indicate that switching, if discovered, is seen as a violation of rules of authenticity. One woman who passed successfully as a man on a conference board for several months was threatened with "real, very physical, very painful rape" when the mostly male group discovered her "real" sex.

Motivation for switching and considerations of authenticity are closely bound up in social ethics. Although the fluidity of gender is recognized as an aspect of cyber interactions, the distinction between "real" and "fictitious" remains tightly writ. The motives that people bring to online interactions include mostly the search for professional, personal and romantic communication.[9]

It is useful to consider bodies and selves in relation to communications technology as they form an apparatus for the production of community (Stone 1993). Agreements about "morality" constitute the basis of community. Morality in interpersonal relations is based on the premise that persons can trust one another, that they can depend on one another to be who and what they say they are. Erving Goffman (1959), in his theories on the presentation of self in everyday life, insisted that the power of manifest impressions lay in the extent to which such impressions evoke "anticipatory socialization." In his words, "The impressions that others give tend to be treated as claims and promises they have been implicitly made, and claims and promises tend to have a moral characteristic" (Goffman 1959: 249). A sustainable moral order is anchored in the ability to imbue collective encounters with shared social meaning. Trust is predicated on stability. An interactional partner who constantly shifts shape not only is unpredictable, but also, through the very act of shape-shifting, repositions the other as well. This can be disconcerting if one is trying to establish a long-term relationship of certain knowable, predictable properties. The tension that arises in online gender switching may be less about the possibility that persons can transcend the physical and author themselves in myriad forms and more about the expectation that we maintain fixed positions that others can depend on. Which leads me to rephrase the question: is the line between "fact" and "fiction" immutable? When is multiplicity not a threat to authenticity?

Back to Alex/Joan. While most persons felt "mind fucked" by Alex's "deception," several expressed feelings of regret at "losing Joan." As one woman puts it: "I know I don't feel like a victim . . . I don't think [Alex] is malicious. What I can't get out of my mind was that he's the same person I've spent hours and hours with [as Joan]. I loved Joan. I feel as if she died" (Van Gelder 1991: 373). These people are not angry about "deception," they are disappointed in the inability of Alex to maintain the fiction-as-reality. He failed at sustaining an acceptable multiplicity of personae. The line gets a bit murky here. It is possible to interpret such responses as a desire for the maintenance of a particular manifestation, regardless of the corporeal match, rather than a concern with multiplicity. The maintenance of successful multiple identities can be quite a feat. Alex himself reports that the burden of maintaining Joan's intense relationships had gotten so heavy that he intended to "kill her off."

The point to consider here is that intent, rather than embodied authenticity, may be the organizing principle for online communicants who are assessing the implications of gender-switching and other forms of self/body multiplicity. For the most part, multiple personalities are a disorder in our culture; we rely on the foundational principle of single selves grounded in single bodies as the source and site of authenticity (Stone 1992). There are occasions where deviations are acceptable, even celebrated, but we demarcate these culturally as "theater" – a realm in which the ability to spin and maintain alternative selves is considered acceptable "fantasy." In the theater the test of authenticity is not a single self grounded in a single body, rather it is the believability of alternative manifestations. In theater, authenticity is seamless multiplicity.

Kendall suggests the case of "Amnesia," a "beautiful pale-skinned young white girl" who claims, "for a little over a year, I got away with pretending to be a woman here – I was one of the most successful pretenders – and even briefly pretended to be her fictional boyfriend simultaneously, too" (Kendall 1998: 136). Amnesia gave up the guise when she met some of her fellow MUDers IRL. Online, however, she continues as Amnesia. In response to Kendall's queries about this, she explains: "'Amnesia' is a woman, and always has been. She is my 'ideal woman'." It is here that the lines between fiction and reality blur. Amnesia, much like corporeal drag queens, is not trying to "be" female; she is performing an image of femininity. The distinction is between the intent to "be" and the intent to "perform." This distinction may be more theoretically and conceptually useful in subsequent research than that between real/non-real and honest/deceitful.

There does appear to be a strain between those users who conceive of cyberspace as a realm in which one is invited to "perform" a variety of alternative realities and those for whom the advantage of electronic communications is the transcendence of time/physical space as a barrier to a range of personal networks. For the latter, one's intent is to remain "intact" as a "real person." Online communications are simply a means to extend the range that this self can travel to meet others. In the former, it is one's performative abilities that count; one's prowess as a choreographer of alternative realities. Problems arise not because one is "performing a fiction" but because the fictional moment breaks down. The production of successful "fictions" requires a mutual willingness to suspend "reality." Spaces that are specifically designated for such are likely to encourage more tolerance of slippage between the corporeal and the cyberreal. In fact, in some of these spaces, those who cannot "enter into the fantasy" are shunned. Bruckman (1993) quotes a character who is describing his MUDing activity as a female: "Did I mention the friendly wizard who turned cold when he discovered I was a male in real life? I guess some people are jerks in real life too" (1993: 3). Here the expectations are inverted. Those who cannot separate real life from "the game" are considered "jerks."[10] Friction appears most intense when there is a clash between those who seek to play/perform and those who privilege "authenticity." The emerging norm, as with any form of theater, appears to be that fiction is acceptable so long as the performance is seamless and enacted in a space designated for multiplicity.

In the introduction to her treatise on the "cyborg," Haraway (1991) asserts: "Social reality is lived social relations." In this culture, distinctions between real/fiction are based on commonly agreed upon "rules" about which categories of difference are "natural" (cf. Zerubavel 1991; Mehan and Wood 1975). Classification schemes that we use to impose meaning and order on interaction become ossified as "reality." Morality consists of the willingness/ability to accept and organize one's behavior in accordance with these "ossified" recipes for interaction. If gender is a primary (read: coded as "natural") institution for organizing social interaction, then boundary transgressions are not only likely to arouse confusion, but to elicit moral outrage from the boundary keepers.

One conclusion that I draw here, or rather, a point suggestive for framing systematic research on cyberfrontiers, is that the earnestness with which gender-policing is conducted in a space in which ready cues are not available indicates that this institution is a fundamental basis for organizing social reality. The primacy of gender as a socially constructed "natural" category of difference is further underscored by the dynamics of crossing. My interpretation is that gender-switching is acceptable when it is intended as play/performance. In other words, as long as we all "really" agree that there is a "natural" (read: physical/biological) referent, then it may be acceptable, even desirable, to "play." The most contested issue at this moment in the history of online communication may be how to establish ways of underscoring real versus fictitious sites so that users can reliably distinguish "real authenticity" from "authentic fantasy." In either case, the notion of an anchored, natural referent remains intact, embodied, and immutable. This dynamic will not erase nor alter traditional gender institutions, rather, successful (read: morally acceptable and/or undetected) gender switching highlights the purity of the conventional form. This is true deception.

"Did you really think you were the girl when I fucked you with the dildo?" my lover wants to know. "I don't really know what I was thinking. I felt like a girl, or at least what I think a girl feels like when she has sex with a very eager boy." I inquire further, "Do you feel like a boy when you wear the strap-on?" She gives me a coy grin and blushes. "Depends on what I'm wearing and what the story is going on in my head." She stretches and then pulls off the calf-length silk skirt she is wearing and continues to undress until she has on only a pair of sheer black thigh-high stockings. "Right now I feel like becoming a dominatrix," she announces over her shoulder as she grasps the harness from the edge of the bookshelf where it is hanging. "When I get back I'm going to want a boy to play with," she adds as she goes in search of her leather jacket. I feel my body stir and look down to see that she already undid the top two buttons of my jeans when she kissed me earlier.

Writing in the body: the experience of form

Yesterday I stopped by the office of a colleague for coffee. I had been running in what turned out to be very humid weather. "I smell disgusting," I mumbled in apology. "Didn't have time to shower. Can you stand to sit with me?" My colleague, a stylish, mid-thirties white woman who insists on making a self distinction between being "of a very feminine gender persuasion" and preferring "acts of pansexuality," opens her desk drawer and pulls out a container of roll-on deodorant. She tosses it to me with a perfunctory look. "I'm shocked!" I drawled. "I didn't think ultra femmes used deodorant, let alone kept it at the office." "How do you think we maintain our no-perspiration reputation under pressure?" she asked, and then continued, "I'm surprised at you, I would have thought that readily available deodorant was a must for any self-respecting drag queen." "I'm raunchy," I claimed in defense. "I like to wallow in bodily fluids, especially sweat." "I take my skin clean," she purred, "I guess that lets you off the hook for today."

Village Voice columnist, Greg Tate, wrote a piece titled, "The Black Lesbian Inside Me" (1995). In it he wrestles the contradictions of what it feels like to have an ex-girlfriend tell him, "You were my great lesbian love affair, the man who solved the mystery of what making love to a woman would be like," with his understanding of himself as an embodiment of centuries of male oppression. In a follow-up to this essay, he is invited to ponder further in a piece he calls, "Born to Dyke" (Tate 1995). He writes up this conversation with fellow author, Lisa Jones:

> Just so no one thinks the irony and outrageousness of a man writing this essay escapes me, yes I do feel weird and conflicted. . . . When I presented my conundrum to Lisa Jones she said, "well I can't write about that scene [Black

Lesbian life] because I'm too much of an outsider." And like, I'm not? To which she replied, "you're an insider by virtue of your desire to want to be inside it." You think I got a snappy answer for that rape-inflected colonialist reading, you got another think coming.

(Tate 1995: 206)

In an appearance in Marlon Riggs' film, *Black Is . . . Black Ain't*, dancer and choreographer Bill T. Jones describes "the woman inside of me." Dance critics, apparently captivated by Jones' attribution of his fluidity and grace to an essentialism he names as "female," cite the line repeatedly for the next several months. Meanwhile, a female performance artist is accosted by a group of lesbians following her impersonation of Elvis, the later years, in a San Francisco club. "You're portraying a man," they chastise the hefty Elvis. "Why are you bringing this into our space?" Presumably "our" refers to a space where women come to get away from men, in either the fictional or the factual form.

How are we to make sense of such seemingly complex gender fluidity in the first instance and such apparent dichotomous rigidity in the latter? Or are we? To this point, I have suggested that the cultural rules about how we "do gender" convey not only the foundational premise that sex is a natural fact, but that variations on this theme, where they occur, are seen as being purely mental maneuvers. The mind–body split again. There are rules for how we can bend gender. Rules that simultaneously allow for the possibility of multiple gender renderings within a single body unit, but reinforce the distinction between fact and fiction. My read is that current online gender dynamics are being conducted and interpreted in accordance with these conceptual clusters: disembodied/multiplicity/fantasy versus embodied/authenticity/reality. The emerging cultural rules that will organize computer mediated communications regarding gender and sexuality are likely to constitute a site for gender-stretching within the context of fantasy. The contest, therefore, may be less about gender *per se*, and more about the emergence of signposts indicating allowable multiplicity. Online gender possibilities are likely to be channeled by the emergent rules for writing the line between fact/fiction. A fundamental dilemma for many online communicants is how to disauthenticate the possibility of multiplicity. Putting gender on (the) line highlights this dynamic as a social construction.

I have suggested that when persons enter cyberspace they bring with them preformulated cultural scripts which they use to map the new territory. In other words, we use existing cultural representations to give meaningful order to uncharted netscapes. As social creatures, our maps or scripts consist primarily of categories for defining and distinguishing self and other and the context for interaction. The categories of distinction, once established in the collective conscience, become social institutions. My central theme is that it is theoretically implausible that the charting of the new frontier of cyberspace will consist of original forms. Rather, the forms of interaction will be shaped by the existing scripts which we will carry over into this realm as the only means that we know for organizing interaction. My observation is that a foundational set of cultural rules intersects body as a site of authenticity with the acceptable self – specifically a single gendered self. Furthermore, computer-mediated communication does not enable a multisensory apprehension of others, thus representations of gender characteristics tend to reproduce stereotypes rather than fluid variations on the form.

The physical anonymity of electronic interactions allows for the possibility that persons will present themselves as the opposite gender from their corporeal form. Precisely because this can occur, regulation is likely to emerge, not because gender-crossing *per se* is problematic, but because multiplicity is. The existing cultural scripts that provide a repertoire for handling multiplicity render it either as pathological disorder or allowable as fiction. Modes of interaction that reflect the carry-over of this script into online communications are already discernible. Far from generating new forms of interaction, these emerging trends are likely to reestablish the connection between the body as locus of identity and a cognitive-emotional apprehension of this state of being as "real." My impression is that the principal organizing theme for the foreseeable future will (continue to) be that we have only one body, therefore we have only one "true" gendered self of which we can be "honestly" aware. To represent this self as something other than that which is consistent with physical form is acceptable only if the performance conforms to mutually understood rules of "fiction." Ultimately, one has either a vagina or a penis, and the presence of one or the other of these physical attributes marks an "authentic" immutable presence in time and space. Or so we will continue to believe.

Disembodied multiplicity

When are our experiences likely to draw us beyond the boundaries of our own pre-conceptions? It strikes me that precisely because electronic interactions are disembodied, this is not a site that is necessarily conducive to the generation of mind-altering experiences. The real act of putting on make-up, trying to steady the hand, the precision of the gestures, the sheer time involved is a physical experience that shapes one's view of what it is to be, in this case, female. Similarly, the pounding of heart and the racing of the pulse that occur when one encounters social hostility because one is physically marked as socially "other" is at the root of an empathetic comprehension of social hierarchy. The "performance" of the "other" by a group of persons who are themselves likely to occupy a position of privilege that protects them from many of the "real" experiences of others is not likely to generate anything other than a reaffirmation of preconceived notions.

Some observers who make the case for electronic communication as a site for the alteration of gender institutions focus primarily on the way in which the act of crossing might lead to a more empathetic understanding of the role of the other (and by inference, an alteration in one's own gendered behavior?). Bruckman (1993) remarks on the high quality of discussion groups regarding gender.

> For participants, MUDing throws issues of the impact of gender on human relations into high relief. Fundamental to its impact is the fact that it allows people to *experience* rather than merely observe what it feels like to be the opposite gender or have no gender at all.
>
> (Bruckman 1993: 4, added emphasis)

Consider the notion of "experience" and who's having it for a moment. According to my theoretical logic, we classify our stimuli by sorting them into meaningful categories. Stimuli become "experience" and encoded as memorable once we have given them a meaningful name. The possible names for our experiences are a product of our existing repertoire of cultural categories. In other words, the meaning that we assign to the occasion is shaped by pre-existing cultural representations. Bruckman describes the story of "Peter" who poses as a female character, SusieQ. SusieQ wears a badge designating herself "Official Helpful Person." Peter reports that "playing a female character has helped him get in touch with the female side of himself" (Bruckman 1993: 5). Note that Peter is not performing as any old "female" but as a stereotypical helpful gal. And note his conclusion that the experience of positioning himself as "helpful" is equal to "female." Bruckman concludes that the "experience of gender swapping in MUDs defamiliarized Peter's real life gender role . . . without makeup, special clothing, or risk of social stigma, gender becomes malleable in MUDs" (1993: 5–6).

My interpretation is that Peter has experienced what Peter as straight-white-middle-class male expects his notion of a particular social type (e.g. helpful female) to experience. It is just as likely that he has reaffirmed his own categorical assumptions about women as it is that he has gained a new understanding of women. Bruckman tells us that Peter played his female character for seven months and then "blew his cover" (his words) because the "experiment had outlived its usefulness."

Kendall (1998), whose fieldwork also takes place in a MUD, fixes the ratio of male to female users as 4:1. She gives the additional demographic information that these users are predominantly white, middle-class, upper-division college students. She considers this a typical composite for similar MUDs. Stone (1992) has this to say about the engineers who are involved in designing virtual reality:

> they are articulating their own assumptions about bodies and sociality and projecting them onto the codes that define cyberspace systems. . . . Many of the engineers currently debating the form and nature of cyberspace are young men in their late teens and twenties, and they are at times preoccupied with the things that have always preoccupied the postpubescent. This group will generate the codes and descriptors by which bodies in cyberspace are represented.
>
> (Stone 1992: 610)

Ironically, while this group is likely to comprehend the possibilities of crossing the multiplicity/inauthenticity boundary, they are also those who are likely to have some of the most conventional views of gender dynamics. Given the composition of users and engineers, it seems likely that a particular view of the "female experience" will be perpetuated, a view that is not likely to be challenged by the presence of alternatives. There aren't likely to be any alternatives except in the form of the fantasy characters which distinguish gaming MUDs and which, precisely because they are designated as "fantasy," reinforce conventional gender dichotomies. As Kendall (1998) concludes, one of the central implications of gender relations in MUDs is the reproduction of the general cultural ideal of "male as natural or normal" (cf. Herring 1993).

Mind over matter: Whose minds? Whose matters?

I have been discussing the conventional forms likely to be reflected in the conceptual scripts held by the average user. There are many users and designers who consider themselves far more radical. The potential for altered forms of interaction lies with those whose own modes of communication break radically with one or more aspects of the conceptual cluster. The most radical of these possibilities would be: disembodied/multiplicity/reality. The pivotal alteration in this case is rewriting the assumption that multiplicity is inauthentic. How and among whom might this revision occur?

I do not have the space here to consider this question fully. I posit however that the (re)production of cultural forms of interaction will be shaped by who is doing the interacting. Or more specifically, by the intersection of the interests among users and the content of the cognitive-emotive maps that shape their world views. The meridian points of cognitive-emotive maps are anchored in one's specific position via cultural constructs that locate people differently. We are a reflection and manifestation of our positions. Gender is a principal cultural box according to which we organize and make sense of our experiences. The very real consequences of centuries of classifying persons according to this simple dichotomy are not likely to be erased by piecemeal "crossings" or play-acting the presumed position of the "other." This is especially unlikely to be the case when the binary has been manifest not only as difference, but also as a very particular hierarchy of privilege and experience. In addition, classification has not been optional; gender nonconformity has been and continues to be one the most predominant bases of discrimination and oppression in this culture.

In the immediate future, it is my sense that the majority of those likely to chart cyberspace also share the composite representations of conventional social stereotypes. The cognitive schemata that constitute their means of mapping reality are limited to the standard representations offered by contemporary cultural entrepreneurs; representations that are indicative of deeply engraved social institutions. There is a reason why so many users note that the conversations on date/chat lines and MUDs tend to "resemble those of male adolescents or locker rooms" (Kendall 1998). It is because this is the basic cognitive-emotional repertoire available to those who comprise the bulk of the user population. These are not vampires who bring an alternative structural perspective. I agree with Stone, a transsubjection of gender will require an alchemy. It will not occur through piecemeal "crossings" or transgressions. These serve mostly to reaffirm the existing boundary/structures. Whether this transsubjection can take place online among the current composite of "typical" users with their particular range of images and perspectives is doubtful. The infusers are more likely to be those who are altergender themselves. This is not likely to emerge as a consequence of online communication *per se*, but rather something that might be "transported" in by those whose imaginations reflect the experiences of passing through embodied spaces in which they are marked as "other."

Scholars writing in the tradition of Foucault note that being queer in America requires one to constantly invent oneself, it is an unpredictable and dangerous mode of existence that has to be made up as one goes along; this process leaves in its wake new cultural forms, new zones of pleasure and new communitarian practices (Halperin 1995). The site of such change is the fusion between embodied experience and the search for a name for such experiences. When the experience and the generation of a name are shared, new form is generated. The potential for collective resonance of such new forms is not in the reaffirmation of a single self/body unit, but as a fusion point across the Cartesian divide – a cognitive-emotive transubstantiation. The online relations that reflect these altered forms are generally enacted in spaces where there is a mutual suspension of the belief that "reality" is connected with one's gendered body. In order to enact alternative forms, one must have comprehending partners. The dance of the queer is a generative improvisation at the same time that it is based on a shared experience of the "unnamed." The line between fact/fiction remains blurred among those who are continually writing themselves – in this case, writing the relationship between the experiences of the body and the (non)possibilities for self in a culture that denies the authenticity of these experiences.

As someone engaged in the enterprise of constructing theories about social forms and the consequences thereof, I am reminded that this is a tricky conceptual place where the ontological premises that I employ to spin theories of a socially constructed space bump up against the very real material consequences that occur when, every single day, through their own actions, millions of people actually rebuild the walls that mark these spaces. David Hume is probably the most insistent of the Enlightenment philosophers in his assertion that the subjective representations that we use to organize and give meaning to our experiences are, just that, subjective constructs without any necessary basis in, or reflection of, a "natural reality." I agree with him – ontologically and epistemologically. However, this does not necessarily lead to the conclusion that anything which can be imagined can and will become immediately manifest; nor that all possible representations have an equal probability of becoming realities. The subjective representations that we use to anchor ourselves meaningfully in what would otherwise be an ontological sea of absurdity, do have weight. Eventually they become islands, even continents. With consequence.

Herein lies both a paradox and a fallacy in what I construe to be the direction of current discussions about the potential of online communication to erase gender as a significant basis for self and social organization: it is possible to mentally transgender or ungender oneself in one's own imagination. It is possible to enact and negotiate this re/degendering through interactions with others. And it may be the case that this is easier to accomplish online. But this does not mean that an institutionalized gender binary – and its consequences – will necessarily cease to exist. Rather the act of transgressing the binary may in fact reinscribe it. Just as the act of jumping off the constructed island and swimming around it may remind us that it's there to be explored, it also reinforces the fact that it's there. The fact is, at the very same historical moment in which it is possible for MCI to air a television commercial showcasing testimonials about the freedom of online communication from persons representing stereotypically oppressed groups – female, black, disabled – it is also true that expressed outrage against gender nonconformity remains a permissible prejudice. Transgendered persons are among the most likely victims of violent crimes in the United States. The perpetrators of these brutal beatings and murders are generally dismissed by the courts (when they are charged at all) on the grounds of justifiable assault due to gender deception.[11] The challenge for the theorist/activist is to retain assumptions of the potential for change implied in the ontological premises of a socially constructed reality without losing sight of the manifest cultural-political realities that shape the (re)generation of these (initially) constructed forms.

Gender is indeed a social construction. But it is an embodied construct. Whatever the bandwidth, whether it be the telephone or online text, when we interact with another with whom we do not have physical contact, we proceed as if they were embodied (Stone 1992). To do so we must conjure an image of them. Gender – based on a conventional female–male binary – is the primary dimension by which we do so. Because this is the imagination that most users bring to online interactions, the reproduction of this institutional binary is likely to endure. An empirical question to ask of cyberspace is whether or not it will eventually afford expansive opportunities to a wide range of individuals for playing with and performing alternative gender relations. Online sites may provide more opportunity for transgendered persons to find, interact and experiment with one another in a "safer space." But the presence of such spaces does not guarantee that the activities and ideas generated in these spaces will be transported into more general cultural spaces – online or in embodied interactions. It is just as likely that these spaces will become ghettos with the consequence of further inscribing differences between "normal" gendering and transgendering.[12]

I conclude with a restatement of the initial question: how does narrowing the bandwidth alter patterns of interaction that have emerged from f2f communication? I have complicated the consideration of this question with the suggestion that sensory perception of physical markers of selfhood is not the main issue – hence interactional forms will not necessarily be altered simply because these cues are not manifest online. Rather, it is the idea of these physical features that serves as a marker for what is considered real – a single self located in a single gendered body. Disembodiment, far from being an occasion for stretching these gendered forms, may in fact result in more stringent attempts to (re)mark what we have come to rely on as a primary basis for structuring interaction. Observed instances of loosening or stretching this form indicate that one reason that existing gender constructs are snapped back into place is that they constitute the basis of another fundamental organizing feature – a single self anchored in a single body. Because gender is considered to be "rooted" in nature, it is represented as the primary link between mind and body. A gendered self is a manifestation of the cultural construct that the self is located in a single, immutable physical referent that can be located in time and space. Therefore, when transgendering does occur it is collectively interpreted in terms of allowable fiction, deceit, pathology, or, in the case of transsexuality, an alteration of the physical referent point.

Each of these interpretations is a variation on the existing institutional form of gender. Change in this institution would include an alteration of relationship between multiplicity and authenticity. Multiple manifestations that are comprehensible as being simultaneously real. Which leads me to wonder how you, the reader, are making sense of my own statements of subjectivity: what explanations are you using to organize this disembodied communication we are having in terms of multiplicity/authenticity and fiction/fact? Do I have a "real" gender, a "real" sexuality that anchors this range of experiences manifest as multiple positions? Is this a "rhetorical fiction"? I can write it. Can I make it real?

I'm reading aloud from this text to my girlfriend who keeps interrupting, "That's not what I said." "It's not supposed to be about quoting you," I try to shush her. "I don't like being misquoted," she pouts. "I did not say to the clerk, 'what's the point of packing,' I said 'what are you trying to communicate,' there's a difference." "OK," I acquiesce and edit the line. She's right, it reads better that way. "But what do you think of the theory?" I continue. "It's hard for me to know because I keep projecting myself into the story," she reflects truthfully. "But honey," I say, "it's not about 'you,' it's supposed to be a composite that will complicate the reader's comprehension of two dimensions; reality/fiction and the idea of a fixed gender identity." "I know that," she retorts. "But still, I hate being misrepresented. And I really can't believe that you are going to tell all our stories and put your real name on this and implicate me as well." She pauses mid-tirade to watch me scribble. "What are you doing now?" she demands. "Writing down what you're saying," I reply. She shrieks and threatens to remove the dinner that she has just set before me. "Stop it!" I try to sound gruff. "You're acting like a spoiled queen." She rolls her eyes at me and returns to the kitchen. "By the way," I holler in an attempt to tease further, "do you think we might ever have lesbian sex?" She pokes her head around the door, "You know I don't identify as a lesbian." She thinks a minute, "but I could maybe get into doing lesbian drag." She ponders a bit more. "Yeah, I could definitely dress the part," she muses, "but whatever would we do?"

Notes

1   An edited version of this article was published in *Women and Performance*, special issue on Sexuality and Cyberspace, vol. 17, 1997. I wish to acknowledge the helpful comments of Judy Howard, Ron Obvious, Kate Bornstein, Theresa Senft and Frances Winddance Twine.

2   Another fascinating case indicative of the salience of gender as a form of social organization with deeply felt cultural implications is the story of a teenager who dated and had sex with several women who presumed their date to be male. When it was discovered that "he" was a physiological "she" several of the women filed charges of "rape." The state supreme court of Colorado is currently hearing the case based on the interpretation that rape includes misrepresentation for the purpose of inducing someone to have sex when they otherwise might not do so (Minkowitz 1995).

3   There is a burgeoning literature on the role of women in determining the shape and influence of technology in personal and cultural spheres. See for instance, Jennifer Light's discussion of "The Digital Landscape: A New Space for Women?" in *Gender, Place and Culture* (1995). These approaches differ from my tack here in that gender as cultural form is treated as a non-problematic given.

4   This should not be read to imply that the subjective assessments of various physical features are fixed. The meaning associated with various physical attributes, especially skin color, differs across time and culture. The point here is that, as a culture, we rely on various physical signs, the meanings of which constitute shared cultural "knowledge," as a source of information about how to position ourselves/others in social interaction.

5   One determinant of how mindless these judgments are is one's relative position in the hegemony of the categorization schemes and one's exposure to difference. A white male who spends most of his time interacting with other white males of similar background and tastes is not likely to be aware of more than the most general of features when he encounters someone less like himself. For those whose circumstances do not allow for the selection of sameness in day-to-day interactions, exposure to the complexities of difference is greater. Thus, the ability to make more discriminating assessments of self/others is a function of the range of categories one has available, which is, in turn, a function of exposure to nuanced difference. Those who interact primarily with persons like themselves are the least likely to have complex categorical schemes of differentiation. This is further shaped by the relative position that one occupies in general institutions of power – those with the most power have the least impetus to pay attention to the nuances of difference.

6   Text as a medium for interpersonal exchange, especially the cultivation of friendship and romance, can be quite rich, as illustrated by the predominance of letters as a form of communication in the nineteenth century. A difference between that social milieu and online communication is that in the former, although one might never have met one's correspondence partner, one had probably been "introduced" to the other through social circles that provided information about the then relevant features of class and gender. Furthermore, simply being able to write and having the leisure to do so was an indicator of one's social standing – an important category of difference at the time. It is possible that Net users also make several assumptions about their interactional partners, especially regarding class (middle, professional) and race (white). Perhaps because centrist positions are assumed, neither of these categories of difference appears to receive the attention that gender does in online communication.

7   I use the term "gender switching" as it is commonly employed among those who retain notions of gender as a binary and, therefore, "crossing" as something that involves "switching" from one binary position to the other. My use of terms such as "transgender" is intended to imply that gender is a social construction with much greater potential for nuance than indicated by the terms "switching" or "crossing."

8   Kendall notes that Previous does not attempt to identify her ethnic or racial identity. She states that the assumption in this MUD is that all participants are white. Race is never explicitly mentioned.

9   Stone reports the observations of an informant who notes that various online services designed to make business transactions simpler have been less successful than planned. "What commercial online information services like Prodigy don't realize is that people are willing to pay money just to connect. Just for the opportunity to communicate" (Stone 1992: 616).

10 Kendall (1998) reports that complaints of harassment are often dismissed in MUDs based on the logic of "this is a fantasy space and anything goes." Her observation is that the prevailing attitude is, "there is no such thing as harassment in a MUD, it's only a game, you can do whatever you want."

11 A report compiled by the US Department of Justice in 1987 states that homosexuals and transgendered persons are the most frequent victims of violent "hate" crimes in the USA. A follow-up study conducted in New York City in 1989 found that 89 percent of these crimes result in no arrest or immediate discharge following arrest.

12 What is already occurring is access among individuals who are geographically isolated

to "alternative" gender communities that exist online. For variation in form to occur in online relations, however, there will need to be considerable interaction between those who bring in altered gender expectations and those who maintain traditional representations of both fact/fiction and male/female. An interesting starting point in this analysis would be the exploration of composites of users within and across queer/ straight spaces. Is there considerable crossover, in which case variations in forms and the dynamics of interaction found in queer spaces might be transported into straight spaces? Or are the traditional ghettos being reproduced in emerging online communities?

References

Adams, Jane M. 1993. "Hot on Wires, Computer Lover Burns Women." *Chicago Tribune* August 8, Section 1: 3.

Bornstein, Kate. 1994. *Gender Outlaw*. New York: Routledge.

Bornstein, Kate. 1997. "Her Son/Daughter." *New York Times Sunday Magazine* January 19.

Bruckman, Amy. 1993. "Gender Swapping on the Internet." ftp://media.mit.edu/pub/asb/papers/gender-swapping.txt.

Butler, Judith. 1990. *Gender Trouble*. New York: Routledge.

Butler, Judith. 1993. *Bodies that Matter*. New York: Routledge.

Gearhart, Sally. 1983. "Female Futures in Women's Science Fiction." In *The Technological Woman*, edited by J. Zimmerman. New York: Praeger.

Goffman, Erving. 1959. *The Presentation of Self in Everyday Life*. New York: Doubleday.

Graddol, David and Joan Swann. 1989. *Gender Voices*. London: Blackwell.

Halperin, David M. 1995. *Saint Foucault: Towards a Gay Hagiography*. New York: Oxford University Press.

Haraway, Donna. 1991. "A Cyborg Manifesto: Science, Technology and Socialist-Feminism in the Twentieth Century." In *Simians, Cyborgs and Women*. New York: Routledge.

Herring, Susan. 1993/1996. "Gender and Democracy in Computer-Mediated Communication." *Electronic Journal of Communication* 3(2). Reprinted in R. Kling (ed.) (1996) *Computerization and Controversy* (2nd edn). New York: Academic Press.

Herring, Susan. 1995. "Posting in a Different Voice: Gender and Ethics in Computer-Mediated Communication." In *Philosophical Perspectives on Computer-Mediated Communication*, edited by C. Ess. Albany, NY: SUNY Press.

Hiltz, Starr Roxanne and Murray Turoff. 1993. *The Network Nation: Human Communication Via Computer*. Cambridge, MA: MIT Press.

Hofstadter, Douglas. 1985. *Metamagical Themas: Questing for the Essence of Mind and Pattern*. New York: Bantam.

Katz, Alyssa. 1994. "Modem Butterfly: The Politics of Online Gender Bending." *Voice* March 15.

Kendall, Lori. 1995. "Net Effects: Identity Performance on MUDs." Paper presented at the Annual Meetings of the Pacific Sociological Association. San Francisco.

Kendall, Lori. 1998. "Are You Male or Female?" In *Everyday Inequalities: Critical Inquiries*, edited by J. O'Brien and J. Howard. London: Basil Blackwell.

Kiesler, Sara, Jane Siegel and Timothy McGuire. 1984. "Social Psychological Aspects of Computer-Mediated Communication." *American Psychologist* 39: 1123–34.

Langer, Ellen. 1989. *Mindfulness*. Reading, MA: Addison-Wesley.

Light, Jennifer. 1995. "The Digital Landscape: A New Space for Women?" *Gender, Place and Culture* 2: 133–45.

Lorber, Judith and Susan Farrell (eds). 1991. *The Social Construction of Gender*. Newbury Park, CA: Sage.

Martin, Biddy. 1994. "Sexualities without Genders and other Queer Utopias." *Diacritics* 24 (2–3): 104–21.

Mehan, Hugh and Houston Wood. 1975. *The Reality of Ethnomethodology*. New York: Wiley.

Minkowitz, Donna. 1995. "On Trial: Boy, Girl?" *10 Percent* July/August.

Neutopia, Doctress. 1994. "The Feminism of Cyberspace." Available from neutopia@umass.edu. Posted on FIST, January 31.

O'Brien, Jodi and Peter Kollock. 1997. *The Production of Reality* (2nd edn). Newbury Park, CA: Pine Forge Press.

Poster, Mark. 1990. *The Mode of Information*. Chicago: University of Chicago Press.

Probyn, Elspeth. 1995. "Queer Belongings: The Politics of Departure." In *Sexy Bodies*, edited by E. Grosz and E. Probyn. New York: Routledge.

Rheingold, Howard. 1993. *The Virtual Community: Homesteading on the Electronic Frontier*. Reading, MA: Addison-Wesley.

Scott, Joan. 1992. "Experience." In *Feminists Theorize the Political*, edited by J. Butler and J. Scott. London: Routledge.

Shapiro, Norman and Robert H. Anderson. 1985. *Toward an Ethics and Etiquette for Electronic Mail*. Los Angeles: Rand Corporation.

Stein, Edward (ed.). 1992. *Forms of Desire: Sexual Orientation and the Social Constructionist Controversy*. New York: Routledge.

Stone, Allucquère Rosanne. 1992. "Virtual Systems." In *Incorporations*, edited by J. Crary and S. Kwinter. New York: ZONE.

Stone, Allucquère Rosanne. 1993. "What Vampires Know: Transsubjection and Transgender in Cyberspace." Transcript from a talk given at the symposium, "In Control: Mensch-Interface-Maschine." Graz, Austria.

Sullivan, Caitlin and Kate Bornstein. 1996 *Nearly Roadkill*. New York: High Risk Books.

Tate, Greg. 1995. "Born to Dyke." In *To Be Real*, edited by R. Walker. New York: Anchor Books.

Van Gelder, Lindsey. 1991. "The Strange Case of the Electronic Lover." In *Computerization and Controversy: Value Conflicts and Social Choices*, edited by C. Dunlop and R. Kling. Boston, MA: Academic Press.

Varley, John. 1992. *Steel Beach*. New York: Ace.

West, Candace and Donald Zimmerman. 1991. "Doing Gender." In *The Social Construction of Gender*, edited by J. Lorber and S. Farrell. Newbury Park, CA: Sage.

Wiley, Juniper. 1995. "NoBODY is 'Doing It': Cybersexuality as a Postmodern Narrative." In *Cyberspace, Cyberbodies, Cyberpunk: Cultures of Technological Embodiment*, edited by M. Featherstone and R. Burrows. Thousand Oaks, CA: Sage.

Wilson, Robin. 1996. "Leading Economist Stuns World By Deciding to Become a Woman." *Chronicle of Higher Education* February 16: A17–19.

Zerubavel, Eviatar. 1991. *The Fine Line: Making Distinctions in Everyday Life*. New York: Free Press.

Part three

Social order and control

Chapter 5

Hierarchy and power

Social control in cyberspace

Elizabeth Reid

The failure of the ideal of complete freedom in cyberspace was an early phenomenon. In the mid-1970s, Allucquère Rosanne Stone writes, "the age of surveillance and social control arrived for the electronic virtual community" (Stone 1991: 91). As Stone describes, the CommuniTree computerized bulletin board was intended to be a forum for intellectual and spiritual discussion among adults. It was an environment where censorship was censured and each user's privacy was both respected and guaranteed by the system's administrators. The community it fostered collapsed under the onslaught of messages, often obscene, posted by the first generation of adolescent school children with personal computers and modems. In the wake of what one participant called the "consequences of free expression" technical means were introduced to enable the system's administrators to monitor users' activities and censor "inappropriate" messages (Stone 1991). As Stone comments, such measures have proved to be necessary concessions to the need to maintain order in virtual communities. This chapter examines the mechanisms for social control which have developed on a type of virtual community known as MUD.

MUDs are networked, multi-user virtual reality systems which are widely available on the Internet. Users of these systems adopt alter egos and explore a virtual world which may depict any imagined environment. The MUD interface is entirely textual; all commands are typed in by the user and all feedback is displayed as text on a monitor. The first MUD appeared in 1978 when Roy Trubshaw, then a student at the University of Essex, England, wrote a computer game which he called Multi-User Dungeon. The name was a tribute to an earlier single-user Adventure-style game named DUNGEN.[1] In 1979, Richard Bartle joined Trubshaw in working on MUD and soon took over the project. The completed program was a fantasy-style game that encouraged players to compete with each other for points earned by going on quests to kill monsters or find treasure. This original game can be seen as a computerized version of the Dungeons & Dragons (D & D) role-playing game first released by TSR Inc. in 1974. Since then many similar programs have been written which bear little if any relationship to D & D in either rules or scenario, and many MUD players in the 1990s prefer to expand the acronym to Multi-User Domain or Multi-User Dimension in recognition of the games' evolution from the style of the original MUD.[2]

Technically, all MUD software programs consist of a database of descriptions of rooms, exits, and other objects including those which represent the users themselves. An example of a MUD locality is the LambdaMOO living room:

> The Living Room
>   It is very bright, open, and airy here, with large plate-glass windows looking southward over the pool to the gardens beyond. On the north wall, there is a rough stonework fireplace. The east and west walls are almost completely covered with large, well-stocked bookcases. An exit in the northwest corner leads to the kitchen and, in a more northerly direction, to the entrance hall. The door into the coat closet is at the north end of the east wall, and at the south end is a sliding glass door leading out onto a wooden deck. There are two sets of couches, one clustered around the fireplace and one with a view out the windows.
>   You see Cockatoo, README for New MOOers, a fireplace, a newspaper, Welcome Poster, LambdaMOO Takes A New Direction, The Daily Whale, a map of LambdaHouse, The Carpet, The Birthday Machine, lag meter, and Helpful Person Finder here.
>   Guinevere, jane, MadHatter, Fred, Obvious, Alex, jean-luc, tureshta, Bullet_the_Blue, Daneel, KingSolomon, lena, Laurel, petrify, Ginger, and Groo are here.[3]

The program accepts connections from users on a computer network, and provides each user with access to that database and with the ability to customize their virtual self by the addition of personal descriptions and social markers such as gender. As Pavel Curtis describes, "users are presented with textual information describing them as being situated in an artificially constructed place which also contains those other participants who are connected to the MUD program" (Curtis 1992). There are many hundreds of MUD programs running on the Internet, each with its own unique database of localities and objects. Some are used as educational tools, others as sites for communication and community-building, others are used (as was the very first MUD program) as games in the style of Dungeons & Dragons. Within each of these systems users can interact with each other and with the virtual environment which the MUD presents to them.

As Curtis (1992) has commented, MUD systems have many of the social attributes of physical places, and many of the usual social mechanisms apply. Users take great care to behave as if the worlds depicted by MUD programs were real. Programming and system tools are utilized and developed to maintain a high level of plausibility and coherence – of realism – in the depiction and behavior of the MUD world. However, it is not the technological interface itself that sustains the willingness of users to treat this simulated environment as if it were real. The technology does not wholly determine the nature of the society, though it may determine the parameters within which that society may develop. MUD communities exist in networks of social relations, which can be supported and structured by technology but are not simply created by it. MUDs act as a tool for the expression of each user's imagination, and mediate between the users' imagination and their communication to others of what they have imagined, but they do not determine what is imagined. The progression of a MUD system from its initial existence as a computer program into a virtual environment habituated by users is the progression of a series of linguistic and cultural acts. Use of a MUD's technological tools to describe an imagined world calls that world into existence. It is the production of knowledge about the virtual environment which produces the environment itself.

The Internet – the realm of electronic impulses and high-speed data highways where MUDs exist – may be a technological artifact, but the virtual reality of a MUD world is a construct within the mind of a human being. Within this construct a representation of a person can be manipulated within a representation of a real or imagined environment, both of which can be manifested through the use of technology. Virtual worlds exist on MUDs not in the technology used to represent them, nor purely in the mind of the user, but in the relationship between internal mental constructs and technologically generated representations of these constructs. The illusion of reality lies not in the machinery itself, but in the users' willingness to treat the manifestation of their imaginings as if they were real.

However, the technical attributes of these virtual places, comments Curtis (1992), do have significant effects on social phenomena, leading to new modes of interaction and new cultural formations. In particular, MUDs tend to fall into one of two categories, commonly referred to by MUD users as "adventure" and "social" MUDs. Whether a particular MUD program belongs in either category is dependent not purely on any technical considerations of its programming or implementation, but on the style of interaction which it encourages. This differentiation is to some extent artificial, and based on averages and general cases. Some MUDs may contain elements of both the "social" and "adventure" style. Nevertheless, the terms are in wide use among MUD users, and point to a key distinction made among users between styles of systems and social interaction.

On adventure-style MUDs there exists a strict hierarchy of technical powers, which usually – though by no means always – coincide with social powers and responsibilities.[4] The person with the most control over the system is the one running the MUD program. He or she has access to every computer file in the program, and can modify any of them. This person is commonly known as the God of the MUD, and has complete control over the elements of the virtual world. Gods may create or destroy virtual areas and objects, and destroy or protect users' characters. The users, on the other hand, have very little control over the system. They cannot build new objects or areas, and have no power over those that already exist. They can interact only with the MUD environment. They can kill monsters, collect treasure, solve puzzles, and communicate with one another. By doing these things, users on adventure MUDs collect points, and once users have a certain number of points they gain certain privileges. With enough points the user may be elevated to the rank of Wizard. Wizards do not have the complete

Table 5.1 Comparison of system privileges on MUDs

Privilege	Title					
	God	Wizard	Privileged user	Basic user (social)	Basic user (adventure)	Guest
Remote messages to all users	✓	✓				
Remote messages to groups of users	✓	✓	✓	✓	✓	
Remote messages to individual users	✓	✓	✓	✓	✓	
Remote messages to Gods or Wizards	✓	✓	✓	✓	✓	✓
Messages to users in the same room	✓	✓	✓	✓	✓	✓
Direct access to the system program and files	✓					
Modify and control objects created by others	✓	✓				
Create new objects; modify and control own objects	✓	✓	✓	✓		
Access to versatile programming language	✓	✓	✓			
Access to simple commands	✓	✓	✓	✓		
Interact with objects	✓	✓	✓	✓	✓	✓
May be subject to a quota on creation of new objects			✓	✓		

degree of control which is available to the God of the MUD. They cannot alter the MUD software itself, but they do have the ability to create and control objects and places within the MUD universe.

Social MUDs are not so strictly hierarchical.[5] While social MUDs have Gods who control the actual software, and Wizards who have privileged powers, these powers in the game universe are not unique in kind but only in degree. Users do not have to fight to gain points and levels before they can build simple objects and create new areas of the game universe. Novice users on a social MUD are able to do these things. They do not have access to the actual computer files of the game program, but they have access to a library of commands that allow them to create and describe objects and areas, and make them behave in certain ways in response to input from other users. The rank of Wizard is not dependent upon gaining points, and elevation to this rank is at the discretion of the Gods. Users of these MUDs are encouraged to interact with and extend the virtual environment rather than compete with and within it for power over it.

The titles given to those who run and administrate the MUD vary from system to system. I have chosen to use the term "God" to refer to the person running the MUD program, and "Wizard" to refer to those users who have been given administrative powers by the God. The technical, administrative, and social powers granted to different types of users also vary between systems. Table 5.1 offers an example of the ways in which privileges may vary between users.

Methods and data

In this chapter I have chosen to concentrate on four MUDs representing four different environments and the two different styles of MUD, although I shall refer briefly to other systems. These four MUDs are known as LambdaMOO, FurryMUCK, Revenge of the End of the Line and JennyMUSH. The first is a social-style MUD, set in a rambling mansion. The second, also a social MUD, involves users in a world in which each individual adopts the persona of an anthropomorphized animal. Revenge of the End of the Line (or EOTL as its users refer to it) is an adventure-style MUD with a medieval flavor, and JennyMUSH is a social MUD used as a virtual support center by survivors of sexual assault.

My primary sources fall into three categories: transcripts of sessions on MUDs, electronic mail sent to me by MUD users, and articles from Usenet newsgroups devoted to discussion of MUD and MUD playing. All quoted extracts have been stripped of identifying information and are included with the permission of the individuals concerned. The original grammar and spelling have been preserved. The MUD systems themselves are referred to by their actual names with the exception of "JennyMUSH." The unique nature of this system and the experiences of its users have led to a great concern with the issue of privacy and the administrator has asked me not to reveal any information that might identify the system.

Disinhibition and sociality

Computer-mediated communication systems have often been described as freeing users from social constraints. Although they often disagree on the effects of decreased social inhibition, some researchers of human behavior on these systems have noted that users tend to behave more freely and spontaneously than they would in face-to-face encounters. Kiesler and Sproull (1986: 1498) describe computer-mediated behavior as "relatively uninhibited and nonconforming." Kiesler et al. (1984: 1129) have observed that "people in computer-mediated groups were more uninhibited than they were in face-to-face groups." The forms that this disinhibition takes differ from one researcher's experience to that of the next. Some have seen an increase in examples of aggressive and disrespectful behavior; others have noted increases in friendliness and intimacy. Behavior on MUDs does seem to conform to these observations. Users do seem to be less inhibited by conventions seen in everyday life. They can be seen to be both more intimate and more hostile with each other than would be socially acceptable in everyday life, particularly when considering that hostility or intimacy may be shown among users who are strangers to one another.

However, being disinhibited is not the same as being uninhibited. MUD users experience a redefinition of social inhibitions; they do not experience the annihilation of them. The social environments found on MUDs are not chaotic, or even anarchic. There is indeed no moment on a MUD in which users are not enmeshed within a web of social rules and expectations. However, the markers of these expectations and rules are not as immediately apparent on MUDs as they might be in actual life. The collection of rights and responsibilities, expectations and obligations that emerge in social situations are expressed by different means in face-to-face and computer-mediated social groups. Until a user has been acclimatized to the communicative conventions of a MUD the virtual environment may seem to be a place where etiquette has been replaced by chaos, and they may therefore assume that within the confines of the MUD anything goes. This tendency toward uninhibited behavior has influenced the conventions that have developed on MUDs. The process of teaching new users the mores of the system and of developing means of dealing with recalcitrant users has resulted in behaviors which differ in both expression and meaning from the conventions we live with in offline life. A set of social behaviors has arisen in which it may be acceptable to talk to strangers, but not one in which the patterns of that talk are not subject to social controls.

The nature of the MUD program encourages a degree of disinhibition. The behavioral influence of the virtual environment is not simply permissive; it encourages. Crucial to the fostering of disinhibition among some users is the fact that they begin their association with the MUD under a veil of anonymity. Users need not be known to others by their real names. They may instead choose to be known by any variety of name or nickname. Some choose to use conventional first names; others adopt more evocative and inventive pseudonyms. The description of the LambdaMOO living room which was quoted earlier ends with a list of the users situated in that room:

> Guinevere, jane, MadHatter, Fred, Obvious, Alex, jean-luc, tureshta, Bullet_the_Blue, Daneel, KingSolomon, lena, Laurel, petrify, Ginger, and Groo are here.

The information which one user can gain about others on a MUD consists of the names by which they choose to be known and the nature of the descriptions which they choose to attach to their virtual self. All that can be known about a user is what he or she chooses to disclose, and every item of information is subject to change.

The initial effect of this pseudonymity is often to provide users with a feeling of safety. Protected by computer terminals and separated by distances of often thousands of kilometers, users feel that the likelihood of any of their fellows being able to affect their "real lives" is minimal. There seems little chance of a virtual action being met with an actual response. There is a sense that no one can be embarrassed, exposed, laughed at or hurt in their day-to-day lives. There are no sticks or stones to contend with, and although words may hurt, users can always resort to the off-switch on their computer. The disinhibition which pseudonymity and a firm boundary between an individual's day-to-day life and their interaction with the group encourages in an Alcoholics Anonymous meeting can also be seen on a MUD. The fact of pseudonymity offers protection; distance strengthens this to make MUDs seem one of the safest possible social environments. This sense of safety enables MUD users to become more expressive than might be acceptable in everyday life.

Curtis (1992) has described increased intimacy on MUDs as a variety of "shipboard syndrome," the result of apparent proximity and the feeling that interlocutors may never meet in everyday life. Since they have little opportunity to interfere with each other's everyday lives the demands of social self-preservation need not inhibit them. MUDs are a world unto themselves, and ships that pass in the virtual night feel little need to anchor themselves in emotional responsibility. Moreover, the MUD community depends on a richness of communication and the creation of social context. The system itself encourages MUD users to become intimate – or at least to simulate intimacy. MUD systems, like any other, abhor a vacuum, and a vacuum on a MUD is seen in a lack of textual exchanges. The MUD universe functions only while users are willing to elicit text from the program and from each other, and are willing to volunteer their own contributions. Communication is necessary to the existence of the MUD and successful MUDs are likely to see a great deal of communication between users, which can then form a basis for familiarity and intimacy. Users on MUDs are likely to be disposed to feel that intimacy with fellow users is a harmless activity, and so be willing to take advantage of those aspects of MUDs that encourage intimacy.

The tendency toward increased intimacy which can be seen on MUDs facilitates the formation of strong personal attachments. Hiltz and Turoff (1978: 101) have noted that some participants in computer-mediated communication systems "come to feel that their very best and closest friends are members of their electronic group, whom they seldom or never see." That this can become so depends on the degree to which users are willing to suspend the usual rules of social self-preservation, and open up to each other. By assuming that the dangers associated with intimacy – the possibility of hurt and embarrassment – can be avoided on MUDs, users can allow themselves to become very close to one another. The safety of MUD friendships increases their worth, and users can, ironically, become extremely dependent upon such relationships. The lack of factors inhibiting intimacy, and the presence of factors encouraging it, can induce deep feelings of attachment in users toward their virtual friends:

> I don't care how much people say they are, muds are not just games, they are *real*!!!

> My mud friends are my best friends, their the people who like me most in the entire world. Maybe the only people who do . . .

> They are my family, they are not just some dumb game . . .

Some of these virtual friendships go beyond the platonic. MUD romances are a well-estab-lished institution, held together by a number of tools and rituals. MUD lovers use the commands with which the MUD system provides them to transform the virtual stage into a set designed to express and uphold their feelings for one another. On social MUDs, the most common action taken by such partners is to set up virtual house together. They create a home, using the MUD program to arrange textual information in a way that simulates a physical structure which they can then share and invite others to share. Tokens are often exchanged, virtual representations of flowers and rings being attached to a user's virtual manifestation through the manipulation of the textual description of the character. More technically gifted users may create objects, which other users can interact with, that textually mimic the behavior of pets and children. These relationships may even be virtually consummated through "netsex," a form of co-authored interactive erotica.

The establishment of networks of social expectation and obligation which is crucial to the development of a social structure on a MUD depends on a factor which can also be a threat to that structure. The tendency toward disinhibition and the accompanying threat of anti-social behavior can be countered by an encouragement of uninhibited sociality. The apparent safety of anonymity encourages users to be expressive, which enmeshes them in a web of relationships. Many MUDs build facilities designed to cement relationships – such as virtual marriages – and decrease anonymity. An example is the "pinfo" (player information) command on FurryMUCK. Users can perform a pinfo query on any other user and may make their own pinfo listing as detailed as they wish. Fields are provided in the pinfo database to allow and encourage users to enter descriptions of their virtual and "real" selves, including such information as real names, email addresses and telephone numbers. Such facilities encourage contactability and accountability, and encourage users to develop a stable presence on the system rather than taking advantage of the potential for ephemerality in both online relationships and virtual identities. The success of these efforts both counteracts and relies on each user's initial tendency toward disinhibition.

Virtual violence

Romances and deep friendships display MUD relationships at their most idyllic, but the lowering of inhibition seen on MUDs has another side. The disinhibiting effects of relative anonymity and physical safety in the virtual environment can encourage the enactment of aggressive and abusive behaviors, and it is at this point that the overt forms of social control which have developed on MUDs come into play. The seeming safety of MUDs can lead some users to use them as a forum for the expression of hostility. MUD systems can "reduce self-consciousness and promote intimacy" but they can also lead users to feel free to express anger and hatred (Kiesler et al. 1984: 1127). This can take the form of "flaming," a phenomenon of computer-mediated communication which has been charac-terized as the gratuitous and uninhibited expression of "remarks containing swearing, insults, name calling, and hostile comments" (Kiesler et al. 1984: 1129). The anonymity of the user behind the pseudonymous character makes the possibility of everyday punishments appear to be limited. The supposed safety of the medium causes the sanction of physical violence to appear irrelevant to virtual actions, although as I shall describe social sanctions are present and often in a textual form that apes physical violence. Nevertheless, the safety of anonymous expression of hostilities and obscenities that would usually incur social sanctions – or a punch in the nose – in a face-to-face encounter encourages some people to use MUDs as a forum for airing their resentment of individuals or groups in a blatantly uninhibited manner.

In some cases harassment of individual users occurs. A harassed individual may face repeated messages from the harasser, and be the object of derogatory descriptions written into objects created purely for that purpose – the virtually physical context can be made to reflect an individual's feelings of hostility as easily as those of intimacy and affection. These electronic monuments to hate can be as upsetting and hurtful to users as the more positive relationships can be sources of support and happiness. Although insults relayed over MUDs may be brushed off just as they may be in actual life, MUDs also provide unique opportunities for personal attacks.

The most striking example of virtual violence that I have come across took place on JennyMUSH. JennyMUSH was a virtual help center for people who have experienced sexual assault or abuse. Users of this MUSH shared a strong bond in their common trauma, and for many of them the MUSH provided their only source of community support. At its happiest, JennyMUSH offered a tremendous example of how MUD programs can be used as valuable social tools. The system was designed with this aim in mind. The chief administrator, or God, of the MUSH was a psychology student whose field of interest is the treatment of survivors of assault and abuse, and the university that she attended fully supported the JennyMUSH project. This official support ensured some degree of security for users of the system.[6]

Nevertheless, official support cannot ensure safety from the less positive aspects of the virtual environment. A single user of JennyMUSH was able to subvert the delicate social balance of the system by using both technical and social means to enact anonymously what amounted to virtual rape. Two weeks after being assigned a character, a user of the system used the MUD's commands to transform him or herself into a virtual manifestation of every other user's fears. This user changed "her" initial virtual gender to male, "his" virtual name to "Daddy," and then used the special "shout" command to send messages to every other user connected to the MUD.[7] He described virtual assaults in graphic and violent terms. At the time at which this began, none of the MUD's administrators, or Wizards, were connected to the system, a fact that may well have been taken into account by the user. For almost half an hour, the user continued to send obscene messages to others. During that time, some of his victims logged out of the system, taking the simplest course to nullify the attack. Those who remained transported their virtual personae to the same locale as that of their attacker. Many pleaded with him to stop, many threatened him, but they were powerless to prevent his attacks.

At the end of that half hour, one of the Wizards connected to the system. He found twelve users connected to the system, all congregated in one place. On transporting himself to that place, he found eleven of those users being obscenely taunted by the twelfth. Quickly realizing what was going on, the Wizard took a kind of vengeance upon the erring user that is possible only in virtual reality. He took control of the user's virtual manifestation, took away from him the ability to communicate, changed his name to "Vermin" and changed his description to the following:

> This is the lowest scum, the most pathetic dismal object which a human being can become.

What had preceded had been painful and ugly – what ensued has been described to me as "virtual carnage." The eleven users who had been victimized by this now impotent one turned upon him and took dreadful virtual revenge. They described all the most violent punishments they would like to enact on this and all other attackers, emoting – both in the conventional sense and in reference to the "emote" command which allows MUD users to textually simulate actions – all the hatred and rage which JennyMUSH had been established to help people deal with.

Since this incident, if such a mild word can be used to describe it, many things changed on JennyMUSH. The system became far more security conscious. The "shout" command, which enabled "Daddy" to send messages to all users connected to the system, was deactivated. The information displayed to all users on connecting to the system was modified to include directions on how to avoid unwanted messages by preventing the MUSH system from relaying messages from a particular user, a facility known as "gagging." New users had to be vouched for by an established user before being given a character, and all users were required to provide the administrator of the MUSH with their legal name and telephone number.

What happened on JennyMUSH could happen on any MUD system, and probably has happened on many.[8] The particular purpose for which JennyMUSH was constructed may have meant that the incident was all the more traumatic for its users, but the same degree of hurt resulting from virtual actions could be brought about on any system. JennyMUSH's experience starkly demonstrates the degree to which users can feel as though they are free to act on feelings and to act in ways which mainstream society hopes to suppress. The cruelty and callousness shown by this abusive user were expressed in a unique form in this virtual environment – he was able to project onto both the virtual environment and the virtual manifestations of other users a kind of violence that may have been all the more distressing for its lack of physicality, and attendant impossibility of fighting back. He was able to shape reality into the forms he wished, and transform it into a reflection of his own cruel intentions.[9]

The kinds of action taken by the other users, and by the Wizards and God of JennyMUSH, use this same ability to reshape reality, this time into forms that create and reinforce social rules and structures. The lesson learnt from this episode on JennyMUSH was described by the MUD's administrator as this:

> We spent so much time trying to make JennyMUSH a place where people could feel free to speak out – we provided anonymity and very few restrictions. Sadly, we didn't foresee the negative aspects such encouragement could have. In the end we discovered that we could not base our little virtual society on "freedom

to" – we had to balance it with "freedom from" and that meant the formation and enforcement of rules and a strict hierarchy of privileges.

The initial reaction of users to the episode on JennyMUSH had the quality of an immediate punishment without any form of due process. The punishment took the form of constraint, a degradation ritual and a mob attack. After the fact, and after emotions had cooled, technical modifications to the system were introduced to reduce the likelihood of another such incident. Most MUD systems offer, as JennyMUSH began to in the wake of the "Daddy" incident, facilities that can be used to silence or banish disruptive users. Some of these facilities are available to all users. They have the option of ignoring, or "gagging," another user. Such a measure does not actually affect the offending user, but prevents the offended one from receiving any messages from that user. By editing his or her personal virtual reality a MUD user can attempt to prevent harassment by severing the links of communication between him or herself and the harasser. Such attempts are not, however, always successful or satisfactory. A determined harasser, realizing that a victim is employing these commands, may simply resume harassment through a new MUD character. Even when nominally successful, these measures are not always felt to be sufficient by victims of harassment. After all, gagging does not prevent the harasser from speaking or being heard by others. The effects of this command are more akin to "ear-plugging" and do not negate the adverse social effects of another's hate-speech. Moreover, as Dibbell (1993) comments, the "gag-and-get-over-it school of virtual-rape counseling, with its fine line between empowering victims and holding them responsible for their own suffering" does not satisfy the needs of all who are advised to employ such measures.

Such measures are, however, the least of those which can be employed against an erring user. Those who persist with unwelcome behavior may be dealt with by the God of the MUD, who has at his or her disposal powers which act to exclude and shame their object. Offenders may be safe from actual physical violence at the hands of those they have victimized, but ostracism is common and social admonition has taken the form of ridiculing and subverting the efforts of disruptive users to actualize their imagined selves in the virtual world. Users who are a continual problem can be not only ignored by their victims, but also punished and even banished by the God of the MUD. If called upon to do so a God can call down virtual fire from heaven – destroying the offending user's character, and disallowing future connections from the particular computer that the offender had been connecting from.

In most cases these technical measures are sufficient. However, users who persist in disruptive behavior, or who counter it by other technical means, can be subjected to public rituals intended to humiliate and punish them, often in the form of a public shaming that utilizes the God's special ability to redesign any aspect of the virtual reality of the MUD. An offending user can be "toaded," a practice that traditionally involves the MUD's Gods or Wizards using their special powers to change the name and description of the user to present an unpleasant appearance (traditionally that of a warty toad) and moving the user to some very public area of the MUD where other users can taunt and chastise him or her. JennyMUSH's treatment of "Daddy" was a classic example of this form of social punishment. This public humiliation is often enough to discourage the user from visiting that particular MUD world again, even if earlier attempts at ostracism had been unsuccessful. Even if a user has not invested sufficient meaning in his or her character to feel hurt by such punishments, they are effective in banishing offenders and appeasing those offended. In these kinds of punishments, power is seen to be at its most absolute. Foucault (1980: 125) has described an effective form of power as one that enables the powerful to "gain access to the bodies of individuals, to their acts, attitudes and modes of everyday behavior." On a MUD, where the physical body is not present, but the virtual body is at the absolute mercy of the Gods, such power exists quite literally. The Gods of a MUD can manipulate a user's virtual manifestation in any way they please. They can reshape it, remake it, remold it, destroy it. From the perspective of the game universe, such acts of power are absolute.

Punishment on MUDs often shows a return to the medieval. While penal systems in the western nations that form the backbone of the Internet – the United States, Europe, the United Kingdom and Australia – have ceased to concentrate upon the body of the condemned as the site for punishment, and have instead turned to "humane" incarceration and social rehabilitation, the exercise of authority on MUDs has revived the old practices of public shaming and torture. The theater of authority in virtual reality is one which demands and facilitates a strongly dramaturgical element. All actions on MUDs must be overt, every nuance of experience must be manifestly represented for it to become part of the play, and so punishment must be flamboyant. The virtual world of a MUD exists in its dramatic strength only in the minds of its users, but the play enacted in the virtual world emulates the physical rather than the mental. The public spectacle of punishment, which Foucault (1986) describes as disappearing from the western political scene between the eighteenth and nineteenth centuries, is alive and well on MUDs.

Hierarchies of power

Social structures on MUD systems are based on control of users' abilities to manipulate the elements of the virtual environment. The haves are those who can control the form of the virtual world depicted by the system; the have-nots are those who can't. Power on a MUD is quite literally the power to change the world. Although all users on the MUDs I have examined have access to tools that allow them to shape the MUD world to some extent, if only by the use of personal descriptions and the taking of virtual actions, no system allows all users access to all commands. User privileges vary between the absolute and the minimal; from the total control over the elements of the MUD universe wielded by Gods to the minimal privileges accorded to users of adventure-style MUDs. There are many good reasons for these limitations. On a large international computer network it would be a security risk to allow any person access to the raw files stored on a computer. A limited amount of hard disk space may make it foolish to allow users to enlarge the MUD database to an unlimited extent. Pragmatic though these reasons may be, they are the basis for a social hierarchy in which greater status corresponds to greater control over the virtual world of the MUD system and greater ability to enrich that system.

Because of their special powers and their special role within a MUD community, Gods and Wizards are frequently the object of special treatment. Many users approach them with, as Curtis (1992: 30) puts it, "exaggerated deference and respect." An example of such treatment was forwarded to me by a Wizard on FurryMUCK:

> Fred pages you with, "Excuse me sir, I hope I'm not bothering you, but could you possibly help me? I'm really new to MUDS, and I've got some pretty dumb questions. If you haven't got time to answer them please don't worry about it, but if you do I would really appreciate it."

Many Wizards and Gods do not spend much time traveling through their virtual domain. Instead, they often retreat to the sanctity of one virtual room. It is to this space – this virtual throne room – that mortal users are called when they wish to speak with the God or Wizard. The protocol for gaining admission to such rooms varies from system to system, but is never non-existent. Most of these rooms cannot be entered without the permission of their owner; entry to some requires the direct intervention of the deity to "teleport" the supplicant to the holy presence. The sign on the door of a Wizard's room on EOTL reads as follows:

> That door leads to Moe's Sanctum Sanctorum. If you knock on it, and he's around, he might invite you in or come talk to you. Lately, though he's been pretty busy, so don't bug him unless you need something. THINK VERY HARD BEFORE KNOCKING. Moe has been known to turn people into barnyard animals if they pester him frivolously.

In some cases the motivation for the creation of such social barriers may simply be to screen out trivial requests from users. Nevertheless, whatever the intention, the power to define what is trivial and to impose punishment for transgressions of that definition lie with the Wizards and Gods. Many preserve a kind of magical or divine distance between themselves and the mortal users of their world. Curtis may be bemused by the deference paid him as the God of LambdaMOO, but such deference is paid and is motivated by the technical and social symbols of power by which Gods and Wizards are surrounded. The basis of authority on MUDs is as medieval as its punishments. Hierarchies are maintained through careful attention to the trappings of power, power which, like medieval kingship, owes its legitimacy to the favor of the Gods. Distance between the rulers and the ruled is carefully maintained. Special spaces are created by virtual rulers to cater to and augment the signs of their power. Virtual analogues of scepters and crowns abound – most Gods and Wizards carry signs of their rank upon them. Divine authority on MUDs is made manifest in technical miracles and virtual symbols of power.

Nevertheless, such power does not always go unquestioned. The legitimacy of power and the enaction of it can be questioned by users, especially when notions of favoritism are introduced. Wizards are created by Gods, and in theory promotion to such a privileged rank is linked to talent. The more a user is able to translate their imagination into the MUD database – the more ingenuity they show in their manipulation of the MUD program – the more likely they are to be promoted to the level of Wizard. A talent for making the MUD more virtually real should be rewarded by being granted greater powers to do so. In practice, however, this may not always be the case. Accusations of Godly and Wizardly prejudice and injustice regularly surface on the Usenet newsgroups devoted to the discussion of MUD playing:

> This mud is TOTALLY LAME! One of the wizzes can't program for shit and only got to wiz coz he rooms with the chief wiz, and another wiz just got the job by having tiny-sex with the chief wiz. I spent DAYS building lots of really cool stuff, really cool descs and everything, and when I showed it to the cheif wiz and asked to get a higher quota he just said "I don't even know you" and refused!!! ARGH!! So I complained and told everbody on the mud what happened and he dests my character and deletes everything I built. I am so sick of wizzes who expect you to brown-nose to get anything.

Gods and Wizards may be the ultimate power within each MUD universe, and may often be the subject of respect and even fawning as users attempt to curry favor and gain privileges, but the atmosphere of respect which often surrounds them can lead them to favor users who are prepared to offer adulation, and to pass over those who are not. The canny wielding of power often means that privileges are bestowed upon those who will uphold the Gods' hegemony; the clumsy handling of this process can threaten that hegemony. The potential for the abuse of power and for unfair treatment of users can create resentment, particularly when there is a conflict between individuals who feel that Gods and Wizards have a duty to behave fairly and those who feel that the administrator of a MUD system has the right to do with it as he or she likes. The number of MUD systems in existence to some extent mitigates the potential for problems, since, as one user replied to the complainant above:

> Look, it's his MUD, he can do what he wants. But if you don't like the MUD, don't play it! If the wiz is an asshole . . . no one will play and the MUD will close. Simple! Sheesh . . .

The common wisdom is that simple economics will make it unrewarding for a Wizard or God to treat users badly, and so most successful holders of those positions will by necessity treat their users reasonably well.

Adventure MUDs: survival of the fittest

Users of adventure-style MUDs must contend with the internal reality of the game world. The characters played are subject to "realistic" forces. On some systems, they grow hungry, thirsty and sleepy, and must find safe places to sleep and rest. They must protect themselves from the ravages of an often hostile climate. They must establish, and often pay for, a safe place to continue their existence while their controlling user is unable to attend to them. Adventure MUD users are driven by the "biological" needs of their characters and by the social and climatic circumstances of the game world. On some systems, users are often confronted with messages from the game program, letting them know that "they" – or rather, their characters – are hungry, thirsty or tired. If users do not satisfy their characters' hunger or thirst those characters will die. If users do not find a safe place for their characters to sleep in, those characters will likely be murdered in their sleep by the mythical monsters that commonly inhabit these MUD worlds – or by another character, provided that the particular game world is one that allows direct combat between users. Before logging out of the game, users must first rent their characters a room in one of the hotels that form a central and basic part of the game world. Renting a room ensures that the character and his or her possessions are kept safe until the user returns to the game. A character left without a rented room may forfeit his or her possessions to unnamed thieves generated by the MUD program, and is vulnerable to the attacks of monsters and other users.

As a consequence of all this, users spend a large amount of time merely making sure that their characters survive. They must continually load themselves with supplies of food and drink before venturing on quests. They must make periodic trips back to the towns of the MUD world to replenish these supplies. They must continually amass treasure – by killing monsters – with which to buy supplies and pay the rent on hotel rooms. It is impossible to play an adventure-style MUD casually. Users who log into the game once a week, and play for only an hour or so at a time, will be continually forced to restart the game. They will never be able to find enough treasure to enable them to pay for the safety of the belongings they buy or win, and so will always lose them to the relentless economics of the game. The least devoted users must, therefore, play often enough and for long enough to maintain their characters' existence. They must, as Alice found in *Through the Looking Glass*, keep running just in order to remain in the same place. Adventure-oriented MUDs, such as LPMUDs and DikuMUDs, demand a basic level of dedication from users. Unlike social style MUDs, such as MUCKs and MOOs, the game itself demands attention. It seems to have a life of its own. A MUCK character remains in stasis when not being controlled by a user, whereas a DikuMUD character can die of starvation, be the victim of robbery or murder, or become part of a marauding Giant Bear's dinner should the user relax his or her vigilance or fail to log into the game before the character's money, and therefore rented safety, runs out.

At the heart of all social structures among users of adventure MUDs lies the hard fact that adventure MUD universes are dangerous. Foucault (1980: 55) has said that "the phenomenon of the social body is the effect not of a consensus but of the materiality of power operating on the very bodies of individuals." Translated into the particular terms of the imagined worlds of adventure-style MUDs this insight has special meaning. There, it is the virtuality of the power of the virtual world operating upon the imagined bodies of individual users that creates the social body of which they are a part. Cooperation is an important element of survival on adventure MUDs. In many cases, users need each other to survive. Particularly strong monsters are more easily defeated by the concerted efforts of a group of users than by one alone. The necessity for cooperative effort has been built into the fabric of the game on many systems. Quests, specific tasks formulated by the Gods and Wizards to test the strength of their users, often demand the application of more skills than one character can have, and so must be undertaken by a group. The economics of the game support group effort. Special commands enable users to form groups, make concerted attacks on monsters and share the experience points gained in shared victories. This technical support and dramatic demand for cooperation between users translates into a social system in which users are expected to aid each other. Many users will guard the possessions which had belonged to a fallen character, and will wait for them to return from the church to which their spirit has gone to pray for reincarnation so that on return they may regain their possessions. This kind of honor system based on favors and debts of gratitude can be especially kind to novice users. The help files on EOTL explicitly encourage users to help the less experienced among them:

> When a newbie begs for some money or help, it is usually expected that you will give what you can. Everyone was a newbie once, and probably got their start through the generosity of other more established users. The least you can do is show the same consideration to future newbies (known as the golden rule). And above all, remember it's just a game . . . but with real people on the other end side.

Such cooperation is not, however, based purely on comradeship. The fact is that users can, if they so choose, cause each other considerable hardship. It is not always altruism that causes users to aid each other, but the prudence of investing in other users' goodwill. Do unto others as you would have them do unto you – that is the rule that prevents many users from taking advantage of the misfortunes of others.

Users are at their most vulnerable when in combat. When fighting a system-generated opponent – a monster or "mobile" – many users will be forced to retreat and use healing potions and spells, or simply rest, before being able to rejoin the fight and eventually kill the monster. It can take several bouts of fighting and healing before the monster can be killed. In the times when a user has retreated, it is possible for another user to come along and kill the now weakened monster while its original opponent is resting. The information on etiquette available on EOTL has this to say about the practice of "kill-stealing":

> Believe it or not, there are certain unspoken rules of behavior on MUDs. . . . It's really bad form to steal someone else's kill. Someone has been working on the Cosmicly Invulnerable Utterly Unstoppable Massively Powerful Space Demon for ages, leaves to get healed, and in the interim, some dweeb comes along and whacks the Demon and gets all it's stuff and tons of xps. This really sucks as the other person has spent lots of time and money in expectations of the benefits from killing the monster. The graceful thing to do is to give em all the stuff from the corpse and compensation for the money spent on healing. This is still a profit to you as you got all the xps and spent practically no time killing it.

Users who break this rule are not popular. Some may be subject to the kinds of punishment and displays of power that Gods and Wizards may call up. Others may be subject to the vengeful attacks of their victims and fellow users.

On some adventure MUDs users' characters are able to kill one another. As far as a character is concerned, another character is as easily a target of the "kill" command as is an orc or dragon. For some users, the possibility of "playerkilling" adds depth and spice to the virtual world. The addition of greater threat and greater danger to the virtual universe enables users to identify more strongly with their virtual persona. The thrill which users describe as a part of such battles, the sheer excitement of adding an unprogrammed human element to the game universe, makes that universe all the more real. Death and danger make the imagined life all the more worth living, and lift the game beyond the confines of the predictable. It is a fear of losing control inherent in a game style that stresses a fight for greater control that makes the game emotionally compelling. Victory in such battles is all the more sweet for the test of a user's skill which it entails.

Nevertheless, not all users need to have the fruits of their imagination challenged to feel that their animation is valid. On the contrary, the intrusion of others' conflicting versions of the world can disturb the imaginative balance of the user. Such conflicting world views are the basis of many power struggles between users. For some playerkilling destroys the mental illusion in which they wish to immerse themselves by connecting to a MUD system. The forceful intrusion of another's imagined reality, an intrusion that can shatter the carefully constructed projections of the victim, inspires great resentment and anger. The practice of playerkilling is looked upon by some users with anger and contempt, as this Usenet article describes:

> Playerkilling is a pointless exercise allowed by some muds, whereby lab geeks with testosterone poisoning kill each other instead of mobiles and pretend that they are better mudders as a result. This collective delusion makes pkers overbearing, obnoxious, and generally no fun at cocktail hour.

In response to this article, another user replied that:

> Playerkilling is the ultimate chessmatch, where you are depending on your knowledge of your capabilities and your mud to match those others who might play. While it is sometimes abused by losers who feel manly by killing newbies, it also seperates the real mudders from the yellow-striped regen waiters who would just as soon wait around to kill a monster that just stands there waiting to die. PKers are neither overbearing nor obnoxious, but they are occasionally arrogant, but then again, being better users, they have a right to be. They never attend cocktail parties because they think those little sandwiches are for wusses.[10]

Playerkilling, then, is an issue surrounded by controversy. On many MUDs, playerkilling is heavily controlled, either by technical or social measures. Some adventure-style MUDs prevent user killing by removing the possibility of it from the MUD computer program. Others simply regulate it. There are two main ways of technically controlling the circumstances under which users may attack each other. The first is to require that users set a "user killer flag" on their character. Only those with such a flag set may be attacked – the program will simply not allow a user to attack another whose killer flag is not set. The second measure is to allow users to attack only those who are close to their own level of competence. On MUDs where a level system is in place, this is commonly implemented. Users who have attained Level 5, for instance, may be able to attack users on Levels 5 and above, but not those on lower levels. At the same time, they cannot be attacked by users on a higher level, unless they initiate the combat – only characters at an equal or lower level may choose to attack them. This prevents victimization, though not foolhardiness. Some systems, however, do not put any technical controls on user killing. The Revenge of the End of the Line is one such system. The help files on EOTL say, with regard to playerkillers, that:

> This is a label given to those users who hunt down and kill other users. These notorious psychopaths usually go on killing sprees, killing lots of users in a short amount of time. User killers have no qualms and no remorse. EOTL's official policy toward user killing is one of tolerance. Wizards can't help you if someone kills you. The best thing to do is to form a lynch mob and massacre the killer to itty bitty bits . . . . User killers usually know Muds like the back of their hands and are extremely dangerous.

Despite this *laissez-faire* ruling on the part of the Wizards and Gods of EOTL, playerkilling is remarkably rare, and the reasons for this lie in the social structure developed among users. Most EOTL users live by an unstated agreement that they should live and let live. Most users are not "psychopathic" playerkillers, and will not initiate battles with those who are not known to enjoy this style of play. Those who do attack without provocation, however, are often hunted down by those who wish to preserve this unspoken rule. The ethics of this kind of justice are incorporated into the game elements. Wanted posters are common in the towns and cities which form the core of EOTL:

MoeTown's Most Wanted

Neighborhood Watch Bulletin

The following people are wanted for malicious mayhem. To collect the reward on one of these people, simply blow a police whistle while in the room with the person. If your call results in the death or capture of the criminal, a representative will pay you at the police station. Police whistles may be bought for 10 coins from the police chief:

#	Perpetrator's name	Current reward:
1	: Voltron (player killer)	39850 coins
2	: Assasin (player killer)	35870 coins
3	: Shadowstrike	25730 coins
4	: Hermes	25090 coins
5	: Shapeless (player killer)	24210 coins
6	: Whittle (player killer)	18690 coins
7	: Bowman (player killer)	14430 coins
8	: Rizzen (player killer)	13420 coins
9	: Time	12640 coins
10	: Bluey (player killer)	5820 coins

As this poster implies, technical measures have been introduced to enable justice to be meted out to user killers. Police whistles are an element of the game which has been coded into its fabric. The social contract that encourages and allows the invention and use of such whistles, is, however, not a technical measure.

Playerkillers are often summarily dealt with by their victims. Adopting the techniques of the enemy's play, irate users can form bands dedicated to hunting down and killing playerkillers. Such a solution seems to be satisfactory to all parties in such conflicts. The appropriation of the playerkiller's style of play by his or her opponents allows all concerned to feel their style of play validated. Dedicated playerkillers do not appear to resent being the victim of playerkilling – in two years of using MUDs and monitoring MUD-related newsgroups, I have found only a few cases of a playerkiller complaining of injustice at the hands of a virtual lynch-mob, though I have found many instances of playerkillers describing with zest the chase they led their pursuers and the enjoyment they experienced in making their quest as difficult as possible.[11] Some have commented on the pleasure they feel at having caused the opponents of playerkilling to join their ranks. The playerkiller's pursuers feel similarly fulfilled. In their eyes, they have not adopted playerkilling as a form of play, but have appropriated such play to serve their own preferred style. Such conflicts have a happy ending – each party feeling their imagined virtual world validated by the outcome.

Social cohesion on adventure MUDs is the result of the Darwinian rule of the survival of the fittest. On the most superficial level, only the strongest and most talented users will survive and flourish on adventure MUDs. It takes time, effort and skill not only to become powerful on such MUDs, but simply to survive on them. At a deeper level, however, it is the most socially fit – the most willing to cooperate – who survive. The social body formed on adventure MUDs is the result of a common consensus to cooperate in fighting against the (im)materiality of the power of the virtual universe operating on the virtual bodies of each individual user.

Social MUDs: cooperative appreciation

On social MUDs, users are not faced with the threats that users of adventure MUDs must contend with. Characters on MUCKs and TinyMUDs are never hungry or thirsty or tired. Instead they provide a tireless mechanism for the exercise of the users' creativity, and for interaction between users. It is this ease of use, rather than the need to protect and maintain their characters, which is the basis of social MUD users' cohesion. On adventure MUDs, social interaction often comes about through expediency, as when characters form gangs the better to slaughter some hapless dragon or infamous playerkiller. By contrast, social interaction on MUCKs and MUSHes is one of the three activities central to the game. In a survey of 583 users on LambdaMOO, users were asked to nominate the activity that took up most of their time on the MUD. The results showed that socializing took up 57.26 percent of users' time, exploring took up 14.63 percent, building 14.14 percent, competitive gaming and puzzle solving 6.99 percent, and other activities 6.98 percent. These three activities – social interaction, creating new elements of the game, and exploring others' creations – complement and reinforce each other. Social interaction serves to create a network of users who constitute an audience for each other's creativity; acts of creation provide the stage for interaction.

In designing TinyMUD, the original social MUD, Jim Aspnes deliberately sought to escape from the competitive confines of adventure-style play. He explains that:

> Most adventure-style games and earlier MUDs had some sort of scoring system which translated into rank and special privileges; I didn't want such a system not because of any strong egalitarian ideals . . . but because I wanted the game to be open-ended, and any scoring system would have the problem that eventually each user would hit the maximum rank or level of advancement and have to either abandon the game as finished or come up with new reasons to play it. This approach attracted people who liked everybody equal and drove away people who didn't like a game where you didn't score points and beat out other users. I think that this effect created a kind of natural selection which eventually led to the current egalitarian ideals.
>
> (Quoted in Rheingold 1993: 162–3)

A successful social space must repel disruptive elements as selectively as it attracts constructive ones. Broadly speaking the technical nature of social MUDs discourages participation by users more interested in competition and adventure and attracts those who prefer exploration, imaginative effort, and socialization. However, whether the 'egalitarianism' that Aspnes claims as a basic ideal fostered on social MUDs actually is so is debatable. In practice, most social MUDs have a hierarchy of users as well developed as those seen on adventure MUDs, complete with Gods, Wizards and variously privileged levels of users. However, these hierarchies are not based on competition and strength, but on interaction and contribution – at least in theory, favoritism occurring on social MUDs as it does on adventure MUDs. Users do not rise to greater degrees of privilege by killing monsters, amassing points and gaining skills, but by inserting themselves into the social and imaginative matrix and becoming indispensable.

Unlike users of adventure MUDs, who must be in regular attendance on their characters in order for those characters to survive and gain greater powers, users of social MUDs are free to enjoy unlimited access to their characters precisely because of those characters' independence of their users. Characters on social MUDs do not need to eat or sleep, and on a user's disconnection from the game the character goes into stasis. Social MUD users are not forced or required to fight for their characters' survival. They are free to play as little or as often as they like. This does, however, lead to infrequent play. On the contrary, for some users it is precisely this freedom from pressure which makes the virtual environment so compelling. Moreover, on social MUDs users are encouraged to contribute to the game in concrete ways – all users can build new places and objects in the virtual world. By making their own parts of the game – by making parts of the game their own – users are drawn into identification with their characters and into a sense of attachment to the game.

Almost without exception, users of social MUDs exercise their ability to create new aspects of the game world. Some users' contributions to the game universe may not be large, consisting of only a few experimental objects, while others' might be extensive and require the investment of much time and thought. Each MUD encourages users to create their own "home," a small section of the game universe with which the user's character is associated, and which is the portion of the game world in which the character appears to be when the user connects to the system. Most users make at least some token attempt to decorate their home with descriptions and objects. Many users extend their home beyond the confines of one virtual building, and go on to create intricate mini-worlds within the greater MUD world. In consequence of this encouragement to build, most social MUDs consist of a hodgepodge of differing environments. Some MUDs have come to insist upon adherence to a particular theme as a prerequisite of a user's promotion to one of the higher levels of game power. Before being allowed to build a greater number of objects, and before being given access to more complex commands and tools with which to build, users must demonstrate an ability to create environments that mesh with the existing game universe. In essence this system of meritocracy involves the relinquishment of one sort of power – the power to do whatever you like – in order to gain coherence and realism.

Many MUDs allow a number of intermediate levels between user and God. The God is able, at his or her own discretion, to increase a user's building quota, or even confer Wizard status upon a user. Some systems allow different levels of building tools to be available to different users, with more complex and powerful commands being available to those the Gods choose to give them to. That privileges are bestowed by the Gods of the system is a vital part of the hierarchy, and the means of its control. Only those who are approved of by the Gods and Wizards can gain greater power within the MUD system – being out of favor means being out of power. Most MUD systems indicate that gaining privileges is a matter of proving that you are worthy of them. The rule on the MUD "MicroMUSE," for instance, is that:

> The quota system for keeping the database at a reasonable size is intended to promote constructive building and efficient use of available resources. Builders engaging on large-scale projects should ask a [Wizard] to inspect their work-to-date, and can then ask for quota increases as needed.

A similar policy exists on LambdaMOO, where the Architecture Review Board, an association of users originally appointed by the Wizards and now elected by the LambdaMOO community, is empowered to decide whom the Wizards shall bestow greater building privileges upon:

> To get a larger quota, you need to talk to some member of the Architecture Review Board. They will take a look at what you've done with the objects you've built so far and decide whether or not they think it would be a net gain for the LambdaMOO community if you were to build some more things.

All users on social-style MUDs have at least a rudimentary ability to add items to the game universe, though the hierarchical system in force on some social MUDs might limit the number of items that novice users can create. But limited powers are powers nonetheless, and this relative egalitarianism is the reason which many users give for their preference for social MUDs. This attitude differs from that taken by many users of adventure MUDs, for whom the elitism of the upper echelons is the source of the desirability of entering those ranks. Compare these two articles from users of the two MUD genres:

> What I like about MUCKs is that I can just go off and build what I like. I can exercise my imagination without sucking up to any Gods or bashing any orcs. I can just do whatever I like straight away.

and:

> The whole point of LPMUds is that once you've made Wizard you know you've earned it. Your privileges are earned, every bit of them. Not like on tinymuds, where ever luser can build his little home and create his little toys. When I meet someone who has made Wiz on an LP...I *know* they've done something to earn it, and if I [make Wizard] other people *know* I've earned it.

In each case, it is access to and legitimacy of power that is the concern of the user. What differs is the perspective taken. In the one case it is the free availability of game powers, irrespective of the user's social position or level of external influence, which is attractive. In the other case it is the difficulty of gaining power and the respect due to those who have persevered which makes it so desirable. Each system serves to attract different types of users, yet each system is based on the exploitation of a common wish for power and influence.

However, many users on social MUDs do not make any attempt to win higher building privileges for themselves. On adventure MUDs, each user is by definition part of a system in which their efforts are geared toward the acquisition of greater wealth and power. On social MUDs the mechanics of the game do not demand that users spend time chasing after material – or virtual – gains. The pressure to be upwardly mobile is far less intense on social MUDs, and so fewer social than adventure MUD users make deliberate efforts of gain entry to the privileged higher echelons. Instead, users on social MUDs tend to form alternate hierarchies, functionally independent of the Wizards and Gods of the world. The economics of hierarchies on social MUDs are based not on competition for rarely bestowed powers but on competition for attention and recognition.

These alternate hierarchies depend on an audience of appreciative and creative fellow-users rather than on competition with other users. Indeed the expressions "fellow user" and "other user" neatly describe the difference between the user hierarchies most common on the two genres of MUD. Social MUD users often seem to see each other as mirrors to reflect the pride and achievement felt by each user toward his or her creations. Adventure users seem more likely to view each other as inimical, as having the potential to shatter that mirror. Alliances between adventurous users are carefully negotiated. Allied users will often devise methods of ensuring each other's loyalty by using spells or holding hostage valued items of treasure or equipment. Betrayal is not unheard of. A user's ally may turn on him or her after the dragon has been killed, and may make off with the dragon's hoard before the victim has time to react. Adventure MUD users tend to view each other with some suspicion. Each user is that mythical anthropological monster – the Other, who may expose and exploit the user, and shatter that user's dreams of power and safety.

Social MUD users are not pressed into these oppositions by a competitive system intrinsic to the MUD program. This is not to say that personal conflicts do not arise or that users do not at times deliberately seek to cause harm to other users or to the virtual world – as JennyMUSH's story demonstrates and Anna DuVal Smith (Chapter 6 in this volume) discusses, users of social MUDs can be quite anti-social. However, conflict is not an inherent facet of social MUDs as it is of adventure MUDs. Hierarchies on social MUDs tend to be socially rather than technically enforced unless episodes such as those seen on JennyMUSH catalyze the evolution of technical controls. Certain stages in the evolution of social control on MUDs seem to be common. The first stage might be characterized as the development of inter-user politics based on the differing balances of power inherent in social and adventure MUDs. The second stage might be the institutionalization of security measures and hierarchies of control over MUD system elements which may be introduced on a MUD in the wake of disruptive episodes.

On social MUDs cooperation is encouraged by the opportunity to extend the virtual world, not by the necessities of survival in it. Users become well known through socializing and through displaying the products of their imagination. Well-known adventure MUD users become so by virtue of attaining high levels of proficiency in the game universe. Well-known social MUD users become so by engaging in social activities on the MUD. Popular users commonly create interesting environments which many users visit and recommend that others visit. They spend a lot of time chatting with others, and many offer advice and aid to new users. These people form the backbone of social MUDs, and may indeed be better known to the majority of users than are the Wizards and Gods who spend most of their time engaged in the more complex work of administering the MUD program.

On some MUDs, this social hierarchy has been written into the game as an alternative track toward officially recognized status. On FurryMUCK and LambdaMOO, highly socially involved users can be rewarded with official recognition of their social importance. Deserving FurryMUCK users may be given an "Official Helper's Badge," a simple MUD object that the character carries around and which identifies him or her as someone to whom users can turn to for help on everything from MUD etiquette to the complexities of building. Special commands have been written into the FurryMUCK program that allow users to view a list of all those who have won such a badge, get information on their areas of expertise, check to see which helpers are currently logged into the MUD, and leave messages for them. Every user who spends some few minutes reading part of the extensive help files available on FurryMUCK will be likely to find these commands and so become aware of who the Official Helpers are. These people are known even by those who have never met them. They are also more likely to become personally well known to a great number of users as they are paged with questions and pleas for help – one character, known as BoingDragon, has achieved almost legendary status through her tireless efforts to help and advise novice users.

Users of social MUDs who enter into the social and creative acts of the MUD will be likely to become popular and well known on that MUD. To achieve that status, considerable time must be invested in learning how to use the particular MUD program on which the game universe is based, and in getting to know fellow users. Anyone who does so invest their time will in consequence be likely to continue to become more involved with MUD. Admiration and respect are addictive. The power of popularity is as great as the power to manipulate worlds. People who feel liked and valued in a particular environment will tend to frequent that environment – that holds true as well for MUDs as for any field of human activity. Involvement leads to popularity, and popularity leads to involvement – users who have established themselves as clever builders and resourceful advisers will find that the popularity they have gained in doing so will keep them coming back to the MUD.

Social cohesion and control

At the heart of many human activities lies the wish for influence and power, for popularity and social acceptance. Power can come in many forms, and different forms are attractive to different people. A desire for sheer physical control can lead people into body building and military corps. A desire for respect and fame can inspire actors and politicians. The forms of power that can be exercised on MUDs vary on each system, and most widely between the two genres of MUD. Adventure MUDs stress user advancement through the attainment of levels or skills through interaction with the game elements and competition with other users. Social MUDs stress user interaction and creativity. The former lends itself to the expression of power through a character's prowess, and the user's resultant powers to affect the game world. Ultimately, users on adventure MUDs strive to help their character achieve a high enough level of expertise to merit their promotion to a position of power over the MUD world. Social MUDs lend themselves more easily to the expression of power through exhibitions of creativity, charm, and knowledge. Almost all social MUD characters have the same powers over the game world – what differentiates them are the ways in which users act through their character to transform the world and to engage other users in supportive relationships.

Each of these different paths to power involve the user in the game. MUDs inspire in users a degree of commitment and emotional investment that makes social continuity and stability possible. Both social and adventure MUDs demand an initial degree of dedication on which to form a basis for status. Adventure MUD users must play the game a minimum of several hours each week just to stay in the game. To advance within the game users must play more often than that. To achieve high levels of expertise they must play very often indeed, and once that level has been achieved users must play – or work – to maintain their position. If a user aspires to Wizardship it is necessary to demonstrate the skills and dedication for which that promotion is deserved. At each level of play on adventure MUDs, time and involvement are demanded, with the level of demand increasing as does the level of investment and reward. As users advance they become more practiced at manipulating existing elements of the MUD, and are rewarded with the power to control those elements and create new ones. Users of social MUDs may also follow a track toward greater, and eventually total, power to manipulate the virtual universe. For most users of social MUDs, however, power over the game universe is not an end in itself. That power is usually freely available, and provides novice users with an immediate reward for playing the game and a reason to continue playing. This free expression of creativity becomes the means to power through social influence. Recognition and popularity among the users of the MUD are won through the creation of novel additions to the virtual world, and through friendly and helpful interaction with other users. Once gained, this renown keeps a user involved.

On social MUDs cooperation is based on a hierarchy of popularity; on adventure MUDs on a hierarchy of strength. Each form of MUD attracts its own set of users, and evokes in those users a willingness to dedicate themselves to the game. While the ultimate reward on all MUDs is the same – to become a God – the paths taken to reach it differ between the two main styles of MUD system. Users of each of these two genres of game must contend with widely different paths to deification. Each path contains its own cohesive elements which center on control and the manipulation of game elements. Power on MUD systems depends on the individual's ability to manipulate the components of the system; privileges consist of increased access to such world-manipulating tools. The degree to which this power is successful is dependent upon users' belief in the value of the MUD world, and the degree to which they have invested meaning and emotion in the objects within it. That the objects and characters stored in the computer files are ascribed value leads to the special treatment of those who can alter those files. Gods' and Wizards' powers depend upon their success in building a system which users view as a virtual world, a system to be interacted with in such a way as to invest emotion in the continued existence of the world and its components. Systems which are so viewed will be more likely to attract users willing to apply their talents and invest their effort in building new areas and objects. The richness of each virtual world leads to its being further enriched.

Within these hierarchical systems of power, social spaces form. Users of MUD systems love and hate in their virtual environments as strongly as they do in face-to-face environments. The manifestation of emotion is made possible by tools that give virtual realism to the imaginings of users. The exercise of imagination is necessary for the creation of a social context within which to act. By utilizing the dramaturgical tools provided by MUD programs, users create the basis for shared social understandings. It is the actualization of imagined reality that makes this possible – nevertheless, it is clear that users' imaginings cease to be acceptable when they threaten the integrity of these shared understandings. Such interaction and such understandings are vulnerable to disruption. This can be traumatic for users: despite the appearance of safety given by pseudonymity and distance, you can get hurt in cyberspace. For imagination to be permitted actualization by other users, it must allow others to maintain the integrity of their imaginings. Violation of that integrity is perhaps the greatest crime on a MUD. What happened on JennyMUSH offers a graphic example of how anonymity and disinhibition may allow users to crush that sense of integrity, and how much anger can be caused by such attempts. The measures taken by the users, Wizards, and Gods of JennyMUSH, both immediately and in the long term, show how order is maintained on MUDs through social and technical conventions. The dramatic expulsion and punishment of errant users serves to reinforce the social structure and reassure victimized users of the value of their commitment. MUD communities rely both on measures of control and on social encouragement of commitment and accountability in users' creativity.

The socio-emotional plots played out on MUDs are only ad-libbed in the immediate instance. Although these systems may seem anarchic and uncontrollable at first glance, they are in fact highly socially structured. Users may play their cultural game according to personal whim, but they play it out on systems that are as subject to the enactment of power and privilege as are more familiar face-to-face social systems. The "theory of technological politics," says Langdon Winner (1986: 22), "suggests that we pay attention to the characteristics of technical objects and the meaning of those characteristics." The meanings with which MUD users literally inscribe the technical objects on a MUD allow the formation of coherent and regulated social groups. The methods used to create physical contexts for sociality on MUD systems are also used to create structures of control which form a context for social hierarchies.

Notes

1   The operating system under which DUNGEN ran allowed filenames to be only a maximum of six letters long, thus the particular spelling of the name.

2   Some would insist that MUD should now stand for "Multi-Undergraduate Destroyer," in recognition of the number of students who may have failed their classes due to too much time spent MUDing.

3   This list of user names was generated by asking a group of people who happened to be logged on to LambdaMOO on 5 November 1993 to volunteer some names which they had used on a MUD.

4   "Adventure-style MUDs" are MUD systems based on the programs known as LP-MUD and DikuMUD.

5   E.g. TinyMUD, MUSH, MUCK and MOO. The names of software variants in the MUD family reflect their evolution from the original "MUD" program: The LP in LP-MUD are the initials of the author of this software; "Diku" is the name of the university at which DikuMUD was developed; MUSH and MUCK are puns on MUD (although the acronym Multi-User Shared Hallucination has been applied after-the-fact to the former); MOO stands for MUD, Object-Oriented. Variants differ in hardware requirements and user commands.

6   More information about JennyMUSH, and in particular a discussion of the consequences to the MUD of participating in my study, can be found in Reid (1996).

7   The shout command, while not unique to JennyMUSH, is not available on all MUDs. On those which do offer it, usage is often restricted to privileged users such as Wizards and Gods.

8 An account of a similar episode on LambdaMOO can be found in a fascinating article by Julian Dibbell (1993).

9 Although I have referred to this user as "he," that being the sex of the character "Daddy," there is no technical reason why the person behind the character could not have been female.

10 The phrase "regen waiters" refers to the time which many players must spend healing (regenerating) before heading back for another bout with a computer-generated monster.

11 Most complaints from playerkillers concern accusations of unfair behavior on the part of Gods or Wizards – that, for instance, they have been unjustly punished for breaking the rules relating to playerkilling.

References

Curtis, Pavel. 1992. "Mudding: Social Phenomena in Text-Based Virtual Realities." *Intertek* 3.3 (winter): 26–34.

Dibbell, Julian. 1993. "A Rape in Cyberspace or How an Evil Clown, a Haitian Trickster Spirit, Two Wizards, and a Cast of Dozens Turned a Database Into a Society." *Village Voice* 38 (51). Online: gopher: well.sf.ca.us Directory: Community.

Hiltz, Starr Roxanne and Murray Turoff. 1978. *The Network Nation: Human Communication via Computer*. Reading, MA: Addison-Wesley.

Foucault, Michel. 1980. *Power/Knowledge: Selected Interviews and Other Writing 1972-1977*, edited by Colin Gordon, trans. Colin Gordon, Leo Marshall, John Mepham, Kate Soper. Brighton, Sussex: Harvester.

Foucault, Michel. 1986. *Discipline and Punish: The Birth of the Prison*, trans. Alan Sheridan. Harmondsworth: Penguin.

Kiesler, Sara and Lee Sproull. 1986. "Reducing Social Context Cues: Electronic Mail in Organizational Communication." *Management Science* 32(11): 1492–1512.

Kiesler, Sara, Jane Siegel and Timothy W. McGuire. 1984. "Social Psychological Aspects of Computer-mediated Communication." *American Psychologist* 39(10): 1123–34.

Reid, Elizabeth. 1996. "Informed Consent in the Study of On-Line Communities: A Reflection on the Effects of Computer-Mediated Social Research." *The Information Society* 12(2): 169–74.

Rheingold, Howard. 1993. *The Virtual Community: Homesteading on the Electronic Frontier*. Reading, MA: Addison-Wesley.

Stone, Allucquère Rosanne. 1991. "Will the Real Body Please Stand Up? Boundary Stories about Virtual Cultures," in *Cyberspace: First Steps*, edited by Michael Benedikt. Cambridge, MA: MIT Press.

Winner, Langdon. 1986. "Do Artifacts Have Politics?" In *The Whale and the Reactor*. Chicago: University of Chicago Press.

Chapter 6

Problems of conflict management in virtual communities[1]

Anna DuVal Smith

In September 1993, tiring of the harassment my female identity received on IRC,[2] I read of MicroMUSE, a MU* reputed to be "nonviolent, noncompetitive and collaborative" because of its mission as an educational tool for children (Leslie 1993: 34; Kelly and Rheingold 1993).[3] Fascinated by the possibilities of self-representation and drawn to a more decorous environment than IRC, I logged in as a guest and shortly thereafter became a registered citizen of MicroMUSE. Within weeks I observed social conflict in this allegedly tranquil community to rival any I had seen or studied in real life as a social scientist and practitioner of mainstream western dispute resolution techniques. For the next two years, first as an ordinary citizen, then as a non-voting member of the governing body, more recently as a voting and technically powered director (in MUD parlance, a Wizard), I observed and participated in the community's interpersonal conflicts, enacting roles of audience, aggressor, target, investigator, reporter, confidante, judge, and conciliator. In this chapter, I report what I learned during that period about the problems, strategies, and techniques of maintaining social order in cyber communities. In particular, I assess the application of well-established real-life tools of conflict management to virtual disputes.

Theoretical background

Various social scientific perspectives have different views of the incidence of conflict and its value in social systems, and accordingly offer different approaches to conflict management. Unitary models (also referred to as "monolithic" and "integration" models) seek and often find system-wide consensus, wherein values, meanings, goals, interests, rules and the like are shared and internally consistent. Individuals have clear under-standings of what things mean and how to behave. They pursue the aims of the system because in so doing they address their own interests (McGregor 1957). This integrated world is one of "harmony and homogeneity" (Martin 1992). Many researchers and managers with this perspective see conflict as rare, disruptive to social integration, and symptomatic of system pathology. It is often attributed to deviants and provocateurs who can be controlled or eliminated by appropriate system design and action (Morgan 1986: 188). The aim of conflict management under this perspective is resolution and prevention for greater system unity (Deutsch 1973; Filley 1975).

This negative view of conflict is shared by others who value harmony – or perhaps power and control – but who view differences and conflict as widespread, natural properties of social systems. Under this frame of reference, conflict management has the same aim as it does for integrationists – minimization and elimination. However, because their conflict management tools act in opposition to individuals and groups, they dominate, suppress or coerce compliance rather than achieve consensus. As many critics of bureaucratic theories of organizations have noted, such managers paradoxically obtain what they hope to avoid by this course of action: less control as people comply in inappropriate ways or find ways to resist (Dalton, 1971 provides an overview of this literature).

The radical model sees differentiation and conflict, too, but takes a positive view of conflict. Trade union leaders, for instance, induce conflict with management as a way to strengthen their position vis-à-vis management (Tannenbaum 1965). Such conflict develops consensus within the subsystem while increasing separation from the other, thus polarizing the system and creating disunity. Ultimately, of course, radicals see conflict as a means to a structural change through a process of dialectics. Thus, the opposing parties, one struggling to maintain the existing order, the other to reverse it, destabilize the system and co-produce change (see Morgan, 1986, especially chapters 8 and 9, for a more complete discussion of this perspective). Whether such conflict is thought good or bad depends on one's moral opinion of the system being destroyed. Certainly conflict that undermines an existing system is dysfunctional to that system, but it is good if the system is evil.

Not all views depend on moral judgment to find positive aspects of conflict. Georg Simmel (1955) saw human relations characterized by ambiguity rather than clarity. The way this plays out in terms of conflict is that social systems are seen always to involve both harmony and dissonance. To him, a completely peaceful social system simply cannot exist because of its incapacity for change and development. Harmony and consensus are not, therefore *per se* good nor is conflict *per se* bad. Rather, both are positive, being necessary for system survival. For example, conflict structures a system, strengthening existing bonds (as within the union in the previous example) and forming new ones as participants become polarized into blocs that persist beyond the conflict. Small conflicts also allow parties to ventilate, reducing the likelihood of larger, destructive conflict. In these and other ways, conflict promotes system endurance and viability (Coser 1956). By this line of reasoning, conflict management aimed at eliminating discord is not only an impossible task, but off the mark. Indeed, even some writers outside the radical school argue for and describe techniques of conflict stimulation (Peck 1987; Robbins 1974). Brown (1983), for instance, explicitly recognizes and integrates both functional and dysfunctional conflict outcomes into a unified model, hypothesizing a curvilinear relationship between conflict intensity and its outcomes. Too little conflict is said to produce a false sense of well-being and low levels of energy, creativity and adaptation. Too much conflict produces antagonism, restricted information flow, low-quality decisions and diversion of effort away from other tasks to deal with the struggle. Either condition may cause system failure. Positive outcomes of conflict and, therefore, system effectiveness are realized in the middle range of conflict intensity, where there is neither too little nor too much. Effective conflict management, then, becomes a matter of either reduction or stimulation as called for by the situation (Brown 1995).

Another property of social systems that is thought to affect their effectiveness is diversity of population in terms of perspectives, skills, knowledge, abilities and the like. One way unitary systems achieve integration is through homosocial reproduction, selecting, socializing and promoting to positions of power similar others. While social similarity produces what Durkheim calls "mechanical solidarity," the stability and inertia can prove fatal when the environment changes and the system lacks the knowledge, skills and abilities necessary to adapt. Pluralistic systems, on the other hand, because they contain a broad variety of perspectives, skills, etc., are more likely to contain the requisite qualities for the new demands of the environment. If granted expression, differences can also generate a multitude of ideas for improving system performance, and greater capacity for their evaluation. Potential benefits of diversity, then, are high quality decision-making, creativity and innovation, and adaptation (Peck 1987; Cox 1991).

However, diversity of values, perspectives, beliefs, interests, knowledge and expectations is also a source of conflict (Pfeffer 1981; Macduff 1994). Pluralistic systems, which are more complex, more elaborately structured than those of the radical model which focuses on dichotomy and opposition, have a vulnerability of their own. As loose networks of people with multiple goals and diverse interests, whose alliances shift over time and across issues, achieving consensus on anything may become insurmountable. A system of extreme heterogeneity, while it may contain the raw material for creativity, flexibility and adaptability, is vulnerable to anarchy and anomie. Social systems operating in environments demanding creativity and innovation thus face an apparent dilemma. If they opt for tranquility either by denying expression of their diversity or by choosing homogeneity, they deny themselves precisely what they need to survive. But if they admit diversity and allow it expression, they may experience too much conflict to be productive and thrive.

And so we come to the Hobbesian question of order: how is society possible?

The unitarist answer is avoidance of conflict through homogeneity. As argued above, this contains the seed of system failure. So, too, does the radical answer, coercion, which is conflict-seeking in its effects if not intent. The pluralist response is the Aristotelian ideal of politics wherein diversity is neither silenced nor avoided, but given expression through constructive conflict management. In the political model of social systems, order is created from diversity by bargaining and consultation that reconciles divergent interests and creates shared understandings (Morgan 1986; Pfeffer 1981). In sum, a social system may be more or less effective depending on its degree of diversity and its strategy for and skill at managing conflict (Cox 1991).

MU*s are social systems which can evolve into symbolic communities, consisting of persistently interacting members with common interests who are linked primarily by symbolic (in this case, electronic) exchange rather than by face-to-face encounters in physical space (Gergen 1991: 214; see also Clodius 1997; Scime 1994). They are also organizations when they are designed to achieve limited objectives through the coordinated activities of their members (Presthus 1978: 1). The manifest goals of these organizations are those designated officially, often set forth in a mission statement. They also have informal or latent goals, which are the aspirations of their members. As with any organization, the two sets of MU* goals are likely to be at least in some degree inconsistent with each other. This research is a case study of an open MU* with limited, formally-determined and stated goals. Evidence is found of significant latent goal incompatibility with the manifest. I argue that such virtual organizations have the same kinds of problems and opportunities brought by diversity that real organizations do. Indeed, to the degree that they are open and attractive to the Internet population, they will be particularly prone to conflict and therefore in special need of effective conflict management techniques. This research also examines the conflict management techniques employed by the organization's members and introduced by the researcher. It concludes that unique features of the virtual world contribute to the problems of conflict management. Unless these problems are addressed by adapting existing techniques or developing new ones, there are limits to the degree of openness and diversity that virtual communities and organizations can tolerate. This, in turn, will affect their ability to adapt to their changing environment.

The setting and the data

MicroMUSE was founded in 1990 under another name as a recreational/gaming MU*, but by 1991 its manifest goals had become educational and a second generation of administrators had adopted its first formal charter (MicroMUSE Charter 1991).[4] The setting is that of Cyberion City and its environs on a cylindrical space station orbiting the Earth. In 1993, guests arrived in the Main Transporter Receiving Station, having been beamed up from Earth. The total population of registered characters was over 2,000 in 1993 (Rheingold 1993: 162), but grew rapidly to over 3,000 by April 1994 (MacDuff, email to Advisory Board, April 18, 1994) after the community received favorable publicity in a number of books and magazine articles. It is impossible to know how many people these characters represented, as some would have been abandoned from lack of interest or loss of Net access and some people would have had more than one character or shared with friends or family. The character population shrank to 1,000 by December 1995 (online statistics) as a result of events which are described below, but since multiple and shared characters are now prohibited, and long inactive ones automatically recycled, this is probably a more reliable estimate of the human population now than 1993's estimate was for that time. The distribution of social characteristics is also not known, but it might be assumed that the largest group of users was male and of college age, since conventional wisdom has it that this is the largest single category of Internet users (Rheingold 1993: 150). The concentration of young men may be declining, along with the population, because of recent concerted efforts to refocus the community on its manifest function and widening access to the Net. Few informal and no formal inquiries are made of a player's race, but nationality and geographic location are frequent topics of conversation. Most players clearly are from the US and Canada, although it is evident that Cyberion City is cosmopolitan, drawing players from western Europe, Asia, Australia, and Latin America. Among the countries known to be represented are Australia, India, Singapore, Taiwan, Thailand, People's Republic of China, Korea, Japan, Mexico, Brazil, Colombia, Czechoslovakia, Finland, England, Ireland, Scotland, Italy, Austria, Poland, and the Netherlands. Two features of MicroMUSE that distinguish it from most other MU*s open to the Internet are its educational focus and deliberate attempt to serve users under the age of 18. As discussed below, these features in interaction with its open-door policy have affected the character of its members' relationships as well as the composition of its population.

The formal organizational structure was changed during the period of this study, but underlying role and class distinctions were constant. The two basic class distinctions are users (or players) and administrators, the latter of whom perform the tasks necessary to keep the community functioning in a technical sense and following the direction outlined in the mission statement. Player characters are of two types. Temporary characters (called "visitors," formerly "guests") lack the ability to create objects or rooms and to change their name. No password is necessary to use one of these and they are recycled when the user disconnects. Permanent characters (called "students" and "members," formerly "citizens") are registered and require passwords to access. They have the technical ability to create structures and processes, and to communicate and move about the community. The administrative structure is too large and complex for description here, but knowledge of the finer distinctions is not necessary to understand the phenomena under investigation.[5] Here, "director" will be used to refer to the class with the greatest authority and technical power, "staff" to other ranks, and "administrators" to all powered ranks. The decision-making bodies will be identified and described as needed.

The sources of data for this investigation are several. As a participant-observer, I spent thousands of hours logged into MicroMUSE and its sister communities, immersing myself in the life of the MUSE for a period of two years. During this time I had thousands of conversations online with guests, registered players, and administrators. In addition to my own notes and transcripts, other users supplied transcripts. Official documents were obtained online and by ftp (file transfer protocol), gopher and the web. I also subscribed to the open-subscription email lists and, later, as a member of administration, I was a party to the closed-subscription lists by which much of the governance of the community is conducted. Finally, there were many email and telephone contacts, and a number of face-to-face encounters, including organized weekend gatherings and impromptu or planned visits by or to fellow MUSERs.

My entry and subsequent involvement in the community as a participant-observer is broadly described in the introduction. As a player, I was initially cautious about revealing my true identity, but became open about it and later my purpose after I made the decision to use the community as a subject of research. I then sought and obtained the consent of the Advisory Board to reveal the identity of their MUSE and make use of the data, but, with a few exceptions, I have used pseudonyms or titles to conceal individual identities.

The problem background

Although many of their projects are about science, MicroMUSE players are free to pursue any topic of interest within the constraints of the community's culture and technical resources. The process of learning, and the learners and their relationships with each other, are more important than any particular subject. Learning is supposed to be fun, self-directed, collaborative, peer- and project-based (Kort 1995). People of all ages and backgrounds are welcomed, but there is a deliberate effort to attract and involve children in kindergarten through grade 12. This effort appears to be successful as my impression is that a large number of the currently registered players are, in fact, minor children, parents, and teachers. In support of its mission, MicroMUSE attempts to provide an environment its administrators deem suitable for children and supportive of learning. Indeed, its Charter states its theme to be "based on an optimistic vision of the 24th century" (MicroMUSE Charter 1994). This vision is optimistic both technically (matter transmission is easily accomplished across the distances of the orbiting space station) and socially (life is supposed to be peaceful with most time spent on scholarly pursuits of discovery, creation, and discussion). Violence, obscenity, racism, pornography, harassment, theft, invasion of privacy, and other kinds of conduct are prohibited (MicroMUSE Bylaws 1994) but not, as the cases below demonstrate, absent.

Player–administration disputes

Nearly the first thing I learned on line about MU*s was the power of the directors. Peter Pan, the 27-year-old unemployed American who introduced me to MicroMUSE, was regularly punished for making frivolous announcements, using foul language in public, and harassing administrators. For this he would be fined, lose the privilege of making announcements to the community, enslaved (a condition that substantially impairs a player's ability to communicate and move), or arrested (forcibly placed in a room with no exits). On occasion, he would be summoned (transported against his will) to a director's office and lectured. On other occasions, he would be punished without being told by whom or why, although he frequently surmised the reason. However, the power of a director is not absolute, as Swagger's case illustrates.

Swagger was a teenager who built an Orgasm Room filled with sex objects to which he apparently invited female players for online sex. When a director discovered this, Swagger was summarily nuked (the MicroMUSE term for complete removal of the character and all its virtual property from the database). Swagger returned as a guest and complained about his treatment on the public channel (a medium of mass communication similar to a Citizens' Band radio channel). He was successful in raising the support of various citizens and staff who believed that he should not have been nuked without an opportunity to defend himself. Two staff cooperated in the re-creation of Swagger's character. At this point, the director whose action had been countermanded objected. A vote of the Executive Board (a body composed of all directors) affirmed the director's original action. Swagger was nuked again, and informed that he had been exiled for a period of two months, after which he could petition for readmission.

Before Swagger's exile by the Executive Board, there was a town meeting presided over by yet a third staff member. About forty people, including Swagger, attended and discussed restrictions on citizen speech, governance, and the justice system. Sentiment was expressed for the election (rather than the appointment) of administrators and/or other means of providing citizen input to the governing body. The attendees also complained about the lack of a meaningful system of justice, alleging power abuse by directors, no opportunity for the accused to defend himself, no trial by jury, and no code of laws (the latter was untrue as everyone was emailed a list of rules upon registration). Shortly thereafter, an unmoderated, open-subscription mailing list was initiated upon which citizens aired their complaints about MicroMUSE and posted various items of general interest, such as the transcript of the town meeting.

One month later, a new Charter was adopted, creating a complex system of governance which included a Citizens Council with a nonvoting representative on the new primary governing body (Advisory Board), and a role for appointed voting advisors who might or might not have technical powers. The 1993 Charter also elaborated and codified the procedure for dealing with rule violations, but did not contain all elements of due process systems sought by the dissidents, such as peer jury trials. It did, however, promulgate the limited right of appeal first granted to Swagger. At about the same time, some of the more disaffected citizens mounted their own MUSE, dubbing it "AntiMicro-Muse," upon which virulent attitudes toward MicroMUSE administrators were expressed. This MUSE was enormously successful for a brief spell, but it was operated in violation of the policy of its system administrator's university, so it was short lived.

The Citizens Council was a complete failure in the opinion of both administrators and players. The election was essentially a popularity contest, and one of the community's most notoriously destructive hackers claims to have stuffed the ballot box to assure a win for his girlfriend. The first Council worked on a few projects, without success, and eventually became completely inactive.

Swagger's petition for readmission was one of the early cases I took on. He was readmitted after an investigation concluded there was no evidence to rebut his assertion, supported by witness statements, that he had reformed. Although he was never again accused of sexual misconduct on MicroMUSE, he did break several other rules, most notably exploiting bugs in the code and using others' characters without their consent. This led to his permanent banishment from MicroMUSE, but he continued to connect illicitly, logging on as characters whose passwords he cracked, and again exploiting code bugs.

Disputes among players

Players naturally have problems with each other as well as with administrators and MUSE policy. Harassment, sexual harassment, assault, spying, theft, and spamming (filling a player's screen with unwanted, meaningless text) are typical complaints. The following cases illustrate the usual course of events in inter-player disputes.

THE TROJAN HORSE. One evening, a stranger named Sinon entered Hecuba's office. After some casual conversation, he gave her a gift. Touched, she accepted it and looked it over. It came with instructions which she followed, whereupon she was spammed by silly material for some minutes. Hecuba thanked the stranger in her return spam, thinking this was a bit of harmless fun. Sinon laughed, saying he could win any spam contest with her because he had a high-speed modem and the edge in technical skill. He then proceeded to demonstrate that he could disable her computer for such a long time that she would be better off disconnecting than waiting for her screen to stop scrolling. When she got control of her computer again, Hecuba spammed him back. Sinon's next present was subjected to a closer scrutiny. Hecuba examined it every way she could and saw only the shadow of an object inside the gift. Curious, she followed instructions again, thinking that at worst, she would have to disconnect to avoid more spam, but this time the game turned into war as this object destroyed nearly everything she owned and then booted her from the MUSE. She reconnected only to see the extent of the destruction, then logged off for the night to lick her wounds. Defeated and depressed, she returned the next day and began reconstruction, but was so ashamed at having been duped that she told no one about it for a long time, not even the director who noticed the shambles of her possessions and asked her about what had happened. Eventually the director pieced the story together and nuked Sinon's character. However, Sinon returned again and again, as each different character he used was discovered to be controlled by him and nuked.

THE HIRED GUN. A similar incident took place on a sister MUSE, one less controlled by its administration than MicroMUSE is. This time the aggressor was an anonymous guest using the public channel to harass other players with obscenities. Outraged players solicited the aid of the aforesaid Peter Pan, who was an accomplished spammer. He executed a single command that flooded the offender's screen for some time, eventually causing him to disconnect. The offender returned in an angry mood, but his retribution was less damaging than Hecuba's Trojan horse as he only dropped a final, huge spam bomb on the channel before leaving for good.

THE SCORPIO MUTINY. A final example of inter-player conflict occurred within a previously collaborative task-oriented team. By way of background, one of the larger and more interesting educational projects on MicroMUSE is Space. Participating players are able to construct ships of various types and fly them in real time and three dimensions to celestial destinations, which may also be of their own creation. Individual space ships are often large, complex structures crewed by multiple players. To make it easy for players to cooperate in the construction and maintenance of such large-scale projects, characters may be created as holding or operating corporations, to which approved players have access. One such group character was Scorpio, which was created to hold the starship ICS Scorpio. Among those using it were two men, Ajax and Achilles, and Achilles' robot. Achilles and Ajax evidently constructed and operated the ship successfully together for some time. If there were any internal power struggles on Scorpio, they did not come to the attention of MUSE administration.

In the fall of 1993, computer memory and disk space limitations caused MicroMUSE administration to decide that the entire space project should be moved to a separate MUSE (MicroMUSE Charter 1994). When this was announced, Ajax lost interest in MicroMUSE entirely and argued for the destruction of the ship. Achilles was opposed, hoping to persuade administration to keep the ship on MicroMUSE as a museum. Announcing he would not be back, Ajax left the MUSE. He returned from time to time, but kept away from the ship. During this period, Achilles mothballed the ICS Scorpio, which was still his home, but eventually decided to take one last voyage. Worried about the risk Ajax posed to the ship and needing a captain, Achilles promoted his former first officer, Nestor, to captain, and demoted Ajax. He also had an administrator remove Ajax from the list of characters who could modify the ship. When Ajax returned to the MUSE, he took a look at the ship's roster and discovered the changes about which he had not been consulted. Believing his ship had been pirated, he gained access to it through Achilles' robot (whose password Achilles had forgotten he had shared with Ajax). Within about an hour, Ajax destroyed the entire ship, with its 120 rooms and objects, and enslaved its robots. He was open about what he was doing, and asked to be nuked when he was finished. Coincidentally and tragically, Achilles was repeatedly trying to connect to the MUSE during this period and failing. When he finally logged in and saw the destruction, he asked a director to rescue his ship from a backup database, but the director refused, saying Achilles should have been more careful about sharing passwords. In the aftermath, all players who lost property in the attack – Achilles, Ajax, Nestor, and others – levied charges against administration for both suspected actions (complicity in certain facets of the affair allegedly motivated by a desire to get rid of these players) and known inactions (failure to stop the destruction once it became known). Ajax was nuked as he requested and the password of the robot changed. A backup copy of the database was eventually made available to Achilles and Nestor, and they began reconstruction, but never regained their former interest in the project or MicroMUSE.

Diversity and social control

These cases do not depict usual player conduct, nor is any one typical of the conflicts observed in the period studied. Rather, they collectively include many elements of the broad range of disputes and have therefore been selected as illustrative of sources of MicroMUSE conflict and the ways in which they were being handled.

Diversity as a source of conflict

Much of the conflict observed arose because of the different meanings of MicroMUSE to its players and administrators, and their diverse values, goals, interests and norms. The following sketches in broad terms some of those different realities.

Beginning with administration, which is responsible for directing the organization towards the fulfillment of its mission, its vision of MicroMUSE was most graphically expressed early in 1994 as the Advisory Board was trying to come to grips with the amount of conflict the community had been experiencing. One director likened MicroMUSE to a science museum which is open to the public but intended for specific educational purposes (D. Albert, email to Inner Circle, February 19, 1994). Under this model, all behavior in the museum is judged in relation to the museum's needs, which are prior to all others. If teachers cannot bring their classes to the museum because a room is openly designated for copulation and teenagers are announcing obscenities on the public address system, or scholars cannot study because of excessive noise, or the building is being vandalized by hoodlums and exhibits destroyed by bombs, then the museum will fail. To survive, virtual communities must protect their primary resources. Being no exception, MicroMUSE administration protects against threats to its physical plant (machine and code) and citizens (Internet gateway and players). Because of its manifest organizational objectives, it must also protect its capital supply (grants and donations), its labor supply (educators and technicians), and its markets (students and their parents). These efforts will come up against players with different perspectives and agendas (often in direct conflict with the museum's) who will resist or try to circumvent them in their own effort to maintain their own autonomy and achieve their own goals. Hence, there is player–administrator conflict as illustrated by the Swagger rebellion.

Turning now to the players, many – particularly those whose expectations of MU*s are shaped by social MU*s such as FurryMUCK or adventure MU*s like BatMUD and Revenge of the End of the Line – have primarily social or recreational interests. Although they do some building and exploring through which they learn some coding and matters of substance, this is not what they really log on for. They come to visit with friends, meet lovers, play games, make toys, have parties, experiment with identity and behavior, act out different feelings, feel powerful, even to heal.[6] To them, MicroMUSE is a play-ground, singles bar, bedroom, coffee house, shopping mall, theater, front porch, therapist's or social worker's office and more. Some are astonished to find that what is tolerated in those real life places is not permitted on MicroMUSE. Swagger, for instance, claimed – possibly disingenuously – that he was unaware of the restrictions. Others, holding that MicroMUSE is not real, being only text from which one can disengage at the flip of a switch, or who subscribe to the hacker ethic,[7] believe that anything technically possible can and should be allowed. To them, MicroMUSE is a game with the rules subject to renegotiation or to being broken for one's own advantage of the sake of discovery. The Trojan horse case and Scorpio's internecine war were fed by this view.

Another vision of MicroMUSE is that of a city-state, a metaphor ironically supported by administration in its decision to represent MicroMUSE as a city and to label its players "citizens." At least some of those expressing this view see the existing form of government as totalitarianism (often calling administration "fascists" or "communists") and hold democracy to be the ideal. A few, who are also extremely vocal, said democracy is an impossible dream because of administration's lust for power. This view reflects the structural pattern of MicroMUSE: division into two parts, with the two halves performing specialized (in this case, reciprocal) functions. Such societies, known as "moities" to anthropologists, work best when power is distributed equally. If one faction is more powerful than the other, there is a tendency to dominate the weaker faction, which then struggles to become stronger so as to avoid domination (Thomas 1984). In MicroMUSE, as in other cybercommunities, ultimate power rests with administration as the party controlling the essential resources of the community – the code and the machine upon which the program runs. Dissident players complaining of fascism were acting in recognition of this asymmetry and the resultant imposition of the stronger faction's vision of the community on the weaker. The rebellion that was sparked by the Swagger case can be understood as a struggle for the right to shape the culture of the entire community (Morgan 1986: 127), and of the player visions described here, this is the one probably responsible for most of the player–administration disputes during the pre- and immediately post-reform period of this study. The large influx of new players attracted by recent publicity and a database swollen to machine capacity put MicroMUSE at a transition point in the fall of 1993. While Swagger's treatment was a cohesive influence in one respect, providing a common cause for diverse elements of the community and mobilizing them to action, the intense political activity during that fall and winter was less about Swagger than the future direction of the community.

The three major interests of those who see MicroMUSE as a city-state were touched on in the town meeting following Swagger's resurrection: freedom of expression and other civil rights, player voice in MUSE government, and justice both through the equitable distribution of resources and due process in administering discipline. Of the three rights Karnow (1994) sees as important for protection of electronic personalities, players with a city-state view most value two – freedom from discrimination and freedom of speech. In fact, most of the administration–player disagreements are, like Peter Pan's, over the content of public communication or public representation of self such as character and object descriptions. They are also the ones most likely to engender open community support for the accused. When a popular player called "Debs" was arrested for a second violation of public obscenity and later exiled when she failed either to agree with administration that her language was inappropriate or to promise to refrain from using such language in public again, the case was discussed for weeks both on and off MUSE. Although much of the discussion was both ill-informed and more accurately characterized as "flaming"[8] than discourse, there were also serious attempts to understand the issues. For example, I received a request to moderate a debate on civil rights in virtual communities and a law student sent me a brief on the First Amendment and cyberspace for discussion by administration. Her argument did not persuade the Advisory Board to end its censorship.

There are, of course, many players who use MicroMUSE for its intended purpose of whose enjoyment of social activities is neither disruptive of nor disrupted by the organization's pursuit of its manifest goals. These players, in fact, probably appreciate and may even rely on administration's attempts to maintain order. For them, Karnow's (1994) first right of electronic personalities – the right to privacy – is primary. When teachers and parents see the safe environment they want for their students and children compromised, and when builders or conversationalists have their activities disrupted by other players' free expression, they often become complainants in MUSE disputes. Debs was reported on both occasions by other players, one of whom was trying to demonstrate the MUSE to educators at a time Debs exercised her right of free speech to utter obscenities on the public channel.

That administration shares these players' high esteem for privacy is shown not only in its rules (entering private space without permission is forbidden, for example), but in a relative absence of monitoring player behavior. Complete permanent logs of commands executed are not made, and only directors have access to the brief transient logs that are made for debugging after a crash. Even then, reading these logs without good reason is considered outside the bounds of propriety, although doing so would make it easier to identify and prosecute miscreants.[9] On the other hand, while administration does not go looking for violations of the rules, either by reading logs or through other forms of surveillance, it does try to prevent them and correct those that come to its attention before players complain. Swagger was caught because an administrator saw the name of his room in the publicly-viewable directory, not because a citizen complained or administration was reading command logs and saw what he was doing in the room. Thus, in terms of the rights discussed by Karnow (1994) as being fundamental to managing the private/public border in cyberspace, the line on MicroMUSE seems rather clearly drawn. On the one hand are administration and the players for whom privacy is paramount; on the other, there are players valuing free speech more and seeking greater influence for themselves that they might be discriminated against less and achieve greater freedom of expression. In late 1993 and early 1994, there were substantial numbers of the latter who were freely and loudly expressing their opposition to the former.

A related source of difficulty is the variety of cultural norms brought into the community by its players. A complex interplay of factors including generation, gender and geographic cross-cultural prejudice and misunderstanding were involved when an adolescent girl from one country and culture accused a man from another of sexual misconduct, a charge he vehemently denied. About the only thing on which there was consensus when the case broke was the girl claimed to be his victim. Some players believed the charge true because "that's the way men are in [that culture]." Others thought the man probably was unaware of how conduct that seemed innocuous to him could be construed by others as injurious. Other views focused on the girl. Some believed she did not fully understand the word she used to characterize his behavior. In their view, his crime, if any, was probably less serious than alleged. Others felt she had merely misinterpreted the man's behavior, and still others questioned her motives, believing the man to be the victim of an immature, and possibly disturbed, teenager's retaliation for a perceived rejection. When it was discovered that the victim of the alleged crime was not the accuser, but someone who was not even a member of the community, this lent credence to the retaliation theory, but still left most of those who were aware of the case distrustful of the accused. As a consequence, he was marginalized. Feeling unwelcome, he redirected his virtual life to other communities, although he did maintain a presence on MicroMUSE and forgave the girl for her role in the affair.

Although it is uncertain whether either of the antagonists in the preceding case supported the notion of a family environment, even those who do so disagree about what that means. For example, a husband and wife from the southern United States once complained about a young man's description that contained a reference to an alcoholic beverage and about swearing in the presence of women players, while college students frequently question why expressions commonly heard in shopping malls, playgrounds and in their own childhood homes are not permitted. Thus, language and behavior disallowed by administration are explained and sometimes defended on several grounds: ignorance of the rules, virtual inequivalence to reality, freedom of speech, and real-world community standards.

In sum, the experience of MicroMUSE suggests several things about virtual communities and conflict. First, to the extent such communities are open to and draw from the Internet's increasingly heterogeneous population with a diversity of values, interests and expectations, they will experience conflict. In addition, when the virtual community has manifest goals, conflict will be greater to the extent that those goals are not understood or shared by members of the community. Third, the social structure of such communities, being one of asymmetrical dependence and power, is an underlying source of conflict and instability. Fourth, given power inequality and a lack of community-wide consensus, administration's strategy for dealing with dissent may have the unintended consequence of increasing and intensifying player conflict behavior. I turn now to this latter point.

Social control

The MUDs studied by Reid (Chapter 5 in this volume) had a medieval system of authority and correction, focusing on the body of the condemned as the locus of punishment. While MicroMUSE has the technical and social devices available to it that Reid's MUDs do, it does not employ them dramaturgically to publicly shame or torture its deviants. In 1993, social controls were more likely to consist of explanations, requests, warnings or lectures in a director's office than public chastisement and humiliation. Technical controls, while they did affect the player's virtual body such as by removing the power the player used to offend (e.g. ability to communicate or move), did not alter the appearance of the offender in order to shame him (a practice known as "toading"). In fact, administration, in keeping with the privacy norm, was loath to report or discuss disciplinary cases in public. The more extreme measures used to tend community borders by gods in Reid's MUDs were, however, frequently used by directors on MicroMUSE: destruction of the offender's character (exile or banishment) and disallowing all connections from the offender's host computer (sitelock) for an hour or two to give the player time to cool down. The sitelock was also sometimes kept in force until the offender's account was canceled by the host system.

That these measures, more modern and humane though they may seem to us than medieval humiliations, have been incompletely successful is evident in the cases described above. Because the Net has so many routes and so many host systems by which to obtain accounts, there are endless ways to defeat the sitelock. Other features of cyberspace and its communities assure that a determined player can return: availability of anonymous guest characters, ease of deception in obtaining email accounts and therefore registered characters, impersonation possibilities because of the casual disregard for security many players have with their passwords, and insecure software. The impotence of banishment and sitelocks is illustrated by Swagger and by Hecuba's assailant, who, as far as I know, may even yet be connecting.

Once exiled players do return, they have both technical and social means to harass other individuals, to disrupt the entire community, and otherwise to challenge the power of administration. Swagger raised community support through the mass media, as did Debs. Players have executed commands or written programs to slow execution of commands ("lag") or crash the computer running MicroMUSE, exploited bugs to destroy database, fraudulently subscribed administrators to hundreds of mailing lists, and harassed and assaulted other players. In other words, much of what they can do to get into trouble in the first place, they can also do to retaliate. Some, of course, amend their behavior and others simply leave, but in the fall and winter of 1993–4, it was evident that a significant share of administrative time and energy was being spent in a ceaseless and escalating battle with users.

Players, too, use both social and technical means to protect and assert themselves, most of which are equivalent to real-life measures. Among these are locking doors and possessions, screening communications, sweeping for listening devices, shunning, ridicule, ostracism, negotiation, and complaining to a person in authority. As the above cases show, there was a frontier ethic of taking the law into one's own hands. Retaliation and counter-retaliation in cycles of escalation were common, and formation of posses and use of hired guns occurred. How many and by what means inter-player disputes were resolved before they escalated to the point where administration became involved is unknown, but cases like the Scorpio mutiny demonstrate the external costs of an informal system of frontier justice: innocent third parties lose intellectual property, administration spends hours investigating and deciding the case and helping with reconstruction, and players lose respect for an administration felt to be unresponsive to their needs.

The reason for this is not just the many conflicts arising from the diversity present and the lack of absolute technical power to expel forever unwanted players. It can also be explained by the way in which administration proceeds when confronted with disobedience to the rules. The Swagger case is informative. Although the director who nuked Swagger originally acted within his authority, his apparent failure to investigate fully and fairly or to give Swagger an opportunity to amend his behavior shocked members of the community and some staff, two of whom countermanded him while acting outside their own authority. Administration as a whole lost respect and the director was under attack in private and public forums, wherein other grievances were raised. Although this was an unusually dramatic case, there were many others in which administration was viewed as acting arbitrarily, capriciously, or discriminatorily and consequently came under vicious, even malicious, attack. When subjected to harsh criticism, personal insults and other acts of revenge, one might be expected to withdraw from the field, defend oneself, or counterattack. All of these reactions were observed to at least some degree. Thus, the charges that administration was unresponsive, remote and unmerciful became self-fulfilling prophecies, fueling still more criticism. The conflict escalated further as the community polarized and each side struggled for control. Administration was on its way to becoming what many in the community all along thought it was – fascist police – rather than the helpful servants, gentle educators, and wise mentors it envisioned of itself. Clearly, MicroMUSE was not the homogeneous community of consensus its powerful administrators wanted. Neither did it resemble the pluralistic vision of society, a web or mosaic of different realities and interests sewn together by conflict (Simmel 1955). Instead, a malignant conflict was becoming intractable (Deutsch 1995: 127). The radical model of dichotomy and opposition in upheaval was a better fit. It was at this point, "after years of adjudicating all manner of inter-player disputes with little to show for it but their own weariness and the smoldering resentment of the general populace" that LambdaMOO's Pavel Curtis turned social control of that community entirely over to the players (Dibbell 1993), effectively altering the balance of power and resolving the structural conflict. Since the Swagger case, MicroMUSE has made some reforms, but it has not taken the democratic path chosen by LambdaMOO.

The reforms

The changes to the Charter passed in 1993 did not effectively address the sources of the conflict identified here, either the competitive relationships produced by plurality and power imbalance or the positive feedback system of conflict management. So, in 1994, several new reforms were introduced. These were designed to define the boundaries of the community more clearly, provide better monitoring of player conduct and more rational sanctions for rule violations, and improve conflict resolution, all of which are among the design elements Ostrom (1990) posits as being essential for robust common-pool resource institutions. One reform was technical and intended to control unacceptable behavior by anonymous visitors. It involved rewriting the server to block nearly all commands entered by visitors. This code modification also significantly curtailed visitor ability to communicate with other players except those designated as "mentors," who act as docents and help visitors register for resident characters. This reform thus protected the machine, code, and users from disaffected players and outsiders with little or no investment in the community.

The second reform significantly altered the process by which new players are introduced to the community. The objective was to reduce conflict caused by diversity by forming a more monolithic society. Like the technical reform, it had a boundary-defining effect. Full membership privileges now required sponsorship by two mentors after a period of socialization. During this period, new players are exposed to the intended culture and complete several tasks, working with mentors to navigate the process and learn rudimentary coding. Theoretically, at least, mentors do not sponsor someone until they know the player is aware of MicroMUSE's mission, accepts the rules and can get around in the MUSE environment. The premise of this reform is that people uninterested in a learning community will not join, while those who stay will be both better informed and more committed by virtue of overcoming a modest hurdle to full status. Thus, self-selection and acculturation would close up the boundaries and produce a more homogeneous population with everyone having at least a little investment in the community.

A third reform institutionalized conflict by providing third-party dispute resolution tools that are used to manage real-life conflicts. This is the subject of the balance of this chapter.

Dispute resolution tools

Ury *et al.* (1988) identify three basic elements of all disputes: interests (the things one really cares about and wants), rights (standards with perceived legitimacy or fairness), and power (the ability to coerce someone to do something against his will). These elements provide three basic strategies for resolving disputes: reconciling interests, adjudicating rights, and exercising power. These strategies have different costs and benefits: the costs of disputing (transaction costs), satisfaction with outcomes, long-term effect on the relationship, and the probability of recurrence. Ury *et al.* (1988) argue that reconciling interests is less costly than adjudicating rights which in turn is less costly than exercising power. This is because reconciling interests tends to result in lower transaction costs, greater satisfaction with outcomes, less strain on the relationship, and less recurrence of disputes than the other approaches. The strategy employed in MicroMUSE in 1993 as described above was counterproductive because it depended on power, either acts of aggression (spamming, destruction of property, etc.) or withholding of benefits (e.g. the sitelock and loss of powers). It accordingly had high transaction costs, produced unsatisfactory outcomes for one or more parties, strained relationships and led to recurrence of conflict since new injuries and disputes were created in the process. The third-party procedures introduced in 1994 were designed to reduce the dependence on power contests by attempting to reconcile interests or adjudicate rights, thus yielding a more effective system of conflict management. In the order in which they are described below, the amount of authority (and, therefore, intrusiveness) of the third-party neutral increases, as does the focus on rights compared to interests.

Mediation is negotiation assisted by a third party who facilitates the disputants' agreement on a solution to their conflict. The success of this approach depends more on the neutral's ability to communicate and influence than to decide, but on-the-spot analysis of rapidly evolving situations and deciding on appropriate ways to proceed are critical. Research into labor mediation has identified two strategies. In deal-making, the mediator figures out what settlement is mutually acceptable to the parties and then manipulates them into adopting it. In orchestration, the mediator enables the parties themselves to discover a settlement that meets their mutual needs (Kolb 1983). The latter approach is more likely to result in settlements that are in the best interests of both parties and is thought to make them less dependent on future third-party intervention than the former. Mediation is commonly used in labor, environmental, community, school, family and divorce, and international disputes, often to keep them from escalating to the more costly rights or power procedures.

Factfinding is a quasi-judicial process in which the neutral conducts an evidentiary hearing and issues a report. Factfinders have the authority to decide the facts of a dispute and may also have the authority to make recommendations for resolution, in which case, the procedure may be termed "advisory arbitration." Typically, if the parties do not accept the factfinder's recommendation, the report is made public. Resolution is theoretically facilitated by the rationalization of the dispute in the first place (determination of the facts and rejection of meritless argument), and by the pressure of public opinion in the second place.

Arbitration is also a quasi-judicial process. It differs from factfinding in that arbitrators issue decisions which, by prior mutual agreement of the parties, are final and binding. It differs from court proceedings in its simplicity and informality which produces results faster and at less cost. The arbitrator's authority flows from and is therefore constrained by the arbitration agreement, which may be a simple *ad hoc* verbal agreement to let a third party make the decision or a more complex one contained in a written contract that also sets forth the rights that are in dispute. Arbitration is widely used in labor and commercial disputes in the United States, but also in less formal settings, such as the family when children take a quarrel to a parent for resolution.

Arbitration was not the procedure of first choice for a number of reasons. First, it requires both parties to give up power procedures entirely. It is therefore more difficult for a party believing itself to hold the balance of power to accept than the other procedures. Second, it is unlikely that the weaker party will accept and use arbitration unless it trusts the stronger one to comply with the arbitrator's directive. In real life, the courts are available to enforce arbitrators' decisions, but litigation is impractical at this time for virtual communities such as MicroMUSE because of its high formality and transaction costs. In view of the superior, though not absolute, power position of administration and the lack of an enforcement agency, I decided not to recommend this procedure for the resolution of player–administration disputes. On the other hand, it offered promise for inter-player disputes if administration would agree to enforce the arbitrator's decision when necessary.

Another reason for favoring factfinding and mediation was that there were few player rights set forth in the 1993 Charter. Rights would therefore have to be more fully elaborated by administration, jointly with the citizens, or by submission to an arbitrator before they could be adjudicated. Interests, on the other hand, can be discovered and reconciled through the other procedures.

Finally, the preliminary diagnosis of social disorder on MicroMUSE suggested that the most important initial objective of intervention was to interrupt the cycle of escalating conflict and improve relations between citizens and administration. Because mediation and, to some degree, factfinding reconcile interests, they are more effective at improving strained relations and preventing recurrence of conflict than is the rights-adjudication arbitration procedure. Thus, the distribution of power, the lack of a mutual understanding of citizen rights and the objectives of the intervention supported the introduction of these two procedures.

The intervention

The essential qualification for dispute resolution practitioners, especially for mediators who depend upon personal power rather than authority, is acceptability to all parties of the dispute. Once a party loses confidence in the mediator, the neutral's usefulness is over. Arbitrators and factfinders also need acceptance because this enhances the likelihood that the parties will accept and abide by their findings and recommendations or decisions. Knowledge of the issues, skill with the process, impartiality and integrity contribute to acceptability, all of which the parties can best discover about the neutral from their own experience with him or her. Using an unknown neutral is risky business in real life, so much so that gaining entry to a relationship is often the most difficult task. In text-based virtual reality, where anonymity and the absence of nonverbal forms of communication impede development of the neutral's personal credibility, where there are no referring organizations and little, if any, experience with these tools, the entry stage is a significant challenge. This proved to be the case in MicroMUSE, where there were a number of false starts. Credibility of both the neutral and the process had to be built over a period of months. A turning point occurred in mid-December 1993 when a sister MUSE was broken into and laid waste in a particularly offensive manner. By this time I had established positive relations both with administrators and those suspected of the attack, so I was invited to observe the investigatory interviews. At the close of those interviews I was asked to write a factfinder's report of findings, opinion, and recommendations, the latter of which were accepted by all parties. This case provided citizens and administration with experience by which they could evaluate the usefulness of third-party techniques in general and the neutral in particular. Submission of disputes to the newly created Citizen Mediator Office soon became routine. The following cases illustrate the application of the two procedures that were introduced in 1994.

The results

A dispute managed by factfinding

In an early case, a player who was an elected member of the Citizens Council was amusing herself by stealing unlocked property. On one of her scavenging trips, she took an object from its owner who was connected at the time and witnessed the theft. The victim followed the thief to her lair, located her own property and uncovered a cache of numerous other objects belonging to others. The mediator was called in by an administrator to whom the crime had been reported. Two mediation sessions were held online, both of which were logged with the knowledge of the participants. The thief did not deny what she had done, but was otherwise uncooperative. At first she scoffed at the notion that it was a crime and blamed her victims for not locking their property up, but later she admitted her actions might have hurt some people. For her part, the victim said she felt both violated by the crime and foolish for not having taken better care of her property. She said she felt the thief not only owed her victims an apology, but also should resign from Citizens Council and help prevent future crimes of this sort by teaching a MUSE course about locks. The thief rejected this proposal, saying that what she did had no impact on her ability to perform her duties of office and that it was administration's responsibility to teach MUSE security. The mediator asked the thief if she had any ideas of her own for acts of restitution, but the thief said she preferred to submit to the will of the Advisory Board, a number of whom she claimed had been members of a previous gang of thieves. Mediation having failed, a report was written to the Advisory Board summarizing the facts and positions of the parties, and making recommendations. A committee was formed which reviewed the evidence and recommendations, and ultimately decided that the thief should be reduced in rank, which would make her ineligible to remain on the Citizens Council, and that she should make amends to the community by an act of her own choosing, subject to the approval of the committee. Eighteen months after this decision, no such act had been made and the thief remained reduced in rank. Although she was implicated in another case at about the same time as this one, there were no further charges filed against her. She continued to connect for some time, but eventually found other MUSEs more to her interest and abandoned her MicroMUSE character. The victim, however, reported that she felt she had regained self-respect when she confronted the thief, and was satisfied with the decision of the Advisory Board committee. Additionally, although the thief made no act of restitution such as would help protect the community from further burglaries, administration did adopt one of the factfinder's recommendations that an article be placed in the online news to remind players to lock their objects and report suspected thefts. The *ad hoc* committee and the process by which the case was handled became the model for the Disciplinary Committee, which was established in May 1994.

A mediated dispute

A later case involved one of the most charming characters on MicroMUSE, a Maas-Neotek robot named Caspian, who is programmed to wander the MUSE, making maps, giving directions, delivering messages, answering questions, and other similar things. One evening a bored player called "Pygmalion" spammed Caspian so badly he crashed. When Faceless, a staff member who maintains Caspian and other MUSE robots discovered this, he checked Pygmalion's record and found that he had been previously warned. He therefore knew that Pygmalion was aware of the prohibition against spamming and had probably agreed not to do it again. Faceless decided he needed to take measures to prevent Pygmalion's willful disregard of the rule again. He therefore arrested Pygmalion, retrieved a log of the spam as evidence, and sent the mediator a report of these actions.

Upon receiving the report, the mediator got in touch with Pygmalion through email, told him he was free to represent himself before the Advisory Board's Disciplinary Committee if he wished, but offered the alternative of mediation, pointing out that the committee usually endorsed mutually agreed-to settlements. She also encouraged him to tell her his side of the story and to suggest a fair outcome. Pygmalion had several responses. First, he complained about the absence of the accused's rights. The mediator explained the reasons for the restrictions and arranged to have the unnecessary ones lifted. Pygmalion also admitted his guilt and told what had happened from his point of view, corroborating Faceless's version of events. He explained he had forgotten he was disobeying an order of an administrator and suggested that a just outcome would be the removal of his ability to invoke the command he used for spamming. His explanation led the mediator to question whether he truly understood why, from administration's point of view, spamming is an unfriendly act. She knew from past experience that administration would not be satisfied with another promise unless Pygmalion knew the reason for the rule as well as the rule itself, so she discussed administration's interests with him. She then asked him if he was willing to restate what he had learned by writing a brief explanation of why spamming is prohibited, especially of robots. Pygmalion agreed to do so. The mediator also informed him that it was not technically possible to remove his power to use the offending command without removing all his membership powers. The matter was left open until Faceless reacted to Pygmalion's explanation.

The mediator forwarded Pygmalion's written explanation to Faceless. He replied that the explanation was satisfactory and that if Pygmalion would make an act of restitution to Caspian and agree this was a last chance, the matter would be closed. Pygmalion accepted these terms, agreeing to write an apology to the robot and a statement to the effect that a third spam offense would subject him to exile. In one of MicroMUSE's more touching moments, Caspian visited Pygmalion in the jail where he listened to the letter of apology and accepted it, saying, "Never mind, Pygmalion," which is his programmed response to expressions of regret. On the strength of the apology and last-chance agreement, Faceless released Pygmalion. The Disciplinary Committee shortly thereafter accepted this mutually agreed-to resolution. There were no further complaints against Pygmalion after this until he, too, abandoned his character . . .

Discussion

Outcomes

These cases illustrate the processes used to attempt reconciliation of diverse substantive and procedural interests with the primary objectives of improving relations and preventing the recurrence of conflict.

In the robot case, Pygmalion's substantive interest was to remain on MUSE (i.e. not have his character recycled) free to pursue his own objectives without undue restriction. He had due process issues of having his case expeditiously and fairly handled, and of having some of the arrest conditions relaxed so he could communicate with other players while his case was pending. For administration's part, its substantive interest was in preventing further abuse of the command queue and other players. It also wanted to prevent social and technical retaliation for perceived injustice and to resolve the case expeditiously. While it may have been faster and taken less effort in the short run simply to recycle the character or to let him languish in jail, none of Pygmalion's interests would have been addressed. Had it taken this power approach, administration would have risked acts of retaliation requiring even more disciplinary actions. In the long run, then, the more labor-intensive process of mediation, because it successfully reconciled all interests of the participants, furthered mutual understanding and respect, and changed the conduct of the miscreant, resulting in a lasting peace. Additionally, it modeled to one of its young users an effective means of managing social conflict and, therefore, was consistent with the educational mission of the MUSE.

In the theft case, once her property was returned, the victim's primary interest was to regain a sense of control and self-esteem. This was achieved in mediation when she confronted the thief on MUSE in real time and later when she was told the results of the Advisory Board's deliberations. Although her specific proposals for resolving the substantive issue of restitution were neither accepted by the thief nor adopted by the Advisory Board, the outcome was not dissimilar: rather than being taught by the thief, citizens received information about locks in the news item; rather than resigning, the thief was de facto removed from the Council by virtue of her reduction in rank; and the community received some protection from future thefts from the news article that contained the self-protection information and may have dissuaded potential burglars by reinforcing a behavioral expectation. Administration experienced the transaction costs of considering and acting on the factfinder's report, but these were mitigated by referring the case to a committee and relying on the neutral's findings, if not her entire set of recommendations. As with Pygmalion, there were no acts of retaliation or repetition, so administration's interest in conflict prevention was addressed. About the only goal of the thief that was achieved was her continued presence on MUSE, albeit at a reduced rank. Procedurally, she had requested a decision by the Advisory Board, perhaps hoping that her friends there would protect her. The integrity of the factfinding process was guarded, however, by appointing a committee composed exclusively of administrators without personal relations with the accused. Thus, the citizen interest in having a fair tribunal was addressed to some degree, although not in the peer-jury form discussed at the October 1993 town meeting. Finally, there was the matter of the thief's position on the Citizens Council. The factfinder recommended that her tenure on the Council be placed before that body, but this was rejected by the Advisory Board, which seemed concerned that this would set a bad precedent and create the expectation that the Council would have authority in future disciplinary matters. In rejecting the factfinder's recommendation, the Advisory Board signaled its unwillingness to cede decision-making authority either to a democratically elected body or to an appointed professional. In conclusion, this case demonstrates the peace-making utility of third-party dispute resolution techniques even when the process does not completely reconcile all the interests of all the parties.

Role of technology

It is difficult to capture in case descriptions the role played by the technology of cyber-space. Even transcripts of online sessions do not fully depict its influence. On the one hand, the frustrations experienced and time consumed can be significant. On the other hand, technology of the community and its environment also makes some things easier to accomplish than in real life. The following are some of the normal consequences of existing technology.

First, mediator/factfinder control of meetings and hearings is significantly impaired by parties connecting from different time zones with different real-life schedules, and by the neutral's inability to isolate the meeting from real-life inter-ruptions, disrupted connections, the need of some users to relog periodically, and lag from various sources. Administrators can forcibly restrict player communications with others as well as inhibit player movement about the MUSE, but even directors are socially and technically powerless over extra-MUSE conditions. The effect of this is to delay the start of meetings, and to interrupt and prolong them, as participants fail to arrive at the appointed hour, leave and return, or leave and fail to return to finish the meeting. Comings and goings disrupt concentration and create the need to repeat or simply to wait until key players return, possibly hours or days later. Mediation is a labor-intensive activity requiring patience anyway, and these conditions make it more so. People at different places in the Net experience different degrees of lag. Those who are lagging the most may be effectively shut out of a group meeting or even a dialogue because of their inability to contribute to the discussion in a timely fashion. Their interests, then, may never be addressed unless the mediator takes care to structure and pace the discussion or to supplement MUSE synchronous communication with asynchronous email. Likewise, it is easy for one or two players to dominate a meeting by virtue of typing skill, a fast, reliable connection, and much to say.[10]

The fact that messages are typed and read, rather than spoken and heard, has several effects. Different people may have the communication edge in this environment than those who do in real life. For example, those who have difficulty expressing themselves or understanding others through speech may be more communicative online while those who have difficulty reading, composing, and typing may be less so.

Typing and lag interact to affect the sequencing of messages, such that one frequently tends to be one or more turns behind in a dialogue, thus one makes statements that appear to have ignored the other party's most recent message, which was itself typed and entered prematurely in an attempt to compensate for lag. Experienced players are accustomed to this and other vagaries of the Net. Most learn not to take offense, but it can be a source of substantive misunderstanding and hard feelings.

Another problem is the quality of the evidence available. Email addresses and logs can be falsified, objects easily destroyed, and passwords cracked. Frequently there are no witnesses to an incident, the complainant has been unable to log what occurred, and no administrator is available to retrieve the transient command log before the evidence disappears. The case then turns on credibility, which is extraordinarily problematic in text-based, multicultural virtual reality where there is an absence of nonverbal communication (except those described textually, either in words or emoticon, which are necessarily consciously chosen)[11] and where meaning is so easily inaccurately conveyed and misconstrued, both unintentionally and deliberately. Nowhere is the problem of finding facts more evident than in the determination of who is responsible for a given act. In an environment where experimentation with identity and role-playing is the norm, deception and detection become a game for some. Under such circumstances it is easy to lose faith in one's evaluative ability and find deception everywhere. Shell (1995) argues that the computer medium itself eliminates much of the warmth of inter-personal contact, making it harder to gauge reactions to ideas under discussion, and that this could lead to misjudging commitments. While there is certainly that risk, my own experience, and that reported by Rheingold (1993), is that interpersonal contacts run the gamut from the detached and impersonal to the intensely passionate. Moreover, players tend to assume distinctive, individual virtual personalities, styles of discourse, and modes of expression. Just as in real life, the more familiar a person is with another, the easier it is to avoid errors due to individual differences (Ekman 1985). Members of the virtual community who know their fellow players' personae should be less vulnerable than outsiders to misjudging their messages. Real-life, face-to-face meetings with online acquaintances are helpful, too, in assessing one's ability to judge virtual human character, although the real character and personality may be quite different from the virtual.

The anonymity and physical separation of cyberspace support social experi-mentation as well as explorations of identity and self. Reid (1994), Rheingold (1993), and others have noted the disinhibition effects on behavior in cyberspace. Being free from experiencing the effects of their behavior on others and free from fear of punishment, players find it easier to speak and act aggressively and dishonestly than they do in real life. This complicates discovery of the truth as well as contributing to the incidence of online conflict. But there is another side to disinhibition, and that is in its encouragement of truth-telling. The protection that physical distance and anonymity gives players supports intimacy and confidences, as well as aggression and deception. It is easier in virtual reality than in the real world to persuade people to confide their needs, desires and secrets. This facilitates reconciliation of differences and discovery of the facts of a particular case.

Other effects of the technology of cyberspace assist the dispute resolution process as well. For instance, although lag can be frustrating and lengthen the time it takes to complete an interview, it also gives one time to think, decide on courses of action and compose one's words. Shell (1995) reports that people may pay more attention to the substantive content of messages on computer screens than to the same content delivered verbally. One would expect such reflection and concentration to improve communication, relationships, and problem-solving. At the least it affords some protec-tion against *faux pas*. In addition, the absence of physical cues and nonverbals can be used by the mediator as well as by the principals, as one does not have to work so hard to overcome barriers of socio-economic differences or to control physical expression of one's own feelings. Another example is the technical ability to make a verbatim record of any interview without the distraction of recording devices, and after an event has occurred to recall and record what is in the buffer. This provides instant and accurate transcripts for later study or evidence, such as in the Pygmalion case. Finally, the ability to multiplex allows one to support, consult, and educate others on private channels, by whispering, paging, and through remote control devices called "puppets,"[12] while simultaneously monitoring or participating in a joint meeting. Thus, caucuses and joint meetings can occur simultaneously as well as sequentially. Multiplexing makes dispute resolution more effective as well as more efficient, because one is more likely to have access to key people, important information and creative ideas during critical moments of the process.

A final case illustrates some of the mediation-enhancing effects of the technology. This case involved a player, whom I shall call "Oedipus," who wrote some code that was unfriendly to the community because it used more than his fair share of bandwidth. I did not observe the incident as it happened, but was able to observe both it and the ensuing confrontation between the member and staff complainants after the fact by virtue of a program that allows me to stay connected to the MUSE even though my own computer is turned off and I am away from my keyboard. The director who later stepped in to back up the complaining staff made a log of his meeting with the two and emailed it to me as evidence that Oedipus had promised to rewrite the offending code. I was thus able to analyze the situation directly, rather than indirectly through another's interpretation, before attempting to mediate the dispute when Oedipus failed to keep his promise. My working hypothesis was that Oedipus was unable to accept his own culpability, and that this made him hostile toward his accusers and resistant to examining and understanding his code. I also concluded that administration's long-term interests would not be satisfied unless Oedipus understood the particular coding problem well enough not to repeat his mistake in the future. These hypotheses were supported when I met separately with each side simultaneously by multiplexing (I spoke with Oedipus while he was detained in the Cyberion City Jail while discussing the situation with administration on an officials-only channel). My objective then became to help Oedipus achieve a degree of understanding satisfactory to administration and sufficient to make an informed commitment, should he choose to make a new one. I knew if I could do this, he would be released as rehabilitated and there would be a good probability he would honor his commitment.

Because of his lingering hostility toward NetRunner (the staff who originally had confronted him), Oedipus refused a joint meeting. However, it was important that NetRunner be well satisfied with Oedipus's knowledge, so I decided not to rely on shuttle diplomacy, but to exploit the technology to create a pseudo face-to-face meeting. I had NetRunner himself explain the problem, but use me as his medium, paging me lines which I then repeated almost verbatim to Oedipus by pasting them unedited into my own "say" command. NetRunner heard for himself what was said through a puppet I placed in the room where I met with Oedipus. He thus could verify the accuracy of what I said and could hear for himself Oedipus's questions and comments, adapting as he, himself, felt necessary to develop Oedipus's understanding.

The strategy was effective. Oedipus was more open to direction emanating from my character, even though the words were not mine, than directly from NetRunner because he could concentrate on the substantive message rather than on his feelings about the messenger. Additionally, because we were in the same virtual space at the same time, the transaction was conversationally interactive. Misunderstandings were immediately corrected and understandings instantly reinforced. This made the effort both effective and efficient. There were external benefits of this session as well, when its log was edited to remove identifying features and later circulated on the mentor mailing list and used in a help file to teach others better coding and, by modeling, coaching techniques.

Evaluation

This experiment was undertaken to assess the usefulness of real-life peace-making tools for improving the adaptability of virtual communities. After the 1993 Swagger case and resultant rebellion, the Advisory Board established a Mediation Office to assist players with interpersonal conflicts and a Disciplinary Committee to review and act on cases of player misconduct. All accused players have the right to controvert and be heard and are not punished for so doing. While they are encouraged to use the mediator, who is familiar with and informs them about the process, they need not do so. If a case cannot be resolved through mediation to the mutual satisfaction of the disputants, it receives careful, systematic, and thorough consideration by a body composed of administrators, none of whom are an immediate party to the complaint. Corrective actions are directed toward rehabilitation and restitution, not punishment. Information about cases is made available on a need-to-know basis on MUSE and off, and the community is kept informed about procedures and Disciplinary Committee actions through news articles circulated on the email list and by ftp gopher and the web. Thus, conflict has become institution-alized through structures and procedures chosen to (1) reconcile the diverse interests of a pluralistic community, both among the community's members and between its members and its administrators, and (2) provide due process for members and administrators accused of misconduct. All of this serves to give expression to conflict, but in a way that is not destructive to the community. Nevertheless, there are indications of problems with the system.

 Criteria for evaluating the effectiveness of due process systems include the fairness and timeliness of the settlement and the ease with which the process is utilized (Aram and Salipante 1981). Taking the procedural criteria first, the Mediation Office acts in the role of ombudsman to educate disputants on and assist them with the process, which itself is not complicated. But for disputants to use the process, they must be aware of it. A case that came to the Office fully 18 months after mediation was introduced clearly demonstrates that the community is inadequately aware of its existence. In this case, a 2-year-old user named "Cassio" felt himself to be slandered in an administrative decision and took his complaint to the director he held responsible. Obtaining no satisfaction and unaware of any other option save leaving the community, he next took his case to the public channel, as Swagger had done 21 months before, and complained bitterly about the director. Eventually the director tired of this and filed a formal complaint of harassment with the Mediation Office. When contacted by a mediator, Cassio expressed surprise that he had any recourse save the political one of raising public opinion or the market one of withdrawing his membership (Hirschman 1970). He subsequently ceased his public criticism of the director, wrote a petition to appeal the administrative decision on the grounds that it was based on hearsay evidence, and offered suggestions about how to make the community better aware of its conflict management options.

A second problem with the system is that cases seem to take a very long time to be resolved. Some of this perception is a function of user expectations in a cyberworld of nearly instantaneous global communications and the inability of some to delay gratification on account of their immaturity. The criticism also has some basis in fact. As described above, existing technology and global usage prolong the process. Little can be done about this except to make users aware of their impact. Another source of the problem is the labor intensity of the process, the community's reliance on volunteer administrators who have real-life commitments taking them off MUSE at times inconvenient for the community, and few players or administrators with the requisite skills, acceptability, or desire to act as conciliators. Increasing community awareness of the program and its needs could help relieve the labor shortage, make community expectations more realistic, and improve actual and perceived timeliness.

Turning now to the substantive criterion, two factors appear to have an impact on the perceived fairness of the settlements. One of these, the evidentiary problem affecting the rationality of outcomes, is discussed above. The other factor is the perceived impartiality of the decision-maker. For the first nine months of my engagement as mediator, I was an unempowered citizen who nevertheless had influence with administration. This gave me credibility with other citizens who perceived me as one of them, but I had to deal with their skepticism about whether I was influential enough to get results. I later accepted a voting and technically powered position on the Board of Directors reasoning that this would both give citizens a powerful voice in MUSE governance (I had veto power) and afford them visible protection when they have grievances against administrators. It also afforded me a degree of independence because, under the Bylaws (1994), directors are not easily removed from office. This solution avoided the problems inherent with employee ombudsman systems wherein the employee advocate is viewed as being under the control of management by virtue of serving at its pleasure. However, it also raised the question of insidious co-optation. It is clear that many members of the community, especially new players, believe I am an enforcer and administrator, not an impartial third party. Because of this, I am not always trusted to mediate interplayer disputes where, as in the Scorpio and Hecuba cases, administration is thought to have an interest counter to the disputants. Acceptability has again become a significant issue.

Additionally, unless players believe they will get a fair hearing when, like Cassio, their grievance is with administration, they will either leave (depriving the community of potentially positive contributions), suffer in silence (depriving the community of indicators of potential problems), or take matters into their own hands, as did Cassio, Swagger, Ajax, and others (Hirschman 1970). In other words, as in real life, unless the third party is viewed as being unaligned with and independent of the goodwill of one side or the other, the conflict management system will be ineffective. The techniques presently employed can continue to resolve many issue-oriented conflicts, particularly if the community is made better aware of the program, the number of mediator/factfinders is increased, and the Office as a whole listens to all sides, respects differences and generally attends to its reputation. But because the asymmetrical power structure of

MicroMUSE is itself the underlying source of much of the conflict, there are some disputes that cannot be resolved without first changing that structure to provide members with more influence (Rapoport 1974). Employing a tripartite arbitration board (consisting of an administrator, an elected member representative, and a third party chosen by the other two) authorized to develop a bill of member rights and resolve inter-player disputes would be a step in that direction and one administration may be ready for now that it has had some positive experience with third-party dispute resolution. Such a step would also move the community toward a more adjudicatory society and less mediative one, an evolutionary step that has been observed in societies elsewhere (Thomas 1984).

Conclusion and summary

This chapter began with the observation of substantial social conflict in the subject virtual community that was, and still remains to a large degree, open to the Internet. It noted a number of features of this world that make conflict more likely and more difficult to manage than in real communities: wide cultural diversity; disparate interests, needs and expectations; the nature of electronic participation (anonymity, multiple avenues of entry, poor reliability of connections, and so forth); text-based communication; and power asymmetry among them. These features and their results are not unique to this community or even to MU*s, as Macduff (1994) made similar observations about email networks. Some features may be limited to synchronous-communication communities such as IRC and MU*s, to MUSEs, or to MicroMUSE in particular: the publicity attendant on MicroMUSE's success, for example, its choice of a mission at odds with perhaps the majority of the Internet's population attracted to such environments, and its decision to be an open-access community. Clearly, though, what MicroMUSE shares with so many other virtual communities and what is at the heart of most, if not all, of its internal disputes, are open boundaries and substantial social diversity, both in degrees uncommonly found in real life. The MicroMUSE experience would thus seem to have lessons for other communities in cyberspace.

This chapter has also argued that cyber communities, like any social system, must include diversity and find some way to integrate it if they are to thrive. Because open cyber communities are likely to be extremely diverse, managing the resultant inevitable conflict is an especially important task. The computer interface, the anarchy of the Net structure, and the power asymmetry of most virtual communities, though, make the task of conflict management especially difficult. If, in their attempts to control behavior, such communities drive out ideas by suppression or exclusion, or escalate into chaos as a consequence of power struggles, their life and purpose will be threatened. To avoid this they must not still the voices of their members, but give them expression. As Scott Peck (1987: 71) puts it, communities must not give up fighting, but learn to "fight gracefully."

Finally, this chapter has demonstrated that several tools from the real world can be adapted by virtual communities to promote the environment of respect and safety necessary for their vitality.

Notes

1 Copyright 1997 by Anna DuVal Smith. All rights reserved. Correspondence concerning this chapter may be addressed to Anna DuVal Smith, Department of Management and Policy Studies, Weatherhead School of Management, Enterprise Hall, Case Western Reserve University, Cleveland, Ohio 44106. Electronic mail may be sent via Internet to axs40@po.cwru.edu.

2 Internet Relay Chat. A "party line" network for chatting in real time.

3 A MUD (Multi-User Dungeon or Multi-User Dimension) is a real-time chat forum with structure (Raymond 1993: 287). MU* is a general class of these virtual worlds including MUDs and their progeny such as MUSHes, MUCKs and MUSEs.

4 "MicroMUSE is chartered as an educational multi-user simulation environment (MUSE) and virtual community with preference toward educational content of a scientific and cultural nature. The MicroMUSE administration works towards the development of MUSE technology to enhance the exchange of ideas, the learning process, and the expression of creative writing for individuals of all ages and backgrounds" (MicroMUSE Charter 1994).

5 Interested readers should consult the 1994 MicroMUSE Charter and, especially, the 1994 MicroMUSE Bylaws for details of the administrative structure in place following the reforms implemented during the term of this study.

6 A psychological analysis is beyond the scope of this paper, but it is worth noting that MicroMUSE's population includes adolescents with developmental issues, adults wrestling with unresolved personal issues, players diagnosed with more serious psychological disorders such as depression, attention deficit-hyperactivity disorder, and substance abuse, and others simply escaping from real life's pressures. Turkle (1995) describes how MU*s, which encourage projection and transference, and offer a place to play and experiment, provide a forum for enacting and working through psychological issues. The MU*, then, is "a medium for working with the materials of . . . life" (p. 188).

7 Belief that information should be freely distributed. A corrolary is that barriers to the free flow of information are evil, thus, central authority and bureaucracy are to be mistrusted and barriers are to be breached. Levy discussed the hacker culture at length in a popular book originally published in 1984.

8 Communicating with the intent to insult or provoke. Also communicating "incessantly and/or rabidly" on some uninteresting topic or with a ridiculous attitude. (Raymond 1993: 181).

9 On some MUSEs (but not MicroMUSE), there is a *1984* Big Brother quality to behavior control as administration logs all commands executed by players suspected of misdeeds.

10 This can be such a significant problem in large meetings where many are vying for the floor that code has been written into the server to allow a meeting's moderator technical control over attendees' ability to speak.

11 An "emoticon," possibly derived from emotion + icon, is an ASCII glyph used in text-based environments such as email, MU*s, and Usenet to indicate an emotional state in order to prevent misunderstandings. Among the hundreds in use are :) ;) and :(which are known respectively as "smiley," "winkey" and "frowney." Deciphering emoticons is facilitated by viewing them with the head tilted to the left.

12 Objects programmed to relay all they see and hear to its owner. Puppets may also be controlled by their owner to move, say, pose, or do anything their owner can do. Thus,

the owner can be in two virtual places at once, the room of the owner and the room of the puppet.

References

Aram, J. D. and Salipante, P. F., Jr. 1981. "An evaluation of organizational due process in the resolution of employee/employer conflict." *Academy of Management Review* 6: 200.

Brown, L. D. 1983. *Managing Conflict at Organizational Interfaces*. Reading, MA: Addison-Wesley.

Brown, L. D. 1995. "Managing conflict among groups." In D. A. Kolb, J. S. Osland and I. M. Rubin (eds) *The Organizational Behavior Reader* (6th edn). Englewood Cliffs, NJ: Prentice Hall.

Clodius, J. (1997, January). *Creating a community of interest: "Self" and "other" on DragonMud*. Paper presented at the combined winter conference on educational uses of MUDs, Teton Village, Jackson, WY. [On-line]. Available *http://dragonmud.org/people/jen/mudshopiii.html*.

Coser, L. A. 1956. *The Functions of Social Conflict*. New York: Free Press.

Cox, T., Jr. 1991. "The multicultural organization." *Academy of Management Executive* 5(2): 34–47.

Dalton, G. W. (1971). Motivation and control in organizations. In G. W. Dalton & P. R. Lawrence (Eds.), *Motivation and control in organization* (pp. 1–35). Homewood, IL: Richard D. Irwin & Dorsey Press.

Deutsch, M. 1973. *The Resolution of Conflict: Constructive and Destructive Processes*. New Haven, CT: Yale University Press.

Deutsch, M. (1995). Commentary: The constructive management of conflict: Developing the knowledge and crafting the practice. In B. B. Bunker, J. Z. Rubin & Associates, *Conflict, cooperation, and justice: Essays inspired by the work of Morton Deutsch* (pp. 123–129). San Francisco: Jossey-Bass.

Dibbell, J. 1993. "A rape in cyberspace or how an evil clown, a Haitian trickster spirit, two wizards, and a cast of dozens turned a database into a society." *Village Voice* 38(51). [Online] gopher: well.sf.ca.us Directory: Community.

Ekman, P. 1985. *Telling Lies: Clues to Deceit in the Marketplace, Politics and Marriage*. New York: Norton.

Filley, A. C. 1975. *Interpersonal Conflict Resolution*. Glenview, IL: Scott, Foresman.

Gergen, K. J. (1991). *The saturated self: Dilemmas of identity in contemporary life*. Basic Books.

Hirschman, A. O. 1970. *Exit, Voice and Loyalty: Responses to Decline in Firms, Organizations, and States*. Cambridge, MA: Harvard University Press.

Karnow, C. 1994. "The encrypted self: fleshing out the rights of electronic personalities." *John Marshall Journal of Computer and Information Law* 13(1): 1–16.

Kelly, K. and Rheingold, H. 1993. "The dragon ate my homework. . . . " *Wired*, July/August: 68–73.

Kolb, D. M. 1983. *The Mediators*. Cambridge, MA: MIT Press.

Kort, B. (1995). *Project based learning and communitas*. [On-line]. Available gopher: cyberion. musenet.org Directory: MicroMUSE/EdNet Articles File: ednet.5.

Leslie, J. 1993. "MUDroom." *Atlantic Monthly* 272(3): 28–34.

Levy, S. 1994. *Hackers: Heroes of the Computer Revolution*. New York: Dell.

Macduff, I. 1994. "Flames on the wires: mediating from an electronic cottage." *Negotiation Journal* 10(1): 5–15.

McGregor, D. M. (1957). The human side of enterprise. *Adventures in Thought and Action: Proceedings of the Fifth Anniversary Convocation of the School of Industrial Management*, M.I.T., Cambridge, MA, April 9, 1957. Cambridge, MA: Technology Press.

Martin, J. (1992). *Cultures in organizations: Three perspectives*. New York: Oxford University Press.

MicroMUSE charter [On-line]. 1991. Available gopher: cyberion.musenet.org Directory: MicroMUSE/Important Documents File: Old 1991 Charter.

MicroMUSE by-laws [On-line]. 1994. Available ftp: 192.1.100.39 Directory: micromuse File: bylaws.

MicroMUSE charter [On-line]. 1994. Available ftp: 192.1.100.39 Directory: micromuse File: charter.

Morgan, G. (1986). *Images of organization*. Newbury Park, CA: Sage Publications.

Ostrom, E. 1990. *Governing the Commons: The Evolution of Institutions for Collective Action*. Cambridge: Cambridge University Press.

Peck, M.S. 1987. *The Different Drum: Community Making and Peace*. New York: Simon and Schuster.

Pfeffer, J. 1981. *Power in Organizations*. Boston, MA: Pitman.

Presthus, R. 1978. *The Organizational Society* (2nd edn). New York: St. Martin's Press.

Rapoport, A. 1974. *Conflict in Man-made Environment*. Baltimore, MD: Penguin.

Raymond, Eric (ed.). 1993. *The New Hacker's Dictionary* (2nd edn). Cambridge, MA: MIT Press.

Reid, E. 1994. "Cultural formations in text-based virtual realities." [On-line]. Unpublished master's thesis, University of Melbourne, Melbourne, Australia. Available http: www.ee.mu.oz.au Directory: papers/emr/index.html.

Rheingold, H. 1993. *The Virtual Community: Homesteading on the Electronic Frontier*. Reading, MA: Addison-Wesley.

Robbins, S. P. 1974. *Managing Organizational Conflict: A Nontraditionalist Approach*. Englewood Cliffs, NJ: Prentice Hall.

Scime, R. (1994) <cyberville> *and the spirit of community: Howard Rheingold – meet Amitai Etzioni*. [On-line]. Available gopher: gopher.well.com Directory: Community File: cyberville.

Shell, G.R. 1995. "Computer-assisted negotiation and mediation: Where we are and where we are going." *Negotiation Journal* 11(2): 117–21.

Simmel, G. 1955. *Conflict*, trans. K. H. Wolff. Glencoe, IL: Free Press.

Tannenbaum, A. (1965). Unions. In J. G. March (Ed.), *Handbook of organizations* (pp. 710–763). Chicago: Rand McNally.

Thomas, Darlene K. 1984. *Dispute Resolution from an Anthropological Perspective* (Occasional Paper 84–1). Washington, DC: Society of Professionals in Dispute Resolution.

Turkle, S. (1995). *Life on the screen: Identity in the age of the Internet*. New York: Simon & Schuster.

Ury, W. L., Brett, J. M., and Goldberg, S. B. 1988. *Getting Disputes Resolved: Designing Systems to Cut the Costs of Conflict*. San Francisco, CA: Jossey-Bass.

Part four

Community structure and dynamics

Chapter 7

Virtual communities as communities

Net surfers don't ride alone

Barry Wellman and

Milena Gulia

Hope, hype, and reality

Can people find community online in the Internet? Can relationships between people who never see, smell, touch, or hear each other be supportive and intimate?

✡ The debate fills the Internet, the airwaves, and especially the print media. Enthusiasts outnumber critics, for as the prophet Jeremiah discovered millennia ago, there is more immediate reward in extolling the future than in praising it. Unfortunately, both sides of the debate are often Manichean, presentist, unscholarly, and parochial.

The Manicheans on either side of this debate assert that the Internet either will create wonderful new forms of community or will destroy community altogether. These dueling dualists feed off each other, using the unequivocal assertions of the other side as foils for their own arguments. Their statements of enthusiasm or criticism leave little room for the moderate, mixed situations that may be the reality. The up-to-the-minute participants in this breathless debate appear to be unaware that they are continuing a century-old controversy about the nature of community, albeit with new debating partners. There is little sense of history.

Brave New Net World?

Enthusiasts hail the Net's potential for making connections without regard to race, creed, gender, or geography. As Amanda Walker asserts online:

mduhn bit

> Every advance in communication changes the nature of reality as we experience it. . . . The Internet is yet another revolutionary method of communication. For the first time in the history of the world, I can have an ongoing, fast-moving conversation with people regardless of their physical location, schedule, or other such constraints. . . . The world is changing, and we're the ones that are doing it, whether we realize it or not.[1]

Phil Patton similarly asserts that

> computer-mediated communication . . . will do by way of electronic pathways what cement roads were unable to do, namely connect us rather than atomize us, put us at the controls of a "vehicle" and yet not detach us from the rest of the world.
>
> (Patton 1986: 20)

John Perry Barlow, co-founder of the Electronic Frontier Foundation, goes further in prophesying the radical and positive social transformation that the Net will bring about:

> With the development of the Internet, and with the increasing pervasiveness of communication between networked computers, we are in the middle of the most transforming technological event since the capture of fire. I used to think that it was just the biggest thing since Gutenberg, but now I think you have to go back farther. . . . In order to feel the greatest sense of communication, to realize the most experience . . . , I want to be able to completely interact with the consciousness that's trying to communicate with mine. Rapidly. . . . We are now creating a space in which the people of the planet can have that kind of communication relationship.
>
> (Barlow *et al.* 1995: 40)

Lost in cyberspace?

By contrast, critics worry (mostly in print, of course) that life on the Net can never be meaningful or complete because it will lead people away from the full range of in-person contact. Or, conceding half of the debate, they worry that people will get so engulfed in a simulacrum virtual reality, that they will lose contact with "real life."[2] Meaningful contact will wither without the full bandwidth provided by in-person, in-the-flesh contact. As Texas commentator Jim Hightower warned over the ABC radio network:

> While all this razzle-dazzle connects us electronically, it disconnects us from each other, having us "interfacing" more with computers and TV screens than looking in the face of our fellow human beings.
>
> (Fox 1995: 12)

Or as Mark Slouka, author of *War of the Worlds: Cyberspace and the Hi-tech Assault on Reality* (1995), worries, "Where does the need come from to inhabit these alternate spaces? And the answer I keep coming back to is: to escape the problems and issues of the real world" (in Barlow *et al*. 1995: 43).

Social networks as communities (virtual or otherwise)

Although they often make broad references to Gutenberg (1455) and McLuhan (1965), both sides of the debate are presentist and unscholarly. Consistent with the present-oriented ethos of computer users, pundits write as if people had never worried about community before the Internet arose. Yet sociologists have been wondering for over a century about how technological changes (along with bureaucratization, industrialization, urbanization, and capitalism) have affected community (Wellman 1988a). Have such changes led community to (1) fall apart, (2) persevere as village-like shelters from mass society, or (3) be liberated from the clasp of traditional solidary groups? Like Jim Hightower today, until the 1950s, sociologists feared that rapid modernization would mean the loss of community, leaving a handful of transitory, disconnected, weakly supportive relationships (Stein 1960). Since then, more systematic ethnographic and survey techniques have demonstrated the persistence of community in neighborhood and kinship groups (e.g. Gans 1962).

More recently, sociologists have discovered that such neighborhood and kinship ties are only a portion of people's overall community networks because cars, planes, and phones can maintain relationships over long distances (Wellman 1988a). They realized that communities do not have to be solidary groups of densely knit neighbors but could also exist as social networks of kin, friends, and workmates who do not necessarily live in the same neighborhoods. It is not that the world is a global village, but as McLuhan originally said, one's "village" could span the globe. This conceptual revolution moved from defining community in terms of space – neighborhoods – to defining it in terms of social networks (Wellman 1988).

Social network analysts have had to educate traditional, place-oriented, community sociologists that community can stretch well beyond the neighborhood. By contrast, members of virtual communities take for granted that computer networks are also social networks spanning large distances (e.g. Rheingold 1993; Jones 1995; Hiltz and Turoff 1993; Stoll 1995). These computer-supported social networks (CSSNs) come in a variety of types such as electronic mail (email), bulletin board systems (BBSs), Multi-User Dungeons (MUDs), newsgroups, and Internet Relay Chat (IRC). All CSSNs provide companionship, social support, information, and a sense of belonging. But do they? The Manichean pronouncements of pundits – pro and con – most likely overstate the actual nature of virtual community life. (Perhaps it is difficult for a pundit to get media attention without unequivocally asserting that virtual community will greatly change life as we know it – for good or ill.) Although naysayers have recently gotten some press (e.g. Stoll 1995; Slouka 1995), most scholarly accounts of online interactions have been quite positive. Although we share this basically positive evaluation, we also suspect that this enthusiasm is partially attributable to the fact that most research has been done by academics and those working for private organizations who have had vested interests in showing that CSSNs work. With the best will in the world, people developing or evaluating online systems want them to work and have invested a large part of themselves in the apparent success of the systems in which they have been involved.

Much of the analysis that does exist is parochial. It almost always treats the Internet as an isolated social phenomenon without taking into account how interactions on the Net fit together with other aspects of people's lives. The Net is only one of many ways in which the same people may interact. It is not a separate reality. People bring to their online interactions such baggage as their gender, stage in the life cycle, cultural milieu, socioeconomic status, and offline connections with others (see for example O'Brien, Chapter 4 in this volume).

Just as previous generations had worried about whether community had been destroyed or transformed by earlier "new technologies" – such as the telephone (Fischer 1992) or the automobile – the pundits of the 1990s have identified the Internet as the ultimate transformer (see the reviews in Wellman 1988a). We think it useful to examine the nature of virtual community in the light of what we have learned about social networks of "real-life" community. Unfortunately, anecdotal assertions about virtual community outweigh careful accounts. These resemble the old genre of "traveler's tales," accounts of adventurous trips from the civilized world to newly discovered, exotic realms. General interest magazines appear weekly with stories about dating or doing witchcraft on the Net. *Wired* magazine appears to run such an account almost every month. *The National Geographic*'s millenium website surveys life in cyberspace.

Unfortunately, there have been few detailed ethnographic studies of virtual communities, no surveys of who is connected to whom and about what, and no time-budget accounts of how many people spend what amount of hours virtually communing. We review here what research there is about virtual community, supplemented with findings from another more widely studied other domain of computer-supported social networks called "computer-supported cooperative work" (reviewed also in Garton and Wellman 1995; Sproull and Kiesler 1991; Wellman *et al.* 1996). To fill in gaps with first-order approximations, we add germane anecdotes and travelers' tales, including our own experiences.[3] Our key questions are:

1   Are relationships on the Net narrow and specialized or are they broadly based? What kinds of support can one expect to find in virtual community?

2   How does the Net affect people's ability to sustain weaker, less intimate relationships and to develop new relationships? Why do Net participants help those they hardly know?

3   Is support given on the Net reciprocated? Do participants develop attachment to

virtual communities so that commitment, solidarity, and norms of reciprocity develop?

4   To what extent are strong, intimate relationships possible on the Net?

5   What is high involvement in virtual community doing to other forms of "real-life" community involvement?

6   To what extent does participation on the Net increase the diversity of community ties? To what extent do such diverse ties help to integrate heterogeneous groups?

7   How does the architecture of the Net affect the nature of virtual community? To what extent are virtual communities solidary groups (like traditional villages) or thinly connected Webs? Are virtual communities like "real-life" communities? To what extent are virtual communities entities in themselves or integrated into people's overall communities?

Question 1: are online relationships narrowly specialized or broadly supportive?

The standard pastoralist ideal of in-person, village-like community has depicted each community member as providing a broad range of support to all others. In this ideal situation, all can count upon all to provide companionship, emotional aid, information, services (such as child care or health care), money, or goods (be it food for the starving or a drill for the renovating).

It is not clear if such a broadly supportive situation has ever actually been the case – it might well be pure nostalgia – but contemporary communities in the western world are quite different. Most community ties are specialized and do not form densely knit clusters of relationships. For example, our Toronto research has found that except for kin and small clusters of friends, most members of a person's community network do not really know each other. Even close relationships usually provide only a few kinds of social support. Those who provide emotional aid or small services are rarely the same ones who provide large services, companionship, or financial aid. People do get all kinds of support from community members but they have to turn to different ones for different kinds of help. This means that people must maintain differentiated portfolios of ties to obtain a wide variety of resources. In market terms, they must shop at specialized boutiques for needed resources instead of casually dropping in at a general store (Wellman and Wortley 1990; Wellman 1992b).

Although much of the current literature shows that one can find various kinds of social resources on the Net, there is no systematic evidence about whether individual relationships are narrowly or broadly based. Our reading of travelers' tales and anecdotes suggests that while people can find almost any kind of support on the Net, most of the support available through one relationship is rather specialized.

In one respect, the Internet has continued the trend of technology fostering specialized relationships. Its structure supports both market and cooperative approaches to finding social resources in virtual communities. With more ease than in most real-life situations, people can shop around for resources within the safety and comfort of their homes or offices. Travel and search time are reduced. It is as if most North Americans lived in the heart of densely populated, heterogeneous, physically safe, big cities rather than in peripheral, low-density, homogeneous suburbs.

Net members have participated in more than 80,000 topic-oriented collective discussion groups by April 4, 1998 (Smith 1998), more than three times the number identified on January 27, 1996 (Southwick 1996; Kollock and Smith 1996). Their topics range from the political (feminist groups etc.), technical (computer hardware and soft-ware groups), to the social (abuse recovery groups, singles groups) and recreational (book reviews, hobby groups, sexual fantasy groups). On synchronous chat modes such as the IRC, people can browse through various specialized "channels" before deciding to join a particular discussion (Reid 1991; Danet *et al.* 1997). Such groups are a techno-logically-supported continuation of a long term shift to communities organized by shared interests rather than by shared place (neighborhood or village) or shared ancestry (kinship group; see the discussions in Fischer 1975; Wellman 1998).

As Net groups can focus on very specific topics, relationships in these virtual communities can be quite narrow, existing mostly for information processing (Kling 1996). The nature of the medium facilitates such relationships since people can easily post a question or comment and quickly receive information in return (Sproull and Faraj 1995). This can be important when efficiency and speed are needed. Everyday examples are the arrangement of group get-togethers, but the Net was also used to marshal resources just after the Oklahoma City bombing in April 1995. Within hours after the explosion, university students in Oklahoma had created special information sites and electronic bulletin boards on the Internet (Sallot 1995). Among other things, these information resources provided a list of names of the wounded, hospitals servicing these wounded, and locations of emergency blood-donor clinics. Not only was this source of information speedy, but some found it more accurate than television news reports. Social movements also have been organized online; for example, striking Israeli university professors have used both private and group messages on the Net to coordinate their fight against the government (Pliskin and Romm 1994; see also Marx and Virnoche 1995).

If the Net were solely a means of information exchange, then virtual communities played out over the Net would mostly contain only narrow, specialized relationships. However, information is only one of many social resources that is exchanged on the Net. Many Net members get help in electronic support groups for social, physical, and mental problems along with information about treatments, practitioners, and other resources. For example, women experiencing the same physical and emotional strains associated with menopause have found online support in knowing that others are going through the same symptoms, feelings, and concerns (Foderaro 1995). Similarly, the Net provides emotional and peer group support for recovering alcohol and drug addicts; the virtual encounters provided by electronic support groups are important supplements to regular attendance at "real-life" meetings or recovery groups (King 1994).

Emotional therapy itself has been explicitly provided through the Net. One psychiatric social worker in New York "sees" dial-in clients on a BBS:

The dynamics of the in-person interactive process itself are missing. But what online work can accomplish is to enable people to begin to explore their own thoughts and feelings without being judged. . . . Because I encounter words on screen only, my sensitivity to style as a communication itself and subtle changes in patterns of "speaking" has been heightened. Knowing what a word means to the "speaker" is particularly crucial where the communication is words on screen only. As a result, I tend to ask about the meaning of more words than I might in person. . . . Email or bulletin boards . . . can open a door for people who would not ordinarily reach out for help.

(Cullen 1995: 7)

Electronic support groups are not the only electronic groups where net surfers can find emotional support and companionship. Peter and Trudy Johnson-Lenz have facilitated online groups for twenty years, working to build self-awareness, mutually supportive activities, social change, and a sense of collective well-being. In 1978 they coined the term "groupware" to describe "computer-mediated culture": "Some parts are embodied in software, other parts in the hearts and minds of those using it" (Johnson-Lenz and Johnson-Lenz 1990: 1). At the heart of their workshops is a "virtual circle," based on non-western traditions of passing around sacred "talking sticks." Software tools rearrange communication structures, vary exchange settings, mark group rhythms, and encourage non-contributing voyeurs to express themselves (Johnson-Lenz and Johnson-Lenz 1990, 1994).

Even when online groups are not designed to be supportive, they tend to be. As social beings, those who use the Net seek not only information but also companionship, social support, and a sense of belonging. For example, while the majority of elderly users of "SeniorNet" reported joining the Net to gain access to information, nearly half (47 percent) had also joined to find companionship. Indeed, the most popular activity was chatting with others. Over a four-month period, the most heavily used features of SeniorNet were email, "forum," and "conferencing" (social uses) while such information access features as "news," "bulletin board," "library," and "database" were the least used. Moreover, SeniorNet provides access to grief counselors who would otherwise be inaccessible. One member noted that "if I am unable to sleep at night, all I have to do is go to my computer and there's always someone to talk to, laugh with, exchange ideas" (Furlong 1989: 149).

There are numerous other examples of the online availability of emotional support, companionship, and advice in addition to information (e.g. Hiltz *et al.* 1986; Rice and Love 1987; Rheingold 1993; Sproull and Faraj 1995). An informal support group sprung up inadvertently in a "Young Scientists' Network" established to provide postdoctoral physicists with job-hunting tips, funding information, and news stories (Sproull and Faraj 1995). Similarly, the private mailing list, "Systers," was originally designed for the exchange of information among female computer scientists, but turned into a forum for companionship and social support (Sproull and Faraj 1995). In another case, the members of a university computer science laboratory use email extensively for emotional support. As much of their time is spent online, it is natural for them to communicate these problems to confidants by email. When confidants receive an online message of distress on their own screens, it is easy for them to respond by email (Haythornthwaite *et al.* 1995).

Emotional support, companionship, information, making arrangements, and providing a sense of belonging are all non-material social resources that are relatively easy to provide from the comfort of one's computer. They usually do not require major investments of time, money, or energy. But skeptics (e.g. Stoll 1995) ask about the quality as well as the narrowness of such support. Consider the following colloquy:

> On the Internet . . . , people would put words like "grin" or "smile" or "hug" in parentheses in a note. It's a code meaning cyberhugs, cybersmiles, cyberkisses. But at bottom, that cyberkiss is not the same thing as a real kiss. At bottom, that cyberhug is not going to do the same thing. There is a big difference.
>
> (Mark Slouka in Barlow *et al.* 1995: 42)

> Yes, there is a difference. But I wasn't without the warmth of my friends. I got a lot of hugs during that period, and I still get them. My community was around me. I mean, it wasn't a case of either/or. I didn't have to give up the human embrace in order to have this other, slightly larger form of human embrace, a kind of meta-embrace. One supplemented the other.
>
> (John Perry Barlow in Barlow *et al.* 1995: 42)

To address this issue, we can only be like Slouka and Barlow and provide anecdotes, rather than more persuasive evidence from controlled experiments, detailed ethnographies, or systematic surveys. There are many examples of online support that are more than ephemeral. For instance, when David Alsberg, a 42-year-old computer programmer, was murdered in New York City, his Net friends organized online to solicit recipes and compile an electronic cookbook whose proceeds support a trust fund for the Alsberg family (Lewis 1994). In another case, when Mike Godwin's belongings were destroyed in a blaze while moving to Washington, his "cyberspace neighbors" on the "WELL" community responded by sending boxes of books to him over six months (Lewis 1994).

In addition to worrying about the reduced bandwidth of the supportive communication provided online as opposed to in-person, some pundits are concerned that the Net may be becoming a repository of misleading information. In 1995, a *Wall Street Journal* article proclaimed that the "pioneers" or veteran users of the Internet were rejecting the electronic medium, overwhelmed by the "sludge" of information that is overpowering Usenet (Chao 1995). Critics worry about the overwhelming number of people "who don't have a clue, who are posting questions because they can, not because they have something to offer" (James Bidzo, president of RSA Data Security Inc. and a twenty-year veteran of online communication, quoted in Chao 1995). This concern is shared by health care professionals who criticize online services for functioning as repositories of erroneous information and bad advice (Foderaro 1995).

Such worries discount the fact that people have always given each other advice. Before life on the Net, people did not always go to experts, be they mechanics for their cars, doctors for their bodies, or therapists for their psyches. For example, the health care literature has many accounts of the "lay referral network," giving community members advice on what their ailments were, what remedies to use, and which doctors or alternative healers to use (Beverly Wellman 1995). To some extent, the Net has just made the process more accessible and more visible to others, including experts whose claims to monopolies on advice are threatened (Abbott 1988).

Yet information supplied over the Net is not like information flows through other relationships, for the Net's speed and potentially greater connectivity can accelerate the spread of (mis)information (Gurak, Chapter 10 in this volume), as people often send messages to scores of friends and to large discussion lists (DLs). For example, the night we were completing a draft of this chapter, we received an email warning from a friend about a "brand-new" "Good Times" computer virus transmitted by email that could destroy our hard disk. Yet we have received the identical warning about the alleged "Good Times" virus eleven times in the past four years. Although the initial warning message was a hoax, the persons who sent it on did so in good faith and were thoroughly alarmed about the possibility of their friends' computers becoming infected. While the speed of the Net allows such information to be disseminated speedily and quickly, fortunately the ability of Net mail systems to maintain logs of who sent and received messages facilitates the correction of misinformation.

It seems as if messages transmitted through the Net can merge the "two-step flow of communication" (Katz and Lazarsfeld 1955) into one step, combining the rapid dissemination of mass media with the persuasiveness of personal communications. The warnings about this non-existent virus usually arrive in clusters, so that when one comes it is likely to be followed by several others. This redundant clustering occurs because messages are broadcast to friends, and such friends are often friends of each other.

Question 2: in what ways are the many weak ties on the Net useful?

Virtual communities may resemble real-life communities in the sense that support is available, often in specialized relationships. But Net members are distinctive in providing information, support, companionship, and a sense of belonging to persons they hardly know offline or who are total strangers. Anecdotes from virtual communities and more systematic accounts of computer-supported cooperative work provide ample evidence of the usefulness of accessing new information from weak ties on the Net (Constant et al. 1996; Garton and Wellman 1995; Harasim and Winkelmans 1990). For example, 58 percent of the messages on an organization's DL came from strangers (Finholt and Sproull 1990; Kiesler and Sproull 1988).

A few commentators have warned about the consequences of making affiliations in an electronic medium teeming with strangers whose biographies, social positions and social networks are unknown (Stoll 1995; Chao 1995; Sproull and Faraj 1995). But Net users tend to trust strangers, much like people gave rides to hitchhikers in the flowerchild days of the 1960s. For example, some Net users hide their identities and addresses by using a remailing service that claims to accept all messages and forward them to designated recipients while hiding the original sender's name and email address. Such a service could be of use to those wanting to disturb the established order or to harass others, yet users must trust the service to keep their identities secret and forward their messages to the intended recipients. The best known service claimed to be in Finland, but for all the users know might have been operated by the CIA, the KGB, the Mafia, or Microsoft.

This willingness to communicate with strangers online contrasts with in-person situations where by-standers are often reluctant to intervene and help strangers (Latané and Darley 1976). Yet by-standers are more apt to intervene when they are the only ones around (and most reluctant when there are many others) and requests are read by solitary individuals, alone at their screens. Even if the online request is to a newsgroup and not to a specific person, as far as the recipient of the request knows, he or she may be the only one available who could provide help. Yet online assistance will be observed by the entire newsgroup and positively rewarded by its members (Kollock and Smith 1996). Moreover, it is easier to withdraw from problematic situations when they are online – all you have to do is "exit" the Net session – than it is to withdraw from face-to-face interactions.

The lack of status or situational cues can also encourage contact between weak ties. Often, the only thing known about others are email addresses which may provide minimal or misleading information (Slouka 1995). The relatively egalitarian nature of Net contact can encourage responses to requests. By contrast, the cues associated with in-person contact transmit information about gender, age, race, ethnicity, lifestyle and socioeconomic status, and clique membership (Garton and Wellman 1995; Hiltz and Turoff 1993). Online interaction can also generate a culture of its own, as when humorous stories (or virus warnings) sweep the Net, coming repeatedly to participants. Indeed, the Net is fostering a revival of folk humor. At times, the velocity and proliferation of this communication can have consequences as when the broad circulation of "Intel Insied" [sic] jokes helped create successful pressure for replacing faulty Pentium computer chips.

Online and offline, weak ties are more apt than strong ties to link people with different social characteristics. Such weak ties are also a better means than strong ties of maintaining contact with other social circles (Granovetter 1973). This suggests that the kind of people you know is more important for obtaining information than the number of people you know. For example, in one large organization, people were better able to solve problems when they received suggestions online from people with a wide range of social characteristics than when they received suggestions from a larger number of socially similar people (Constant et al. 1996).

Question 3: is there reciprocity online and attachment to virtual communities?

It is a general norm of community that whatever is given ought to be repaid, if only to ensure that more is available when needed. Repayment of support and social resources might be in the form of exchanges of the same kind of aid, reciprocating in another way, or helping a mutual friend in the network. For example, the real-life communities of the Torontonians we are studying are reciprocal and supportive overall. Almost all can get a wide range of help from somewhere in their network. Their diversified portfolios of ties provide access to a wide variety of network members and resources (Wellman and Nazer 1995).

The problem of motivation for giving support in a virtual community arises when we consider that many of the exchanges that take place online are between persons who have never met face-to-face, have only weak ties, and are not bound into densely knit community structures that can enforce norms of reciprocity. Some analysts have suggested that the greater the social and physical distance between the support seeker and provider (i.e. the weaker the tie), the less likely that reciprocity will take place. This suggests that there may be little motivation for individuals to provide assistance, information, and support to physically and socially distant others on the Net since they are less likely to be rewarded or provided with support in return (Thorn and Connolly 1987; Constant et al. 1996).

Nevertheless, there is substantial evidence of reciprocal supportiveness on the Net, even between weak ties (Hiltz et al. 1986). Constant et al.'s (1996) study of information sharing in an organization suggests two explanations for this reciprocity (see also Constant et al. 1994). One is that the process of providing support and information on the Net is a means of expressing one's identity, particularly if technical expertise or supportive behavior is perceived as an integral part of one's self-identity. Helping others can increase self-esteem, respect from others, and status attainment.

Meyer's (1989) study of the computer underground supports this social psychological explanation. When they are involved in illegal activities, computer hackers must protect their personal identities with pseudonyms. If hackers use the same nicknames repeatedly, this can help the authorities to trace them. Nevertheless, hackers are reluctant to change their pseudonyms regularly because the status associated with a particular nickname would be lost. With a new nickname, they would have to begin the process of gaining the group's respect all over again. If they are not seen to contribute, the hackers would not be recognized as community members.

Norms of generalized reciprocity and organizational citizenship are another reason for why people help others online (Constant et al. 1996). People who have a strong attachment to the organization will be more likely to assist others with organizational problems. Such norms typically arise in a densely knit community, but they appear to be common among frequent contributors to distribution lists and newsgroups. People having a strong attachment to an electronic group will be more likely to participate and provide assistance to others. As Kollock and Smith (1996) argue:

> Whatever the goal of the newsgroup, its success depends on the active and ongoing contributions of those who choose to participate in it. If the goal of the news-group is to exchange information and answer questions about a particular topic, participants must be willing to answer questions raised by others, summarize and post replies to queries they have made themselves and pass along information that is relevant to the group.
>
> (Kollock and Smith 1996: 116)

Group attachment is intrinsically tied to norms of generalized reciprocity and aiding mutual friends. People having positive regard for the social system in which requests for assistance are embedded are likely to show respect for that system by offering their help either directly to others who have helped them in the past or to total strangers (Constant *et al.* 1996). Rheingold, a regular participant of the WELL community, writes that "the person I help may never be in a position to help me, but someone else might be" (Rheingold 1993: 60). Moreover, one of us has observed that those who have contributed actively to the BMW car network get their requests for advice answered more quickly and more widely. That is probably why people reply to the entire group when answering an individual's question.

In addition to aiding self-expression, organizational attachment, and generalized reciprocity, the Net's technological and social structures facilitate providing social support in other ways. The logistic and social costs of participating in electronic gatherings is relatively low if people have a personal computer (Sproull and Faraj 1995). People can easily participate within the comfort and safety of their own homes or offices, for any length of time they choose, and at their own convenience. Moreover, it can be quite easy to provide assistance to others when the group is large. The accumulation of small, individual acts of assistance can sustain a large community because each act is seen by the entire group and helps perpetuate an image of generalized reciprocity and mutual aid. People know that they may not receive help from the person they helped last week, but from another network member (Rheingold 1993; Barlow 1995; Lewis 1994).

Question 4: are strong, intimate ties possible online?

Even if weak ties flourish in virtual communities, does the narrower bandwidth of computer-mediated communication work against the maintenance of socially close, strong ties? When people chat, get information, and find support on the Net, do they experience real community or just the inadequate simulacra about which Jim Hightower and Mark Slouka have warned?[4] The test is to see if the Net creates and sustains the socially close, strong, intimate ties that are the core of community. Personal relationship theorists tell us that the stronger a tie, the more intensely it exhibits these characteristics:

- (1) a sense of the relationship being intimate and special, (2) with a voluntary investment in the tie and (3) a desire for companionship with the tie partner;

- (4) an interest in being together as frequently as possible (5) in multiple social contexts (6) over a long period;
- (7) a sense of mutuality in the relationship (8) with the partner's needs known and supported;
- (9) intimacy often bolstered by shared social characteristics such as gender, socio-economic status, stage in the life cycle, and lifestyle.

(Perlman and Fehr 1987; Blumstein and Kollock 1988)

In practice, many strong ties do not contain most of these characteristics. For example, intimates living abroad may rarely be seen or offer social support, while many frequently seen relationships are with neighbors and co-workers whose relationships rarely are intimate, voluntary, or supportive (Wellman *et al.* 1988). So this list of nine characteristics is more a typology with which to evaluate the strength of online relationships than it is an accurate depiction of the actual nature of strong ties.

Strong online ties have many characteristics similar to strong offline ties. They encourage (4) frequent, (3) companionable contact and are (2) voluntary except in work situations. One or two keystrokes are all that is necessary to begin replying, facilitating (7) reciprocal mutual (8) support of tie partners' needs. Moreover, the placelessness of email contact facilitates (6) long-term contact, without the loss of the tie that so often accompanies geographical mobility.

But if the relationships are companionate and supportive, are they (1) truly intimate and special enough to be strong ties, and do they tend to operate (5) in multiple social contexts? Part of the fears of pundits about the inability of the Net to sustain strong ties is wrongly specified. Pundits, both enthusiasts and critics of virtual community, usually speak of relationships as being solely online. Their fixation on the technology leads them to ignore the abundant accounts of community ties operating both online and offline, with the Net being just one of several ways of communicating. Despite all the talk about virtual community transcending time and space *sui generis*, much contact is between people who see each other in person and live locally. Our research into a less trendy communication medium, the telephone, found that Torontonians spoke more with people who live nearby than they did with those far away. Their calls filled in the gaps between in-person meetings, and made arrangements for future get-togethers (Wellman 1996).

Yet some relationships are principally sustained online. Can they be strong? Some analysts have argued that the comparatively low bandwidth of computer-mediated communication cannot by itself sustain strong ties (Beniger 1987; Jones 1995; Stoll 1995). They argue that without physical and social cues or immediate feedback, email can foster extreme language, difficulties in coordination and feedback, and group polarization (Kiesler and Sproull 1992; Hiltz and Turoff 1993). Perhaps the medium itself does not support strong, intimate relationships; or as neo- McLuhanites might say, the medium may not support the message (McLuhan 1965). Thus Clifford Stoll (1995: 24) worries that intimacy is illusory in virtual community: "Electronic communication is an instantaneous and illusory contact that creates a sense of intimacy without the emotional investment that leads to close friendships."

The debate is not yet resolved because scholarly research thus far has focused on the presence of supportive, intimate relationships in online work situations rather than in virtual communities. (However, as noted above, the supportiveness of online co-workers has been an unexpected outcome of what had originally been seen as an instrumental, limited-bandwidth medium focused on the exchange of information.) In one study, some participants came to feel that their closest friends were members of their electronic group, whom they seldom or never saw (Hiltz and Turoff 1993). Walther (1995) similarly argues that online relationships are socially close, suggesting that groups of people interacting on the Net become more personal and intimate over time. He points out that most research experiments analyze social interactions within a limited time frame, missing the nuances of later interactions and the potential for relationships to grow closer over time. He argues that the medium does not prevent close relationships from growing but simply slows the process. Relational development takes longer online than in face-to-face interactions because communication is usually asynchronous (and slower) and the available bandwidth offers less verbal and non-verbal information per exchange. Walther's experiments comparing groups of undergraduates online and in-person meetings suggest that over time, online interactions are as sociable or intimate as in-person interactions. In other words, the Net does not preclude intimacy.

There has been little systematic analysis of the nature and longevity of online intimacy, other than experiments with university students or serendipitous observations of intimacy observed in computer-supported cooperative work (reviewed in Garton and Wellman 1995). Despite lurid media reports, there may not be much anti-social behavior online other than uttering hostile "flaming" remarks and "spamming" individuals and DLs with profuse junk mail. However, social psychological studies report that CSSNs seem to foster uninhibited discussion, non-conforming behavior, and group polarization (Kiesler et al. 1985; Sproull and Kiesler 1991; Walther et al. 1994). Studies of Usenet groups (e.g. Kollock and Smith 1996) report extensive free-rider "lurking" (reading others' comments without contributing). Although lurking does not support the group, because it is not easily observed online it is less detrimental to group morale than is similar behavior in face-to-face situations.

With respect to longevity, there are no statistics of (6) how long lasting are Internet relationships, although one study shows that people are more apt to participate actively in those online groups that they perceive to be long lasting (Walther 1994). We do note that the durability of real-life strong ties may be more pastoralist myth than current reality. For example, only 27 percent of Torontonians' six socially closest real-life community ties remained close a decade later (Wellman et al. 1997).

To be sure, there are numerous anecdotes about anti-social behavior online, such as confidence men betraying the innocent, entrepreneurs "spamming" the Net with unwanted advertisements, online stalkers harassing Net members, and scoundrels taking on misleading roles. The most widely reported stories seem to be about men posing online as women and seducing other women (e.g. Slouka 1995), but the accounts suggest that these are probably rare incidents. Moreover, masquerading can have a playful, creative aspect allowing people to try on different roles: such systems as the real-time

IRC (Reid 1991) and the asynchronous EIES (Hiltz and Turoff 1993) encourage role-playing by permitting participants to communicate by nicknames.

A much greater threat to community relationships is the ease by which relationships are disrupted. The literature on flaming shows that the narrower bandwidth of communication facilitates the misinterpretation of remarks and the asynchronous nature of most conversations hinders the immediate repair of damages.

What of (5) multiplexity, the strengthening of relationships through interactions in multiple roles and social arenas? In multiplex relationships, a neighbor may become a friend, or a friendship may broaden from a single shared interest. The Net supports both narrowly specialized and broadly multiplex relationships. Usenet groups and distribution lists focus on special interests, although online relationships often broaden over time. For example, one of us has observed that frequent participants on the BMW DL know little about each other besides the model of car they drive and their level of expertise about repairs. Indeed, the rules of that DL forbid comments unrelated to BMWs.

Our observations of such groups suggest that many online interactions are what Wireman (1984) calls "intimate secondary relationships": informal, frequent and supportive community ties that nevertheless operate only in one specialized domain. Although Wireman formulated her analysis on the basis of in-person groups, such as voluntary organizations, they are quite relevant to the understanding of relationships online.

Question 5: how does virtual community affect "real-life" community?

Several writers have expressed fears that high involvement in virtual community will move people away from involvement in real-life communities, that are sustained by face-to-face, telephone, and postal contact. Certainly there are stories of "cyberaddicts" whose great involvement in online relationships turns them away from real-life relationships with family and friends (Hiltz and Turoff 1993; Barlow 1995; Rheingold 1993; Kling 1996; *Newsweek* 1995). Addiction may even create "cyber-widows" as when O'Neill (1995) reports: "I was coming home later and later. My wife thought I'd started drinking again. I lose all sense of time once I get online. I'm an addict."

Such fears are misstated in several ways. For one thing, they treat community as a zero-sum game, assuming that if people spend more time interacting online they will spend less time interacting in "real life." Second, such accounts demonstrate the strength and importance of online ties, and not their weakness. As we have seen in the previous section, strong, intimate ties can be maintained online as well as face-to-face. It is the siren call of the virtual community that appears to be luring some people away from "real life." We believe that critics who disparage the authenticity of such strong, online ties are being unwarrantedly snobbish in disregarding the seriousness with which Net participants take their relationships.[5]

Third, we suspect that the excitement about the implications of email for community implicitly sets up a false comparison between email-based virtual communities and face-to-face-based real-life communities. In fact, most contemporary communities in the developed world do not resemble rural or urban villages where all know all and have frequent face-to-face contact. Rather, most kith and kin live further away than a walk (or short drive), so that telephone contact sustains ties as much as face-to-face get-togethers (Wellman *et al.* 1988). Indeed, even community members living in the same neighborhood rely on telephone contact to maintain relationships in-between face-to-face encounters (Wellman 1996). While people now take telephone contact for granted, it was seen as recently as the 1940s as an exotic, depersonalized form of communication (Fischer 1992). We suspect that as online communication becomes widely used and routinely accepted, the current fascination with it will decline sharply. It will be seen much as telephone contact is now and letter writing was in Jane Austen's time: a reasonable way to maintain strong and weak ties between people who are not in a position to have a face-to-face encounter at that moment. Indeed, there are times when people prefer email contact to face-to-face contact because they can better control their communication and presentation of self, and they do not have to spend time at that moment dealing with the other person's response.

Fourth, people do not neatly divide their worlds into two discrete sets: people seen in-person and people contacted online. Rather, many community ties connect offline as well as online. It is the relationship that is the important thing, and not the communication medium. Email is only one of multiple ways by which a relationship is sustained. For example, a set of university computer scientists intermingle in-person and email communication, often using email to arrange in-person get-togethers (Haythornthwaite *et al.* 1995; Finholt and Sproull 1990). In another example, employees in a small office communicate by email while they physically work side-by-side. This allows them to chat while giving the appearance of working diligently at their computers (Garton 1995). In such situations, conversations started on one medium may continue on others. As with the telephone and the fax, the lower bandwidth of email may be sufficient to maintain strong ties between persons who know each other well. Thus "invisible colleges" of scholars communicate over wide distances through email and other media (Kaufer and Carley 1993), while kinship networks use the Net to arrange weddings and out-of-town visits.

Fifth, although many online relationships remain specialized, the inclusion of email addresses in messages and DL headers provides the basis for more multiplex relationships to develop between participants (Rheingold 1993; King 1994; Hiltz and Turoff 1993). For example, King's survey of recovering addicts on electronic support groups reported that 58 percent of respondents made contact with other Net acquaintances by phone, postal mail, or face-to-face (King 1994). His findings corroborate Walther's aforementioned hypothesis (1995): the longer an addict frequented the electronic support group, the more likely the addict was to contact others offline. Such multiplexity has also been found elsewhere: "During and following Conference '72, a very significant portion of the participants altered their business and vacation travel plans so as to include a face-to-face meeting with one another" (Hiltz and Turoff 1993: 114).

As in this situation, the development of multiplexity can involve the conversion of relationships that operate only online to ones that include in-person and telephonic encounters. Just as community ties that began in-person can be sustained through email, online ties can be reinforced and broadened through in-person meetings. In the absence of social and physical cues, people are able to meet and get to know one another on the Net and then decide whether to take the relationship into a broader realm. For example, in a newsgroup devoted to the topic of planning weddings, one of us observed a woman explaining that some of her guests would include people she has never seen but has known for some time from the Net.

In sum, the Net supports a variety of community ties, including some that are quite close and intimate. But while there is legitimate concern about whether true intimacy is possible in relationships that operate only online, the Net promotes the functioning of intimate secondary relationships and weaker ties. Nor are such weaker ties insignificant. Not only do such ties sustain important, albeit more-specialized, relationships, but the vast majority of informal interpersonal ties are weak ties, whether they operate online or face-to-face. Current research suggests that North Americans usually have more than 1,000 interpersonal relations, but that only a half-dozen of them are intimate and no more than 50 are significantly strong (Kochen 1989; Wellman 1992b). Yet, in the aggregate, a person's other 950+ ties are important sources of information, support, companionship, and a sense of belonging.

Question 6: does the Net increase community diversity?

To this point, we have considered the ability of the Net to support community ties. But a community is more than the sum of a set of ties: its composition and network structure affect how it supplies companionship, supportiveness, information, and a sense of identity.

Consider two types of communities. The traditional communities of pastoralist nostalgia have been densely knit, village-like structures composed of socially similar community members. Their composition and structure gives them the communication capacity to coordinate and control the supply of supportive resources to needy community members. Yet they tend to be all-encompassing, with less scope for innovation. In contemporary western societies, such traditional communities are typically found in isolated rural areas or enclaves of poor immigrants (e.g. Gans 1962), but even such communities have significant ties with the outside world (Allen and Dillman 1994).

Most contemporary western communities do not resemble preindustrial villages for they are socially diverse, sparsely knit, and well connected to the outside world (Wellman *et al.* 1988). These are only partial communities which do not command a person's full allegiance. Rather, each person is a limited member of multiple communities such as kinship groups, neighborhoods, and friendship circles. These heterogeneous, low-density communities do not control members as well as community villages, for disgruntled participants can always shift their attentions to other arenas. Although such communities do not control resources as well as village-like structures, they are better at acquiring resources from elsewhere. The multiple, ramifying communities expose each member to a more diverse set of social worlds, with heterogeneous, non-redundant sources of information and social support (Fischer 1975).

Although MUDs and similar role-playing environments at times resemble village-like structures in the ways they capture some participants' attention (see Chapters 5 and 6 by Reid and DuVal Smith in this volume), people rarely spend their full time in these environments. Rather, the tendency of the Net is to foster participation in multiple, partial communities. People often subscribe to multiple discussion lists and newsgroups. They can easily send out messages to personal lists of their own making, perhaps keeping different lists for different kinds of conversations. Moreover, they can vary in their involvements in different communities, participating actively in some, occasionally in others, and being silent "lurkers" in still others.

Such communities develop new connections easily. The Net makes it easy to ask distant acquaintances and strangers for advice and information via email (distribution lists, newsgroups, etc.). When one's strong ties are unable to provide information, one is likely to find it from weak ties. Strong ties are more likely to be socially similar and to know the same persons; hence they are more apt to possess the same information. By contrast, new information is more apt to come through weaker ties better connected to other, more diverse social circles (Granovetter 1973).

The Net encourages the expansion of community networks. Information may come unsolicited through DLs, newsgroups, and forwarded messages from friends who "thought you might like to know about this." Friends forward communications to third parties, and in so doing, they provide indirect contact between previously disconnected people who can then make direct contact. Newsgroups and discussion lists provide permeable, shifting sets of participants, with more intense relationships continued by private email. The resulting relaxation of constraints on the size and proximity of one's "communication audience" on the Net can increase the diversity of people encountered (Lea and Spears 1995).

The Net's relative lack of social richness can foster contact with more diverse others. The lack of social and physical cues online makes it difficult to ascertain whether another Net member has similar social characteristics or attractive physical charac-teristics (Sproull and Kiesler 1986), and Net norms discourage asking outright if someone is high or low status, handsome or ugly. (As one pooch in a *New Yorker* cartoon says to another, "On the Internet, nobody knows if you're a dog." [Steiner 1993]) Thus the Net's lack of in-person involvement can provide participants with more control over the timing and content of their self-disclosures (Walther 1995). This allows relationships to develop on the basis of communicated shared interests rather than be stunted at the onset by perceived differences in social status (Hiltz and Turoff 1993; Coate 1994).

This focus on shared interests rather than on similar characteristics can be empowering for otherwise lower-status and disenfranchised groups. Consider, for example, "Amy's" situation in Douglas Coupland's novel, *Microserfs*:

> [Amy] told me that all her life people had only ever treated her like a body or a girl – or both. And interfacing with [her virtual lover] Michael over the Net [where she used the gender-obscure alias, "Bar Code"] was the only way she could ever really know that he was talking to *her*, not with his concept of her. "Reveal your gender on the Net, and you're toast." She considered her situation. "It's an update

of the rich man who poses as a pauper and finds the princess. But fuck that princess shit – we're both *kings*."

(Coupland 1995: 334)

As Amy/Bar Code observes, social characteristics do not disappear entirely from the Net. Women, in particular, may receive special attention from male Net members and may feel uncomfortable (or be made to feel uncomfortable) in participating actively (Herring 1996; O'Brien, Chapter 4 in this volume). This may well be a function of the high ratio of men to women on the Net (Pitkow and Kehoe 1995).

Possibilities for diverse communities depend also on the population of the Net having diverse social characteristics. Yet a survey of "Web users" in spring 1995 found that women comprised less than one-fifth of their sample, although the proportion of women users had doubled in the past six months (Pitkow and Kehoe 1995; the authors note that their convenience sample may not be representative). The survey reported that about two-thirds of sampled Web users had at least a university education, had an average household income of US$59,600, and three-quarters lived in North America (Gupta *et al.* 1995).

Because most friends and relatives live a long drive or airplane ride away, it is often easier to maintain relationships online than it is to get together face-to-face (Wellman *et al.* 1988). Indeed, people's allegiance to the Net's communities of interest may be more powerful than their allegiance to their neighborhood communities because those involved in the same virtual community may share more interests than those who live on the same block. Howard Rheingold expresses his attachment to the parenting conference on the WELL in the following terms:

People you know as fierce, even nasty intellectual opponents in other contexts give you emotional support on a deeper level, parent to parent, within the boundaries of "Parenting", a small but warmly human corner of cyberspace.

(Rheingold 1993: 18).

Community on the basis of shared interests can foster another form of homogeneity. Despite the medium's potential to connect diverse cultures and ideas, we suspect that people are generally drawn to electronic groups that link them with others sharing common interests or concerns. Sole involvement in one Net group may have a de-individuating effect, where the lack of information about personal characteristics may promote attraction between people only on the basis of their membership in that group (Lea and Spears 1992).

Question 7: are virtual communities "real" communities?

Despite the limited social presence of online links, the Net successfully maintains strong, supportive community ties, and it may be increasing the number and diversity of weak ties. The Net is especially suited to maintaining intermediate-strength ties between people who cannot see each other frequently. Online relationships are based more on shared interests and less on shared social characteristics. Although many relationships function offline as well as online, CSSNs are developing norms and structures of their own. They are not just pale imitations of "real life." The Net is the Net.

The limited evidence available suggests that the relationships people develop and maintain in cyberspace are much like most of the ones they develop in their real-life communities: intermittent, specialized, and varying in strength. Even in real life, people must maintain differentiated portfolios of ties to obtain a wide variety of resources. But in virtual communities, the market metaphor of shopping around for support in specialized ties is even more exaggerated than in real life. Indeed, the very architecture of computer networks promotes market-like situations. For example, decisions about which newsgroups to get involved in can be made from topical menus listing all available choices, while requests for help can be broadcast to a wide audience from the comfort of one's home rather than having to ask people one-by-one. Thus while online ties may be specialized, the aggregate set of ties in virtual communities are apt to provide a wide range of support.

The provision of information is a larger component of online ties than of real-life ties. Yet despite the limited social presence of online ties, companionship, emotional support, services, and a sense of belonging are abundant in cyberspace. Furthermore, while it is not possible to send material goods over the ether, the Net supports arrangements to supply goods as well as services. The mechanism or functions involved with maintaining supportive network ties exists in both virtual and "real life" community networks. Like other forms of community, virtual communities are useful means of both giving and getting social support.

Virtual communities differ from real-life communities in the basis upon which participants perceive their relationships to be intimate. People on the Net have a greater tendency to base their feelings of closeness on the basis of shared interests rather than on the basis of shared social characteristics such as gender and socio-economic status. So they are probably relatively homogeneous in their interests and attitudes just as they are probably relatively heterogeneous in the participants' age, social class, ethnicity, life-cycle stage, and other aspects of their social backgrounds. The homogeneous interests of virtual community participants may be fostering relatively high levels of empathetic understanding and mutual support (Lazarsfeld and Merton 1954; Marsden 1983).

The architecture of the Net may encourage significant alterations in the size, composition, and structure of communities. Although no study has yet provided a count of the number of ties in virtual communities, the Net's architecture supports the maintenance of a large number of community ties, especially non-intimate ties. Discussion lists and newsgroups routinely involve hundreds of members while it is easy for individuals to send hasty notes or long letters to many friends and acquaintances. The distance-free cost structure of the Net transcends spatial limits even more than the telephone, the car, or the airplane because the asynchronous nature of Net allows people to communicate over different time zones. This could allow relatively latent ties to stay in more active contact until the participants have an opportunity to get together in-person. By supporting such online contact, the Net may even foster more frequent in-person meetings between persons who might otherwise tend to forget about each other.

With regard to the structure of communities, the Net is nourishing two somewhat contradictory phenomena. Specialized newsgroups, discussion lists, and the like foster multiple memberships in partial communities. At the same time, the ease of group response and forwarding can foster the folding-in of formerly separate Net participants into more all-encompassing communities.

Operating via the Net, virtual communities are glocalized. They are simultaneously more global and local, as worldwide connectivity and domestic matters intersect. Global connectivity de-emphasizes the importance of locality for community; online relationships may be more stimulating than suburban neighborhoods. At the same time, people are usually based at their home, the most local environment imaginable, when they connect with their virtual communities. Their lives may become even more home-centered if they telework (Wellman et al. 1996). Just as before the Industrial Revolution, home and workplace are being integrated for teleworkers, although gender roles have not been renegotiated. The domestic environment of teleworkers is becoming a vital home base for neo-Silas Marners sitting in front of their computer screens. Nests are becoming well feathered, and teleworkers will be well situated to provide the eyes on the street that are the foundation of neighboring (Jacobs 1961).

Pundits worry that virtual community may not truly be community. These worriers are confusing the pastoralist myth of community for the reality. Community ties are already geographically dispersed, sparsely knit, connected heavily by telecommunications (phone and fax), and specialized in content. There is so little community life in most neighborhoods in western cities that it is more useful to think of each person as having a personal community: an individual's social network of informal interpersonal ties, ranging from a half-dozen intimates to hundreds of weaker ties. Just as the Net supports neighborhood-like group communities of densely knit ties, it also supports personal communities, wherever in social or geographical space these ties are located and however sparsely knit they might be.

Both group communities and personal communities operate online as well as offline. Thus Wellman gets widely distributed email daily from his group communities of BMW aficionados and social network analysts. He reads all of these groups' online discussions, and all of the groups' members read his. Messages to group communities narrowly focus on the concerns of that group (Hiltz and Turoff 1993). For example, no one else in the social network analysis group is interested in BMWs, and vice versa.

At the same time, Wellman maintains an email address file of over 800 members of his personal community. As the creator, maintainer, and center of this network, he is the only one who initiates communications with this personal community. Usually, correspondents respond privately to his messages, although some email programs facilitate replies to all those who received the message. By its very nature, this personal community cuts across the specialized, partial group communities. Hence such personal communities provide the basis for cross-cutting ties that link otherwise disconnected social groups.

It is even possible that the proliferation of computer-mediated communication may produce a counter-trend to the contemporary privatization of community. In the twentieth century, community has moved indoors to private homes from its former semi-public, accessible milieus such as cafés, parks, and pubs. People in the western world are spending less time in public places waiting for friends to wander by and to introduce friends to other friends (Wellman 1992a). Even the French are going out to cafés much less often (*Economist* 1995). Instead, by-invitation private get-togethers and closed telephone chats have become the norm. This dispersion and privatization means that instead of dropping in at a café and pub and waiting for people they know to drop by, people must actively get in touch with community members to keep in contact. The result probably is a lower volume of contact among community members.

Computer mediated communication accelerates the ways in which people operate at the centers of partial, personal communities, switching rapidly and frequently between groups of ties. People have an enhanced ability to move between relationships. At the same time, their more individualistic behavior means the weakening of the solidarity that comes from being in densely knit, loosely bounded groups (Wellman 1997).

Yet virtual communities provide possibilities for reversing the trend to less contact with community members because it is so easy to connect online with large numbers of people. For example, one of us has a personal "friends" list of eighty persons and frequently sends them jokes, deep thoughts, and reports about life experiences. Such communication typically stimulates ten to twenty direct replies, plus similar messages sent out by others to their online friends. Communities such as online chat groups usefully stimulate communication in another way. Because all participants can read all messages – just as in a barroom conversation – groups of people can talk to each other casually and get to know the friends of their friends. "The keyboard is my café," William Mitchell enthuses (1995: 7).

Thus even as the Net might accelerate the trend to moving community interaction out of public spaces, it may also integrate society and foster social trust (Putnam 1995). The architecture of the Net facilitates weak and strong ties that cut across social milieus – be they interest groups, localities, organizations, or nations – so that the cyberlinks between people become social links between groups that otherwise would be socially and physically dispersed (Wellman 1988b).[6]

We have concluded this chapter more like pundits and tellers of tales than like researchers. As others before us, we have argued often by assertion and anecdote. This is because the paucity of systematic research into virtual communities has raised more questions than even preliminary answers. As one of Bellcore chief technologists noted, when "scientists talk about the evolution of the information infrastructure, . . . [we don't] talk about . . . the technology. We talk about ethics, law, policy and sociology. . . . It is a social invention" (Lucky 1995: 205).

It is time to replace anecdote with evidence. The subject is important: practically, scholarly, and politically. The answers have not yet been found. Indeed, the questions are just starting to be formulated.

Acknowledgments

A preliminary version of this chapter was presented to the annual meeting of the American Sociological Association, Session on "Reinventing Community," Washington, DC, August, 1995. We have benefited from the advice of our current colleagues on the Computer Networks as Social Networks project: Janet Salaff, Dimitrina Dimitrova, Emmanuel Koku, Laura Garton, and Caroline Haythornthwaite. We appreciate the advice provided by the editors of this book and by our computer science colleagues in the now-completed Cavecat and Telepresence projects: Ronald Baecker, William Buxton, Marilyn Mantei, and Gale Moore. Financial support for this chapter has been provided by the Social Science and Humanities Research Council of Canada (General and Strategic grants), Bell Canada, the Ontario Ministry of Science and Technology, and the Information Technology Research Centre. We dedicate this chapter to science-fiction personage, the late Judith Merril, who surfed the Net for fifty years until her death in 1997.

Notes

1 Message on the Net to the Apple Internet Users distribution list, August 3, 1995. Fittingly, the message was forwarded to Wellman in Toronto by Steven Friedman, a DL member and friend of Wellman's who lives in Israel. Yet the interaction is not solely a product of virtual community. The relationship between Wellman and Friedman developed out of a close childhood friendship of Wellman's wife and was reinforced when the Wellmans spent April 1995 in Israel.

2 We put "real life" in quotation marks because we believe that interaction over the Internet is as much real life as anything else. However, we continue to use "real life" in this chapter because it is useful to make the contrast between online relationships and other types of community ties.

3 We focus in this chapter on computer-mediated communication (CMC) systems that are primarily text-based and are primarily used for personal and recreational reasons. These include both synchronous and asynchronous modes of CMC such as the Internet, dialogue or chat lines (i.e. Internet Relay Chat), email, newsgroups, bulletin board systems, commercial networks such as America Online or Prodigy, MUDs, MOOs, etc. Although some of these systems are strictly speaking not part of the Internet, they are rapidly becoming connected to it. Hence unless we are making special distinctions, we refer here to the sum of all these systems as the "Internet" or simply, "the Net." Indeed, the Net has never been a single entity. Rather, it is a "network of networks," a form first identified by Craven and Wellman (1973). We exclude here analyses of picturephones, videoconferencing, and other forms of video-based computer-mediated communication that now are largely used in large organizations or experimentally by academics. For information on desktop video-conferencing, see Garton (1995).

4 Devotees of computer science and science fiction are already aware that virtual community members in the near future may interact via simulacra. Instead of sending text messages, animated figures will interact with each other (*Communications of the ACM* 1994). Several preliminary chat systems using graphical "avatars" already exist, such as *AlphaWorld*

on the Internet and *WorldsAway* on the *CompuServe* network. Non-graphical (text-based) "agents" have proliferated rapidly on the Net since 1995. Although these agents have largely been used to search the World Wide Web for relevant information, they should soon have the capability of interacting with the Net denizens (from files to humans) they encounter (Morris 1998).

5 Our own study of "real-life" community in Toronto provides support for accepting people's own accounts of strong ties. We asked study participants to distinguish between their intimate and less strong relationships, and we independently coded for intimacy ourselves. The correlations were extremely high (> 0.90) between the participants' own reports and our "expert" coding.

6 Of course all inter-group contact may not be benign. The Guardian Angels, a volunteer group formed in 1979 to patrol public spaces in New York City, have created "Cyber-Angels" to patrol the Net for "suspicious activity" that might indicate crimes against children or inter-group hatred. As the privatization of in-person community has emptied the streets, the Guardian Angels are going where the action is (*Atlanta Journal-Constitution* 1995).

References

Abbott, Andrew. 1988. *The System of Professions: An Essay on the Division of Expert Labor*. Chicago: University of Chicago Press.

Allen, John and Don Dillman. 1994. *Against all Odds: Rural Community in the Information Age*. Boulder, CO: Westview Press.

Atlanta Journal-Constitution. 1995. "Angels to Patrol the Net." August 6.

Barlow, John Perry. 1995. "Is There a There in Cyberspace?" *Utne Reader* March–April: 50–6.

Barlow, John Perry, Sven Birkets, Kevin Kelly and Mark Slouka. 1995. "What are we Doing On-Line?" *Harper's* August: 35–46.

Beniger, James. 1987. "Personalization of Mass Media and the Growth of Pseudo-Community." *Communication Research* 14: 352–71.

Blumstein, Philip and Peter Kollock. 1988. "Personal Relationships." *Annual Review of Sociology* 14: 467–90.

Chao, Julie. 1995. "Net Loss: The Pioneers Move On." *Toronto Globe and Mail* June 20.

Coate, John. 1994. "Cyberspace Innkeeping: Building Online Community." Online: tex@sfgate.com

Communications of the ACM. 1994. Special issue on Intelligent Agents 37 (July).

Constant, David, Sara Kiesler and Lee Sproull. 1994. "What's Mine Is Ours, or Is It? A Study of Attitudes about Information Sharing." *Information Systems Research* 5: 400–21.

Constant, David, Lee Sproull and Sara Kiesler. 1996. "The Kindness of Strangers: The Usefulness of Electronic Weak Ties for Technical Advice." *Organization Science* 7(2): 119–35.

Coupland, Douglas. 1995. *Microserfs*. New York: Regan Books.

Craven, Paul and Barry Wellman. 1973. "The Network City." *Sociological Inquiry* 43: 57–88.

Cullen, Diana List. 1995. "Psychotherapy in Cyberspace." *The Clinician* 26 (summer): 1, 6–7.

Danet, Brenda, Lucia Ruedenberg and Yehudit Rosenbaum-Tamari. 1997. "Hmmm . . . Where's All That Smoke Coming From? Writing, Play and Performance on Internet

Relay Chat." In *Network and Netplay: Viirtual Groups on the Internet*, edited by Sheizaf Rafaeli, Fay Sudweeks and Margaret McLaughlin. Cambridge: MIT Press.

Dantowitz, Aaron and Barry Wellman. 1996. "The Small World of the Internet." Presented to the Canadian Sociology and Anthropology Association, June, St. Catharines, Ont.

Economist, The. 1995. "Mais où sont les Cafés d'Antan?" June 10: 50.

Finholt, Tom and Lee Sproull. 1990. "Electronic Groups at Work." *Organization Science* 1: 41–64.

Fischer, Claude. 1975. "Toward a Subcultural Theory of Urbanism." *American Journal of Sociology* 80: 1319–41.

Fischer, Claude. 1992. *America Calling: A Social History of the Telephone to 1940*. Berkeley, CA: University of California Press.

Foderaro, Lisa. 1995. "Seekers of Self-Help Finding It On Line." *The New York Times* March 23.

Fox, Robert. 1995. "Newstrack." *Communications of the ACM* 38(8): 11–12.

Furlong, Mary S. 1989. "An Electronic Community for Older Adults: The SeniorNet Network." *Journal of Communication* 39(summer): 145–53.

Gans, Herbert. 1962. *The Urban Villagers*. New York: Free Press.

Garton, Laura. 1995. "Linking Social Networks: A Case Study of Communication Media Use in One Organization." Report to Centre for Information Technology Innovation. Laval, Que, June.

Garton, Laura and Barry Wellman. 1995. "Social Impacts of Electronic Mail in Organizations: A Review of the Research Literature." *Communication Yearbook* 18: 434–53.

Granovetter, Mark. 1973. "The Strength of Weak Ties." *American Journal of Sociology* 78: 1360–80.

Gupta, Sumit, Jim Pitkow and Mimi Recker. 1995. "Consumer Survey of WWW Users." Web site: http://www.umich.edu/sgupta/hermes.html. August 10.

Gutenberg, Johann. 1455. *The Bible* ["Forty-Two Line" or "Mazarin" edition]. Mainz: At the printer's shop. [Note: Original author's names disputed; exact publication has been out of print for a while.]

Harasim, Linda and Tim Winkelmans. 1990. "Computer-Mediated Scholarly Collaboration." *Knowledge* 11: 382–409.

Haythornthwaite, Caroline, Barry Wellman and Marilyn Mantei. 1995. "Work Relationships and Media Use: A Social Network Analysis." *Group Decision and Negotiation* 4(3): 193–211.

Herring, Susan C. 1996. "Gender and Democracy in Computer-Mediated Communication," in *Computerization and Controversy: Value Conflicts and Social Choices* (2nd edn), edited by Rob Kling. San Diego, CA: Academic Press.

Hiltz, Starr Roxanne and Murray Turoff. 1993. *The Network Nation* (2nd edn). Cambridge, MA: MIT Press.

Hiltz, Starr Roxanne, Kenneth Johnson and Murray Turoff. 1986. "Experiments in Group Decision Making: Communication Process and Outcome in Face-to-face Versus Computerized Conferences." *Human Communication Research* 13(2): 225–52.

Jacobs, Jane. 1961. *The Death and Life of Great American Cities*. New York: Random House.

Johnson-Lenz, Peter and Trudy Johnson-Lenz. 1977. "On Facilitating Networks for Social Change." *Connections* 1(2): 5–11.

Johnson-Lenz, Peter and Trudy Johnson-Lenz. 1990. "Rhythms, Boundaries, and Containers: Creative Dynamics of Asynchronous Group Life." Report to Awakening Technology.

Johnson-Lenz, Peter and Trudy Johnson-Lenz. 1994. "Groupware for a Small Planet," in *Groupware in the 21st Century*, edited by Peter Lloyd. London: Adamantine Press.

Jones, Steven. 1995. "Understanding Community in the Information Age," in *Cybersociety: Computer-Mediated Communication and Community*, edited by Steven Jones. Thousand Oaks, CA: Sage.

Katz, Elihu and Paul Lazarsfeld. 1955. *Personal Influence*. Glencoe, IL: Free Press.

Kaufer, David and Kathleen Carley. 1993. *Communication at a Distance: The Influence of Print on Sociocultural Organization and Change*. Hillsdale, NJ: Lawrence Erlbaum.

Kiesler, Sara and Lee Sproull. 1988. "Technological and Social Change in Organizational Communication Environments." Working Paper. Carnegie Mellon University.

Kiesler, Sara and Lee Sproull. 1992. "Group Decision Making and Communication Technology." *Organizational Behavior and Human Decision Processes* 52: 96–123.

Kiesler, Sara, Lee Sproull and Jacquelynne S. Eccles. 1985. "Pool Halls, Chips, and War Games: Women in the Culture of Computing." *Psychology of Women Quarterly* 9: 451–62.

King, Storm. 1994. "Analysis of Electronic Support Groups for Recovering Addicts." *Interpersonal Computing and Technology* 2(July): 47–56.

Kling, Rob. 1996. "Social Relationships in Electronic Forums: Hangouts, Salons, Workplaces and Communities," in *Computerization and Controversy: Value Conflicts and Social Choices* (2nd edn), edited by Rob Kling. San Diego, CA: Academic Press.

Kochen, Manfred (ed.). 1989. *The Small World*. Norwood, NJ: Ablex.

Kollock, Peter and Marc Smith. 1996. "Managing the Virtual Commons: Cooperation and Conflict in Computer Communities," in *Computer-Mediated Communication: Linguistic, Social, and Cross-Cultural Perspectives*, edited by Susan Herring. Amsterdam: John Benjamins.

Latané, Bibb and John Darley. 1976. *Help in a Crisis: Bystander Response to an Emergency*. Morristown, NJ: General Learning Press.

Lazarsfeld, Paul and Robert Merton. 1954. "Friendship as Social Process," in *Freedom and Control in Modern Society*, edited by Morroe Berger, Theodore Abel and Charles Page. New York: Octagon.

Lea, Martin and Russell Spears. 1992. "Paralanguage and Social Perception in Computer-Mediated Communication." *Journal of Organizational Computing* 2: 321–42.

Lea, Martin and Russell Spears. 1995. "Love at First Byte? Building Personal Relationships Over Computer Networks," in *Understudied Relationships: Off the Beaten Track*, edited by Julia T. Wood and Steve Duck. Thousand Oaks, CA: Sage.

Lewis, Peter H. 1994. "Strangers, Not Their Computers Build a Network in Time of Grief." *New York Times* March 8.

Lucky, Robert. 1995. "What Technology Alone Cannot Do." *Scientific American* 273 (September): 205.

McLuhan, Marshall. 1965. *Understanding Media*. New York: McGraw-Hill.

Marsden, Peter. 1983. "Restricted Access in Networks and Models of Power." *American Journal of Sociology* 88: 686–717.

Marx, Gary and Mary Virnoche. 1995. "'Only Connect': E.M. Forster in an Age of Computerization." Presented to the American Sociological Association, Washington, DC, August.

Meyer, Gordon. 1989. "The Sociological Organization of the Computer Underground." Master's thesis, Department of Sociology, Northern Illinois University, Dekalb, IL.

Mitchell, William. 1995. *City of Bits: Space, Time and the Infobahn*. Cambridge, MA: MIT Press.

Morris, John. 1998. "User Interfaces." *PC Magazine*, June 9: 162–63.

Newsweek. 1995. "Cyberaddicts." December 18: 60.

O'Neill, Molly. 1995. "The Lure and Addiction of Life On Line." *New York Times* March 8.

Patton, Phil. 1986. *Open Road*. New York: Simon & Schuster.

Perlman, Daniel and Beverley Fehr. 1987. "The Development of Intimate Relationships," in *Intimate Relationships*, edited by Daniel Perlman and Steve Duck. Newbury Park, CA: Sage.

Pitkow, Jim and Colleen Kehoe. 1995. "Third WWW User Survey: Executive Summary." Report to Graphic, Visualization and Usability Center, Georgia Institute of Technology.

Pliskin, Nava and Celia T. Romm. 1994. "Empowerment Effects of Electronic Group Communication: A Case Study." Working Paper, Department of Management, Faculty of Commerce, University of Wollongong.

Putnam, Robert. 1995. "Bowling Alone: America's Declining Social Capital. *Journal of Democracy* 6: 65–78.

Reid, Elizabeth M. 1991. "Electropolis: Communication and Community on Internet Relay Chat." Honours thesis, University of Melbourne.

Rheingold, Howard. 1993. *The Virtual Community: Homesteading on the Electronic Frontier*. Reading, MA: Addison-Wesley.

Rice, Ronald and Gail Love. 1987. "Electronic Emotion: Socioemotional Content in a Computer-Mediated Communication Network." *Communication Research* 14(February): 85–108

Sallot, Jeff. 1995. "Internet Overloaded after Bombing." *Toronto Globe and Mail* April 27.

Slouka, Mark. 1995. *War of the Worlds: Cyberspace and the High-Tech Assault on Reality*. New York: Basic Books.

Smith, Marc. "Netscan: A Tool for Measuring and Mapping Social Cyberspaces." April 4, 1998. Website: http://netscan.sscnet.ucla.edu/index.html.

Southwick, Scott. 1996. "Liszt: Searchable Directory of E-Mail Discussion Groups". Report to BlueMarble Information Services, January 27. Website: http://www.liszt.com.

Sproull, Lee and Samer Faraj. 1995. "Atheism, Sex and Databases: The Net as a Social Technology," in *Public Access to the Internet*, edited by Brian Kahin and James Keller. Cambridge, MA: MIT Press.

Sproull, Lee and Sara Kiesler. 1986. "Reducing Social Context Cues: Electronic Mail in Organizational Communication." *Management Science* 32: 1492–512.

Sproull, Lee and Sara Kiesler. 1991. *Connections*. Cambridge, MA: MIT Press.

Stein, Maurice. 1960. *The Eclipse of Community*. Princeton, NJ: Princeton University Press.

Steiner, Peter. 1993. "On the Internet, No One Knows You're a Dog." *New Yorker*, July 5.

Stoll, Clifford. 1995. *Silicon Snake Oil: Second Thoughts on the Information Highway*. New York: Doubleday.

Thorn, B.K. and T. Connolly. 1987. "Discretionary Data Bases: A Theory and Some Experimental Findings." *Communication Research* 14: 512–28.

Walther, Joseph B. 1994. "Anticipated Ongoing Interaction Versus Channel Effects on Relational Communication in Computer-Mediated Interaction." *Human Communication Research* 20(4): 473–501.

Walther, Joseph B. 1995. "Relational Aspects of Computer-Mediated Communication: Experimental Observations Over Time." *Organization Science* 6(2): 186–203.

Walther, Joseph B., Jeffrey F. Anderson and David W. Park. 1994. "Interpersonal Effects in

Computer-Mediated Interaction: A Meta-Analysis of Social and Antisocial Communication." *Communication Research* 21(4): 460–87.

Wellman, Barry. 1988a. "The Community Question Re-evaluated," in *Power, Community and the City*, edited by Michael Peter Smith. New Brunswick, NJ: Transaction Books.

Wellman, Barry. 1988b. "Structural Analysis: From Method and Metaphor to Theory and Substance," in *Social Structures: A Network Approach*, edited by Barry Wellman and S.D. Berkowitz. Cambridge: Cambridge University Press.

Wellman, Barry. 1992a. "Men in Networks: Private Communities, Domestic Friendships," in *Men's Friendships*, edited by Peter Nardi. Newbury Park, CA: Sage.

Wellman, Barry. 1992b. "Which Types of Ties and Networks Give What Kinds of Social Support?" *Advances in Group Processes* 207–35.

Wellman, Barry. 1996. "Are Personal Communities Local? A Dumptarian Reconsideration." *Social Networks* 18: 347–54.

Wellman, Barry. 1997 "An Electronic Group is Virtually a Social Network," in *The Culture of the Internet*, edited by Sara Kiesler. Hillsdale, NJ: Lawrence Erlbaum.

Wellman, Barry. 1998. "The Network Community," in Networks in the Global Village, edited by Barry Wellman. Boulder, CO: Westview Press.

Wellman, Barry and Nancy Nazer. 1995. "Does What Goes Around Come Around? Specific Exchange in Personal Community Networks." Presented to the International Social Network Conference, London, July.

Wellman, Barry and Scot Wortley. 1990. "Different Strokes From Different Folks: Community Ties and Social Support." *American Journal of Sociology* 96: 558–88.

Wellman, Barry, Peter Carrington and Alan Hall. 1988. "Networks as Personal Communities," in *Social Structures: A Network Approach*, edited by Barry Wellman and S.D. Berkowitz. Cambridge: Cambridge University Press.

Wellman, Barry, Janet Salaff, Dimitrina Dimitrova, Laura Garton, Milena Gulia and Caroline Haythornthwaite. 1996. "Computer Networks as Social Networks." *Annual Review of Sociology* 22: 211–38.

Wellman, Barry, Renita Wong, David Tindall and Nancy Nazer. 1997. "A Decade of Network Change: Turnover, Mobility and Stability." *Social Networks* 19: 27–50.

Wellman, Beverly. 1995. "Lay Referral Networks: Using Conventional Medicine and Alternative Therapies for Low Back Pain." *Sociology of Health Care* 12: 213–38.

Wireman, Peggy. 1984. *Urban Neighborhoods, Networks, and Families*. Lexington, MA: Lexington Books.

Chapter 8

Invisible crowds in cyberspace

Mapping the social structure of the Usenet[1]

Marc A. Smith

The Usenet is a quintessential Internet social phenomenon: it is huge, global, anarchic, and rapidly growing. It is also mostly invisible. Although it is the largest example of a conferencing or discussion group system,[2] the tools generally available to access it display only leaves and branches – chains of messages and responses. None present the trees and forest. With hundreds of thousands of new messages every day, it is impossible to try to read them all to get a sense of the entire place. As a result, an overview of activity in the Usenet has been difficult to assemble and many basic questions about its size, shape, structure and dynamics have gone unanswered. How big is the Usenet? How many people post? Where are they from? When and where do they post? How do groups vary from one another and over time? How many different kinds of groups are there? How many groups successfully thrive and how many die? What do the survivors have that the others lack? How do different social cyberspaces connect and fit together to form a larger ecology?

There is no shortage of questions. But we lack a historical record of the transformations of social cyberspaces just at the point when network interaction media are being widely adopted.[3] Cyberspace is changing the social physics of human life, broadening the size and power of group interaction. But without base-line measures of online activity, we are unable to assess if the groups being selected for study or the periods studied are typical for the groups in question. Without a general typology of these spaces there has been no systematic way to contrast research findings and integrate the results of separate research projects. The virtual blackout that cloaks interaction through networks has limited many prior studies to a narrow focus on a specific group over short periods of time (Lewenstein 1992; Pfaffenberger 1996; Phillips 1996), or on individual participants rather than the social space as a whole (Turkle 1996). As a result, attempts to broadly characterize general social processes have been based on limited samples (McLaughlin 1995). While the details of individual experiences and the events occurring in individual groups are important, research should look both at the details of individual groups and at the emergent social structure that grows out of the aggregation of tens of thousands.

Social cyberspaces can be mapped by computer-assisted analysis. In this chapter I report on the initial results of Netscan, a software tool I designed that gathers an ongoing stream of Usenet messages and maintains a database of information drawn from the header of each message. It then distills measures of activity and relationships in any collection of newsgroups selected for study.[4] This is an initial attempt to survey this emerging social landscape and address some of the limitations of existing tools for exploring them.

Data drawn from group interaction in cyberspace offer some unique opportunities for the study of social organization. One of the unique features of network-mediated communication is that almost all interactions leave behind a durable trace: electronic tracks that can provide detailed data about what vast numbers of groups of people do online. Unlike research on face-to-face social relations, online data gathering can be automated and collected over an extended period of time from vast numbers of social spaces, involving millions of people and tens of millions of messages. Longitudinal research on social cyberspaces can illustrate the ways network interaction media, and the social institutions that have emerged in them, have changed over time (Rice 1982). And, because these messages are often created in a casual manner, these data offer insight into the everyday world of many people. Online spaces become self-documenting "natural settings." And while there are a number of possible back channels of communication that limit claims to the completeness of these data, digital artifacts have the advantage of being exact copies of the messages the participants wrote or read themselves.[5] Because online interactions are often archived in their entirety, at least for a short while, the contents of entire collections of messages exchanged by a group can be examined and studied.[6] Computer-generated message headers and accurate copies of message content have even been found to be more reliable sources of data about communications activities than alternative self-reporting surveys (Bikson and Eveland 1990).

The Usenet

There are a number of reasons to start an investigation into the structure of social cyberspaces with the Usenet. Created in 1979 at the University of North Carolina, as an alternative to services available through the more elite ARPANET, the Usenet initially connected only two computers and handled a few posts or messages a day (Harrison 1995). It is now the third most widely used form of interaction media on the Internet (behind email and the World Wide Web) in terms of users. Growing from 15 newsgroups, which contained messages that collectively took up 15 kilobytes per day in 1979, the Usenet now contains more than 14,347 newsgroups carrying 6 gigabytes of messages per day. On an average day, 20,000 people post 300,000 messages. In the 150 days ending November 15, 1997 1.1 million people[7] posted at least one message each for a total of more than 14 million unique posts.[8]

The Usenet also has the largest geographic scope of systems of its type, drawing participants from nearly every corner of the globe.[9] By reviewing the email addresses of the people who post to the Usenet we can crudely measure the location of posters around the globe. While not every nation has a large population participating in the Usenet, there are few that are completely absent. Of the 250 officially recognized Internet domains, 238 are reserved for nations and recognized sovereign entities. Of those, only 33 countries have zero messages in the Usenet.[10] A significant majority of people post from the United States but the system is extremely international, drawing 59 percent of its participants from outside the US (see Table 8.1). Remarkably, the fifteenth most common region is anonymous – messages which lack headers that identify the author of the post. Information about the author of a Usenet message is stored in the FROM: line of the

Table 8.1 Top twenty national domains appearing in the Usenet

Rank	Country	Number of posters	% of total Usenet population
1	United States[11]	714,757	40.694
2	Taiwan	99,150	5.645
3	Germany	38,848	2.212
4	Britain	31,657	1.802
5	Canada	30,116	1.715
6	Australia	17,801	1.013
7	Japan	16,322	0.929
8	Italy	15,203	0.866
9	France	14,673	0.835
10	Netherlands	13,251	0.754
11	Spain	10,013	0.570
12	Finland	9,178	0.523
13	Sweden	7,994	0.455
14	Norway	7,250	0.413
15	Anonymous (Blank)	6,624	0.377
16	Poland	6,277	0.357
17	Russian Federation	6,252	0.356
18	Denmark	6,015	0.342
19	Korea (South)	4,708	0.268
20	Belgium	4,547	0.259

header. Without much trouble this line can be intentionally modified or damaged so that the author cannot be identified. This is only the most obvious and clumsy form of anonymity practiced in the Usenet. More sophisticated forms of anonymity use properly formatted addresses that point to non-existent people.

The number of people simply reading the Usenet remains a mystery but it seems safe to assume that more people read the Usenet than actively participate in it. Measurements of readership are difficult to generate because only active participants leave artifacts that can be studied.[12] Newsgroups have many silent observers for every active poster (Terveen *et al.* 1997). If we assume a ratio of 20 passive participants to each active one, there could easily be more than 20 million people reading the Usenet at least once a year.[13]

The Usenet helps structure the interactions between these millions of participants by organizing every message into a branching tree structure. As seen in Figure 8.1, each newsgroup is located within one of a number of "hierarchies" which broadly categorize all

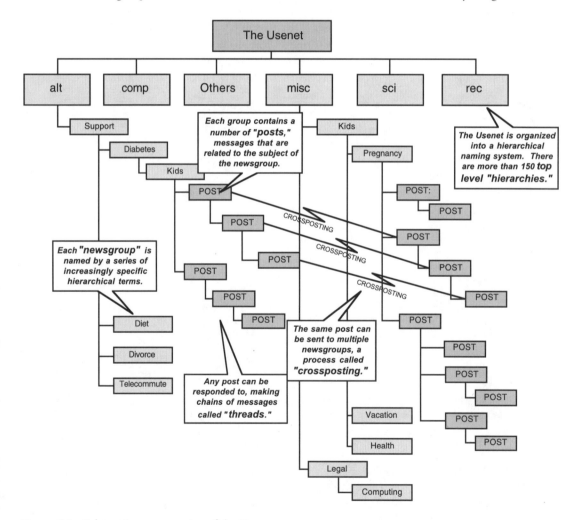

Figure 8.1   Schematic representation of the Usenet

of the topics covered in the Usenet. There are 143 widely distributed hierarchies, but a group of 8 (alt, comp, misc, news, rec, sci, soc, and talk) are the historical core of the Usenet (Salzenberg 1992). Newsgroups are named in loose accord with a number of conventions that describe their topic and goals. Groups start with one of the hierarchy names and then add words separated by periods that increasingly narrow the scope of the group, for example, "comp.lang.perl.misc," "alt.support.diabetes.kids," and "misc. kids.pregnancy."

Each newsgroup contains a collection of posts that are organized into "threads" – chains of posts linked like paper clips to one another. Any post can be "crossposted," a practice that places a copy of the message in a number of separate newsgroups.[14] Each post contains a "header" that automatically records a range of information about the post, including the email address; user name and organizational affiliation of each message's author; the subject of the message; a number that identifies each message uniquely; the date and time the message was posted by the author; a list of all the newsgroups it is intended to be distributed to; and information that locates the message within a chain of other messages.[15]

More than its size, scope, or structure, it is the Usenet's technical and social organization that makes it of particular interest. The Usenet can be divided into two main components: the technical and physical infrastructure, the computers, wires, phone lines, and software; and the social and technical structure of its content, the system of interconnected newsgroups, threads, and messages. Both the technical and social structure of the Usenet, analogous to the phone system and the conversations that take place through it, are decentralized and organized as a commons. These qualities play an important role in shaping the kinds of groups that form within it.

In contrast with systems run and managed by a single organization, the Usenet is not a commercial product and has grown without central planning or control. No single individual, group or cabal is in complete or even dominant control. None of the more than 300,000 computers around the planet that act as Usenet hosts is the central point of the entire system. Each system owner, from information system managers at large corporations and universities to individual hobbyists, decides what part of the feed to accept and what to pass on and to whom. Usenet members agree simply to accept and pass along the "feed" – the collection of messages currently being shuttled between all the Usenet "hosts" in the world. The Usenet is like an informal bucket brigade, as shown in Figure 8.2. Someone who wants to carry the contents of the Usenet only has to convince a person who already receives it to pass it along to them. The technical structure of the Usenet shares many of these qualities with the Internet itself, both are social and technical achievements that exist only because of widespread informal agreements to minimally cooperate with local partners.

This technical infrastructure is the foundation for the formation of the Usenet's social structure: tens of thousands of social spaces or "newsgroups" devoted to a huge range of interests and groups. Each newsgroup is potentially a place where people can collectively produce something that none could have created by themselves. Some are practical and convenient sources of technical support and information. Others provide entertainment, a sense of connection, membership, and mutual support. From around the

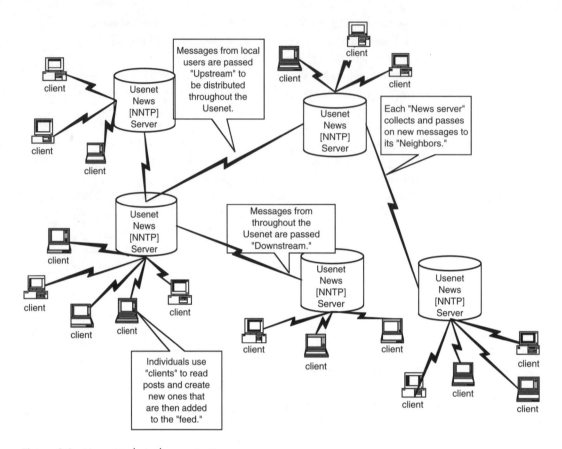

Figure 8.2 Usenet technical organization

planet, expectant mothers swap stories about their experiences in misc.kids.pregnancy, programmers with problems they can't solve on their own find guidance in comp.lang. perl.misc, video game fans offer tips to one another in comp.sys. ibm.pc.games.strategic. Newsgroups are the source of public goods, the resources produced in them are available to any one even if they do not pay for or contribute to their creation.

However, the potential for creating collective projects in these network commons does not guarantee their success. As Mancur Olson (1965) noted, "if the members of some group have a common interest or objective, and if they would all be better off if that objective were achieved, it [does not necessarily follow] that the individuals in that group act to achieve that objective." Common sense would suggest that none of the groups created through network interaction media should succeed. Nearly anonymous people from around the world with no prior introduction independently request or contribute time and expertise and freely give the result away to anyone interested without payment or coercion. Such a fanciful social organization would seem doomed to failure.

This challenge is even greater in the Usenet, since many of the resources that groups usually rely on to help maintain themselves are oddly transformed or missing. The distributed technical architecture of the Usenet has far-reaching implications for the kinds of social organizations that form within it. Most conferencing systems (for example, message boards in America Online) and alternative network interaction media (like email, chat, and MUDs) are centralized and "owned" by a single person or institution. Because they occupy a central location in their system, owners of these spaces have the ability to limit people's access and filter their contributions. In the Usenet few of the spaces are "owned" in this way.[16] As a result, it is almost impossible to stop someone from posting a message to a newsgroup or reading the messages that are already there. No one can be banned and no one can be gagged.[17] Any and every user of the Usenet potentially wields an equal and large amount of control over the entire system. This makes the Usenet about as pure a case of social anarchy as can be found in the real world. The lack of boundaries ensures that newsgroups remain a kind of commons where their contents are publicly available to any and all who are interested (Kollock and Smith 1996).

Given the challenges, it is not surprising that the tens of thousands of newsgroups that make up the Usenet are not uniformly pleasant, useful, or even entertaining. In many cases a newsgroup is a barren or cacophonous space that may yield less value than the effort it takes to be there. Many groups seem to be dedicated to non-cooperative interaction: people fill them with challenges, insults, irrelevant advertisements and lures for scams. On balance there may even be more useless material than good. The focus on failures has led to a common cliché in Usenet discussions – "Imminent death of the Usenet predicted" (Raymond 1993). But after seventeen years of repeated announcements of its impending demise, the reality is that the Usenet is a robust social institution that permanently teeters on the brink of chaos. The Usenet displays an impressive robustness,[18] sustaining useful social interaction in the face of (or perhaps because of) anarchic organization, rapid growth,[19] and intentional attacks.[20] The undeniable fact is that many people find islands of quality interaction and access valuable resources through media like the Usenet.[21] The question is not why many of these collective projects fail, but why as many that succeed do so.

Variation in social cyberspaces

But how many successes are there? The question is difficult to answer; what constitutes "successful"? An alternative and more tractable question is what kinds of interaction patterns are present in each newsgroup? What immediately becomes clear is that social cyberspaces are not all the same. The following takes each logical level of the Usenet – hierarchies, newsgroups, posts, posters, and crossposting – looking at the range of variation across the system as a whole from data collected from November 1, 1996 to January 18, 1997.

Hierarchies

Each hierarchy varies in terms of the number of groups it contains, the number of messages those groups receive, and the number of people who contribute those

Table 8.2 Top twenty hierarchies appearing in the UCLA Usenet feed

Rank	Hierarchy	Description	# Groups
1	alt:	"Alternative" groups	5,339
2	comp:	Computer related	884
3	rec:	Recreational	677
4	clari:	Clarinet commercial news service	584
5	uiuc:	University of Illinois, Urbana Champagne	406
6	microsoft:	Microsoft	355
7	fj:	Japanese Kanji groups	353
8	ucb:	University of California, Berkeley	335
9	ucla:	University of California, Los Angeles	328
10	de:	Germany	313
11	tw:	Taiwan	279
12	soc:	Social issues	258
13	bit:	Bitnet gateway newsgroups	230
14	sci:	Science	203
15	zer:	More German groups	191
16	uw:	University of Washington	169
17	sfnet:	Finland	151
18	aus:	Australia	132
19	misc:	Miscellaneous	131
20	relcom:	Russian	131

messages. As seen in Table 8.2, of all the hierarchies, "alt" is by far the largest. The "alt" hierarchy is dedicated to a range of subjects that fall outside the range covered by the other categories. "Alt" possesses 29 per cent of all newsgroups, 22 per cent of all the postings, and 24 per cent of Usenet participants. This may be because the "alt" newsgroups are a political sub-continent of the Usenet, governed by a different and less restrictive process for the creation of new newsgroups.[22] This means that the most active area of the Usenet is not covered by the same political regime that rules the others. It does not mean that this activity equates to quality, value, or user satisfaction. But it does suggest that the difference in social regulation plays a role in the difference in activity.

Newsgroups

It is not easy to measure the exact number of newsgroups. The Usenet's architecture, essentially an amorphous distributed database, causes it to look different depending on the news server from which it is viewed, making claims to the completeness of any study questionable. Since every local news server's feed is partial (almost no single news server takes every newsgroup), a truly complete picture of the Usenet may be impossible to generate.[23] Netscan studies show more than 79,000 newsgroups exist worldwide (although many may be only locally distributed). Of these, my study collected data on the 14,347 groups carried in the UCLA news server's feed.[24]

Posts

Newsgroups do not all receive the same number of messages. A full fifth of the newsgroups studied were entirely empty.[25] Many newsgroups (42 percent) held fewer than 100 messages in the ten-week period studied. A significant mid-range of newsgroups (23 percent) contains between 100 and 1,000 messages over this period. The remaining messages are distributed throughout a smaller set (7 percent) of "super newsgroups" that contain more than 1,000 posts. At the very top of the scale are a tiny collection of 163 newsgroups (~1 percent) that range from more than 1,000 to as many as 250,000 messages over the entire period. In general, the Usenet is mostly filled with small newsgroups with a moderate amount of message traffic.

The three largest, and seven of the top ten newsgroups in terms of numbers of messages, are devoted to job announcements (Table 8.3). While these job-related groups, many with a specific regional focus, are the largest throughout the entire Usenet, they have dramatically fewer participants than smaller groups dedicated to other topics. Many of the messages in these groups are posted by commercial organizations soliciting job applications for technology-related positions and are more like broadcast channels than social interaction spaces.

Table 8.3 Top ten newsgroups in terms of message volume, November 1, 1996 to January 18, 1997

Rank	Group	#Posts	#Posters	Poster-to-post ratio	Crosspost degree	#Articles crossposted
1	misc.jobs.offered	232,612	5,184	0.022	793	217,845
2	biz.jobs.offered	217,472	3,227	0.015	648	202,977
3	ba.jobs.offered	210,562	2,249	0.011	433	169,611
4	misc.jobs.contract	98,803	2,353	0.024	481	95,731
5	alt.jobs	76,605	1,438	0.019	537	76,600
6	ba.jobs.contract	29,077	1,139	0.039	246	27,850
7	news.newusers.questions	27,332	12,012	0.439	827	6,470
8	comp.sys.ibm.pc.hardware.video	25,293	5,576	0.220	374	8,579
9	tx.jobs	20,741	931	0.045	335	19,394
10	comp.sys.ibm.pc.games.strategic	20,482	5,055	0.247	221	7,987

Posters

The groups of people that contribute to Usenet newsgroups are usually very small, mostly fewer than 50 people. About a quarter of all newsgroups attract between 50 and 500 people. These groups may be the most productive and stable of all newsgroups. There is some indication that face-to-face groups can maintain self-organized cooperative relationships fairly easily when group sizes remain small, usually below 150 people (Orbell and Dawes 1981; Messick and Brewer 1983). One effect of the ways network-mediated communication alters the economies of interaction may be to double or triple this maximum level, allowing cooperative groups to expand to include as many as 500 or 600 active people and many thousand more passive participants. A few newsgroups are huge, drawing thousands of different participants. Further research may be able to determine if these larger groups are more or less stable and cooperative than smaller groups.

On average, there are four messages contributed to the Usenet for each poster. But posting behavior is far from normally distributed. Posting behavior resembles a Poisson distribution, starting at a peak of 42 percent of all posters who posted only a single message in the ten-week period studied and falling off steeply with a tiny fraction posting more than 200 messages. The broadest pattern of activity is sparse and sporadic, 96 percent of posters posted fewer than 30 messages in the period. Remarkably, the 99.55 percent of people who posted fewer than 200 posts are responsible for only 63 percent of all messages. In contrast only 0.04 percent of all posters posted more than 200 posts. But this group created 37 percent of all the messages contributed in the study period. This small group of active posters is probably composed of non-human posters (i.e. control messages and spam).

The most popular newsgroups, where the most people contribute messages, focus on topics related to the Usenet itself, employment opportunities, and aspects of personal computer use. These groups are good examples of the way the Usenet is used to sustain mutual support groups that can draw upon a vast population. But not all newsgroups, even those that contain large numbers of messages, are places where social interaction occurs. Some are barren, completely abandoned by everyone. Others can be kinds of broadcast channels, cleared of interaction in order to let announcements stand out from the clutter.

One rough measure of the quality of interaction in a newsgroup is its poster-to-post ratio (see Figure 8.3). Some newsgroups are characterized by a high poster-to-post ratio, that is, one in which many different people write most of the messages. A newsgroup with a lower measure indicates that just a few participants are contributing a disproportionate number of messages to the newsgroup. A measure closer to one indicates a lack of turn-taking social interaction since each person writes only one message. This means that no one responds to a response, a sign of the turn-taking structure indicative of direct social interaction (Sacks *et al.* 1974). Yet newsgroups with high poster-to-post ratios are not necessarily barren and useless. Newsgroups set aside for announcements only, where discussions are discouraged to provide an uncluttered place for messages of higher priority, can have a high poster-to-post ratio.

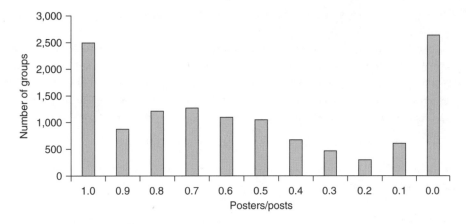

Figure 8.3 Distribution of poster-to-post ratio for all newsgroups, November 1, 1996 to January 18, 1997

A poster-to-post ratio measure closer to zero indicates that a newsgroup has very few active participants who contribute many messages. Most of the "clari.*" newsgroups have a very low poster-to-post ratio. These groups are part of a commercial news service called Clarinet that piggybacks on the Usenet to distribute wire service news stories and financial information. In "clari.*" groups a single poster, the Clarinet news service, alone posts thousands of messages.

Extremely high or low poster-to-post ratios indicate a lack of interaction between participants in a newsgroup. A poster-to-post ratio in the middle range is not a guarantee of social interaction (a number of people may post more than once and still not be talking to each other) but measures at either extreme are solid indications of a lack of turn-taking style interaction. While newsgroups are generally thought of as interactive places, only

Table 8.4 Top ten newsgroups in terms of poster population, November 1, 1996 to January 18, 1997

Rank	Group	#Posts	#Posters	Poster-to-post ratio	Crosspost degree	Crosspost volume
1	news.newusers.questions[26]	27,332	12,012	0.439	827	6,470
2	comp.os.ms-windows.win95.misc	16,875	7,189	0.426	516	9,879
3	comp.sys.ibm.pc.hardware.video	25,293	5,576	0.220	374	8,579
4	misc.jobs.offered	232,612	5,184	0.022	793	217,845
5	comp.sys.ibm.pc.games.strategic	20,482	5,055	0.247	221	7,987
6	comp.sys.ibm.pc.hardware.chips	12,005	4,394	0.366	303	6,021
7	comp.os.ms-windows.nt.misc	10,337	4,377	0.423	341	5,553
8	comp.sys.ibm.pc.games.action	11,525	4,329	0.376	265	6,931
9	comp.os.ms-windows.win95.setup	7,792	4,202	0.539	286	5,305
10	comp.sys.ibm.pc.games.rpg	12,590	4,201	0.334	243	6,113

60 percent of all newsgroups have poster-to-post ratios that indicate conditions that allow for interaction.

Of the ten largest newsgroups all, with the exception of misc.jobs.offered, have poster-to-post ratios in the middle range, an indication that these groups are characterized by many participants each contributing a number of messages (Table 8.4). This reflects the general purpose of these newsgroups where people ask and answer technical questions pertaining to the configuration and operation of personal computers and popular games played on them.

Daily and weekly cycles

On an average day, 300,000 messages are posted by 18,000 posters. Messages arrive at the rate of about 3,500 messages an hour, written on average by 1,200 posters. At its peak, 400,000 messages are created per day by 44,000 posters. Messages are not contributed at a steady rate throughout the day. In fact, the Usenet has a weekly cycle of activity that builds during the workweek and falls off over the weekends, suggesting that many people access the Usenet from their workplaces. This may challenge the belief that recent network growth has been predominantly driven by home consumer use.

As seen in Figure 8.4, the fairly stable weekly pattern found in November dissolves in December, where usage rises continuously until just before Christmas Day (December 25), which was one of the lowest activity days in the study. In contrast to Christmas, which is celebrated more globally, the relatively normal activity on Thanksgiving (November 28, 1996) may be an indication that activity outside the United States, where Thanksgiving is not usually celebrated, is a significant portion of overall Usenet activity.

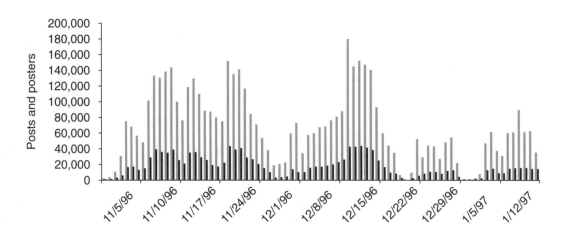

Figure 8.4 Daily rates of messages and participants in the Usenet, November 1, 1996 to January 18, 1997

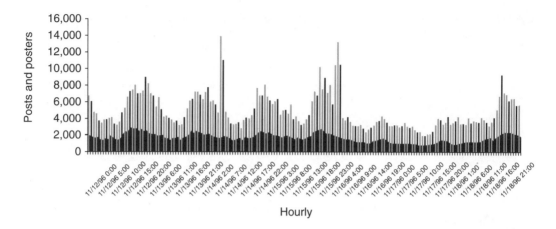

Figure 8.5 Hourly rates of messages and participants in the Usenet, November 12, 1996 to November 18, 1996

Each day, as illustrated by Figure 8.5, activity in the Usenet begins to rise at about four o'clock in the afternoon Greenwich Mean Time (GMT).[27] This is about eleven o'clock in the morning on the East coast of the United States, eight o'clock in the morning on the West coast. Each day the lowest points of activity occur during the European day and North American night. But even at its low points, the Usenet is always active, an indication of both the global scope of the participants in the Usenet and the way asynchronous communication allows people to interact at any time of the day or night.

Crossposting connections between newsgroups

Through the practice of crossposting, newsgroups are densely interconnected with one another, forming large neighborhoods of interrelated topics.[28] These connections can be measured in two ways. First, each newsgroup is connected to a certain number of other newsgroups. This is the crossposting degree. A related but separate measure is the crossposting volume, the count of the number of posts the groups shares through crossposting with other newsgroups. A newsgroup could be connected to many other groups but share only a small portion of its messages with them, or a newsgroup can be connected to only a few newsgroups, but share many of its messages. Most interfaces to the Usenet present each newsgroup as if it were distinct and isolated. But very few newsgroups are in fact islands, only 798 (6 percent) of the active newsgroups are not connected to any other newsgroups at all. While most newsgroups are connected to only a few others they are often directly connected to one of the core newsgroups. A core newsgroup is one to which most other newsgroups are connected. Because of the presence of these core groups, no newsgroup is more than a few "steps" apart from any other. On average, a newsgroup is connected to 50 other newsgroups. At the top end of the spectrum, 588 (4 percent) are connected to more than 200 other newsgroups. While

Table 8.5   Top ten newsgroups in terms of crossposting degree, November 1, 1996 to January 18, 1997

Rank	Group	#Posts	#Posters	Poster-to-post ratio	Crosspost degree	#Articles crossposted
1	news.answers	4,350	670	0.154	992	4,346
2	alt.forsale	4,745	1,881	0.396	960	4,727
3	alt.business	10,236	1,533	0.150	835	10,208
4	news.newusers.questions	27,332	12,012	0.439	827	6,470
5	misc.jobs.offered	232,612	5,184	0.022	793	217,845
6	alt.retromod	182	32	0.176	762	182
7	alt.sex	2,128	1,216	0.571	724	2,087
8	alt.business.misc	11,699	1,525	0.130	720	11,671
9	misc.entrepreneurs	14,760	2,485	0.168	700	12,016
10	misc.misc	7,957	1,536	0.193	677	7,255

only 15 percent of all groups are connected to more than 100 other groups through crossposting, these massively crossposted newsgroups are the core of the Usenet, containing 69 percent of all the messages posted during the study.

This dense level of interconnection gives the Usenet the ability to act as a powerful social information switch. Questions that appear in one newsgroup are likely to be seen by someone who has a connection with a more appropriate newsgroup, who then forwards the message or redirects the questioner to a proper newsgroup.

The top ten most crossposted newsgroups are not necessarily the most active or populous newsgroups (Table 8.5). But their high levels of interconnection make these groups the crossroads of the Usenet. At the same time, high levels of crossposting are indications that a newsgroup lacks a clear boundary, possibly indicating the lack of focused content and a stable population. More distinct boundaries may be necessary for the emergence of social ties that characterize groups that are closer to what is commonly understood to be a "community."

In practice, when posters crosspost many messages to another newsgroup they can effectively merge into the same group. Readers and participants in each closely crossposted newsgroup are effectively members of a single larger meta-newsgroup. There is good reason to believe that there are far fewer meta-groups than distinctly named newsgroups since 58 percent of newsgroups crosspost more than 50 percent of the messages they contain. Remarkably, in one-third of all newsgroups, 100 percent of the messages are crossposted to (or from) other groups.

Using crossposting records, it is possible to generate network maps of the interconnections between Usenet newsgroups.[29] Crossposting patterns can be more intuitively represented as a network map (Krackhardt *et al.* 1994; Becker *et al.* 1995; Cox and Eick 1995; Krebs 1996). The patterns of a newsgroup's connections to others may indicate a great deal about the newsgroup (Rice 1995). It is beyond the scope of the

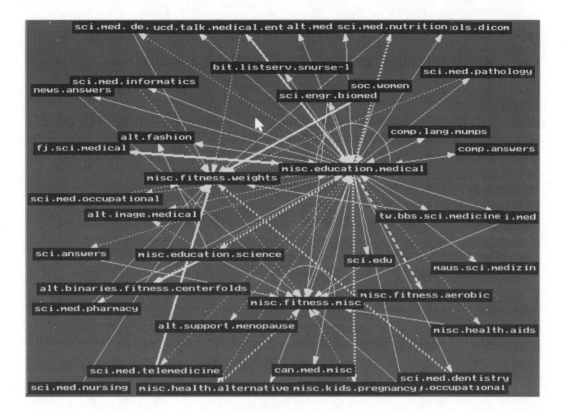

Figure 8.6 The misc.education.medical crossposting neighborhood, November 1, 1996 to January 18, 1997

current project, but a map of the interconnections of all the newsgroups is entirely feasible.

These maps can highlight some unexpected connections between newsgroups. For example, in Figure 8.6, an unexpected connection between alt.fashion and misc.education.medical is created by recurrent discussions of the health effects of dieting. These maps illustrate the ways cultural topics and interests are clustered together and can be useful guides to direct observation of related groups.

Discussion

These initial results illustrate some important features of the Usenet. Within the sample I examine, the average newsgroup has about 100 messages a week, contributed by fewer than 50 different people. Nearly all of the messages in a majority of newsgroups are crossposted to other newsgroups, and each group is connected to 50 other groups on average. On an average day, 18,000 people contribute 67,000 messages to the Usenet. In an average hour, 3,500 messages are written by 1,200 people. The high rates of interconnection between newsgroups through crossposting means that there are fewer newsgroups than there are newsgroup names. A majority of newsgroups crosspost more than 50 per cent of their messages, making them interconnected to the point that they agglomerate into larger meta-clusters. Mapping these clusters is a key direction for future research. The highly interconnected nature of the Usenet may be the quality that accounts for its extraordinary robustness.

Future directions

These measures begin to answer some basic and important questions about the ways human groups work when computers and networks mediate them. A variety of improvements in the Netscan software promises additional information about the social and technical structure of the Usenet. Future study may be able to show how distributed cooperation works in network interaction media. The existing database can be analyzed further to reveal information about the patterns of posting behavior, the connections between individuals and between newsgroups, and the life cycles of individual newsgroups. Other forms of network interaction media including other conferencing systems, email (either from the perspective of an individual or a mailing list), and some forms of real-time chat systems and MUDs, could be studied, allowing comparative analysis of different network interaction media. Two areas of research, on the presence and size of core groups of posters and the structure and length of the threads in newsgroups, stand out in particular.

Some newsgroups are populated by a core of dedicated participants who contribute much of the value found in the group.[30] A core group of posters can act as a means of socialization, ensuring that group experiences and lessons are conveyed to the next generations of participants. The presence or absence of a core group who produce a significant and disproportionate amount of the participation may explain why some newsgroups are more ordered and productive than others. Core posters, who make up only a few percent of most newsgroup's population, post more than twenty times the average amount of messages, target their messages more finely, and are more likely to be responded to (Terveen *et al.* 1997).

Another measure that captures a newsgroup's quality of interaction is the thread-to-post ratio. Newsgroups in which the dominant form of interaction is the contribution of announcements that receive no commentary will have a very high thread-to-post ratio: each thread will contain only one post. Newsgroups in which the dominant form of interaction is a fairly straightforward pattern of questions asked and answered will have thread-to-post ratios near 0.5, each thread will have one question and one answer. If the measure is lower, the newsgroup is more likely to be characterized by long threads which may be an indicator of discussions characterized by disagreement, divergent opinions, or ambiguous subjects that cannot be neatly characterized. Initial results show that 11 million of the 14 million messages posted in the 150 days ending November 17, 1997 are "thread heads" – initial posts that indicate the beginning of a new chain of conversation. This means that only about 3 million (21 percent) messages receive any replies at all.

Content analysis of message bodies could lead to studies that map the diffusion of topics through the Usenet and other communication media. Such data could assist studies of informal communication networks and the transmission of folk beliefs (Shibutani 1966) as well as the development of academic disciplines (Bayer *et al.* 1990). Studying message content could allow for the measurement of social problems like mass mailings, or "spam," that clutter many newsgroups.

Ethical issues

Digital artifacts are incomplete and potentially dangerous. There are reasons to be cautious about research using data collected from network interaction media. These data refine and extend the means of surveillance that are already a disturbing trend in such systems. For all of the potential benefits, using data of this sort requires consideration of the possible impact of such research on the people studied. Data that maps the activities of thousands of individuals around the world raise serious issues about privacy, property, and the responsibilities of researchers to the members of the online groups they study. The information available through machine analysis of the artifacts of network interaction can uncover social spaces, subjecting them to a kind of panoptic surveillance (Poster 1990).

In effect, such research produces maps that reveal in great detail a social space that has previously been cloaked. Is the creation of such a map an invasion of privacy? The answer depends largely on the nature and status of the Usenet and other social cyberspaces. Are these public spaces, like city streets or plazas, where we have lower expectations and protections of our privacy? Or are these private or semi-private spaces where people have an expectation of privacy? Even if Usenet is a "public" space or a commons, are all actions in it subject to aggregation and analysis? If many people have a high expectation of privacy, do those expectations deserve respect regardless of the technical realities? Or do new technical tools change and shift the nature of this space, forcing participants to recognize a change in its character?

As networks and computers insinuate themselves into more and more aspects of everyday life, the use and interpretation of these records raise a range of ethical and legal issues concerning the protection of individual privacy (Clarke 1994).[31] The goal must be responsible and ethical research practices that allow researchers to derive much of the value of this information, without eroding the privacy of participants. But researchers have a responsibility to consider the impact of their work. It can be argued that some information should not be gathered even if it is easy and possible to do so. King argues for balancing the amount of deception and disclosure practiced in the process of data collection with the extent to which the data are anonymized (King 1996).[32] He also notes a perverse effect of online studies: research that violates an online group's sense of privacy may leave "scorched earth" behind for prospective participants and future researchers as participants seek more private online spaces to carry out their group's business or simply scatter under the scrutiny of researchers. The bright light of social science research can create an unpleasant glare for participants drawn to a dimly lit online space. And, as Reid notes, this effect can occur even when researchers comport themselves responsibly but draw other researchers to the space they studied (Reid 1996). The light cast by researchers can also act as a beacon for others, making the space all but useless for its participants. Online researchers have the potential of becoming social locusts, descending on online spaces and rendering them barren.

The stakes are even higher when research reveals information that can be linked to specific individuals, even more so if an individual's diverse and unrelated activities can be drawn together into a unified dossier of all their activity (Clarke 1994). Researchers may have a responsibility to anonymize both the identities of the participants in an online group and the location of the online space itself.

As with many issues related to computer networks, the issue may already be moot. Regardless of whether researchers include personal identification or identify specific newsgroups, anyone can now generate similar reports on individuals and newsgroups with DEC's Alta Vista service (http://www.altavista.digital.com/) or with Deja News (http://www.dejanews.com/). Alta Vista, like half a dozen similar services, allows users to enter a person's name or email address and get a list of all the messages that person contributed to all Usenet newsgroups since the service started collecting data in March of 1996. Deja News goes a step further, explicitly offering a "Poster Profile" report that lists the number of times the person selected posted to the Usenet over a period of time, the percentage of postings that were responded to as well as a breakdown of each newsgroup the person posted to and the number of messages the person posted there.[33] This profile can be seen as a very informative aid in the evaluation of the merit of a poster's message or as an invasion of privacy. Regardless, these services do create a dramatic change in the balance between self-exposure and self-disclosure.

Groups may find that there are benefits to operating within a system that is surveilled by network services like AltaVista, DejaNews, and Netscan. The data collected about group activity may help groups that are studied to see themselves. The data collected about group dynamics can be reflected in the user interface to these spaces providing information about the overall population and group sizes, level of interaction, and the internal connections and structure of the groups that are missing from existing systems. Offering this information directly to the users of these media may return to the participants some of the information that is lost when communicating through network interaction media.

Acknowledgments

This research was made possible by the generous support of the Microsoft Advanced Research and Virtual Worlds Groups. I want to thank Christine Morton, Eli Smith-Morton, and Theta Pavis for their enduring support, encouragement, and guidance.

Notes

1 Direct correspondence to Marc A. Smith, Department of Sociology, University of California, Los Angeles, CA 90095–1551 (smithm@ucla.edu).

2 Conferencing systems are distinguished from alternative network interaction media like email, discussion lists, chat, MUDs, and graphical worlds, by their collections of messages created by a group of people that are organized around topics, "threaded" into chains of responses and replies, and exchanged asynchronously. Other conferencing systems include PicoSpan (used on the WELL), Caucus, and a variety of BBS systems. The major commercial services – AOL, CompuServe, and MSN – also offer discussion groups.

3 Broadly, it can be argued that all kinds of digital artifacts, like bank balances, credit reports, and architectural designs, are social. But not all cyberspaces are social in the sense of primarily providing a venue for interaction between people.

4 The system is publicly accessible at http://netscan.sscnet.ucla.edu/. David Faraldo and Alex Brown were instrumental in implementing Netscan. This study was conducted using data collected from the UCLA campus news server (news.ucla.edu). News servers collect and store messages in Usenet newsgroups and send specific messages in response to requests made by news clients. News is exchanged via the Network News Transport Protocol (NNTP) and is often managed by a server known as Internet Network News (INN). See RFC 1036 for definition of message headers, and RFC 977 for definition of NNTP.

5 Usenet interactions are embedded in a larger set of communications ties. Most Usenet participants have access to alternative channels of communication (email, IRC, MUDs, WWW, telephone, face-to-face interaction, etc.) none of which is visible in the data Netscan uses. In many cases, interactions that start in Usenet newsgroups are continued in more private email discussions.

6 Through most of the history of the Usenet some of its content has been archived, but much of the Usenet is routinely erased after a period of a few days or weeks. As a result, there are no clear long-term measures of its growth, content, and dynamics. Although some of the data can be reassembled from scattered pieces, a complete picture of the early history of Usenet may be difficult to reconstruct.

7 This number is actually a count of the distinct email addresses used to post messages to the Usenet.

8 Because of crossposting, many of these messages were duplicated in more than one group. If messages are counted each time they occur in any newsgroup, more than 19 million messages were distributed. This means that about 40 percent of the Usenet is composed of redundant information. This value may be even higher as 9 percent of all Usenet messages are quoted text (segments of prior messages) reproduced in responses (Brewer and Johnson 1996).

9 Although commercial providers like AOL and MSN claimed 9 million and 2 million users respectively in 1997, it is likely that these figures are significantly inflated and do not reflect the real number of users who participate in these system's conferencing areas. Furthermore, these systems are far more geographically bounded (serving mostly North America and Europe) than the Usenet.

10 Zero messages originated from the following domains: Antarctica, Bangladesh, Belize, Bouvet Island, Burundi, Buthan, Chad, Congo, Equatorial Guinea, Guadeloupe (Fr.),

Guam (US), Guinea Bissau, Guyana, St. Kitts Nevis Anguilla, Korea (North), Lesotho, Liberia, Malawi, Martinique (Fr.), Nauru, Norfolk Island, Northern Mariana Isl., Palau, St. Pierre and Miquelon, Rwanda, Solomon Islands, Svalbard and Jan Mayen Is, Tadjikistan, Tanzania, Tokelau, Tunisia, Virgin Islands (British), Wallis and Futuna Islands.

11 The value for the United States is a total of the com, net, edu, org, us, gov, mil, and usa domains; this is not entirely accurate, because many com domains are accessed from outside of the United States.

12 For ten years Brian Reid of the DEC West Coast Research Lab ran a program that generated reports that came to be known as "Arbitrons." Through the cooperation of a large group of system administrators, Reid received information on the number of newsgroups, the number of postings in each group, the number of bytes in those posts, and the number of "readers" for each group. It is the measure of readership that was most often contested. Reid's method involved a sample that may not have been representative and used multipliers to estimate the total size of the Usenet population that may have been dramatically off. Still, even if the magnitudes of Reid's data are mistaken, the process he used to measure the Usenet remained relatively constant throughout his study making the relative measures useful. For a discussion of the many potential flaws in these measurements see http://www.tlsoft.com/arbitron/statistical_error.html.

13 Network measurement is a fairly new and somewhat inexact art in which significant differences of opinion and methodology continue to exist. Estimates of the number of people online, for example, vary from tens of millions to over one hundred million people in 1998. While the exact figures are not unimportant, the general trend is indisputable; people are adopting computer-networked media at an impressive rate (see RFC1296, www.mids.com, www.nw.com and ftp://ftp.isoc.org/isoc/charts/hosts3.ppt). Sampling methods and survey research may offer some insight into readership patterns, a possible future direction for further research.

14 Crossposting creates a non-directional tie between two or more newsgroups. The data included in each message's header do not identify from which group a post originates. As a result, all connections between newsgroups are bi-directional. No data are available to determine if a group exports more messages than it imports.

15 Netscan collects the From, Date, Newsgroups, References, Message ID, Hosts, and Subject elements from the header of every message in every group and creates a database from the information. This database was used to generate the measures presented here. In this study I ignore the body of the messages exchanged, and focus on the structure of social interaction, not its content. Analyzing message content in aggregate can be a difficult task because of the vast storage requirements imposed by the heavy message traffic in the Usenet. However, message content can be investigated using widely available computer textual analysis methods that can be quite sophisticated (Weber 1984; Damashek 1995). These techniques represent a direction for future work. The results of computer textual analysis methods cannot replace ethnographic study of social cyberspaces but can be a powerful complement to such research.

16 Usenet newsgroups can be "moderated" which allows only messages specifically approved by the newsgroup's owner to be posted to the newsgroup. Only about 1,544 (10 percent) of newsgroups are moderated. Many Usenet users are aware that the moderation feature can be fairly easily circumvented.

17 There are reception filters, known as killfiles, which allow a particular poster's messages to be screened out of a newsgroup for a particular reader. The posts remain available for others who have not filtered out that poster.

18 Network interaction systems like the Usenet continue to grow in use even in the face of newer and flashier network media where others have become extinct. The World Wide Web has all but killed the older Gopher protocol. But the Usenet, email, IRC, and MUDs seem to have a future as integrated components of the WWW.

19 During the history of the Usenet, waves of new users have flooded in repeatedly, first as universities opened access to the Internet and thus the Usenet to student populations, and again as commercial online services and Internet Service Providers have made network access a consumer commodity. Each wave has challenged the existing structure and traditions of the Usenet and resulted in the fashioning of new ones.

20 Attacks and chronic problems include spam, cancelbots, topic, and newsgroup name drift. Spam is the term used for messages that are mass mailed or posted throughout the Usenet without regard to the topics of the groups. Cancelbots have been developed as a response to this kind of shotgun littering. They are automated methods for deleting offensive messages. However, the solution may be more of a problem than its inspiration since they introduce the possibility of censorship. Name and topic drift occurs when the content of a discussion shifts but its subject title does not. This erodes the coordination system that keeps the millions of messages sensibly organized.

21 One application of this research may be to provide better clues as to where these islands are located. Related research and applications identify the Web sites most frequently mentioned in a newsgroup (Hill and Terveen 1996). Other applications focus on ways to collect and apply the reactions of prior readers of online materials to allow groups to review and recommend material to one another automatically (Brewer and Johnson 1996).

22 With the exception of newsgroups in the "alt" hierarchy, new newsgroups are created through a fairly elaborate electoral process. In exchange for following this process ratified newsgroups gain wider distribution. While no Usenet site is required to accept or pass along all newsgroups, by informal agreement many sites carry any newsgroup that passes the electoral hurdle. In contrast, newsgroups in the "alt" hierarchy can be created at a moment's notice by anyone who desires to. The trade-off is that many Usenet sites refuse to carry "alt" newsgroups entirely or carry only select newsgroups. Many "alt" newsgroups must develop a moderately strong following before they will be widely distributed, posing a chicken-and-egg like start-up problem. Still, many "alt" newsgroups succeed and are widely available.

23 The problem is complicated by the fact that some news servers will list newsgroups that they do not actively carry. A possible solution to this problem is to connect Netscan to multiple servers or to run multiple copies of Netscan at sites around the world. These copies could exchange information with one another to generate as complete a picture of the entire Usenet as possible.

24 This level of coverage seems to be fairly equal with a range of commercial providers of Usenet feeds for consumer use. Few servers attempt to collect a feed for every possible group, waiting for a request for a particular group instead.

25 This figure may be significantly inflated. The count of empty groups reflects the message holdings of the single news server used in this study. In some cases newsgroups are created globally but contain messages that are distributed only regionally, making the message traffic within them invisible from other parts of the world. Measures of non-zero newsgroups are likely to be more reliable.

26 Many commercial Internet providers automatically direct their customers to

news.newusers.questions for support, funneling thousands of people into the Usenet and this newsgroup every month.

27 Since messages are contributed from all over the world, each time stamp has been adjusted to GMT to provide a uniform basis for comparison.

28 Newsgroups are also connected to other groups when they share the same poster or reader regardless of whether they have been crossposted together.

29 Network maps are created in conjunction with the social network analysis tool Krackplot (http://www.contrib.andrew.cmu.edu/~krack/).

30 One indication of a group's level of organization is the existence of documents that document some of the group's goals and history. For example, in many Usenet newsgroups Frequently Asked Questions (FAQ) files contain lists of answers to the most common questions and issues raised in a particular newsgroup. These files can save the regular participants of a newsgroup the irritation of having the same topics and questions come up continuously. They also provide a valuable resource for anyone just starting to explore the topic of the newsgroup. There are 1,623 (14 percent) newsgroups with a FAQ listed in the main repository for FAQs, the RTFM site maintained by MIT ("RTFM" is the canonical answer to common, trivial, or annoying questions on the Internet and means roughly "Read the Manual". The site is located at ftp://rtfm.mit.edu/pub/usenet/). The remaining newsgroups may be well organized and useful, but the presence of a FAQ is an important sign of the maturation of a newsgroup.

31 Whenever people interact with other people or organizations through any computer system they may leave a durable mark. Phone calls, banking and credit transactions, library loans, video rentals, airline reservations, magazine subscriptions, utility bills, and other forms of electronic records are routinely cataloged and analyzed for a variety of purposes.

32 I follow King's lead by avoiding all identification of individuals in this chapter.

33 Messages that contain an optional X-No-Archive Header are not archived by the Deja News service, allowing anyone who is well informed enough to opt out of the archival service. The Netscan analysis tool also honors this convention.

References and further reading

Bayer, A. E., J. C. Smart and G. W. McLaughlin. 1990. "Mapping intellectual structure of a scientific subfield through author cocitations," *Journal of the American Society for Information Science* 41(6): 444–52.

Becker, Richard A., Stephen G. Eick, and Allan R. Wilks. 1995. "Visualizing Network Data," *IEEE Transactions on Visualization and Computer Graphics* 1(1): 16–21.

Bikson, T. and J. D. Eveland. 1990. "The Interplay of work group structures and computer support," in J. Galegher, R. Kraut and C. Egido (eds) *Intellectual Teamwork: Social and Technical Bases of Cooperative Work*. Hillsdale, NJ: Lawrence Erlbaum.

Brewer, Robert S. and Philip M. Johnson. 1996. "Collaborative Classification and Evaluation of Usenet," Collaborative Software Development Laboratory, Department of Information and Computer Sciences, University of Hawaii, Honolulu, HI, Unpublished manuscript.

Clarke, Roger. 1994. "The Digital Persona and Its Application to Data Surveillance," *The Information Society* 10(2): 77–92.

Cox, Kenneth C. and Stephen G. Eick. 1995. "3D Displays of Internet Traffic," in Nahum Gershonand and Stephen Eick (eds) *IEEE Symposium on Information Visualization*. IEEE Computer Society Press, October.

Cox, Kenneth C., Stephen G. Eick and Taosong He. 1996. "3D Geographic Network Displays," *Sigmod Record* 24(4).

Damashek, Marc. 1995. "Gauging Similarity with n-Grams: Language Independent Categorization of Text," *Science* 267 (10 February): 843–8.

Danowski, J. 1982. "Computer-mediated communication: a network-based content analysis using a CBBS conference," in M. Burgoon (ed.) *Communication Yearbook* (vol. 6). Beverly Hills, CA: Sage.

Danowski, J. 1988. "Organizational infographics and automated auditing: using computers to unobtrusively analyze communication," in G. Goldhaber and G. Barnett (eds) *Handbook of Organizational Communication*. Norwood, NJ: Ablex.

Eick, Stephen G. 1996. "Aspects of Network Visualization," *Computer Graphics and Applications* 16(2): 69–72.

Harrison, Mark. 1995. *The Usenet Handbook: A User's Guide to NetNews*, Sebastopol, CA: O'Reilly & Associates.

Hess, Charlotte. 1995. "Untangling the Web: The Internet as a Commons, 1996," Paper Presented at the "Reinventing the Commons" Workshop, Transnational Institute, Bonn, Germany, November 4–5.

Hill, Will and Loren Terveen. 1996. "Using Frequency-of-mention in public conversations for social filtering," unpublished manuscript: http://weblab.research.att.com//phoaks.cscw96.ps.

Hiltz, S.R. and Turoff, M. 1993. *The Network Nation: Human Communication via Computer*. Cambridge, MA: MIT Press.

Jones, Steve G. 1995. "Understanding Community in the Information Age," in S. G. Jones (ed.) *CyberSociety: Computer-Mediated Communication and Community*. Thousand Oaks, CA: Sage.

Kiesler, Sara. 1986. "The Hidden Messages in Computer Networks," *Harvard Business Review* January–February: 46–60.

King, Storm. 1996. "Researching Internet Communities: Proposed Ethical Guidelines for the Reporting of Results," *The Information Society* 12(2): 119–28.

Kling, Rob. 1996. "Social Relationships in Electronic Forums: Hangouts, Salons, Workplaces and Communities," in Rob Kling (ed.) *Computerization and Controversy: Value Conflicts and Social Choices* (2nd edn). San Diego, CA: Academic Press.

Kollock, P. and M. A. Smith. 1996. "Managing the Virtual Commons: Cooperation and Conflict in Computer Communities," in Susan Herring (ed.) *Computer Mediated Communication: Linguistic, Social and Cross-Cultural Perspectives*. Amsterdam: John Benjamins.

Korenman, Joan and Nancy Wyatt. 1996. "Group Dynamics in an Email Forum," in Susan Herring (ed.) *Computer Mediated Communication: Linguistic, Social and Cross-Cultural Perspectives*. Amsterdam: John Benjamins.

Krackhardt, D., Blythe, J. and McGrath, C. 1994. "KrackPlot 3.0: An Improved Network Drawing Program," *Connections* 17(2): 53–5.

Krebs, Valdis. 1996. "Visualizing Human Networks," *Release* 1.0 (12 February).

Larson, Ray R. 1996. "Bibliometrics of the World Wide Web: An Exploratory Analysis of the Intellectual Structure of Cyberspace," http://sherlock.berkeley.edu/asis96/asis96.html.

Lewenstein, Bruce V. 1992. *The Changing Culture of Research: Processes of Knowledge Transfer*. Office of Technology Assessment (OTA) Contract no. I3–4570.0, 28 December.

Marsden, Peter V. 1990. "Network Data and Measurement," *Annual Review of Sociology* 16: 435–63.

McLaughlin, Margaret. 1995. "Standards of Conduct on Usenet," in S.G. Jones (ed.) *CyberSociety: Computer-Mediated Communication and Community*. Thousand Oaks, CA: Sage.

Messick, David M. and Marilynn B. Brewer. 1983. "Solving Social Dilemmas," in L. Wheeler and P. Shaver (eds) *Review of Personality and Social Psychology* (vol. 4). Beverly Hills, CA: Sage.

Olson, Mancur, Jr. 1965. *The Logic of Collective Action*. Cambridge, MA: Harvard University Press.

Orbell, John and Robyn Dawes. 1981. "Social Dilemmas," in G.M. Stephenson and J.M. Davis (eds) *Progress in Applied Social Psychology* (vol. 1). New York: Wiley.

Pfaffenberger, Bryan. 1996. "'If I Want It, It's OK': Usenet and the (Outer) Limits of Free Speech," *The Information Society* 12: 365–86.

Phillips, David J. 1996. "Defending the Boundaries: Identifying and Countering Threats in a Usenet Newsgroup," *The Information Society* 12: 39–62.

Poster, Mark. 1990. *The Mode of Information: Poststructuralism and Social Context*. Chicago: University of Chicago Press.

Quarterman, John S. 1990. *The Matrix: Computer Networks and Conferencing Systems Worldwide*. Bedford, MA: Digital Press.

Raymond, Eric (ed.). 1993. "The On-Line Hacker Jargon File" (ver. 3.0.0), ftp: rtfm.mit.edu. Also published as *The New Hacker's Dictionary* (2nd edn). Cambridge, MA: MIT Press.

Reid, Elizabeth. 1996. "Informed Consent in the Study of On-Line Communities: A Reflection on the Effects of Computer-Mediated Social Research," *The Information Society* 12: 169–74.

Rice, Ronald E. 1982. "Communication Networking in Computer-Conferencing Systems: A Longitudinal Study of Group Roles and System Structure," in M. Burgoon (ed.) *Communication Yearbook 6*. Beverly Hills, CA: Sage.

Rice, Ronald. 1995. "Network Analysis and Computer-Mediated Communication Systems," in Stanley Wasserman and Joseph Galaskiewicz (eds) *Advances in Social Network Analysis*. Thousand Oaks, CA: Sage.

Rice, Ronald E., August E. Grant, Joseph Schmitz and Jack Torobin. 1990. "Individual and Network Influences on the Adoption and Perceived Outcomes of Electronic Messaging," *Social Networks* 12: 27–55.

Rodgers, Everett M. 1987. "Progress, Problems and Prospects for Network Research: Investigating Relationships in the Age of Electronic Communication Technologies," *Social Networks* 9: 285–310.

Sacks, Harvey, Schegloff, Emanuel A., and Jefferson, Gail. 1974. "A Simplest Semantics for the Organization of Turn-taking for Conversation," *Language* 50: 696–735.

Salzenberg, Chip. 1992. "What is Usenet?", ftp: rtfm.mit.edu.

Schelling, Thomas C. 1960. *The Strategy of Conflict*. Cambridge, MA: Harvard University Press.

Shibutani, Tamotsu. 1966. *Improvised News: A Sociological Study of Rumor*. Indianapolis, IN: Bobbs-Merrill.

Sproul, L.S. and Kiesler, S.B. 1991. *Connections: New Ways of Working in the Networked Organization*. Boston, MA: MIT Press.

Terveen, Loren, Will Hill, Lynn Cherny and Steve Whittaker. 1997. "Quantifying Online Conversation," Unpublished manuscript.

Turkle, Sherry. 1996. *Life on the Screen*. New York: Simon & Schuster.

Waskul, Dennis and Mark Douglass. 1996. "Considering the Electronic Participant: Some Polemical Observations on the Ethics of On-Line Research," *The Information Society* 12: 129–39.

Wasserman, Stanley and Katherine Faust. 1994. *Social Network Analysis: Methods and Applications*. Cambridge: Cambridge University Press.

Weber, R. 1984. "Computer-aided Content Analysis," *Qualitative Sociology* 7(1–2): 126–47.

Wellman, Barry, Janet Salaff, Dimitrina Dimitrova, Laura Garton, Milena Gulia and Caroline Haythornthwaite. 1996. "Computer Networks as Social Networks: Collaborative Work, Telework, and Virtual Community," *Annual Review of Sociology* 22: 211–38.

Whittaker, Steve. 1996. "Talking to Strangers: An Evaluation of the Factors Affecting Electronic Collaboration," ATT Labs, Murray Hill, NJ.

Whyte, William H. 1988. *City: Rediscovering the Center*. New York: Doubleday.

Chapter 9

The economies of online cooperation

Gifts and public goods in cyberspace[1]

Peter Kollock

The Internet is filled with junk and jerks. It is commonplace for inhabitants of the Internet to complain bitterly about the lack of cooperation, decorum, and useful information. The signal-to-noise ratio, it is said, is bad and getting worse.

Even a casual trip through cyberspace will turn up evidence of hostility, selfishness, and simple nonsense. Yet the wonder of the Internet is not that there is so much noise, but that there is any significant cooperation at all. Given that online interaction is relatively anonymous, that there is no central authority, and that it is difficult or impossible to impose monetary or physical sanctions on someone, it is striking that the Internet is not literally a war of all against all. For a student of social order, what needs to be explained is not the amount of conflict but the great amount of sharing and cooperation that does occur in online communities.

Rheingold (1993) has described interaction in one online community (the WELL) as consisting of a gift economy, in which help and information is offered without the expectation of any direct, immediate quid pro quo. Even in more anonymous settings, such as Usenet discussion groups, there is a surprising amount of free help and information given out, often to complete strangers whom one may never meet again.

In comp.sys.laptops, a discussion group on Usenet devoted to notebook computers, it is commonplace for participants to contribute detailed specifications and reviews of new models as they come onto the market. Participants also respond to questions that other users post with detailed advice and answers to technical questions. Personal computer consultants will offer similar advice for about $40 per hour. In comp.lang.perl, a discussion group devoted to the computer language Perl, participants routinely help others out with their technical questions and contribute new computer code for others to use. An accomplished Perl programmer can charge $75 per hour. In a number of online discussion groups for lawyers, participants routinely offer each other detailed legal advice concerning cases on which they are working (Simon 1996). The lawyers report that they often refuse to give similar information over the phone or charge up to several hundred dollars an hour for the same advice.

Why would anyone give away such valuable advice? What can explain the amount of cooperation that does occur in online communities? In this chapter I wish to analyze how the economies of cooperation change as one moves to the Internet. I argue that there are fundamental features of online interaction which change the costs and benefits of social action in dramatic ways.

Because the metaphor of gift-giving has been used to describe online interaction and exchange, I will begin with a brief discussion of the concept of the gift. I then discuss social dilemmas – situations in which individually reasonable behavior leads to collective disaster – and in particular examine the challenge of providing public goods (to be defined below). Subsequent sections detail the shift in the economics of cooperation, discuss the motivations that drive contributions and collaboration, and provide two striking examples of online collective action. I close with a strong caution against assuming that the shifting economics of online interaction guarantee high levels of cooperation.

Gifts

What is a gift? Carrier (1991: 122) expands on the classic work by Mauss (1935) to define a gift as (1) the obligatory transfer, (2) of inalienable objects or services, (3) between related and mutually obligated transactors.

Unpacking this further, a gift transaction involves a diffuse and usually unstated obligation to repay the gift at some future time. Gift exchanges should not involve explicit bargaining or demands that the gift be reciprocated, but a relationship in which there is only giving and no receiving is unlikely to last. The contrast to a gift exchange is a commodity transaction, in which no obligation exists after the exchange is con-summated – the bottle of water purchased at a convenience store does not create an obligation to buy something there again. A gift is also tied in an inalienable way to the giver. This is to say that gifts are unique: it is not simply *a* sweater, but rather *the* sweater-that-Bill-gave-me. In contrast, commodities are not unique and derive no special value having been acquired from person X rather than person Y – a pound of flour is a pound of flour is a pound of flour when purchased at a supermarket. Finally, gifts are exchanged between individuals who are part of an ongoing interdependent relationship. In a commodities transaction, the individuals are self-interested, independent actors (Carrier 1991).

Another distinction between gifts and commodities is made by Bell (1991), who focuses on how individuals can increase the benefits of their exchanges. In a gift economy, benefits come from improving the "technology of social relations" by, for example, increasing the range and diversity of one's social network. In commodity economies, the benefits come from making improvements in the technology of production. Thus, gift economies are driven by social relations while commodity economies are driven by price. It is also important to note that gift exchange and commodity transactions are ideal types, and any economy will be a mix of these two types of exchange as well as many intermediate cases between them.

Using these definitions, are the acts of sharing information and advice that we see on the Internet examples of gifts in a strict sense? While gift giving as classically defined certainly occurs in the Internet (e.g. colleagues emailing each other useful information), much of the help and sharing that occurs is actually different than traditional gift exchange. When people pass on free advice or offer useful information, the recipient is often unknown to them and the giver may never encounter the recipient again. Thus, the usual obligation of a loose reciprocity between two specific individuals is difficult or impossible. Indeed, gifts of information and advice are often offered not to particular individuals, but to a group as a whole. Gifts of information might be offered to a group that has a clearly defined membership (a private discussion list, for example) or to groups that are more loosely defined – for example, information posted in a Usenet discussion group. Even more striking, if the information is posted on a World Wide Web page, there may be only the most tenuous sense of the group – the information may be offered to an unknown set of recipients.

The relative or absolute anonymity of the recipient makes it all the more remarkable that individuals volunteer valuable information – one cannot realistically count on the reciprocity of the recipient in the future to balance the gift that has occurred. While a balanced reciprocity with a particular individual may not be possible, there is a sense in which a balance might occur within a group as a whole. When, for example, skilled programmers who participate in the Perl discussion group volunteer an answer to a tricky programming question, they may have no expectation of being helped in return by the recipient. They may, however, feel entitled to, and believe they will receive, help from some other member of the group in the future.

This kind of network-wide accounting system, in which a benefit given to a person is reciprocated not by the recipient but by someone else in the group, is known as "generalized exchange" (Ekeh 1974). To offer an example from face-to-face interaction, if I help a stranded motorist in my community, I do not expect that motorist to return the favor, but I may hope and expect someone else in the community to offer me aid should I be in a similar situation (cf. Yamagishi and Cook 1993).

This system of sharing is both more generous and riskier than traditional gift exchange. It is more generous because an individual provides a benefit without the expectation of immediate reciprocation, but this is also the source of risk. There is the temptation to gather valuable information and advice without contributing anything back. If everyone succumbs to this temptation, however, everyone is worse off than they would have been otherwise: no one benefits from the valuable information that others might have. Thus, generalized exchange has the structure of a social dilemma – individually reasonable behavior (gathering but not offering information) leads to collective disaster.[2]

Public goods

In particular, many of the benefits provided in cyberspace have the quality that they are public goods, which are goods that anyone might benefit from, regardless of whether they have helped contribute to their production. A public good is defined by two characteristics. First, it is to some degree nonrival in that one person's consumption of the good does not reduce the amount available to another. One person's viewing of a fireworks display, for example, does not reduce what can be seen by another person. Second, a public good is to some degree nonexcludable in that it is difficult or impossible to exclude individuals from benefiting from the good – one receives the benefits of a national defense system regardless of whether one pays taxes. In most cases a public good will exhibit these two qualities to some degree only; pure public goods are the exception.

Everyone in a group may be made better off by the provision of a public good, but that in no way guarantees that it will be produced. Because excluding others from consuming the public good is difficult or impossible, there is the temptation to free-ride on the efforts of others, enjoying a public good without contributing to its production. Of course, if everyone tries to free-ride, the good will not be produced and everyone suffers, hence the social dilemma.

Providing public goods poses two key challenges. The first is the issue of motivation: getting individuals to contribute to the provision of a public good despite the temptation to free-ride. The decision not to contribute may spring from at least two sources – the desire to take advantage of someone else's efforts (greed), or an individual may be willing to cooperate but feel that there is not much of a chance that the good will be successfully provided and so does not want to waste his or her efforts (a concern with efficacy). The second challenge is one of coordination: even if a group of individuals are motivated to contribute toward a public good, they will need to coordinate their efforts and this will involve its own set of difficulties and costs.

Because the costs and benefits of providing some types of public goods change radically in online environments, so too do the dynamics of motivation and coordination. The next section will explore these shifts in the economies of cooperation.

Digital goods

Online communities exist within a radically different environment. The setting is (1) a network of (2) digital (3) information, and each of these three features drives important changes. It is a world of information rather than physical objects. Further, it is digital information, meaning that it is possible to produce an infinite number of perfect copies of a piece of information, whether that be a computer program, a multimedia presentation, or the archives of a long email discussion. As Negroponte (1995) put it, the setting is one of bits rather than atoms. And finally, this information is being produced not in isolation, but in an interwoven network of actors.

To draw the contrast differently, Carrier (1991: 130) argues that "in societies of the gift, gift relations are oriented to the mobilization and command of *labor*, while in capitalist societies commodity relations generally have been oriented to the mobilization and command of *objects*" (emphasis in original). In online communities, exchange relations are oriented to the mobilization and command of information.

The fact that online communities exist in a network of digital information means that there are significant changes in the costs of producing public goods, in the value of public goods, and in the production function of a public good, i.e. the relationship between the amount contributed toward a public good and the proportion of the public good produced.

Changes in costs

Online interaction can reduce the costs of contributing to the production of a public good in numerous ways. Consider, for example, collective protest designed to change the policy of an organization (Gurak, Chapter 10 in this volume; Mele, Chapter 12 in this volume). Even if one believes in the goals of the protest, the temptation is to let others do the work and avoid even such small costs as composing and sending off a letter of protest. To the extent costs are lowered, the more likely it is that individuals will take part in the collective action.

To take the example of a protest letter, Gurak (Chapter 10 in this volume) demonstrates how online interaction reduced the costs of sending a letter out to near zero. Sample letters were sent around the Internet so that individuals did not have to write their own. The usual cost savings of email also meant that there was no need to prepare an envelope, add a stamp, and walk down to the postbox to mail the letter. Online petitions were also circulated in which all one had to do was add one's name to the list and then forward it on. In this case the cost savings may seem trivial – how much effort, after all, does it take to mail a letter of protest? Yet reducing a small cost to near zero can have profound behavioral effects. Consider, as an example, the difference in television viewing habits caused by a remote control. The costs of getting up and changing the channel are very small, but reducing the costs still further (to essentially zero) by use of a remote control creates a dramatically different pattern of channel surfing. A small change in costs can have a disproportionate impact on behavior.

Coordination costs can also be reduced as a result of online interaction. Meeting with other people involved in a social protest or finding out information about the current situation and future plans can become trivially easy online. The formation of a new discussion group in Usenet devoted to a protest, for example (Gurak, Chapter 10 in this volume), creates a natural meeting place for those interested in the issues, and an easy way of distributing information. People can meet, plan, and discuss issues without regard to physical location or time.[3]

Changes in benefits

The value of a public good can also shift as one moves to online interaction. The fact that many of the public goods produced on the Internet consist of digital information means that the goods are purely nonrival – one person's use of the information in no way diminishes what is available for someone else. It also becomes easy and very cheap to distribute information across the Internet. While these feature are troubling for those concerned with intellectual property rights, they also create powerful incentives for groups interested in providing public goods. Once produced, the good can benefit an unlimited number of people. This is unlike physical public goods – there is a large though strictly finite limit to the number of people who can benefit from a fireworks display, a lighthouse, or even national defense. If an individual is motivated in even a small way to benefit the group as a whole, the fact that digital public goods are purely nonrival can be a significant incentive to contribute toward the public good.

And while the provision of many public goods requires the actions of a group (e.g. staging a social protest, writing a new operating system), the nature of a digital network turns even a single individual's contribution of information or advice into a public good. Any piece of information posted to an online community becomes a public good because the network makes it available to the group as a whole and because one person's "consumption" of the information does not diminish another person's use of it. This is a remarkable property of online interaction and unprecedented in the history of human society.

Thus, a clever bit of programming in a Perl discussion group, advice on how to cope with a serious illness posted to a discussion list, or a collection of restaurant reviews gathered onto a Web page can end up benefiting an unlimited number of people. In contrast, consider the same goods in the absence of a digital network. An individual or group may have useful advice on dealing with Alzheimer's patients but the information may remain known only to the group and their local contacts. Eventually the information may diffuse through people's social networks as they talk to each other or write letters, but this may take time and has its own set of costs associated with it. Even if the group is motivated to try to distribute the information widely as an act of cooperation, the costs of doing so may be huge. Few groups have the resources, for example, to publish a national magazine or buy commercial time on the radio or television. And even if such ambitious actions were possible, commercials eventually stop airing, magazines are lost, and it is difficult or impossible to keep the information current and let others add to the information. An online support group solves each of these challenges and each piece of new advice or information becomes instantly available to the group as a whole.[4]

Changes in the production function: the new ubiquity of privileged groups

The provision of public goods usually requires the concerted effort of a group. Sometimes most or all the members of a group must help out to produce the good. At other times, the good may require the efforts of only a smaller subgroup within the community. This relationship between the proportion of the group contributing to a public good and the proportion of the public good that is produced is known as the production function.[5]

I discussed above that a remarkable characteristic of the Internet is that any piece of information posted to an online group becomes a public good. A second remarkable characteristic is that the size of the group necessary to produce many public goods is often reduced to one. Groups in which an individual is able and willing to pay the costs of providing a public good by himself or herself are known as "privileged groups" (Olson 1965: 49–50).

Until the advent of online interaction, privileged groups were considered an unusual exception – most public goods required the actions of a group. While very small privileged groups can easily be imagined (someone planning a party for friends), very large privileged groups, while logically possible, were so rare and exotic that they were the stuff of legends. A famous example of a public good provided by a single individual within a huge group is retold by Hardin (1982):

> Consider the actual case of billionaire Howard Hughes, whose tastes ran to watching western and aviation movies on television from midnight to 6:00 AM. When he moved to Las Vegas where the local television station went off the air at 11:00 PM, his aides badgered the station's owner to schedule movies through the night until the owner finally challenged a Hughes emissary: "Why doesn't he just buy the thing and run it the way he wants to?" Hughes obliged, paid $3.8 million for the station, and ran movies until 6:00 AM. The potential audience for these movies was a quarter of a million people.
>
> (Hardin 1982: 42; the story was originally reported in *Time*, April 8, 1974: 42)[6]

What makes this story newsworthy is that it took the resources of one of the world's most wealthy persons to create a public good that could benefit hundreds of thousands of individuals. This is no longer newsworthy – a single individual with access to a thousand dollars of computer hardware can now produce information and Web content that might be viewed by and benefit a potential audience of millions.

The fact that many digital public goods can be provided by a single individual means that in these cases there are no coordination costs to bear and that there is no danger of being a sucker, in the sense of contributing to a good that requires the efforts of many, only to find that too few have contributed. Thus, an important category of costs is eliminated, as is the fear of contributing to a lost cause. And while the fact that something has the quality of a public good has usually meant that it might be difficult to motivate individuals to produce it, in the case of a privileged group the fact that one's solitary contribution becomes a public good can actually serve as a positive motivation for the person to provide it – there is the hope that it will be seen by and benefit a potentially huge audience.

Shifts in the economies of production mean that individuals are able to produce many public goods on their own. And the decrease in contribution and coordination costs as well as the potential amplification in the value of the contribution (because of the huge audience) makes it more likely that an individual will experience a net benefit from providing the good.

Motivations for contributing

The specific effects of changes in the costs and benefits of online cooperation will depend on what general motivations are driving the decision to cooperate. In this section I discuss a list of possible motivations for providing public goods. I begin by examining motivations that do not require any assumptions about altruism or group attachment. In other words, these motivations rest on self interest (either short term or long term). I then discuss possible motivations for this kind of cooperation that relax the assumption of egoism and take it for granted that individuals care to some degree about the outcomes of others.

One possibility is that a person is motivated to contribute valuable information to the group in the expectation that one will receive useful help and information in return; that is, the motivation is an anticipated reciprocity. As I discussed above, it is sometimes the case that reciprocity will occur within the group as a whole in a system of generalized exchange. This type of network-wide accounting system creates a kind of credit, in that one can draw upon the contributions of others without needing to immediately reciprocate. Such a system, in which accounts do not need to be kept continually and exactly in balance, has numerous potential benefits (Kollock 1993). If each person shares freely, the group as a whole is better off, having access to information and advice that no single person might match. A loose accounting system can also serve as a kind of insurance, in that one can draw from the resources of the group when in need, without needing to immediately repay each person.[7]

While participants may accept the existence of outstanding debt, there is likely to be some sense that there should be a rough balance over time. Someone should not simply take without ever contributing to the group. Members may eventually shun those who never give or conversely make an effort to help those who have contributed in the past (helping the "good citizens" of the group). Indeed, some observers (Wellman and Gulia, Chapter 7 in this volume; Rheingold 1993) have reported that individuals who regularly offer advice and information seem to receive more help more quickly when they ask for something.

If the possibility of future reciprocation is the motivation driving an individual's contribution, then the likelihood of providing public goods will be increased to the extent individuals are likely to interact with each other in the future and to the extent that there is some way to keep track of past actions (for example, by making sure contributions are seen by the group as a whole or by providing archives of past actions and contributions). Identity persistence is also a very important feature in encouraging contributions based on reciprocity. If identities are not registered to particular users and stable across time, and if there is no record of past actions and contributions, an account of past contributions, however loose, cannot be kept (Kollock 1996, 1998). A final feature that would encourage reciprocity over time is a well-defined and defended group boundary (Ostrom 1990; Kollock and Smith 1996). If the population of a group is extremely unstable, there is the temptation to come into a group and take advantage of its resources and then leave. Contributing something to the group today in hopes of taking something back later amounts to making a loan to the group. If the recipients of the loan leave, the system of generalized exchange breaks down.

A second possible motivation is the effect of contributions on one's reputation. High quality information, impressive technical details in one's answers, a willingness to help others, and elegant writing can all work to increase one's prestige in the community. Rheingold (1993) in his discussion of the WELL lists the desire for prestige as one of the key motivations of individuals' contributions to the group. To the extent this is the concern of an individual, contributions will likely be increased to the degree that the contribution is visible to the community as a whole and to the extent there is some recognition of the person's contributions. The inherent nature of online interaction already means that helpful acts are more likely to be seen by the group as a whole. And the powerful effects of seemingly trivial markers of recognition (e.g. being designated as an "official helper") has been commented on in a number of online communities. In addition, each of the features that encourage reciprocity – ongoing interaction, identity persistence, knowledge of previous interactions, and strong group boundaries – would also work to promote the creation and importance of reputations within an online community.

A third possible motivation is that individuals contribute valuable information because the act results in a sense of efficacy, that is, a sense that they have some effect on this environment. There is a well-developed research literature that has shown how important a sense of efficacy is (e.g. Bandura 1995), and making regular and high quality contributions to the group can help individuals believe that they have an impact on the group and support their own self-image as an efficacious person. If a sense of efficacy is what is motivating someone, then contributions are likely to be increased to the extent that people can observe changes in the community attributable to their actions. It may also be the case that as the size of the group increases, one will be more motivated to contribute because the increasing size provides a larger audience and a potentially greater impact for one's actions.

For none of these three motivations do we need to assume that the individual is altruistic – simple self-interest is enough. However, it may sometime be the case that an individual values (at least to some degree) the outcomes of others. In this case a fourth possible motivation is need, that is, one may produce and contribute a public good for the simple reason that a person or the group as a whole has a need for it. Rheingold (1993) again draws from the WELL in giving examples of members producing software tools for the community's use after the need for such tools had been discussed. If someone's or some group's needs are what motivates an individual, then their contributions will likely be increased to the extent that the needs of the group are clearly known and communicated. An ongoing record of the group's discussion is useful here, as are central meeting places (e.g. a "public square") where important issues and needs can be discussed and displayed.

More generally, an additional possible motivation is the attachment or commitment one can have to the group. In other words, the good of the group enters one's utility equation. In this case one contributes to the group because that is what is best for the group – individual and collective outcomes are thus merged and there is no social dilemma. However, complete devotion to a group is rare. It is much more likely that even if an individual feels an attachment to the group, it will be moderated by other desires and the price of helping the group. A literal altruist – who works for the good of others without any regard to self – is very rare indeed. Nevertheless, to the extent that someone feels an attachment to the community, that person's contributions will likely be increased to the extent that the goals of the community are developed, clearly articulated, and communicated to the members.

In all the cases mentioned above, whether the motivation is based on some form of self-interest or altruism, the kinds and quantities of public good produced will be sensitive to the costs and benefits involved. This is the theme from the first part of the chapter, and it is worth stressing again that regardless of what motivation or mix of motivations is driving a person's actions, the shifting economies of online cooperation will make many kinds of public goods possible and profitable that otherwise would not be.

As a last example of these effects, consider the impact of the fact that the distributions costs for a piece of information can be near zero. While it may be the case that many people spend time and effort producing goods they intend to contribute to the group, another path to the production of public goods is as a simple side-effect of private behavior. People may need to write a particular computer program for their own use with no thought to anything other than solving their particular problem at hand. Having written the program, the costs of now sharing and distributing it with others may be near zero: they can simply post it in an appropriate discussion group or other online community. Here again, the ease with which this can be done, and the manifold benefits it might have for others and for themselves, mean that the fruits of one's private workshop can be distributed to the world.

Illustrations

While I have made the point that many digital public goods can be provided by single individuals, other public goods certainly require the coordinated actions of a group. In order to explore the additional challenges that are created when a group must act in concert to produce a public good, and in order to illustrate the dynamics I have been discussing, I will describe two striking examples of online collective action. The case studies are the 1996 effort to wire California's elementary schools for Internet access, known as NetDay 96, and the production of a new computer operating system, known as Linux, through the use of voluntary labor.

Linux: the "impossible" public good

Consider the following goal: to create a clone of a powerful and complex computer operating system by asking programmers from around the world to donate their time and effort to the project. The operating system would be made available free to anyone who wanted it, regardless of whether they had contributed to the project.

Such a project seems doomed to failure. The temptation to free-ride is huge for two separate reasons. First, because the program (should it be successfully developed) would be made available to anyone at no cost, there is the temptation to let other people write the program and then enjoy the fruits of their labor. Second, even if one were willing to contribute to the project, there is a very serious risk that the project would fail if not enough people contributed their efforts. The risk of contributing to a lost cause could dissuade even those who wanted to support the project. Remarkably, this goal was accomplished. In a little over two years time a clone of the Unix operating system named Linux was created.

Linux began in 1991 as a private research project of a computer science student in Finland who wanted to write a Unix-like system for his 80386 computer. His name is Linus Torvalds and in the early history of the project he wrote most of the code himself. After a few months of work he had succeeded in developing a version of the program that was reasonably useful and stable. There was still a tremendous amount of work to be done, but the fact that his program was now usable encouraged a great number of people to contribute to the project. By the beginning of 1994 Linux had become a powerful and useful operating system and was officially released as version 1.0. It is available free to anyone who wants it and is constantly being revised and improved through the volunteer labor of many programmers.

How can we account for the production of such an improbable public good? The question has been asked to Linus Torvalds in a number of interviews, and his comments and the comments of others involved in the project suggest a number of reasons why the Linux project succeeded.

One of the points made by Torvalds and others was the ability of the Internet to facilitate collaboration. Early in the project Torvalds made use of the Internet to get help with the development of the program and to gather suggestions and advice about the features the program should contain. As people began to experiment with his program they sent in bug reports to let Torvalds know about problems with Linux. Some programmers also sent in computer code with their bug reports in order to fix the problem. Eventually, people volunteered to write new code for the program in order to expand its list of features and usefulness. Here we see the reduction in communication and coordination costs that was mentioned above – online interaction made it easy to send in comments and suggestions and to keep everyone who was interested up-to-date on the current state of the program. Torvalds flatly states that "without net access, the project would never have even gotten off the ground" (Torvalds 1993).

But these savings in the costs of communicating and collaborating are not enough to explain the success of Linux. There are a great many programs that would be useful for the Internet community and yet have not been developed in the same decentralized way as Linux. Torvalds has stated that programs which are collaboratively developed on the Internet usually share two features:

> (a) Somebody (usually one person) wrote the basic program to the state where it was already usable. The net community then takes over and refines and fixes problems, resulting in a much better program than the original, but the important part is to get it started (and channeling the development some way). The net works a bit like a committee: you'll need a few dedicated persons who do most of the stuff or nothing will get done.

> (b) You need to have a project that many programmers feel is interesting: this does not seem to be the case with a lot of the application programs. A program like a word processor has no "glamour": it may be the program that most users would want to see, and most programmers would agree that it's not a simple thing to write, but I also think they find it a bit boring.
>
> (Torvalds 1993)

The first feature implies that the shape of the production function also played a role – even though many people were needed for the eventual success of the project, the ability of a small number of people (or even one) to get the project under way may be crucial. The second feature suggests that the intrinsic interest and challenge of the project can be important. If people find the task interesting and useful for themselves, then the production of the larger public good must deal with issues of coordination but not motivation: the project was interesting for many programmers and they were helping to develop something that would be personally useful to them. Indeed, as programmers began to contribute code to the project, their contributions were often directed at making the operating system useful for themselves (e.g. writing device drivers for the operating system so that they could use hardware and peripherals that were of interest to them). Once these subprograms were developed, it was very easy to share the work with the entire Linux community because of the extremely low costs of posting and distributing the information.

A key reason why people were willing to share their work was the fact that the Linux project was put under a particular copyright agreement known as the GNU General Public License.[8] Under the terms of this copyright agreement the source code for the program would be freely available to anyone.[9] Further, anyone who modified the program was required to add the modification to the source code and make it available to all. The arrangement creates an incentive structure in which programmers are encouraged to contribute modifications to the program because they are assured that everyone will have access to their contributions and that they will have access to any modifications other people have made, either currently or in the future. This helps create a healthy generalized exchange system. Further, because the source code is available to all, it is open to the inspection and critique of others. This makes the programmer's contribution public and creates an informal monitoring system as others review the code. Thus, there is an incentive to contribute well-written code.[10]

NetDay 96: a modern barn raising

In 1995 John Gage of Sun Microsystems and Michael Kaufman of KQED in San Francisco came up with an audacious idea: to wire all of California's public and private schools for connection to the Internet using an army of volunteers. The campaign focused on a single day – March 9, 1996 – when most of the actual wiring would take place. The event was a classic example of a public good – the potential gains to the schools and to the communities as a whole were great, but those benefits would be enjoyed regardless of whether one volunteered for the project. Thus, there was the temptation to free-ride on others' efforts, but if everyone tried to free-ride, the campaign would fail. Because this was a public good that could only be provided by the efforts of a very large group, there was the additional challenge of trying to recruit and coordinate the large number of volunteers that would be needed. Even if one could assume that there were thousands of willing contributors, there would still be the problem of distributing them across different schools, assuring them that their efforts would not be in vain, training them, and keeping both volunteers and schools up-to-date on how things were progressing.[11]

Remarkably, the effort was in large part a success and generated the endorsements and attention of prominent business, community, and political leaders. On NetDay itself, over 2,500 schools were wired by approximately 20,000 volunteers (Colvin 1996). While the goal of wiring every California school was not reached on NetDay 96, the effort was successful enough that further NetDay events were held in California, and similar programs have been set up in all the US states and in several other countries.

Even more striking was the fact that the NetDay organization had no offices, budget, paid staff, mailings, or even a receptionist to answer the phone.[12] Instead, the overarching promotion, recruitment, and coordination for the campaign was carried out via the World Wide Web. In order to save time, effort, and money, the plan was to use the Web as a decentralized organizing tool. The Web site was carefully designed to facilitate the recruitment and coordination of volunteers and took advantage of the shifting economies of online interaction as well as new software technologies that had been developed by a number of companies.

One of the most innovative features of the site was a clickable map of California that listed every school in the state and provided a visual representation of the level of volunteer activity at each school. By repeatedly clicking on an area of the map, people could zoom in on their own county, city, neighborhood, and even block to search out schools in their area. Schools were represented by colored dots, with a red dot signifying that the schools had no volunteers for NetDay, a yellow dot indicating one to four volunteers, and a green dot indicating more than four volunteers. The data were updated hourly, and so the map provided an up-to-date visual accounting of volunteers across the state. This made it easy for volunteers to discover where they were needed and for schools to track the number of volunteers who had signed up to help their school. The map also had the additional effect of advertising the fact that many people had already volunteered and that more were doing so every day. This is an important point because even if people are willing to contribute to a public good, they may not want to participate unless they know enough others will contribute to make the event a success.[13]

As one zoomed in on the map to view a particular neighborhood, any of the dots representing schools could be selected. This brought up a Web page for the school that provided basic information and allowed one to sign up as a volunteer, organizer, or sponsor. Volunteers entered personal information onto an online form and listed the skills they had as well as any additional comments. Once volunteers signed up, they were automatically added to a list on the school's page. Their names, email addresses, skills, and comments were listed. Online sign-up forms were also available for those who wished to be sponsors or organizers for the event. Sponsors were responsible for purchasing the wiring kits that each school would need and for providing technical assistance. Online descriptions of the wiring kits and order forms were also provided on the site so that ordering the kit for the school could be done as easily and quickly as possible. Organizers were responsible for contacting the school, contacting the registered volunteers, and arranging a meeting of the volunteers prior to NetDay.

Thus, the school Web pages made it easy for volunteers to see what help was needed, to sign up, to contact the school and other volunteers, to inform the school and other volunteers of their skills and experience, and to keep up-to-date on organization efforts. Further, all of this was accomplished in a decentralized way without any staff.

Information that would be needed for the effort was also made available via the Web – everything from To Do lists for volunteers and organizers to a large Frequently Asked Questions file was provided. There was also the issue of training the volunteers. Even though it was hoped that individuals and organizations with technical expertise would be on hand to help with the installation, not everyone would have experience installing this particular kind of wiring, and some volunteers would want to learn about the process before showing up on NetDay. To meet this need, an online wiring installation guide was created that provided pictures, animation, and detailed step-by-step instruction for wiring the classrooms.

The campaign also advertised endorsements and corporate supporters on the Web site. The list of endorsements was an impressive roster of leaders in government, education, and business. From the standpoint of the person making the endorsement, adding his or her name was trivially easy, involving almost no time or effort, and the long list of dignitaries helped to provide legitimacy for the campaign. A list of corporate supporters was also provided, and the corporations were ranked according to how many volunteers from the company were participating. Research on social dilemmas and public goods has demonstrated that people are more likely to cooperate if their actions are public (Kollock 1998). This list made the support of companies public, while inviting comparisons and competition between companies. The list also served as an acknowledgment of the efforts of top companies.

It is important to note that while a great deal of the organization occurred online, there were also many face-to-face meetings. In particular, the California Department of Education organized regional meetings for schools and districts who wanted information or assistance with NetDay activities. At the school level, face-to-face meetings were also common among school officials, organizers, and volunteers. Thus, the NetDay Web site facilitated local organization and meetings rather than completely supplanting them.[14]

The Web site provided a database that displayed and updated information on volunteer activities without the need for any staff. Online resources also reduced the costs of signing up for the campaign as well as contacting other volunteers. The color-coded map served to assure others that many people were involved in the project, helped direct volunteers to where they were needed, and allowed everyone to keep track of the current status of efforts. And the nature of digital information also made it extremely cheap to distribute information to anyone who was interested and to broadcast such things as the rankings of corporate supporters and list of endorsements. Consider how expensive each of these functions would be if organizers had to rely on mailings, or had to buy time on radio, television, or in newspapers.

The usual benefits of digital goods were also a factor in that informational resources – such as the installation guide, To Do lists, and the Frequently Asked Questions file – once produced were available to an unlimited audience. The resources could also be produced with fewer individuals than would be the case if the material had to be physically published and distributed. This demonstrates again changes in costs and the production function as one moves to digital goods. The online resources helped create a quickly organizing and highly efficient federated system that supported more conventional face-to-face meetings at the local school level.

NetDay is also an interesting case in that it demonstrates the use of digital goods in the service of producing a physical good. Unlike most of the other illustrations discussed in this chapter, the final public good was not some type of digital information, but rather physically upgraded classrooms. NetDay demonstrates that the economies of online interaction can be used to facilitate the production of some physical goods as well.

The limits of online cooperation

The previous examples were designed to illustrate the ways online interaction can significantly reduce the costs of providing some public goods. However, I do not wish to imply that online interaction solves all problems of cooperation and collective action. The shifting costs, benefits, and production functions of online interaction make a certain class of public goods more likely, but it is important to recognize the requisites of this online cooperation in order to appreciate its limitations.

Torvalds suggested that Linux was successfully developed in part because Linux was considered inherently interesting and because one person was able to write the core of the program. Each of these features suggests limits to the decentralized co-operation of the Internet. A new operating system has been created, but it is far less likely that equally useful, but much less interesting, programs such as a word processor or spreadsheet will be collaboratively developed by a network of volunteers. I would also hazard to guess that if NetDay had been directed toward patching the roofs and repairing the plumbing of schools – an equally important but less technologically interesting goal – the turnout would have been significantly less.

Torvalds' second point implies another limitation. The nature of digital goods and the economies of online interaction mean that many public goods can be produced by small groups or single individuals. But many public goods, even digital public goods, require the coordinated activities of a large group from the very beginning. Such public goods are less likely to be produced, though NetDay demonstrates that a very large project requiring close coordination among thousands can be orchestrated and augmented via online interaction.

It is also true, of course, that many of the public goods a healthy community requires are physical in nature and cannot be provided solely through online interaction. Roads, hospitals, and schools must be built and maintained, and while the Internet can certainly facilitate the production of physical public goods (again, as demonstrated by NetDay), in the end bricks and mortar must be laid.

Thus, as remarkable as the products of online cooperation and collaboration have been, it may be that we have been picking the "lowest hanging fruit" – supplying interesting digital goods that can be provided by single individuals while ignoring duller, more complex, but no less useful public goods. I do not mean to slight the benefits that online interaction has brought, and further advances in hardware, software, and connectivity may reduce the cost of producing public goods still further and create new "low-hanging fruit." Nevertheless, it is crucial to avoid an empty-headed extrapolation from current success to utopian visions of fully cooperative communities.[15]

It is also useful to consider what changes in the structure of online communities might encourage or discourage online cooperation. One place to start is the previous discussion on motivations. Although a number of different motivations for contributing to a public good were discussed, three structural features are common in many of the cases and can be regarded as the basic features required of any successful online community (Kollock 1996). These features are ongoing interaction, identity persistence, and knowledge of previous interactions. If members of a group will not meet each other in the future, if there is no stability in the names and identities that people adopt, and if there is no memory or community record of previous interaction, it will be very difficult to create and maintain a cooperative online community.[16]

Among the other structural features discussed that can encourage cooperation are making sure that contributions are visible and that contributors are recognized for their efforts, and well-defined and defended group boundaries. To make a broad statement, to the extent an online community lacks each of these features, we can expect that cooperation and collective action will be less likely.[17] Of course, if a certain motivation turns out to be especially significant in people's decision to cooperate, then the structural features that encourage this motivation will be particularly important. For example, if most people contribute information and advice because they anticipate receiving information at a later point in time, then well-defined group boundaries will be particularly important because a successful generalized exchange system requires a reasonably stable population.

As a final note, it is important to point out that a cooperative group is not always a good thing for the wider society. The very same economies that enable people to collaboratively build software and plan school improvements also make it easier for violent and racist groups to organize and collaborate. To the extent one wishes to fight against such groups, then the lessons of this chapter need to be inverted in order to discourage group cooperation.

Conclusion

This has been a chapter on incentive structures, but incentive structures are not the same thing as actual motivations. Thus, an important direction for additional research is identifying which motivations in particular are driving people's decisions. Detailed case studies of online collective action are one way of addressing this question, and the chapters by Gurak, Uncapher, and Mele in this volume provide valuable information on the motivations and structural conditions necessary for collective action.

Future research should also examine the importance of various structural features: are strong group boundaries important, for example, and if so, does this imply a higher rate of contributions (or better quality information) in a closed mailing list versus a Usenet newsgroup? Are public goods less likely to be provided when they require the contributions of a large group versus being able to be provided by a single individual? The pattern of reciprocity in online groups is another important research topic. Do people who have helped in the past receive more help when they are in need? Does a strong group boundary encourage a healthy generalized exchange system? Such studies will be increasingly important as our lives move more and more into online worlds.

The purpose of this chapter was to begin to map out an explanation for the striking amount of cooperation that exists in online communities. This is not to say that online cooperation is inevitable or expanding. Nor is it to say that online cooperation and collective action is always a benefit to the larger society. However, the changing economies of online interaction have shifted the costs of providing public goods – sometimes radically – and thus changed the kinds of groups, communities, and institutions that are viable in this new social landscape.

Notes

1 Direct correspondence to Peter Kollock, Department of Sociology, University of California, Los Angeles, CA 90095–1551 (Kollock@ucla.edu). This chapter complements an earlier article (Kollock and Smith 1996) on "Managing the Virtual Commons." The earlier article discussed the basic social dilemmas that occur in online interaction, using Usenet discussion groups as the case study. It used as its framework Ostrom's (1990) work on common pool resources. The present chapter concentrates specifically on public goods and the shifts in the costs and benefits of providing public goods.

2 See Kollock (1998) for a review of research on social dilemmas, and Kollock and Smith (1996) for a fuller discussion of social dilemmas in online interaction. The link between generalized exchange and social dilemmas is investigated by Yamagishi and Cook (1993).

3 Another cost that can be associated with collective action is the cost of bargaining (Heckathorn 1996). The effects of online interaction on bargaining costs are more uncertain, and it is unclear whether the costs of bargaining are accentuated or attenuated (cf. A. Smith, Chapter 6 in this volume).

4 See Slatalla (1996) for a description of an online support community for those caring for Alzheimer's patients.

5 Strictly speaking, the production function refers to the level of resources that are

contributed rather than the number of actors that are contributing. See Heckathorn (1996) for a very useful analysis of production functions and the provision of public goods.

6 Of course, this example assumes other people also valued late-night westerns.

7 One hears stories, for example, of people who have faced an impossible deadline for a report and have turned to their online network to gather the information necessary to quickly complete the task.

8 The license was developed by the Free Software Foundation: http://www.gnu.ai. mit.edu/copyleft/gpl.html.

9 The source code is the plain text version of a computer program before it is digested by a compiler into instructions for the computer. Having the source code means that the inner workings of a program can be examined, studied, and modified by a programmer.

10 I note in passing a few other features that may have contributed to the successful development of Linux. Torvalds depended on a set of software tools (the GNU tools) that had previously been developed in a similar collaborative project. Bentson (1995) also suggests that the project was helped by the fact that there was a fairly large population of programmers to draw from who had the requisite skills. He also suggests that the prevalence of personal computers may have helped in that programmers had more freedom to explore and experiment on their own systems rather than monopolizing and potentially introducing buggy software into larger mini and mainframe computer system.

11 Note that coordination for NetDay posed a more severe challenge than the coordination of the development of Linux because NetDay was organized around a particular day when most of the activities needed to be accomplished.

12 The only phone number that existed was a single number with a voice mail system that provided basic information.

13 The possible effects of advertising the number of current volunteers brings up some interesting strategic concerns. Might it be better, for example, to wait until a certain number of people had volunteered before making the map public during the early stages of the campaign? In this way new potential volunteers would not confront a map devoid of contributors, which could discourage them from signing up. This is, in fact, the strategy of many fund raising campaigns – they are not publicly announced until a significant proportion of the goal has already been met. And there is also the possibility of using deceit: organizers could inflate the number of reported volunteers early in a campaign in order to encourage others to join. (Of course, I do not mean to imply in any way that the number of volunteers reported for NetDay was inaccurate.) For a general discussion of the dynamics of such "critical mass" phenomena, see Schelling (1978).

14 Local organization and coordination with school officials was not as great as it should have been during the first NetDay. California's second NetDay (on October 12, 1996) placed an emphasis on coordinating more closely with local schools and giving them more time to prepare and train volunteers (Pool 1996).

15 Purveyors of utopian visions rarely seem to realize the irony of the term itself. Coined by Sir Thomas More in 1516, "utopia" literally means "not a place," that is, a place that cannot be.

16 These three features turn up repeatedly in the research literature of social dilemmas (Kollock 1998). Axelrod (1984), for example, identifies them as the most important prerequisites for cooperation.

17 This list of features partially overlaps the list of design principles Ostrom (1990) identified in her study of communities managing common pool resources (see also Kollock and Smith 1996).

References

Axelrod, Robert. 1984. *The Evolution of Cooperation*. New York: Basic Books.

Bandura, Albert (ed.). 1995. *Self-Efficacy in Changing Societies*. Cambridge: Cambridge University Press.

Bell, Duran. 1991. "Modes of Exchange: Gift and Commodity." *Journal of Socio-Economics* 20(2): 155–67.

Bentson, Randolph. 1995. "The Humble Beginnings of Linux." *Linux Journal* 11(March), http://www.linuxjournal.com/lj/issue11/history.html.

Carrier, James. 1991. "Gifts, Commodities, and Social Relations: A Maussian View of Exchange." *Sociological Forum* 6(1):119–36.

Colvin, Richard Lee. 1996. "Volunteers Wire 2,500 Schools on NetDay." *Los Angeles Times* 10 March: A-1.

Ekeh, Peter P. 1974. *Social Exchange Theory: The Two Traditions*. Cambridge, MA: Harvard University Press.

Hardin, Russell. 1982. *Collective Action*. Baltimore, MD: Johns Hopkins University Press.

Heckathorn, Douglas D. 1996. "The Dynamics and Dilemmas of Collective Action." *American Sociological Review* 61(2): 250–77.

Kollock, Peter. 1993. "'An Eye for an Eye Leaves Everyone Blind': Cooperation and Accounting Systems." *American Sociological Review* 58(6): 768–86.

Kollock, Peter. 1996. "Design Principles for Online Communities." In *The Internet and Society: Harvard Conference Proceedings* also available at http://www.sscnet.ucla.edu/soc/faculty/kollock/papers/design.htm).

Kollock, Peter. 1998. "Social Dilemmas: The Anatomy of Cooperation." *Annual Review of Sociology* 24: 183–214.

Kollock, Peter and Marc Smith. 1996. "Managing the Virtual Commons: Cooperation and Conflict in Computer Communities." In *Computer-Mediated Communication: Linguistic, Social, and Cross-Cultural Perspectives*, edited by Susan Herring. Amsterdam: John Benjamins.

Mauss, Marcel. 1969 (1935). *The Gift*. London: Routledge & Kegan Paul.

Negroponte, Nicholas. 1995. *Being Digital*. New York: Knopf.

Olson, Mancur, Jr. 1965. *The Logic of Collective Action*. Cambridge, MA: Harvard University Press.

Ostrom, Elinor. 1990. *Governing the Commons: The Evolution of Institutions for Collective Action*. New York: Cambridge University Press.

Pool, Bob. 1996. "NetDay 2 Puts more L.A. Schools Online." *Los Angeles Times* 13 October: B–12.

Rheingold, Howard. 1993. *The Virtual Community: Homesteading on the Electronic Frontier*. New York: Addison-Wesley.

Schelling, Thomas C. 1978. *Micromotives and Macrobehavior*. New York: Norton.

Simon, Stephanie. 1996. "Internet Changing the Way Some Lawyers Do Business." *Los Angeles Times* 8 July: A–1.

Slatalla, Michelle. 1996. "Who Can I Turn To?" *Wired* 4(5): 116–19, 184–8.

Torvalds, Linus. 1993. "The Choice of a Gnu Generation: An Interview with Linus Torvalds." *Meta* 1(November): http://www.au.com/meta/history/interview.html.

Yamagishi, Toshio and Karen S. Cook. 1993. "Generalized Exchange and Social Dilemmas." *Social Psychology Quarterly* 56(4): 235–48.

Part five

Collective action

Chapter 10

The promise and the peril of social action in cyberspace

Ethos, delivery, and the protests over MarketPlace and the Clipper chip[1]

Laura J. Gurak

In April 1990, Lotus Development Corporation announced a product called Market-Place: Households. MarketPlace was to be a direct mail marketing database for Macintosh computers and would contain name, address, and spending habit information on 120 million individual American consumers. After MarketPlace was announced, computer privacy advocates began investigating the product. Although most of the data contained in MarketPlace were already available (data were provided by Equifax, the second largest credit reporting agency in the United States), privacy advocates felt that MarketPlace went far beyond current standards for privacy protection.

From Lotus's first announcement until months after it canceled the product, the Internet was full of discussions about MarketPlace; soon, debates about the privacy implications of MarketPlace and suggestions for contacting Lotus began to circulate. People posted Lotus's address and phone number, the email address of Lotus's chief executive officer (CEO), and also gave information about how to request that names be removed from the database. Some people posted "form letters" that could be sent to Lotus. Notices were forwarded around the Internet, reposted to other newsgroups, and sent off as email messages. In one case, a discussion group was formed specifically to discuss the product. As a result of the Internet-based protest, over 30,000 people contacted Lotus and asked that their names be removed from the database. The product, which had been scheduled to be released during the third quarter of 1990, was never released. In the end, many acknowledged the role of online action in stopping the release of MarketPlace. Some subsequently called it a "victory for computer populism" (Winner 1991).

A few years later, another action took place in cyberspace. The case of the Clipper chip is based on a long history of encryption technology. Encryption involves the use of a mathematical algorithm to "scramble" electronic messages. The message sender encodes the message and sends it out across the electronic medium; the person on the receiving end must then use the corresponding decryption algorithm to descramble the message so that he or she can actually read and understand it. Encryption is used for security and privacy purposes, and its use dates back well before electronic technology.

The controversy, however, surrounding the Clipper chip involved the federal government's proposed use and ownership of the encryption algorithm. Clipper is the name of a specific encryption chip that could be inserted in a telephone handset. When a call was made, the transmission would be scrambled, then descrambled at the receiving end. The technology itself is not what caused privacy and free speech advocates on the Internet to become alarmed. Instead, the problem, as they saw it, was with who would own the "key," or descrambling algorithm, and who would regulate exactly which kinds of encryption programs could be used and exported from the US. The government, under the Clinton administration, proposed that all encrypted messages should ultimately be able to be deencrypted by the government for security purposes. Privacy and free speech advocates, however, did not (and still do not) agree, and in February 1994, a group of privacy advocates organized an Internet-based petition drive, which generated approximately 47,000 signatures. The purpose of this petition was to defeat Clipper chip policies being considered at that time. As with the MarketPlace case, a community of privacy advocates used the Internet to disseminate technical information and organize people with common values about privacy and encryption.

This chapter analyzes the MarketPlace and Clipper protests from a rhetorical perspective. I argue that two rhetorical features, powerful and quick delivery on computer networks and a strong community *ethos*, were critical to both social actions because these features sustain such actions in the absence of traditional face-to-face methods of establishing presence and delivering a message. I argue that what we see in both of these cases is truly the proverbial double-edged sword. On the one hand, these cases illustrate the promise of online communication for crossing physical boundaries and allowing people of common interests and goals to meet and act across space and time. Yet at the same time, the MarketPlace and Clipper cases illustrate a certain peril: the very same features of delivery and *ethos* that allowed for these actions also encouraged a kind of insularity and the spread of inaccurate information, with participants trusting "the Net community" even in the face of some obvious factual errors.

Research in computer-mediated communication has long noted this dichotomy: the technology provides the opportunity for more people to communicate, but at the same time it appears to encourage a tendency toward what has been called "uninhibited behavior" (Hiltz and Turoff 1993; Sproull and Kiesler 1986; Rice and Love 1987). Yet these studies were primarily conducted in the context of discrete organizations or experimental settings. The promise and peril illustrated by MarketPlace and Clipper extend beyond individual organizations to the broader political and social sphere. Moreover, the peril in these cases is not over individual instances of flaming; it is about the exclusionary power of strong community *ethos*, propelled by rapid delivery across corporate, organizational, and national boundaries.

Social and political action on the Internet is still somewhat novel, yet the trend appears to be toward an ever-increasing use of cyberspace as a political arena. Much ado has been made in the popular press about the notion of cyberdemocracy; in fact, many localities and states have "electronic democracy" projects, and citizens can now write to most local and national representatives via the Internet. At issue, therefore, is how traditional rhetorical activities (such as speeches, public debates, and protests) conducted in these new online spaces differ or are enhanced or problematized by the uses of computer-mediated communication technologies. Rhetorical discourse, for example, has until very recently functioned primarily in the world of physicality. The MarketPlace and Clipper cases illustrate that while there is great promise in this new technology, participants should also be aware that the very nature of communication in cyberspace may encourage a speedy response when in fact more research on the topic may be in order. The rhetorical dynamics of online communities certainly do allow many citizens to participate, but concerns about dominance and exclusion should make us aware as we continue to design and use these systems.

I begin with a short section describing my research method. Next, I introduce the rhetorical concepts of *ethos* and delivery, which should be helpful for the non-rhetorician and the rhetorician alike, as I use these terms in a somewhat non-traditional fashion. This section is followed by the case analysis, which examines the promise and then the peril of delivery and *ethos* in cyberspace.

Rhetorical analysis of cybertexts

The Lotus and Clipper studies were conducted using rhetorical criticism triangulated with standard qualitative research methods including participant observation (done online) and interviews. For both projects, I collected all available electronic texts of the Lotus and Clipper chip controversies by searching the Internet, downloading files, and performing a brief analysis to determine content integrity. The texts are from sources including Usenet newsgroups, bulletin boards, discussion lists, email, and messages received by members of Congress and other officials. Texts were then analyzed for their rhetorical features, including the speaker's use of *ethos* (appeal by character), use of *logos* (logical argument), structure of the discourse (deductive or inductive), style (formal or informal), and speed of delivery.[2]

Along with performing textual analysis, I observed the online forums and interviewed organizers and participants of the electronic forums. For both studies, this process involved tracing "header" information (information in the "To," "From," and "Subject" lines) of an electronic message in order to locate the author(s) of the postings. I conducted interviews primarily via email and telephone.

I have considered material from a publicly accessible electronic forum to be published material and have treated this material as such, excerpting from text and citing with footnotes. Yet even though my use of this material is criticism and thus would no doubt fall under the fair use provisions for copyright, I have made one significant change in this material: I have not used real names of the authors of these Internet postings. Instead, except in cases where I obtained explicit permission or where the person is a public figure, I have changed authors' real names to pseudonyms, indicated by the use of square brackets within the texts themselves and the use of quotation marks in the footnoted citations. Thus, I have cited Internet postings with accuracy and with respect for privacy balanced by a belief that material posted to publicly accessible Internet forums can and should be used by scholars and researchers.[3]

Ethos, delivery, and online rhetoric

The features of *ethos* and delivery are not new in the public speaking arena; both have been important since the early Greek rhetorics of Plato and Aristotle. But online, *ethos* and delivery take on new significance.

Based on their comments and on email addresses, many of the participants were computer or other professionals, often with specialized knowledge and tacit under-standings about computer privacy. The character and quality in which these values were expressed is evident in what in rhetorical terms can be called the *ethos* of the discourse. In each case, protest postings reflect a certain group *ethos*: in the Lotus case, this *ethos* was a personal, angry, and antagonistic voice; in the Clipper case, the group *ethos* was also angry at times but was also highly technical. In either case, the group *ethos* appealed to others of similar persuasion and made it easy to spread the word and attract others with similar beliefs into the protest community.

In classical rhetoric, *ethos* is associated with the credibility and character of the speaker. *Ethos* is one of the three modes of appeal – *pathos*, *ethos*, and *logos* – that make up Aristotle's system of invention. For Aristotle (1991), *ethos* was part of this broader inventional scheme of "finding in any given case the available means of persuasion" (1356a) and required speakers to "find" and assume the appropriate character traits for a given argument (1378a). The notion of *ethos* was also a part of the Roman rhetorical tradition (Cherry 1988: 255), with Quintilian's sense of the rhetor as "a man of good character and courtesy" (Meador 1983: 166) or Cicero's (1970) belief that wisdom must be accompanied by eloquence (B.I. C.II).[4]

While rooted in classical rhetoric, however, *ethos* is also a contemporary concept used widely to describe the character, tenor, or tone of a rhetor. In general discussion, one often hears references to "the *ethos*" of a particular public figure or time period. Along with this common usage, the concept has played a continued role throughout the contemporary rhetorical tradition. Throughout this chapter, the notion of *ethos* is based on these long-standing definitions: the values and character of the speaker(s) expressed in what has been called "a characteristic manner of holding and expressing ideas" (Halloran 1984: 71).

The focus of *ethos*, especially in the classical tradition, however, has primarily been on individual speakers. Yet in both the Lotus and Clipper cases, *ethos* was also a group quality, one which characterized the entire group by its collective sense of character and values. This notion of group *ethos* has been noted by Halloran (1982: 62), who suggests that the "word *ethos* has both an individual and a collective meaning. It makes sense to speak of the *ethos* of this or that person, but it makes equally good sense to speak of the *ethos* of a particular type of person, of a professional group, or a culture, or an era in history." Furthermore, *ethos* can be extended to the group persona created by communication technology.[5] Thus, the *ethos* of both the Lotus and Clipper cases highlights the claim that "*ethos* is not measurable traits displayed by an individual; rather it is a complex set of characteristics constructed by a group, sanctioned by that group, and more readily recognizable to others who belong or share similar values or experiences" (Reynolds 1993: 327, emphasis original). During the Lotus protest, for example, electronic texts served to create and maintain a "cyber-*ethos*" among community members. Electronic texts were characterized by a group *ethos* of sarcasm, blame, anger, and concern for personal privacy, which arose out of and reflected the character and values of the individual speakers and the community. Group *ethos* can also leave out or ostracize those who do not agree with the majority, and this problem is often enhanced by the specialized nature of electronic discussion lists.

Although *ethos* is most often used to refer "to the character of an age, era, society, or culture, something like *zeitgeist*" (Reynolds 1993: 327, emphasis original), there are two additional ways of considering *ethos* that are also of special significance to online discourse. The first is the relationship of *ethos* to ethics. It is not just the projection of a speaker or group's character, but his or hers, or the group's, actual moral and ethical character that is relevant to both the effectiveness and the quality of the speech. In online discourse, the ethical character of the speaker often goes unchallenged; the sense of trust among some people as members of "the Internet community" is often based on a person's stated professional affiliations and subsequent contributions to life on the Internet. Individuals, such as the person who sent out a form letter in the Lotus case, are often accepted as moral and credible even though the many Internet receivers of the message have never met the message's author(s) and in fact cannot be sure authors are who they say they are.

Another aspect of *ethos* comes from the actual etymology of the Greek word, which, when translated carefully, becomes "a habitual meeting place," thus invoking *ethos* as an "image of people gathering together in a public place, sharing experiences and ideas" (Halloran 1982: 61). Once this aspect of *ethos* as "space, place, or haunt" has been recognized, we can begin to see *ethos* "as a social act and a product of a community's character" (Reynolds 1993: 327); in other words, we can see that people come to acquire a community *ethos* by inhabiting the space and learning its unique communication characteristics. Nowhere could this concept be more obvious than in the specialized newsgroups and other electronic forums on the Internet, where outsiders are regularly "flamed" until they have come to understand and assimilate the community *ethos*, and where, as both the Lotus and Clipper cases illustrate, community *ethos* is the basis for what information other online participants will accept and believe.

In the Lotus and Clipper cases, *ethos* functioned hand-in-hand with the delivery medium of computer-mediated communication. Delivery is the fifth of the five components, or canons, of rhetorical discourse,[6] and it traditionally involved gestures, facial expressions, vocal intonations, and other physical actions and "body language" involved in giving a speech. The relationship between *ethos* and delivery in rhetorical theory is well noted and is quite obvious: one's perceived credibility and persona are inherently linked to the way in which one delivers a speech.

In electronic discourse, this relationship is equally important, but in a somewhat altered and novel fashion; hence Bolter's (1993: 97) suggestion that "electronic writing compels us to reconsider the classical concept of delivery." Certainly since radio and television, and even more significantly in cyberspace, delivery no longer means the oral presentation of a speech; rather, delivery is now bound up in the *medium* of distribution. Delivery in cyberspace means multiple, simultaneous transmissions of messages across great distance and without regard for time. Furthermore, this cyber-delivery allows and even promotes interaction between the original message author and other online participants through email, interactive live chat sessions, and bulletin boards or Usenet newsgroups; in other words, electronic technology "has made the fifth canon of delivery (medium) take on the urgency of simultaneous communication" (Welch 1990: 26). Where *ethos* was once conveyed to a room or town square full of people via a speaker's physical gestures, it is now sent across the world, conveyed through ASCII characters, signature files, and strong language, to thousands of individuals who can immediately respond. Often, it is those of similar interest who are attracted to a certain message, and in this fashion, communities of social action, such as the MarketPlace or Clipper forums, come into existence.

Although traditional rhetorical theory offers little of substance on the fifth canon of delivery,[7] work by Kaufer and Carley (1993, 1994) provides useful concepts for explaining how delivery functions in cyberspace. In their study of communication at a distance, they note the features of reach, asynchronicity, durability, and multiplicity. These features, along with speed, time, and specificity, are the major components in electronic delivery and provide a language for describing delivery in cyberspace.

The promise of delivery and *ethos* in cyberspace

The promise of communication and social action in cyberspace is clear from both the MarketPlace and Clipper cases. In both instances, the speed and reach of online delivery along with a powerful community *ethos* made the issues clear and immediately accessible to thousands of people concerned about computer privacy. Propelled by their common concerns, these people continued to use the Internet to spread their messages. This feature of online communication is promising, because it allows people of common interest to mobilize quickly. This process also has direct implications for democratic action: it is cheaper to send email than to travel to a physical location, and it is certainly faster to send messages in cyberspace versus surface mail. In addition, online communication is efficient, because participants can talk directly to others who share their values and concerns. In the beginning of each action, this online delivery and common *ethos* allowed both actions to come into focus quickly and easily, reaching across time and space to the specialized spaces on the Internet. Messages soon reached thousands of people of common values and interests, and this feature brought the issues into focus in short order.

In the MarketPlace case, for example, an article about the product which originated in the *Wall Street Journal* was quickly disseminated across the networks and became the focus for the early postings in this protest. In many computer conferences, for example, excerpts from this article appeared almost immediately. RISKS Digest, an online newsletter focusing on risks to the public in computing, for example, contained three postings about Lotus MarketPlace. Another electronic site, the Electronic Frontier Foundation (EFF) forum on the Whole Earth 'Lectronic Link (WELL) network, also contained a reference to the *Journal* article:

> Topic 71 – New Lotus product puts millions of Americans under scrutiny. by [Tom K ___] [email address deleted] Wed, Nov 14, 1990 (01:33) 292 responses

> Tuesday's (10/13) WALL STREET JOURNAL carried a Section B front page story about Lotus Corporation's new product. The name escapes me, but the product is a disk(s) with the names of millions of Americans, categorized by demographics and buying habits.[8]

By simply typing in messages and issuing the appropriate commands to post them, participants were able to bring the article to the attention of thousands (if not more) readers just one day after the article appeared in the paper. Although the *Journal* has a larger overall number of readers than the network conferences, delivery in cyberspace brought the issue of Lotus MarketPlace to the attention of a specific audience: people with a concern for computer privacy who knew how to use the networks to spread a message.

It is impossible to say how many people saw these and other early postings. Although one may obtain a reasonable count of the average number of readers to certain kinds of computer conferences, it is impossible to know how many people saw the postings by way of secondary sources. If people were to read the RISKS article, for example, and think it relevant for colleagues at work, they could copy the message from the conference and redistribute it via email or repost it to an internal company bulletin board. Delivery in cyberspace thus is much more than the speed of electronic postings; it is also the exponential process of cutting and pasting messages from one site to another and passing these messages along to numerous other cyberspaces.[9]

These examples illustrate the power of online delivery for defining and focusing an exigence and drawing together a community. Within 24 hours after the *Wall Street Journal* article, word spread throughout cyberspace about the Lotus product, and before long, specialized discussion groups on MarketPlace sprang up across the Internet. Word spread not only to those who read the conferences but also by forwarded messages via email to an unknown number of people throughout cyberspace. Because it is so easy to forward and repost notes to computer conferences or as email, delivery in cyberspace helped the controversy come into sharp focus and to do so quickly.

In the Clipper case, a similar form of delivery took place, serving again to focus the issue by quickly bringing together like-minded individuals into a community which was against the adoption of the chip. In April 1993, the Clinton administration proposed the Clipper chip as a voluntary standard for telecommunications encryption. Shortly thereafter, a number of advocacy groups began to organize. For example, a group calling itself the Digital Privacy and Security Working group, comprised of "a coalition of communication and computer companies and associations, and consumer and privacy advocates," was formed in May; this group sent a letter to President Clinton questioning the Clipper chip. Computer Professionals for Social Responsibility (CPSR) also sent a letter to President Clinton in May, stating that the group disagreed with some statements of the Digital Privacy and Security Working group. Later in May, CPSR filed a suit "challenging the secrecy of the government's Clipper chip encryption proposal" (CPSR 1993b).

All of these activities were discussed and monitored on the Internet. As in the Lotus case, specialized Usenet newsgroups, such as alt.privacy.clipper, formed quickly. Other newsgroups focusing on computers and privacy soon contained discussions, or "threads," about the Clipper chip. For example, on April 16, the day the administration announced the proposed standard, the actual statement by the White House Press Secretary was available on many Internet sites. The statement, along with another CPSR announcement from the same time period, was widely reposted, appearing, for example, in the Computer Privacy Digest, the Privacy Forum Digest, and the RISKS Digest. By late May, postings about the Clipper chip were quickly making their way across the Internet. As in the Lotus case, these postings echoed far and wide across cyberspace within a very short time. One such note indicated that the author had obtained a faxed copy of a Clipper-related letter from Representative Edward Markey to Secretary of Commerce Ron Brown. This participant then describes how he is crossposting his note to "a few mailing lists . . . related to privacy, encryption, clipper chip, etc."[10] Similarly, another participant notes the many lists where Clipper information can be found:

> For anyone interested, the majority of the debate is going on in the new group alt.privacy.clipper; you can also find it in comp.org.eff.talk, sci.crypt, alt.privacy, alt.security, alt.security.pgp, comp.dcom.telecom, and stray offshoots in a dozen other groups.[11]

In both the MarketPlace and Clipper cases, then, the speed, reach, and simultaneity of online delivery assisted in focusing the online actions in short order. Similar communities of common interest would take months or even longer to organize through traditional rhetorical means or even through more modern forms such as direct mail. But delivery in cyberspace helped bring people together within hours or days of important events and provided accessible meeting places that spanned distance and time for communities of mutual interest.

Speed of delivery alone, however, will not move people to action. In cyberspace, it was the combination of electronic delivery and a strong community *ethos* that focused both protests in their early stages. This *ethos* is a combination of shared technical values and shared attitudes toward the technology in question. Such a common *ethos* was important in focusing the early postings into more cohesive online protests. This *ethos* is a powerful feature in online social action, because it allows people of similar interests and concerns to communicate easily. Participants in both cases were able to assume that others in the newsgroups or lists understood certain technical concepts and agreed with certain premises; a newsgroup focused on computer privacy, for example, is inhabited by participants who are concerned about privacy and want to protect their rights. Thus, participants do not have to spend time making introductory remarks or defending the premises of their statements. This "instant *ethos*" made it easy to reach many individuals of similar values in short order, and when combined with online delivery allowed for both protests to focus quickly.

For example, the first posting on another MarketPlace-related discussion group illustrates the common values and technical knowledge assumed by the writer:

> Tuesday's (10/13) WALL STREET JOURNAL carried a Section B front page story about Lotus Corporation's new product. The name escapes me, but the product is a disk(s) with the names of millions of Americans, categorized by demographics and buying habits.
>
> Lotus claims the new product will simply make it easier for smaller businesses to engage in the same direct marketing (e.g. direct mail and telemarketing) practices used by larger firms. But is this in the public interest, to have all of this personal information floating around without opportunity even for rebuttal and susceptible to amateur modification? Does evening the playing field for business create more equity for the persons whose data is the commodity at issue?
>
> Lotus says you can get off their disks in the conventional way, by calling the various direct marketeers, or by calling Lotus. First you have to know about it, however, and the removal process is, so far, unverified.
>
> It's ironic that the company founded by Mitch Kapor, who has done so much for personal privacy and commonsense law regarding the rights of information workers, consumers, and producers, now is foisting this sweet little package on the American people.
>
> Comments?[12]

This passage begins with tacit assumptions about technical knowledge and privacy. The issue of a possible misuse by "amateur modification" assumes that others not only understand the technical aspects of such a phrase (the ability of someone to crack the data encryption scheme used by Lotus), but also understand and to some extent agree with its implications. In other words, beyond its assumption about readers' technical knowledge, this statement assumes a shared belief in "unethical people" who will try to crack the encryption scheme built into MarketPlace. Lotus Corporation spokespeople surely would have disagreed with the very basis of the implicit argument of such phrases, suggesting that the encryption scheme cannot be broken and that no one would really want to do such a thing because this information is already available from other sources; the participants in these online privacy forums, however, assume this unstated information as a given.

These assumed premises about privacy are also apparent in the speaker's questions, when he asks whether it is "in the public interest, to have all of this personal information floating around without opportunity even for rebuttal and susceptible to amateur modification?" The suggestion that it is a problem to have personal information "floating around" reflects the common values this participant assumes about other members of these privacy newsgroups and lists. Furthermore, when this participant suggests that Lotus is "foisting this sweet little package" on consumers, he displays an anger and sarcasm that was also common among privacy advocates.

Assumptions about technical knowledge and computer privacy in the Lotus case thus allowed for the creation of short, direct messages that assumed the community *ethos* and appealed to other participants in these computer conferences. In addition, an authoritative and ironic voice offered a strong challenge to Lotus's claims and invited other readers to join the debate. Participants spoke to a community with whom they shared technical expertise and values about computer privacy. In other words, the highly specialized nature of online communities allowed rhetorically effective messages with an appealing group *ethos* to be sent out to others of similar thinking. This community *ethos*, combined with the speed of electronic delivery, played a major role in the initial exigence that developed around the Lotus product.

The early postings in the Clipper case also exhibited a strong community *ethos*, which, like the MarketPlace case, shared a similar rhetorical configuration: "a characteristic manner of holding and expressing ideas" (Halloran 1984: 71). As was true with the MarketPlace postings, this *ethos* was powerful because of the highly specialized nature of online spaces. Early Clipper postings used highly technical language; for example, in response to the April 16 announcement of Clipper, one participant posted the following series of questions to others in the privacy community. These questions clearly assume a level of technical knowledge ("V. 32 modem;" "Huffman compression") even though the author admits in the beginning of his message that he "isn't a cryptographer and doesn't play one on TV":

> 1. What's an "encryption" device? Is a V.32 modem one? Without another modem it's pretty hard to figure out what's going on. What about programs such as compress? With out the "key" of the compress/decompress program it's a bit difficult to decode compressed files.
>
> . . .
>
> 5. What if I use some sort of Huffman compression and transmit the frequency table in a separate message? Common algorithm but without the "key" in the form of a frequency table it'll be a bit difficult to figure out.[13]

Another early Clipper-related message also invokes the same technical *ethos* and community awareness of other readers when the author indicates that "as you may know,"

> for some years I have been pushing for a **token–pin–challenge based encryption system** for session as well as password encryption & this IMHO answers many questions posed by the C[lipper] C[hip].
>
> (emphasis added)[14]

Similarly, the author of another posting assumes that other participants are familiar with a 1987 article in a collection published by the Association of Computing Machinery, when he suggests that "now would be a good time for all to re-read [author's] 'Reflections on Trusting Trust,' which was published as an ACM Turing Award lecture."[15] All of these assumptions reflect the professional background, interests, and political points of view common to these lists and conferences. This common *ethos* among participants gave rise quickly and broadly to an online action against Clipper.

Along with technical language, the community *ethos* in the Clipper protest involved a level of sarcasm and anger similar to the Lotus protest. The first section of a posting from the April 27 issue of the Computer Privacy Digest, for example, is overt in its feelings about Clipper:

****

DEFEAT THE BIG BROTHER PROPOSAL! JUST SAY F!CK NO TO THE PRIVACY CLIPPER!

***[16]

This message assumes the community *ethos* by exhibiting anger and concern over "Big Brother" and relates this concern to Clipper, which it sarcastically calls the "privacy Clipper."

Once both protests came into focus, certain electronic form letters and petitions began to become prominent. A shared *ethos* made participants inclined to sign or act, and the reach and power of delivery made it easy for them to do so. In both cases, it was not long before a few texts became widely reposted and distributed. Once participants learned of MarketPlace and later Clipper, they could and did easily use email to write directly to the CEO of Lotus or the President of the United States.

In the protest over MarketPlace, the most prominent posting was "the Seiler letter," which, although initially posted to only a few sites, was soon widely available on the Internet as participants copied and reposted it across the Internet. Seiler, a computer professional at a New England computer firm, posted a long note about MarketPlace to a few Usenet newsgroups. His note contained a lengthy introduction followed by the word-for-word text of a letter Seiler had sent to Lotus. This sample letter provided an address and appropriate names to contact at Lotus, and encouraged readers to "pass this message along to anyone whom you think might care."[17]

Before long, Seiler's note had spread over cyberspace. His note was posted to newsgroups, reposted to others, and forwarded on email. Seiler himself says "[I] very quickly started getting echoes – quite literally, as I received a number of copies back again with long forwarding lists – sometimes entirely inside the company, and sometimes from the outside."[18] The preface to one of these messages illustrates exactly how extensively postings were traveling across cyberspace:

The next entry is a long one sent to me by my good friend [S___ S___], who is the policy advocate for the activist Telecommunications Workers Union in British Columbia. He took it off a net somewhere.[19]

In this example, Seiler's note was taken from a newsgroup or other Internet source ("off a net somewhere)" by a "policy advocate" (S___ S___) in British Columbia, forwarded back to the US as email to the above participant, and then posted by this participant to a new online forum. Embedded in the full posting are other header messages, indicating that the author's friend "S___ S___" took the note from an online forum called the Progressive Economists' Network. According to a story in *PC Week*, in which Seiler was interviewed, the note "reached computer buffs as far afield as Saudi Arabia" (Fisher 1991).

Seiler's message appealed strongly to a collective *ethos* of anger and concern over MarketPlace. It was selected, out of many electronic messages, over and over again until it became a prominent posting in the debate. Such a process gave great power to online participants, for it allowed them to select a representative message by community consensus and redistribute this message with great reach. The protest over MarketPlace cohered in large part around the Seiler and other postings as they moved, as one participant put it, "like an electronic wave going 'round the world."[20] This was a wave built by many individual actions, not one individual or group posting or organized plan. This process represents a great promise for open communication in cyberspace, because it promotes rapid reposting and is not hampered by the sort of gatekeeping functions so common to the mass media.

The Clipper debate also inspired form letters that were also reposted across the Internet, appearing on most of the privacy and Clipper newsgroups. A petition begun by CPSR ultimately became, like the Seiler letter, a prominent text in the protest. The petition came to represent the attitudes and concerns of participants; in addition, it offered a built-in process to simplify participation: with the few keystrokes it would take to type the phrase "I OPPOSE CLIPPER" and press "send," individuals could "sign" the petition. The petition began with the phrase "Electronic Petition to Oppose Clipper . . . Please Distribute Widely," and then provided these simple instructions for signing (CPSR 1993a):

> To sign on to the letter, send a message to:
>
> Clipper.petition@cpsr.org
>
> with the message "I oppose Clipper" (no quotes)
> You will receive a return message confirming your vote.

Attached to these instructions was a letter to President Clinton, to which all of the electronic signatures would be attached.

The Clipper petition was also circulated widely. Although initially posted by CPSR, the petition appeared on virtually all privacy, encryption, and computer-related newsgroups, then quickly spread across the Internet to other newsgroups, lists, and email addresses. Like the Seiler letter, the petition to oppose Clipper was posted and reposted via the speed and reach of online delivery. Note the following, for example, which is a reposting of the Clipper petition to PACS-L, an electronic discussion list for librarians:

From owner-pacs-l@UHUPVM1.UH.EDU Thu Feb 3 08:46:24 1994
Date: Thu, 3 Feb 1994 14:46:24 CST
From: [Greg D___] [email address deleted]
Subject: Re: Petition to Oppose the Clipper Chip
To: Multiple recipients of list PACS-L <PACS-L@UHUPVM1.bitnet

———————————Original message——————

This is an interesting item that has cropped up on every second list I subscribe
to ;-(. . . [21]

Like the Seiler letter, the Clipper petition made its way across cyberspace, providing
focus for the debate. In addition, the petition offered an immediate mechanism for
gathering signatures. This feature could be very powerful to future online activists,
lobbyists, and others.

The peril of delivery and *ethos* in cyberspace

Although delivery and *ethos* in cyberspace suggest great promise for online social action,
these rhetorical dynamics also require us to view cyberspace with a critical eye. These
features may at the same time encourage the spread of inaccurate information and
promote an insider status that leaves out dissenting voices.

Let us revisit the Seiler letter and Clipper petition. In each case, these texts were
widely posted and became prominent in the debates. Yet as this section illustrates, online
communities often become self-selecting and may not challenge information obtained in
cyberspace forums. Instead, participants choose to believe and subsequently post and
repost because certain messages appeal to their shared values. The speed and ability to
rapidly edit and repost heightens this process, so that messages with strong appeal may be
reposted widely with very little critical review of the informational content. This ability
to appeal to shared values is very helpful in terms of allowing people from vast distances
to come together in virtual space, but on the other hand it can and often does promote
insularity. The Seiler letter and, even more dramatically, the other widely circulated
message protesting MarketPlace, for example, contained numerous inaccuracies, which
were rarely if at all challenged by other participants. In fact, the process of reposting to
other privacy groups on the Internet only added to the inaccurate information, as new
information was added with each reposting.

Seiler's letter, for example, states the following:

Second, pass this message along to anyone whom you think might care. To me, this is
not just a matter of privacy. Lotus is going to sell information behind our backs – we are
not allowed to dispute their data or even know what it is. Worse, **Lotus is going to sell
rumors about our income. Still worse, they will do it on a scale never before achieved.**
This should not be tolerated. Please help to stop Lotus.

(emphasis added)[22]

Lotus was not selling "rumors about our income." Rather, the company obtained income range information from credit giant Equifax and incorporated this range into the database. Furthermore, it is questionable whether Lotus MarketPlace would spread this information "on a scale never before achieved." Although the product did in fact have serious privacy implications, the scale of distribution would probably not have exceeded the everyday distribution of information by companies such as Equifax or TRW. Yet since Seiler's information came not from Lotus itself but rather from sources within the online privacy community, the letter is not completely accurate. The appeal of *ethos*, however, was more powerful to online participants than was the desire for accurate information. Indeed, the preface to this letter begins by noting that Seiler did not check his "facts" with Lotus but rather with someone who had "an excellent reputation on the Internet."

A more detailed and striking example of inaccuracy is illustrated in the following passage from the other dominant posting:

Lotus "Household Marketplace":

In one one [*sic*] database, the combined knowledge may include such things that we normally expect to consider private:

o   family members' names, gender, and ages (!)
o   address and home phone number
o   annual salary
o   debt-to-earnings ratio
o   net worth (house, cars, misc. household items)
o   investment portfolio (stocks, CD's, etc.)
o   self and spouse employer info
o   health and life insurance plan info
o   schools attended by my children
o   kind of car(s) I own
o   kind of computer I own   ⎫
o   kind of stereo equipment I own   ⎬ from "warranty"
o   kind of video equipment I own   ⎪ registrations
o   kind of household appliances I own   ⎭
o   who knows what else? . . . [23]

This list is an exaggerated and inaccurate account of MarketPlace. In fact, most of the items on this list, such as kind of car or computer owned, were not included in the Lotus database. Even items that were included are reported inaccurately here; for example, this list says "annual salary" when what MarketPlace actually contained was a salary range for each household. Furthermore, none of the MarketPlace data came directly from warranty cards (although the data provided by Equifax may at one time have been compiled based on warranty information). Nonetheless, because the author(s) of the above list were under no obligation to check sources, the posting is inaccurate and adds to an already emotive and extreme *ethos*. The strong belief in other community members can easily promote inaccuracies, which, given the rapidity of online delivery, can easily grow and become compounded with each new posting.[24] Within weeks, both messages had wide circulation and had in essence become dominant in the MarketPlace debate. The power of delivery and the appeal of *ethos* provided for these texts to circulate widely, despite their inaccurate information, because these postings resonated with others on the Internet. Subsequently, the online protest soon had generated over 30,000 complaints to Lotus Development Corporation.

Furthermore, there existed a tacit trust in what participants thought of as "the Internet community." In both cases, this involved trust for the online community versus distrust of "Big Brother" in the form of Lotus or the government. This trust in community allowed Larry Seiler, who was clearly opposed to his personal information being pressed onto CD-ROM and distributed by Lotus, to post his home address across the Internet:

> 198 L___ Street
> B___, MA ___[25]
> December 6, 1990
>
> Lotus Development Corp.
> Attn: Market Name Referral Service
> 55 Cambridge Parkway
> Cambridge, MA 02142
>
> Dear Marketeers,
>
> I do not want my name included in your "Household Marketplace" CDROM database, nor that of anyone in my family, at any address I have ever lived at. To be specific, please make sure that the following entries are **NOT** included in your database:
>
> any last name (especially Seiler, S___, P___, or Z___) at 198 L___ Street, B___ MA
>
> any Seiler family name at 53 O___ Street, W___ MA
>
> any Seiler family name at 77 R___ Road, H___ MA [26]

The apparent contradiction in Seiler's letter was noted by a few participants on one conference, where the following exchange took place:

> **Interesting that Seiler did not mind his name and address and a narrow expression of his political views going on over any network.** That's a lot more telling than a single entry in a CD-ROM.[27]
>
> . . .
>
> A telling point . . . which I'd been mulling over. As we discovered in the Journalists' topic, **there's a perceived community implicit in any electronic network** (even a broad one like the Internet) that does not exist in a mere mailing list. Part of it is the cultural tradition of mutual respect which has emerged over most conferencing systems . . . [28]
>
> (emphasis added)

This "cultural tradition" extended itself to the text of Seiler's letter as well, which also contained an overt expression of his belief in one member of the "Internet community":

> In interviews, Lotus has said that individuals will NOT be able to correct their own entries, or even see what they are. I didn't try to confirm this in my call to Lotus, but I did confirm that the person who reported it – R___ S___ of [company name deleted] – has an excellent reputation on the internet. Also, everything he said that I checked with Lotus is absolutely accurate. Further, the Wall Street Journal has reported on it – saying that the database has ages, marital status, and other such personal data as well.
>
> (emphasis added)[29]

This trust in a perceived community was a large part of what made the Lotus protest successful. The Seiler letter was spread far and wide, with little concern for the fact that the accuracy of his information came from someone with no connection to Lotus Corporation but rather who had "an excellent reputation on the internet."

In the Clipper case, a slightly different but no less troublesome form of insularity was involved in CPSR's petition. Although the petition, researched and carefully distributed by CPSR, was perhaps more technically accurate than the material surrounding the MarketPlace protest, it nonetheless offered a strong *ethos*, and because participants could sign it quickly with a few keystrokes, the content was rarely, if ever, challenged. Although some privacy advocates did in fact raise questions about CPSR's dominance in the debates, this discussion did not inspire much, if any, challenge to CPSR's position. Participants seemed to sign the petition without doing any sort of background research, and some people noted that this tendency might make the government less likely to take the petition seriously. It appeared that participants trusted CPSR and were bound together by a common *ethos* that distrusted government.

Beyond the petition, certain postings did not even need an author's name to inspire this trust. In the Clipper protest, this trust was evident in the mass reposting of an anonymous message. Shortly after the announcement of Clipper, the government decided that it would hire a company called Mykotronx, a manufacturer based in Torrance, California, to be the primary manufacturer of the chips. In October, a long posting suddenly appeared on the privacy discussion groups and soon spread to other sections of the Internet. This posting contained detailed financial and other corporate information about Mykotronx, and included this comment from its anonymous author:

> Here are excerpts of the general ledger of Mykotronx, the Torrance Based Big-Brother outfit that is going to make the Clinton Clipper wiretap chip. I have left off their chart of accounts numbers, since you don't care about that. Do not reveal the source of this document (me) to anyone[30]

The author of the posting had used simple Internet tools to remain anonymous. Yet even though the posting did not contain any indication as to its origin, the information was widely accepted as true by others who trusted the Internet privacy community.

Both cases thus illustrate that in cyberspace, certain voices/texts can easily become dominant, whatever their level of accuracy. Thus, it can be argued that while both cases show the great potential for individual expression and free speech on the Internet, this model is not without its problems. The power of community *ethos* is heightened in cyberspace. Postings that appeal to community standards and are perceived as important, true, and credible will, if these two cases stand as examples, be reposted widely and quickly. Those participants who do not agree are often left on the side, and there is nothing inherent in the structure of the Internet itself to suggest otherwise. In fact, the current structure of the Internet is very much the classic double-edged sword: while it allows many people to connect with each other across space and time, it may also, especially in the discrete communities of Usenet newsgroups and discussion lists, offer fertile ground for unchecked information and insularity.

Summary: beyond promises and perils

Perhaps the most obvious promise of communication in cyberspace is that the new technology holds great potential to provide space for many more voices than have ever before had access to such a powerful communication medium. Television, though its reach is vast, cannot be interacted with, and most people do not have the power to purchase a television station or even buy air time. Call-in radio programs also cannot compare to the growing number of Internet newsgroups, chat sessions, and mailing lists. Part of this potential lies in the fact that delivery with these new communication technologies is extremely efficient. The speed and reach of one email message with a single keystroke is vast, and is also extremely targeted: online participants can reach thousands of other people who are specifically interested in a certain topic.

Furthermore, the current Internet structure flattens hierarchies, allowing people to correspond with each other regardless of corporate position or rank. In the Lotus case, for example, people did not need corporate credentials or even an appointment to send email to Jim Manzi, the then-CEO of Lotus. And in the Clipper case, many participants sent email expressing their anger and concern about the proposed encryption standard directly to President Clinton, Vice President Gore, and other public officials. Even within online communities themselves, hierarchy is often flattened, especially in the non-moderated conferences and newsgroups where there are no official gatekeeping structures in place. The current shape of the Internet seems to thus offer the potential for expressions from the *vox populi*.

Yet these same features also bring with them many potential problems and difficulties. Online, it appears that speed may supersede accuracy and that the beliefs of the community may preside over the responsibility of citizens to make informed decisions. In our age of rapid-fire response, it is easier to simply send off a quick email than it is to research a decision. This cumulative behavior, promoted by the highly specialized nature of online communities, does not always cultivate an open atmosphere and instead may leave out those who are on the margins and do not assume or feel comfortable with the prevailing community *ethos*. Furthermore, the flattened hierarchies and open forums of the Internet can promote the spread of inaccurate information.

How then should we consider the future of online social action? If it is true that all technologies bring with them both promise and peril, what can we do to inspire more of the promise and less of the peril? At the risk of sounding too much like a pure academic, let me suggest that we begin by aggressively performing close case studies of actions such as MarketPlace and Clipper. These sort of online actions are still very new, and the complexities of these and other cases could provide needed data for designers, funders, and government bodies involved in the new national information infrastructure (or whatever the Internet of the future may be called). Social scientists, rhetoricians, language scholars, and others from the traditionally humanistic perspective should work together with computer scientists and industry or government agencies to bring this needed perspective into the policies of cyberspace.

Notes

1 Portions of this chapter appear in *Persuasion and Privacy in Cyberspace*, published by Yale University Press (see Gurak 1997)
2 This method is based on neo-Aristotelian criticism, focusing on the five canons of rhetoric.
3 The use of electronic texts and the electronic forum for rhetorical analysis presents a number of novel methodological issues, from copyright and fair use questions to technical concerns of retrieving and storing texts (see Gurak 1996 or Appendix in Gurak 1997).
4 Greek and Roman rhetorics, specifically those associated with Aristotle and Quintilian or Cicero, had distinctly different ideas about *ethos*, however. Whereas Aristotle's rhetoric spoke primarily of finding the available means and using them, Romans such as Quintilian or Cicero placed far greater emphasis on the rhetor as someone who embodied civic good (Johnson 1984). Yet my point here is that the general notion of *ethos* as character has been a strong part of the entire classical tradition and has been carried down into contemporary rhetorical theory.
5 In discussing the online technology of hypertext, for example, Bolter (1993: 107), noting that "what we mean by the voice of a text was in ancient terms [called] *persona* or *ethos*," suggests the existence of a "hypertextual voice."
6 In classical rhetoric, delivery was one of five canons, or parts, of the rhetorical system. Ethos, for example, was part of the first canon of invention. The next two canons, arrangement and style, involved how a speech was organized and in what stylistic manner it was constructed. The final two canons, memory and delivery, were important to ancient rhetors, for whom public speaking involved a good memory and an ability to deliver before a live audience.
7 Both the fourth canon of memory and the fifth canon of delivery have traditionally received little theoretical treatment (except for the limited work of elocutionists during the eighteenth century); Connors (1993: 65) notes that "the status of the last two [rhetorical canons], memory and delivery, has always been problematic."
8 "K_____, Tom." Electronic message to Whole Earth 'Lectronic Link computer conference, Electronic Frontier Foundation conference, topic 71 (Lotus MarketPlace). 14 Nov. 1990. Message no. 0. 1:33 PST.

9 This entire process would take only a minute or two using fewer than ten key strokes, thus providing one illustration of the explanatory power of Kaufer and Carley's (1994) principles of distance communication in relation to delivery. First, the principle of multiplicity, which they define as "the number of communication partners that can be communicated with at the same time," is illustrated by the many people who read and coalesced around the early postings. Second, availability of these messages to anyone at any time shows the "asynchronicity": the freeing of network participants "from having to work at the same time," thus overcoming the distances of both time and space (Kaufer and Carley 1994: 34).

10 "U___, Harry." Electronic message to Computer Privacy Digest 2.38. 27 April 1993. Posted 25 April 1993 18:17:58.

11 "G___, Tom." Electronic message to Computer Privacy Digest 2.37. 27 April 1993. Posted 24 April 1993 22:20:36 GMT.

12 "K___, Tom." Electronic message to Whole Earth 'Lectronic Link computer conference, Electronic Frontier Foundation conference, topic 71 (Lotus MarketPlace). 20 Dec. 1990. Message no. 153–154. 19:22 PST.

13 "P___, Brice." Electronic message to Privacy Forum Digest 2.12. 17 April 1993. Posted 16 April 1993 16:59:16.

14 "R___, B. Roger." Electronic message to Privacy Forum Digest 2.13. 22 April 1993. Posted 18 April 1993 09:44:41. Note: "IMHO" is a common online acronym for "in my humble opinion."

15 "L___, Adam S." Electronic message to Privacy Forum Digest 2.15. 30 April 1993. Posted 24 April 1993 13:03:46.

16 "N___, Todd." Electronic message to Computer Privacy Digest 2.38. 30 April 1993. Posted 28 April 1993 19:16:01.

17 Seiler, Larry. Electronic letter distributed to many sites on the Internet. Excerpted here from author's original posting and used with permission. 2 Dec. 1990.

18 In various edited forms, I have documented numerous "echoes" of Seiler's letter, including December 20 on the WELL and December 30 on both Telecom Digest and Telecom Privacy Digest.

19 "K___, Tom." Electronic message to Whole Earth 'Lectronic Link computer conference, Electronic Frontier Foundation conference, topic 71 (Lotus MarketPlace). 20 Dec. 1990. Message no. 153–154. 19:22 PST.

20 "D___, Robert C." Electronic message to Telecom Privacy Digest 2.11. 23 Jan. 1991. Posted on 23 Jan. 1991 7:32:32 PST.

21 "D___, Greg." Electronic message to PACS-L electronic mailing list. 3 Feb. 1993 14:46:24 CST.

22 Seiler, Larry. Electronic letter distributed to many sites on the Internet. Excerpted here from author's original posting and used with permission. 2 Dec. 1990.

23 Exact author unclear; excerpted from the following posting: "D___, Robert C." Electronic message to Telecom Privacy Digest 2.11. 23 Jan. 1991. Posted on 23 Jan. 1991 7:32:32 PST.

24 Because of the nature of online writing and delivery, it is difficult to know how to properly give credit for certain online postings. The above list is an example. The excerpt of this posting used here has actually been copied by two people before being pasted into the final note. I have given credit to the person who posted the final note, although this person is not the author of the passage cited here.

25 I have removed Seiler's home address to protect his privacy.

26 Seiler, Larry. Electronic letter distributed to many sites on the Internet. Excerpted here from author's original posting and used with permission. 2 Dec. 1990.

27 "T___, Mike." Electronic message to Whole Earth 'Lectronic Link computer conference, Electronic Frontier Foundation conference, topic 71 (Lotus MarketPlace). 21 Nov. 1990. Message no. 25. 06:33 PST.

28 "S___, Bart." Electronic message to Whole Earth 'Lectronic Link computer conference, Electronic Frontier Foundation conference, topic 71 (Lotus MarketPlace). 22 Dec. 1990. Message no. 71. 18:07 PST.

29 Seiler, Larry. Electronic letter distributed to many sites on the Internet. Excerpted here from author's original posting and used with permission. 2 Dec. 1990.

30 Anonymous. Information on Mykotronx Corporation received from anonymous source. Posted to various sites on the Internet in May 1993. Available via anonymous ftp from ftp.cpsr.org/cpsr/privacy/crypto/clipper/mykotronics_info.txt.

References

Aristotle. 1991. *On Rhetoric: A Theory of Civic Discourse*. Translated by George A. Kennedy. New York: Oxford University Press.

Bolter, Jay David. 1993. "Hypertext and the Rhetorical Canons." In *Rhetorical Memory and Delivery*, edited by J. F. Reynolds. Hillsdale, NJ: Lawrence Erlbaum.

Burke, Kenneth. 1969. *A Rhetoric of Motives*. Berkeley, CA: University of California Press.

Cherry, Roger D. 1988. "*Ethos* Versus Persona: Self-Representation in Written Discourse." *Written Communication* 5(3): 251–76.

Cicero. 1970. *De Oratore*. Translated by J.S. Watson. Carbondale, IL: Southern Illinois University Press.

Connors, Robert J. 1993. "'Actio': A Rhetoric of Written Delivery (Iteration Two)." In *Rhetorical Memory and Delivery: Classical Concepts for Contemporary Composition and Communication*, edited by J.F. Reynolds. Hillsdale, NJ: Lawrence Erlbaum.

CPSR. 1993a. Electronic Petition to Oppose Clipper: Computer Professionals for Social Responsibility.

CPSR. 1993b. NSA Seeks Delay in Clipper Case: Computer Professionals for Social Responsibility.

Fisher, Susan E. 1991. "What Do Computers Know About You?" *PCWeek* 11 February: 156–7.

Gurak, Laura J. 1996. "The Multifaceted and Novel Nature of Using Cybertexts as Research Data." In *Computer Networking and Scholarship in the 21st Century University*, edited by T. M. Harrison and T. D. Stephen. Albany, NY: SUNY Press.

Gurak, Laura J. 1997. *Persuasion and Privacy in Cyberspace: The Online Protests over Lotus MarketPlace and the Clipper Chip*. New Haven, CT: Yale University Press.

Halloran, S. Michael. 1982. "Aristotle's Concept of *Ethos*, or if not His Somebody Else's." *Rhetoric Review* 1(1): 58–63.

Halloran, S. Michael. 1984. "The Birth of Molecular Biology: An Essay in the Rhetorical Criticism of Scientific Discourse." *Rhetoric Review* 3(1): 70–83.

Hiltz, Starr Roxanne and Murray Turoff. 1993. *The Network Nation: Human Communication Via Computer* (revised edn). Cambridge, MA: MIT Press.

Johnson, Nan. 1984. "*Ethos* and the Aims of Rhetoric." In *Essays on Classical Rhetoric and*

Modern Discourse, edited by R. J. Connors, L. S. Ede and A. A. Lunsford. Carbondale, IL: Southern Illinois University Press.

Kaufer, David S. and Kathleen M. Carley. 1993. *Communication at a Distance: The Influence of Print on Sociocultural Organization and Change*. Hillsdale, NJ: Lawrence Erlbaum.

Kaufer, David S. and Kathleen Carley. 1994. "Some Concepts and Axioms about Communication: Proximate and at a Distance." *Written Communication* 11(1): 8–42.

Meador, Prentice A. Jr. 1983. "Quintilian and the 'Institutio oratoria'." In *A Synoptic History of Classical Rhetoric*, edited by J. J. Murphy. New York: Random House.

Reynolds, Nedra. 1993. "'*Ethos*' as Location: New Sites for Understanding Discursive Authority." *Rhetoric Review* 11(2): 325–38.

Rice, Ronald E. and Gail Love. 1987. "Electronic Emotion: Socio-emotional Content in a Computer-mediated Communication Network." *Communication Research* 14(1): 85–105.

Sproull, Lee and Sara Kiesler. 1986. "Reducing Social Context Dues: Electronic Mail in Organizational Communication." *Management Science* 32: 1492–512.

Welch, Kathleen E. 1990. "Electrifying Classical Rhetoric: Ancient Media, Modern Technology, and Contemporary Composition." *Journal of Advanced Composition* 10(1): 22–38.

Winner, Langdon. 1991. "A Victory for Computer Populism." *Technology Review* May–June: 66.

Chapter 11

Electronic homesteading on the rural frontier

Big Sky Telegraph and its community[1]

Willard Uncapher

Montanans appreciate communication, and it is not hard to see why. Vast distances and low population density make it difficult to establish social or business communication, or to create economies of scale to lower costs (Parker and Hudson 1992; Hudson 1984). Little wonder that places like Montana have long been a favorite proving ground for distance education. With only twelve towns with a population of over 10,000 in the 1980 and 1990 US Census, most civic life in Montana was organized in terms of much smaller towns. Few of Montana's many one- and two-room schools were located in towns listed in the 1980 US Census data, which detail only towns with a population of 2,500 or greater. Montana has only one Congressman.

At the same time, the expanse of the state is immense. The two counties near Dillon, for example, are larger than the state of Connecticut and Rhode Island combined, but with a population totaling only 8,000. The local school bus route through the Big Hole Valley where I did much of my interviewing is the longest in the United States.

Given this low population density, it is no wonder that statewide there are still over 100 one-room schools in Montana (with more in nearby Wyoming and Idaho). Even though the schools might have only some 20–40 students, some students still have to travel over 25 miles to school every day. Home schooling exists beyond even the reach of the one-room school. Class levels in the one-room school generally progressed from Kindergarten through eighth grade. While the one-room school might physically have more than one room, generally all the students would be taught in one communal room with older students helping teach the younger, directed by a teacher and an assistant or two. Two- or three-room schools would have a few more teachers and rooms. High schools tend to serve as magnet schools, and one of the most difficult questions for many a Montanan family is whether to board their high school age child, or to temporarily split up the family in some way. In an isolated school as at Polaris, MT, which had only eight students, a teacher might not see another adult for the duration of the whole day.

Big Sky Telegraph (BST): a brief history

By the late 1980s, however, Montana telecommunications activists, such as Frank Odasz, began to express a renewed belief that new information technology would allow rural people to telecommute, create new service jobs, provide better access to market information for existing businesses, improve health care, and in general allow for the local pooling of information and resources so as to enrich the collective cultural, economic, and educational environment. Decreasing computer and modem costs, and the ability to pool transmission and hence reduce transmission costs via bulk store-and-forward systems (such as FidoNet), all suggested an untapped potential. Maybe the time really was right for a new kind of economy, and for new kinds of communities to reintegrate, revitalize, and re-humanize local culture. Maybe it was time to set up enhanced communities.

The initial concept, proposed by Frank Odasz, was to create an "online network" to link together the one-room schools of Montana. Odasz, now an assistant professor of computer education at Western Montana College, realized that most of these one-room schools already had computers, mostly rudimentary Apple II/e's, relics of an ever earlier age (circa 1982) when state and federal administrators had felt that computers should be included in every school to provide self-paced learning modules, some clunky educational games, to become a tool to develop computer literacy in what was supposed to be known as the "computer age." Now these computers sat silent in the corner. After all, what could these computers do that books and a good teacher couldn't? A good teacher was more flexible and reliable than any Apple II/e ever could be. Part of the excitement of the BST project was to take computers that comparatively could do so little and turn them into globalizing information search, retrieval, and sharing devices. All one needed to do, Frank Odasz imagined, was to add modems, a central computer to switch the calls, staff, training, and hopefully a way to keep telecommunication costs down.

Meeting needs

Frank wanted the Telegraph to stay close to demonstrated needs. "As much as possible, we have tried to stay as close as possible to actual needs. What does a rural teacher really need? Resources, lesson plan, contact with other teachers, contact with libraries and resource providers. OK, and some means of social access." Frank saw the need, knew of the technology, but was unsure how to proceed. After all, as he would later tell me, when he had gotten his Master's of Instructional Education only a few years before, the only computer that was considered important in his school was the mainframe, and the bigger the better. Inspired in part by Naisbitt's best-seller, *Megatrends* (1982), Odasz believed that a revolution was about to occur and that it would lead to decentralization, new rural opportunities, and new ways of thinking. Odasz approached Col. Dave Hughes (retd) of Colorado Springs, Co., a nationally known proponent of and expert on computer conferencing for community development with his idea about setting up a conferencing system in Western Montana. Hughes in turn was fascinated by the larger community picture.

Hughes also intensely disliked the notion that technology use could precede needs, that computers were a solution looking for a problem, that a well-meaning benefactor would simply bring the fruits of the "advanced" world to "backward" people. Hughes agreed that the rural teachers had a real, unmet need to communicate that a computer network could solve. He could see why an earlier attempt to bring ranchers and farmers computers linked to a central agricultural database had been such an abysmal failure. The people pushing their new communication gadgets seem to forget that ranching, farming, and merchandising were serious businesses, and that anyone who was staying in business must have already forged a good communication network. A rancher learns something from a ranch trade magazine or a broker tells friends about it over the telephone, and together they could hash out its significance. "Most every night we telephone, or visit," said one rancher.

While market conditions, technologies, and products change quickly, do they really change so quickly that ranchers who measure investment cycles in terms of seasons would fall behind if they do not get some market information for a day or two? The truth is that when an innovative device or practice pays off, it doesn't take all that long to be adopted, despite what ranchers and farmers say about their own traditionalism. In 1981, only a few, pioneering ranchers had satellite disks out beside their homes to catch the new television and cable networks; a year later the idea had taken off like wild fire. It was either adopt or stick to two television stations or fewer. Computer conferencing and database searches seemed an OK idea but would it really pay off? "Eliminating telephone tag" by adopting email and computer conferencing didn't seem a priority to the ranchers I spoke with. Those farmers and ranchers who had been foolish enough to buy one of those dedicated terminals to the interstate database got burned when the service collapsed. When I asked one County Extension agent what he thought of online communities and services, he leaned back and pointed to that useless, but expensive hulk of a terminal at the corner of the room: a relic of misplaced optimism in computer access.

Hughes realized that if one could get the teachers of these communities online, they could possibly serve as a bridge to "informatizing" the rest of the community, providing both an example and a point of access. For Hughes the real source of information for a rural community would not come from some massive database, but from the experience and knowledge of local people themselves. Lower costs made the time ripe for a new strategy: get people with needs online and allow those online to redefine how the technology was organized. Going online, Hughes taught his networking students, could not be understood simply reading about it in a book, or hearing a lecture; one had to go online for oneself. There was no substitute to actually sitting at terminal and doing it oneself. Going online was bound to be a lot simpler and more fun than most people at the time might have thought – and at the same time a lot more ordinary. If one was to reach out to rural communities, then starting with the schools made excellent sense since they played a central role:

> in many small towns in America, the concept of "community" is so strong, that nothing is "just" school, or government, or business, or private group. Schools are frequently a social center, a place where other elements of the community can do their own thing so long as the kids are educated and the school gym is available for the basketball games scheduled.
>
> (Hughes 1989)

While only teachers would get subsidized phone rates, and then only for a trial period, BST was open and free to the public from the very beginning, whether they were from the local geophysical community, or dialing in long distance.

Gathering resources

Over a period of several months, Dave Hughes taught Frank Odasz online at 300 baud between Montana and Colorado, how to set up and organize the computer conferencing software and hardware, and together they drew up expanded plans about how the new system might also become regional computer conferencing system, and establish a network of other networks. Finally, during Thanksgiving 1987, Hughes packed up his van with equipment and software, and headed for Dillon. He later stated that as the equipment was unpacked and tested, he did his best to stand back and watch. He wanted the people involved with the project to be able to construct and configure the system itself. Later Hughes would proudly point there was no local "data priest" (DP: the unaffectionate term for systems operators who in the mainframe era ran complex computer systems according to arcane rules and access schemes). He saw in Frank and Reggie Odasz ordinary people (at least as far as computers were concerned). Their assistant sysop (systems operator) Elaine Garrett, ordinarily a professional hunting and fishing guide, was invited into the project particularly because she was one of the few people who had had experience with an IBM computer. If the knowledge base was local then the power associated with that knowledge could stay local as well.

Initial funding was provided in part by M. J. Murdock Charitable Trust of Vancouver, Washington, for administration and hardware, and the Mountain Bell Foundation of Montana (US WEST) to provide limited 800 toll-free telephone number for instate teachers. Later, other companies and foundations would provide additional resources, such as the twenty modems given by Apple Computers. Mountain Bell, the regional representative of US WEST, had been interested in the Big Sky Telegraph from the beginning, and while they did not rush in head over heels with funding, they did slowly increase funding, perhaps seeing a service that would increase telecommunications traffic and services. According to Hughes, *online* communication was instrumental in even getting the seed money grant from US WEST since Hughes had contacted people he knew online, such as Tony Sees-Pieda, the Denver-located Mountain Bell Public Relations official who then moderated a regulatory public policy conference on Hughes's Chariot BBS: members of one virtual community helping another with real resources.

However, the long-term goal was to make the communication network self-supporting, as well as reproducible. This meant that the sysops would gradually encourage the teachers and their community to make an investment of even only $10/20 a month to keep the system running. Users would ultimately have to pay some kind of access fee. Indeed, the subsidized 800 number was valid only during an initial set-up period. After that even the teaching community would have to pay. If a teacher wanted to take a course on accessing the BST, it could cost $60 for college credit, $25 for non-credit, self-study, free. A business-oriented version was listed at $120. However, even to this anyone with a modem or Internet connection can log on, check out the general discussion areas, download a few files, and contribute. Visitors are issued an online ID almost automatically.

Big Sky Telegraph goes online

The Telegraph officially went online in January 1988 and took off immediately, making use of pre-existing communication networks between the teachers, and their communities. According to Hughes,

> In the first 40 days of it being up, it has been called 1,612 times by people – 75% of whom are total novices – all over that rural dispersed state of Montana. They have left 975 messages which is a message-to-call ratio of over 60%. *That* meets my standard for "user friendliness" of a dial up system.
>
> (Hughes, EIES, C685:153:275, 2/19/88)

Teachers learned about the system through ground mail, during the bi-annual (face-to-face) teacher conferences, and later through anyone who knew about it. Teachers in the isolated one-room schools across the state would be sent through the mail a $125 modem with a letter telling them how to open the Apple case, install the thing, run the software, and dial up Big Sky Telegraph. Once connected (with maybe some additional help provided over the telephone, or on occasion, a site visit), a teacher could continue learning online skills by taking credit or non-credit online keyboarding classes to explain how to minimize online costs, how to figure out what the connection was doing, how to download messages for later use, how to send messages, or find a message to read. It was a big step for many teachers just to realize that they wouldn't break the Telegraph by pushing one key, or by being unexpectedly disconnected.

The concept of computer conferencing and virtual communities was new on the Montana frontier. As Dave Hughes stated in a posting on the WELL in San Francisco,

And the MINUTE the first wave of callers (about 23 I recall) realized that this was far, far more an "online meeting place" for a "peer" group, and less a "data base", one-on-one teacher–pupil relationship, the joy was unbounded among those remote teachers and the word spread like wildfire.

(Hughes, Telecom Conf. Topic 393, Jan 15, 1989)

By the following August, over 7,000 messages had been exchanged between 300 people, and more than 30 teachers had completed the accredited formal online training, with more taking classes. The online architecture was gradually redesigned by the users themselves, with the less knowledgeable drawing on the skills of those who knew more: teachers teaching teachers.

Online discussions focused on promoting online and offline community building, improving educational resources for students, teachers, and the community, and of course celebrating all those teachers who had made that uncanny step into the online worlds. Critical comments were avoided according to many of the participants I spoke with, not particularly because the teachers feared offline repercussions, but because they wanted to support the empowering aspects of the medium. The Telegraph was a virtual community in part because its members were encouraged to have a sense of belonging (Cohen 1985). Newcomers would find their mailbox promptly filled with greetings from Frank, Reggie, or other teachers. A list of online facilitators was available. Have a math problem, then why not send some email to Otis Thompson, Western Montana College Mathematics Professor and Apple computer and software expert! Teachers could leave their email addresses and telephone numbers online to be general resource people. This in turn facilitated offline learning, and after all, many of the teachers would meet one another at one of the two joint teacher conferences held each year.

The Telegraph organized the direct circulation of educational software and library materials so that materials rather than having to be sent back to the regional library to be lent out again, could be forwarded directly to whomever needed it next. An MIT mathematics professor taught concepts of Chaos Theory to rural schools using the Telegraph, and a forestry department administrator would come online to answer fire prevention questions from the students and the general public as Smoky the Bear. Students at least initiated pen-pal correspondence, and lesson plans were shared. In the ideal situation, the educational needs of a specific dyslexic child could be raised online, and teachers could send one another the books and teaching materials that the community already had while offering general encouragement and advice, all without having to go through the County Education Superintendent or the Teaching College. Decentralized resource sharing was clearly a way to do more with less.

RuralNet

And just as it had promised, the Big Sky Telegraph sought to include the rest of the regional community and its economy. Cyber-activist and columnist Gordon Cook and Dave Hughes spoke of a community development in terms of a chair with three legs

— education, business, and civic. Take away one of the legs and the chair would fall over. Genuine community development has to have the participation of all three sectors, and the Big Sky Telegraph was seen as one way to provide such a common space and common project. Hughes would refer to his long-term vision of this project as RuralNet, an interstate, decentralized, low-cost electronic network to facilitate economic, business, and civic development. Odasz probably described the vision best as

> optimal collaboration allowing citizens, schools and communities new to infra-structural issues to work together with multiple existing networking projects, by sharing information on what does or doesn't work, on an ongoing basis, transcending traditional borders and cooperative barriers.

However, from the beginning, the initiators realized that it would take time for some real-life communities that didn't speak to one another offline to feel at home together online: different communities would need their own online space, a space where they could feel at home, a space where they could meet people with whom they felt comfortable. A rancher coming online for the first time might not feel too at home in a virtual room full of school teachers. Neither might retail business managers.

To solve this problem, the founders of BST partitioned the computer in such a way that users could dial the same access number, and then face a menu presenting the different login choices: BBS for educators, HRN for the Headwater Regional Network's business partition, AKCS for Internet access, Gold for tourist information partition or later Community Access Services, and so on. Each of these partitions was a unique, self-sufficient bulletin board system running on the same server. These were the different communities, each with some resources all their own and some held in common. In addition, some users might be so privileged as to have a personal login and directory. Hughes had configured the server with XENIX, a PC version of Unix rather than PC-DOS to make these multi-user choices more stable and easily available. This structure allowed the partitions to easily share a common community database. Each of the partitions would run the same BBS software, a customized version of XBBS, however, so that learning how to navigate one partition would make navigating another partition easier.

On the school side of this zoned community, a bulletin directory updated the Telegraph community with system announcements, position papers, and messages of important general interest. Different conferences would be devoted to different topics. The Open Classroom conference discussed general educational concerns, the Science conference developed science projects, a Writing conference provided an arena for creative writing experiments, and so on. A few community conferences would be found nearby, including, for example, one for Displaced Homemakers, another for the Western Educators Conference, another for health issues. And of course there was the Kid Mail conference for students trying to find virtual pen-pals, and a Coffee Shop conference for jokes and comments that fit nowhere else.

The business and community end of things was much less stable, presumably because of three factors. First, there was no perceived need that could be met only by the

Telegraph. As Frank said, "Now we're in economic development. I don't know that the economic development people know what information [these] people really need." I talked with several regional "development" people who could see the value of the network, and saw that developing such electronic networks might ultimately lead to new jobs, new efficiencies and markets for existing businesses, and new cultural resources. And yet how could they develop these things by themselves. The main focus for the business and civic users would be immediate practicality. The promotional literature from the Telegraph 1988–93 suggested that BST's business services could include: Online Conferencing, Electronic Mail, Office to Office Document Transfer, Personalized Interface, Access to regional databases, and even, presumably on a very limited basis, such advanced services as scanning and desktop publishing.

If a local, non-educational community group could manifest a clear need to the Telegraph's administrators, then a distinct partition could be added. The Headwaters Regional Development group, for example, based on the support of the seven Southwest Montana development agencies, would try their hand at developing a partition, as would several tourist agencies, but these areas would take time to develop, and with differing degrees of success. In the context of a larger, pre-existing media ecology, most of the business and civic leaders already had the financial resources to pick up the phone and the social network to know who to call. In one instance, secretaries were discretely and unofficially designated to go online and pick up email and files rather than have the directors go online directly. If one online benefit was to eliminate phone tag, then these directors already had a working system: secretaries to take and send messages and documents while the directors went to face-to-face meetings.

General local community interest developed. In between pumping gas at the 'Gas 'n Stop' and doing chores, Sue Roden, with a beehive hairdo and plenty of character, would dial in to the Big Sky Telegraph on an old PC borrowed from the Women's Resource Center in Dillon. She had come to tiny Lima, MT, situated on a valley road near the border to Idaho with her husband while he developed his ministry. Even though she would get lessons in the mail about how to use the computer, and occasional visits from people who knew BST, often she turned to passing truckers and tourists for help. One time when the online community couldn't figure out why her software wouldn't work, a passing truck driver explained that she had to "un-write-protect" her disks. She ran her computer like a public access center: if you would pay the telephone bill, you could get online from Lima. She enjoyed talking to people, and downloading files. One of the main reasons she was interested in this online world, she explained, was the hope for "a second job, a second income." What about virtual communities? She responded, "As for community, well the Reverend has an active one, and as for free time, there wasn't much."

Indeed, research showed that one of the most important and successful non-teacher user groups of the Telegraph were found from the women's groups and non-traditional students. Carla Hanson, after going back passing her own high school equivalency exams, encouraged her friends to take their own high school equivalency exams and to get online. While two men had started with her effort, it was six of her women friends who finished, and successfully passed the exams. Carla Hanson suggested that in the new economy women needed to be able to make their own money and decisions. During these hard times, women wanted to have their own skills, and their own ability to be successfully independent. While sensitive, personal issues would usually be conducted outside of public conferences, the public conferences provided information about where people could go to find out about new jobs, how to deal with spouse abuse, and how to deal with or prevent health problems. Carla and her friends were proud of having gone online, and Frank Odasz certainly tried to build pride as well. Jody Webster at the Women's Resource Center admirably explained:

> Some of it is attitude. All your skills aren't the physical skills, like typing or shoveling. A lot of it is attitudinal skills. [wu: "social skills. . . . "] yeah. communication skills: how to ask for a raise, or how to ask for a job or not ask for a raise; the fact that you need to sell yourself; the difference between self-esteem and conceit. When I grew up a lot of the things would have been immodest or conceited, and now you can say the same things in a different way, and you are simply letting people know something about you. You didn't say "I."

The online community allowed for the articulation of an "I" whose identity could be balanced between self-esteem and conceit. It was thus suggested that the vitality of an online persona and the pride associated with going online could translate into changed self-esteem and vocational effort offline.

The first adoption dip

Still, after a time, adoption rates stalled in a number of communities. Many local one-room schools did not come online. With 114 potential schools, only some 30 or more schools were actively involved two years later. Those teachers who did go online spoke highly of the experience and of the potential for decentralized resource sharing. The prospect of going online seemed so positive and cost-effective that it seemed surprising that any teachers would wait. Was the problem really simply one of rural computer "illiteracy" or of "penny wise pound foolish" budgets? What was keeping teachers offline?

The easiest answer was structural: there were not enough modems, nor enough teachers who knew the system, nor enough information about what was involved, nor enough money to make the local connections. Put another way, five structural problems appeared to be factors: cost of equipment, limited availability of computers, vast physical distances, limited local computer skill, and high cost of telecom services. However, most of the school had computers, and grants would cover initial equipment and connection costs. Connection costs could be kept down since a teacher need only dash online, do the online transactions as quickly as possible, and leave. Lack of skill could be a problem. Perhaps the diffusion of innovations network became too tenuous far from Dillon, and the reinforcement too infrequent (Rogers 1983). Many of the teachers, and community activists such as Jody Webster, program director of the Women's Resource Center, who were online had already been exposed to computer networking somewhere else, often through the Federal Forest Service. They knew what the water was like before they jumped in.

Upon investigation, the reasons appeared more complex. There were cases where teachers had taken an online course, knew how to use the system, had access to a computer and modem, had funds from grants to make the connections, but still didn't use it. Why would skilled teachers with resources not go online? Addressing this problem would prove key to the rest of my study.

Lessons learned: cultural complexity on the cyberfrontier

It became clear that I would have to stand back and look more analytically at the larger picture, to look at how the Big Sky Telegraph was imagined and signified in society, at the more subtle factors that had put these machines in the hands of the teachers, students, and activists in the first place. It is perhaps too easy while studying virtual communities such as those described in this book to overlook the extent to which the virtual community is one community among many, and how communities influence one another. A striking feature of a virtual sociology (or more accurately a sociology that includes virtual spaces) is how these new communication technologies can alter the organization of power so that it eludes or augments traditional hierarchical constraints in unexpected ways.

Both popular and academic/professional accounts of the Big Sky Telegraph and networked enhanced communication in general were polarized over the issue of centralization and decentralization. Locally, the issue of centralization proved more profound even than the question of technology itself. After all, the ranchers weren't afraid of technology, what with their tractors, their satellite dishes, their microwave ovens, and their cars. Ranchers and farmers wanted to be able to fix what they had, and computers didn't fit that bill (did satellite dishes?). If it could be shown that a new technology really would help bring more power locally then there was a good chance that someone in the household would adopt it. If this was the case, then why not simply suggest that the Big Sky Telegraph, and computer networks like it, were ideal means of decentralizing and localizing, that it would not be like the television, that necessary evil whose content all too often seemed controlled in the boardrooms of New York and the production studios of Los Angeles. Decentralization was the very promise of the Telegraph, and Frank Odasz and all the teachers were constantly promoting this aspect.

In many ways, the scholarly split about the de/centralizing impact of computer-based communication mentioned was manifested in the rural communities themselves. Was this continuity an artifact of my own perspective, indicative of the influence of one group on the other, or perhaps indicative of a deeper, common problem? It is the conclusion of my study that both trends of centralization and decentralization are occurring simultaneously, but in relation to different commodities, and that individuals in local communities are divided over the impact of the technologies in terms of these conflicting economies. While much has been made of the new "information economy" as defining a new economic and communications era (Machlup 1962; Bell 1973; Porat 1977), I would argue that we conflate the organization of material and information commodities at our peril, particularly as social researchers. Indeed, it would appear that there are two distinct economies, or organizational poles within the larger economy. As will become clear later, it appeared that the complexity and creativity of the emerging systems of cyberspace seem strongly engendered and self-organizing by the impact of this split (Kauffman 1995; Cowan *et al*. 1994).

On the one hand, where information and access to information is the coin of the kingdom, traditional hierarchies are coming apart, and with them new patterns of decentralized and decentralizing opportunities are emerging. Accelerating changes in markets, knowledge bases, and resource access is undermining rationalized, top-down, bureaucratic, management (Zuboff 1988). Giant centralized operations producing movies or widgets often seem to be struggling to keep up with competitors who need less and less initial capital and who are small enough to keep up with changes in the complex and open distribution mechanisms for information. Where once there were 3 major television networks, now people go to video stores if they don't like what the 30–500 cable channels are showing, or else they hit up some other communication channel, such as the Internet. As the bandwidth of the Internet and digital transmission lines increases, there should be even more selection, beyond the narrow choice of a few hundred, generally well-financed cable or satellite networks.

The new worker in this scenario is supposed to become more self-directed, more flexible, more holistic, a better collector of information, active in local "quality circles," and comfortable and skillful with being in closer touch with both higher management and customers (e.g. Toffler 1981; Pine 1993). Middle management finds the "middle" getting smaller and itself increasingly excluded from production and income. After all, information technology can mediate more and more of the complex operations of producing and organizing products for markets. With digital packet switching, and the increasing power of humble computers to act as local switching nodes, traditional telecommunication and information hierarchies are collapsing into increasingly geodesic networks, into a decentralized infrastructure of bypass and local pathways (Uncapher 1995a; Huber 1987; Huber *et al*. 1992). For local, rural communities this decentralization can mean: increased, more direct, more interactive access to resources, as well as ways to share information locally. Why wait for some higher up to provide information? Get or give it yourself, more informally, more individually, and more timely. Decentralization also portends in this scenario increased regional employment where traditionally defined isolation no longer matters. A database for hunting information can be as easily located in a rural area as in an urban center.

On the other hand, using this new information still means getting access to material resources, including capital/credit. Many of the individuals I interviewed reminded me that while capital might be "immaterial," if someone won't give it to you, and you can't earn enough of it, then you can't get access to the things that capital provides. Even using online resources to find out about funding and resource opportunities becomes problematical as more and more competition develops for these resources, as more people get online and as this information gets relayed to the offline populace. Information and material jobs increasingly can be contracted out to small, often under-funded individuals firms. Material production and distribution follows the logic of immense economies of scale. It is at the transnational, not even the national, that immense wealth and opportunities are organized, and communication technologies are making this global organization of material production possible. Even national telecommunication giants, like the Italian state-owned STET, are finding that they are no longer big enough to be major players in the global telecommunication markets (Uncapher 1995b). Just because workers are "self-directed, more flexible, more holistic, better educated, etc." doesn't mean they will be well paid for their labor. It means that without these attributes workers won't even be able to participate in the job market! As the critics would have it, does a Big Sky Telegraph represent the first step of local becoming techno-peasants hoeing the digital fields of the transnational corporations?

Local debate about the impact of information technologies tended to take one side or the other, and these debates in turn merged into older, archetypal configurations examining issues of change and continuity, opportunity and exploitation, dependence and independence, locals and outsiders, money and resources. Frank Odasz did what he could to associate the image, the "myth" of the Big Sky Telegraph with the "independent cowboy spirit." Getting online would transpose a user to an electronic frontier of individual freedom and community responsibility. The American Frontier so essential to the American spirit had not been lost, as Turner (1894) had supposed, nor relocated to a few rogue outposts like Montana (Kemmis 1990). Rather, it now existed in a fractally enfolded cyberspace beyond the easy reach of centralized authority (Bey 1991: 108–16). And the traditional values of the Frontier might finally re-emerge as a bioregionalism enhanced by appropriate technology (Sale 1991; Van der Ryn and Cowan 1996).

While the short-term result of adopting computer conferencing would be a better sharing and acquisition of resources, new skills, new occupations, and a new lease on life for the local economy, what will happen in the long run, who will control the local economy then? One rancher pointedly told me that he worried that a generation of "button pushers" (his term) would not be able to dig a ditch for themselves. People would not be able to control their own destiny. They couldn't even fix these things when they broke. Other rural people told me they were interested in the Telegraph because they felt they had no other choice in a changing economy than to adopt and adapt this new technology.

Owner-operator ranchers and farmers spoke about new communication technologies in terms of scale. There was a scale to how things were done. Ranchers do some things on a large ranch that they can't on a smaller one, and vice versa. Vichorek reports:

> It seems to me that Montana ranchers and farmers fit into niches at different scales. For example, on the local scale, each ranch and farm is tailored to local conditions. . . . On a larger scale, farmers and ranchers are involved in a sort of worldwide economic ecology.

> (Vichorek 1992: 10)

Despite the prejudice of some outsiders that ranchers and rural people in general would not be cognizant of the forces of globalization, the truth was in fact just the opposite. While a city-based wage laborer can try to believe that the fruits of his or her labor are constrained by national and local economies alone, rural people look to global markets. When I asked one rancher about globalization, he pointed over to a tractor and said, "on the outside it says 'Made in America,' but I know the parts for it come from all over the world." The market for agricultural products and livestock are global, and anyone who plans to stay in business had better follow where the market is going.

If anything, then, the Big Sky Telegraph signified the new economy to traditionalists. BST was a lead dog in a global hunt, even if the well-meaning folk connected at the Telegraph weren't too aware of the larger picture; for many traditionalists, the picture was one of convergence and centralization. Bill Gillan of the Gillan Ranch in Colstrip, Montana, noted:

> The trend is for big outside money to come in and buy big ranches. We don't know where the money comes from. It might be the Japanese, or drug dealers, or maybe only doctors and lawyers looking for a tax write-off. . . . This sort of big money investment drives the price of land up, sometimes up to three or four times the productive value. . . . I might be the last generation of owner-operator on this ranch.
>
> (Vichorek 1992: 53)

In what was something of a surprise to me, ranchers generally said they were not opposed to Japanese and foreigners buying ranches, such as the Zenchiku ranch outside of Dillon, so long as they were kept as working ranches. Ranchers and farmers pointed out that Montana has had a history of outside land investment since even before Lewis and Clark came around the bend, whether they were nineteenth-century Wall Street robber barons or Japanese firms looking for a direct source of specialty Kobe beef. The specter of media moguls and financial tycoons buying up the land for vast country estates, however, angered locals who foresaw the decline in subsidiary income. The "new" economy seemed less and less place or respect for what they were doing, and the fruits of that economy seemed to go to the wealthiest somewhere else. The 1990 Montana Farm and Ranch Survey produced by Montana State University reported that one-third of the farmers and one-fifth of the ranchers expected to quit within the next five years for financial reasons.

We might take a cue from rural people on issues of scale as we analyze the impact and potential role of cyberspace on rural landscapes. Indeed, scale has become an important issue for many anthropologists and sociologists seeking to take stock of the cultural aspects of globalization (Barth 1978; Hannerz 1992), and for good reason. While traditional sociology tends to locate power in terms of place – the person at the big desk has more power, is at a higher strata than those on the production floors down below – the shift toward the dynamic process in the information economy refocuses issues of control in terms of such entities as "niche" and "rates of change." Shifts in the global/local economy can quickly undermine the wealth of those not prepared to move to the new niche (e.g. Davidow and Malone 1992). The fact that the naive notion of intrinsic identity is being redefined, although not without controversy, by an interest in the process of identification, whether it is the intellectual object constructed by reading (Derrida 1974), the scientific object constructed by socially situated scientists (Bijker *et al.* 1987; Haraway 1989), or even the physical object constructed by intention and attention (Thurman 1984; Varela *et al.* 1991), should help focus a virtual sociology exploring events like the dynamics of the diffusion of the Big Sky Telegraph not simply on an interplay of static power relationship, but on power as an activity which constrains and facilitates other activities as these relationships redefine themselves.

Social groups and the scale of communication

The great poles of social organization then seem to play out the tensions between a centralizing global and the decentralizing local not on one massive battlefield, but in terms of various scaled zones that exist dynamically in between them. Unlike the flat social network envisioned by most social network and diffusion of innovations theorists (e.g. Rogers and Kincaid 1981; Granovetter 1982), contemporary hierarchy theorists look to scale and constraint, to how entities at local, smaller scales generally function more quickly than those the larger scale, but are in turn restrained (in various degrees and fashions) by the larger scale, by what in essence is a more slowly changing environment (Ahl and Allen 1996; Allen and Starr 1982). When the larger scale entities begin to change rapidly, it is usually because they have found some functional way to make use of the dynamics of their component systems (Arthur 1994). Given that the way each of these levels (and society itself) develops as a function of communication, so changing the means of communication, the media ecology changes the organization of society, and the leverage of any entity within it. Virtual communities appear to be playing a key role in this move to a more dynamic, complex social system. And it is the conclusion of this research that the dynamics of adoption, or more accurately of the development of communities in cyberspace, reflects conflicts at several different scales.

In line with Fernand Braudel's analysis (1981–4) of the global economic system into (1) local material production and consumption, (2) regional market economy, and (3) global-capitalist economy, I identified four scales of demographic and cultural organization with which to analyze how virtual communities like Big Sky Telegraph fit their environment/s: (1) personal/user, (2) local, (3) municipal/regional, and (4) outsider/global. Individuals and their activities can be active at different contexts and scales simultaneously since any given action can contribute to different levels of organization at the same time. A federal land agent working at a municipal or outsider level could also be a parent. It is the roles that function at different scales.

Private lives in a public world

The personal/user scale focuses on how the private and public intersect. At this level of inquiry into communities in cyberspace, processes develop by which identities are internalized and desires externalized, a locus of great interest by those investigating, for example, issues of technological embodiment in cyberspace (Stone 1995; Featherstone and Burrows 1995), as well as the personal sense of security and wholeness (e.g. Giddens 1991; Bauman 1992). However, these concerns are not new. Consider Hannah Arendt who wrote in 1958:

> The distinction between a private and public sphere of life corresponds to the household and the political realms, which have existed as distinct, separate entities at least since the rise of the ancient city-state, but the emergence of the new social realm, which is neither private nor public, strictly speaking, is a relatively new phenomenon.
>
> (Arendt 1958: 28; cf. Nguyen and Alexander 1996: 109)

If the reasons that adoption of BST tapered off were not simply structural, another possibility lay with the complex public/private nature of the medium. Even if the Big Sky Telegraph was initially directed to the rural educational community, perhaps the general online public intimidated teachers. Openness, particularly in the rural setting, might work to the local educational community's advantage when these outsiders, whether they be local, national, or international, had resources or answers to share. No sooner did the Telegraph open than the word went out in the telecommunications/online community that an interesting project was under way in Montana. Callers from Japan, USSR, Europe, and around the Americas logged in during this period beginning 1988. Facilitated by Hughes's enthusiastic, larger than life persona, "the Cursor Cowboy," and Odasz's own travels, word of the new project spread to other electronic bulletin boards and early Internet outposts, such as the WELL in San Francisco, Meta-Net in Washington, DC, and the EIES network in New Jersey, and online visitors would often become information resource sharers.

I initially supposed that one strong inhibitory factor of the adoption of BST would be teacher fear of panoptic eavesdropping. What if a parent strongly disagreed with something that a teacher said? Public spaces, even virtual ones, evolve in the context of a complex sets of rules and assumptions serving to maintain a balance between trust and power. Groups often develop because of the way they control access to the private, back space; media can certainly change this (Meyrowitz 1985). When these online worlds are so close to offline ones, prudence is often the better part of valor.

However, users of the Telegraph uniformly stated they were not overly concerned about the public/private nature of the online communities. In one scenario I presented, a county supervisor of education or parent objects to something that a teacher writes online. Teachers need the support of the county supervisor, particularly in the face of volatile local opinion, and it rarely pays to rile up the parents. However, teachers and other users felt at this point that anything that improved local communication would be welcomed. Teachers said they had nothing to hide and would not mind having the supervisor overhear just how hard the teachers had to work! In fact, most of the regular users at least stated that they looked forward to more local participation and improved local and regional communication.

Local scale: paying for the connection

The local level reflected the organization primarily of the small town, population 50–300, situated in the midst of primary extractive, agricultural, or pastoral regions, although this scale of organization could also be found hidden as a subgroup within more urban areas. The schools at this level went only to the primary level, from nursery school to eighth grade. People generally had to travel a distance to get things done, 5–20 miles to the post office, school, or retail stores. Group activity at this level tended to be very issue oriented: should they raise local taxes, expand the school library, improve the road, and so on? or else concerned with the public/private lives of individuals. Issues served to weave the community together. The key players would be ranchers, farmers, local land management officials if present, service providers such as small retail stores, and of course the various groups associated with the schools: teachers, parents, students, and school board members. Along with controversies over collective land use, a perennial, central decisions had to do with the local school budgets. Ranchers and farmers were the key tax payers, and school spending was often the most important and expensive item on the local budget, it was also the site not only of an economic debate, but a cultural one.

Since the Big Sky Telegraph sought to be self-supporting, it intended to rely finally on the community resources to provide the mere $10–30 a month for the connections. Small as this amount might be, it opened the door to debate about what role the Telegraph should have. The Montana tax structure in the late 1980s had evolved to use a variety of property taxes in place of income or sales tax, a scheme that had made some sense when the giant mineral companies like Anaconda had anchored the economy, but which now made the land rich but cash poor ranchers and farmers wince at even a few cents tax increase. Without a sales tax, there wasn't much chance to directly capture any of the tourist income, and any mention of a new tax was greeted with suspicion. No one believed the promises of some state legislators that if a sales tax were granted, the property taxes would be substantially lowered. Hence, the introduction of this new device might mean that it would have to be paid for by the local ranchers and farmers, and other substantial taxpayers, who could suppose that the BST might incur additional costs in the future, tie up valuable teacher time with an unknown and unproved project, and, as was examined a moment ago, help facilitate the introduction of economic forces of centralization and globalization that seemed to be undermining the local economy, and with it local values, local traditions, and local culture. Teachers would need more than their own teacher support group to break through.

Ranchers spoke of themselves as the upholders of the Montana way of life as well. In this view, federal land management employees, teachers, even merchants might come and go, but it is up to the ranchers to decide the future of the state since they can provide continuity to its past. If ranching and farming families cannot always control their own economic destiny, if key economic decisions are being made in an increasingly vast, global theater, at least they can manage their collective symbolic destiny, something which outsiders can't penetrate without local guides. Economic conditions continue to change. Many felt that being traditional had kept them in business. When I asked one rancher if the people who didn't lose their ranches during the recent economic decline were more traditional, he replied, "Had to be. Throwing their money away. They couldn't pay for it [the new gadgets, services, and products]. The banks encouraged them."

Ranchers, farmers, and rural business people often did know about the Telegraph, but thought of it vaguely as a system for educators. There had perhaps been community presentations at the schools where a teacher or Telegraph associate would demonstrate connecting to BST, leave handouts, and encourage non-school uses. Were there computers available in the homes of the ranchers? I could find no statistical data on this, and the absence of a local computer repair infrastructure suggested not. However, my own interviews revealed that there were some computers in the homes. In this gendered, rural society where ranching was done by the men, bookkeeping in turn was done by their wives, who were of course interested in economical, reliable, labor-saving devices. It was thus the wives who were among the first to want to get access to computers, and it was they who seemed best situated to understand and use this new technology. Still without much extra income, a machine that could do a few spreadsheets, simplify letter writing, and interest the kids in newer technologies seemed a bit extravagant. But they were in a number of the houses I visited. Children and their education for the future were also considerations in getting a home computer, and several ranchers joked they intended to learn computers and networking from their children.

The notion that the teachers could serve as a bridgehead to bring computer networking to the rural communities was problematical. The teachers did indeed serve a central role in the community; however, they also were the bearers of all kinds of symbolic attributes that made moving ideas from them up into the community difficult. Local sources stated that rural teachers at the time of this study were about 95 percent women, making some $11,000–13,000 per year, barely a living wage. Those who took up the challenge were either wed to the job, or using it as part of a second family income. Since the teacher was such an obvious member of the community and one who dealt with children, she often found it difficult to socialize in bars or other places that might compromise her moral standing. Going online, therefore, offered a new avenue for socializing, and the movement of the teacher from a known position – considered by some to be a lowly one – to something unknown. Given their subservient status in the community, could the teachers be the ones to informatize the rest of the community? Marsha Anson, a minister's wife in Wise River and who was studying to be a school librarian, noted, "They [the teachers] are overworked to start with, and then to become information people for an entire community is too much to expect for what they are making, and for the time they have."

Indeed, a virtual teaching community would clearly transform the teachers themselves. Several teachers suggested that virtual community reinforced their sense of themselves as a community with shared needs. They were not simply teachers in a classroom, or teachers in a local community, but teachers who needed to develop a community of their own. One teacher confided that she felt these online communities might provide good tools with which to unionize the labor of teachers. A dangerous idea, I admitted, one that might not be supported nor funded by the local school boards. The teacher in question later left her teaching position to take up union organizing full time, one example, perhaps, of the impact of the Big Sky Telegraph on the teachers. Put another way, the online community of teachers began to resemble what I have been calling the municipal level or scale – interested in planning and sharing structures that could encompass different local communities.

Municipal scale: fragmentation and integration

The municipal or regional level in general was associated with urban centers, such as Dillon, Butte, and Bozeman, Montana, with populations more in the range of 3,000–6,000. Here one found the regional offices of the agricultural, technical agencies and other social services. Group activity at this level tended to be more abstract, trying to establish collective rules and frameworks, including those necessary to promote the educational, environmental, or financial resources of disparate local level organizations. High school and college instruction functioned at this level given that they would have to accommodate students from very different backgrounds. A bank and retail chain stores might be located in a very rural region, but often they functioned at a municipal or outside scale by using information technologies to link them into larger scale financial, legal, and cultural constraints about the deployment of people and capital. I would claim that it is at this municipal level that most virtual communities are developing as a kind of meta-community that must tolerate and even encourage open-ended diversity.

The introduction of virtual communities and information technologies was looked to with more hope at the municipal or regional level than at the local. The (agricultural) extension agent, the county education supervisors, and the social activists, etc., all wished they could have more reach into the local communities. Using radio shows and occasionally making 100-mile journeys were time consuming and often ineffective. While sending out brochures describing a service or product might act as a beginning, the real activity of these agencies was actually interactive: answering questions, directing clients to resources, setting up support groups. The business leaders further wanted to find new ways to broadcast the good news about the region to the outside world (to tourists, businesses seeking to relocate, etc.). All would support a cost-effective way to provide better cultural/educational environment in general, such as for the schools.

However, individuals at this level tended to find it more difficult to get institutions around them to change. According to hierarchy theory, the higher the organizational level, the slower the change but the greater the resources and the greater the impact when things do change (Allen and Starr 1982: 13). A ranching family with a little extra cash could simply go out and buy a new satellite dish or a computer, but a city school would have to fill out requisition and funding forms, which in turn would be handled by a bureaucracy devoted to making the hard decisions about how to manage limited financial resources. Ironically, while the ratio of computers per student in the rural one-room schools was say 1 computer per 20 students, the magnet high schools at the time of this study would have only 1 per 100, and the colleges, say, 1 per 500. These higher levels might have more financial resources in some absolute sense, but they were committed to projects that did not want to be defunded and hence took longer to change.

At the same time, while things might change or metabolize more slowly at a higher scale, the impact on the lower, faster moving scales was more profound. Several other electronic networking activists who worked at the state level suggested that BST might have made quicker headway if they had tried to diffuse the Telegraph through the county superintendent and other such officials. The reasoning was not that superintendents could more easily contact all the schools in their charge, but rather, that the superintendents would have more status and therefore more say *vis-à-vis* the local school boards and their communities. While BST may have been functioning internally according to many definitions of a community in cyberspace, it was not really functioning externally on the municipal level as a coherent community. The teachers in the one-room schools would have to influence their local community directly, while the influence of this virtual municipal community as a whole on the local community would have to wait.

Outsider/global scale: computer conferencing in a Brave New World

Wait for what probably would have to include some influence from the outsider or global level. I am interested in the term "global" as an indicator of the importance of a globalized capital flow, or more broadly, as part of the global cultural flows model that explores the disjunctive, sometimes chaotic confluence of a global financescape (flow of capital), mediascape, ethnoscape (flow of peoples, including tourists, temporary laborers, refugees, immigrants and emigrants to regions), technoscape (flow of technological ideas, expertise, and actual items), and ideoscape (a flow of ideas about social and personal goals, from inflections on the meaning of democracy, nationalism, and theocracy to personal self-mastery) (Appadurai 1990; Uncapher 1995b). Properly conceived, these flows influence but do not determine one another, leading to all kinds of unexpected local configurations.

In some ways the consideration of the outsider level *vis-à-vis* the Big Sky Telegraph helps to problematize the notion of grassroots. While the premise of the BST was that local people could create their own local network and find new ways to empower their local communities and themselves, the impetus for these changes came in part outside of the community. After all, knowledge of how to run a Unix server, command of the resources to buy all the modems, the production of the modems themselves, suggest some outside influence. Once the Big Sky Telegraph becomes a key component to developing a local, grassroots model, how is this model to be circulated? As it was, much of the strongest support and recognition came from outside of Montana.

Outsiders, who include tourists, researchers, investors, and various change agents, have even more tenuous local links. Outsiders can often command great economic and political forces unavailable to more localized levels, but may not know local or municipal culture. They could include land speculators and investors, manufacturers looking for labor meeting certain specifications, or federal government managers. Outsiders tend to be project-oriented on the local scene, wanting to get specific things accomplished, a hunting trip, help setting up a computer-mediated conferencing system, and so on. As such, the outsider's goals can be empowering to the local community, serving to expand the flow of money and ideas, or else constrictive, using economic influence to limit local opportunities or exploit them unfairly. The greater the lack of integration at the municipal level with other municipalities, the more vulnerable the municipal level can be to predatory outsider practices.

Developing physical infrastructure is generally something that is not done at local level: outsiders usually build the roads, whether they are made of pavement or fiber optic cable. Rural regions needed general upgrading of telecommunication facilities, the elimination of multi-party service, lifeline rates, equitable cross-subsidy from immediately profitable urban areas to encourage rural enterprise and thus the health of the state as a whole, extended service areas that reflect that geographically extended way of life, and ultimately the upgrading of line capacity (Parker and Hudson 1992). Shared multi-lines, for example, could not be used reliably for digital transmissions since any one of the parties might unknowingly disconnect someone else. While goals like these were accepted there was no real consensus about how they should be accomplished: regulated cross-subsidy, deregulated competition, or something in between? Estimating and quantifying economic and non-economic returns from telecommunications investment often makes questionable assumptions (Hudson 1984). Local activists suggested that the state public utilities commissioners did not understand that the telephone involved much more than simple voice communication. Whatever the truth, the commissioners would stand at the boundary of the regional and the outsider levels, looking not simply to their constituents, but also to what other state commissioners were doing (Parker and Hudson 1992: 63), and making compromises with a multinational corporation like US West.

The network nodes, such as the Big Sky Telegraph, were linking up local communities with global partners. For example, several ranches in the area, such as Zenchiku Ranch outside of Dillon, had been bought by the Japanese who wanted a good supply of hormone-free, fatty beef. They would raise the beef locally and would then have it sent directly to Washington state for export, using computers to provide both inventory and communication advantages. Likewise, teachers had access to international online public through their modems. And the Telegraph did put Dillon and Western Montana College on the map as it were. When I went to the InfoTech conference held in Dillon under the auspices of the Big Sky Telegraph, I met people there from around the United States and abroad.

So BST was in a way an early outpost of the International Digital Economy. As such, one would expect that BST would have some influence on the development of new online opportunities. That kind of conclusion cannot yet be explored at this stage of history. However, several individuals have told me that what they learned while using the Big Sky Telegraph was instrumental in providing them interest, direction, and skills to pursue new livelihoods. One administrator left to start a computer sales and repair shop, another set up a computer-enhanced camping supply manufacturing factory, and so forth. Another state-wide community communication activist spent important time working with the Telegraph. It is hard to trace these links since it is hard to ever locate digital workers. The *Montana Business Quarterly* calls the new telecommuters "lone eagles," suggesting that they are important in Montana's entry into the digital or information economy (Jahrig 1995). But what about the kinds of exploitation that might come with the new communication networks?

During my interviews, there was little local concern about the expansion of Taylorist "piece work" potentially associated with computer communication (Robins and Webster 1986). In this critical scenario, workers stay at home or in isolated factories, and are paid simply by the number of pieces they produce, whether sweaters, handwritten mass mailings, and so on. There is a potential for exploitation of local labor forces when employers fail to provide living wages, job security, health benefits, pensions, and so on. Global corporations can locate some production in a region with low pay, and move on when the wages rise. When markets change or the local labor becomes more expensive, then the investor could pull out. My informants from all sides were not particularly worried. They said that first they wanted outside investment and the jobs that would bring. If it turned out that the outside investor was trying to take unfair advantage of locals then they would eventually organize for adequate compensation. Joked one farmer, "We might use something like this Telegraph you have been telling us about."

Conclusion: frontier days in cyberspace

Individual community networking systems are being overtaken by the very success and technology they helped spawn. The Internet generally can provide better, more adaptable interface, a more standardized software, and hence more support, and cheaper connections. One of the goals of the Big Sky Telegraph has been to provide a model that would be adaptable to people who did not have access to powerful computers, and new users to the Internet must generally use complex, multi-tasking equipment, especially if they want to invoke a direct Slip/PPP connection that makes the point and click of World Wide Web browsing possible. After all, the rural people had to find ways to keep their connection costs down, and a ten minute call just to town might cost an arm and a leg. There are special service charges for most of the 800 numbers to national online providers. The Big Sky Telegraph continues as a beacon to developing regions in the world where commuter technology like the Internet remains too expensive, demands the skills of an unavailable systems manager, or where communication costs are prohibitive.

In a way, the introduction of the Internet has caused hand-wringing in many of the early populist, grassroots networks around the world. If they move to more graphic intensive interfaces, then many humble computer users might be left behind, able to use email, and to request files, but not much more. Where does a service provider draw the line, at the level of a Windows 3.1/Mac interface or with a multi-tasking central processing unit (CPU)? Do rural people *need* the Internet, and if not, why make that the entry level? The Internet is also undermining the centrist topology of the Freenet or community network itself. Rather than have one machine where community messages and files are located, why not make use of distributed Usenet news hierarchies, with some messages circulating at the community level, some at the state level, and some in accordance to some non-Euclidean logic of inclusion. All a server like the Big Sky Telegraph then need do is subscribe to the message group, and redistribute the files and messages.

At this point, the Big Sky Telegraph is trying to adapt to this new media environment, and trying to maintain enough funding and personnel to keep up with changing user and community needs. External forces want the personnel at the Big Sky Telegraph to announce whether they are a community network, an educational network for schools, and access center, or whatever. Consider that educational institutions (including students and teachers) get discounted access to the Internet. If BST uses the subsidized rates, then how are they to bring the rest of the community in without unfairly competing with the new generation of Internet providers beginning to move into the rural areas. Philosophically, the people associated with the Big Sky Telegraph have seen all the community as their teachers and students and have fought making this distinction. "We are a K-100 school." A Windows/Mac level BBS called the Montana Educational Network (MetNet) was established with Montana Office of Public Instruction funds to provide information to officially recognized teachers and students, and to them alone, and with an expensive 1–800 service, they have had fewer long distance connect worries.

The model of the Big Sky Telegraph which seeks to bring the whole community together is still important. Teacher concerns are often rancher concerns, and vice versa. Further, the Telegraph has become a repository of skills and examples about how to estab-lish communities in cyberspace. Frank Odasz concluded that a successful community network needed:

1 pragmatic use of existing resources – using what you have while you have it;
2 to keep focused on existing needs – not to become a little bit of everything to everyone;
3 to make the interface appropriate to the users – teachers want one thing, administrators another, business people something else;
4 to allow the users to redefine the system themselves – if it is to be a community, then those who have suggestions or are willing to make an effort should be heard, and this is a strong way to keep people involved;
5 to make it new – have something new on the system every time someone logs on so they will want to keep coming back;
6 to make use of every communication channel possible – learning about computer networking and virtual communities does not just take place online, it involves physical visits and other media, including books like this one;
7 to keep the system adequately funded – never an easy task;
8 to involve the business, educational, and civic communities together – that is, to get the local geophysical community thinking about things that they could do only using computer-enhanced communication.

As the other contributions to this volume have made clear, going online involves many new social and cognitive skills and orientations. Frank Odasz and others on BST suggested that going online encouraged informality, maybe even a new sense of play and responsibility. For Frank Odasz this led to emergent properties he felt he was discovering on an individual scale:

It's more a consciousness thing than anything else. And I'm in the business of teaching new ways, new levels of thinking, new levels of intellectual interaction. Communicating with a person in writing seems to be unfathomable to many of these people . . . who know business letters, but know nothing about the written word beyond the business letter. And a business letter is stodgy. You are limited. You've got to be kind of conservative. Whereas online tends to be a pretty different animal – being more folksy, more intimate in a hurry, more mind to mind; and I leave spelling mistakes in. Sometimes I do. Just for the heck of it.

So as I think about this more and more, at East Germany and Russia, and . . . and what I'm doing, and it's like consciousness. Not hardware or software, not purposeful communication, so much as consciousness of new possibilities. And that's what the computer seems to open up, is literally new levels of conscious, interactive . . . new levels of interaction for consciousness for partnership.

Two economies

The Big Sky Telegraph developed in the context of not just one emerging information economy, but two. Two economies and economic structures seemed trying to consume one another, one based in the global economies of scale of the material world, the other using the possibilities of decentralization and renewed localism available using the Internet, and the information economy in general. Just as highly mediated grassroots organizations might increasingly be able to draw on global resources and key leverage points to restrain global corporations, corporations which still have to fit into the context of local decisions, so global corporations will be able to draw on their own financial and informational background to influence local politics.

How will the growth of different virtual communities, tethered to different extents to regional groups, change this? While some might see these conflicts in static terms, we need to research the emergent properties of how going online affects the community of communities, of how real and virtual economies influence one another, including the impact this has for everyday people, their businesses, their cultures, and their local communities. While researchers, politicians, and philosophers can elaborate the implications of either one of these economies, clues to what might emerge can be found in the communities of Western Montana. To understand these changes we need to study not only online communities, nor offline communities using online technologies, but the way in which all these different worlds work and communicate together.

Note

1 Much of the following research is based on material originally collected as part of a long master's thesis (gopher://gopher.well.sf.ca.us:70/00/Community/communets/bigsky. txt). Please consult this paper for fuller methodological treatment. Research has since expanded to other communities and organizational levels. Any ethnographic project is part

collaboration, so I should recognize this investigation would not have been possible without the material, intellectual, and compassionate help of many activists and individuals, particularly Frank Odasz, Reggie Odasz, Jody Webster, Gerry Bauer, Mike Jatczynsky, Dave Hughes, Bob and Nash Shayon, Stan Pokras, members of the WELL, and the Electronic Networking Assoc. As an investigator I hope that I have not only reported the organization of communication, but also helped to facilitate it. Big Sky Telegraph: mac.bigsky.bigsky.dillon.mt.us. Gentle with the Internet link, please.

References

Ahl, Valerie and T.F.H. Allen. 1996. *Hierarchy Theory: A Vision, Vocabulary, and Epistemology*. New York: Columbia University Press.

Allen, T.F.H. and Thomas B. Starr. 1982. *Hierarchy: Perspectives for Ecological Complexity*. Chicago: University of Chicago Press.

Appadurai, Arjun. 1990. "Disjuncture and Difference in the Global Cultural Economy." *Public Culture* 2(2): 1–24.

Arendt, Hannah. 1958. *The Human Condition*. Chicago: University of Chicago Press.

Arthur, Brian. 1994. "On the Evolution of Complexity," in George Cowan, David Pines and David Meltzer (eds) *Complexity: Metaphors, Models, and Reality*. Proceedings volume in the Santa Fe Institute studies in the sciences of complexity, 19. Reading, MA: Addison-Wesley.

Barth, Frederik (ed.). 1978. *Scale and Social Organization*. Oslo: Universitetsforlaget.

Bauman, Zygmunt. 1992. *Intimations of Postmodernity*. London: Routledge.

Bell, Daniel. 1973. *The Coming of Post-Industrial Society: A Venture in Social Forecasting*. New York: Basic Books.

Bey, Hakim. 1991. *T.A.Z. The Temporary Autonomous Zone, Ontological Anarchy, Poetic Terrorism*. Brooklyn, NY: Autonomedia.

Bijker, W.E., T. Hughes and T. Pinch (eds). 1987. *The Social Construction of Technological Systems: New Directions in the Sociology and History of Technology*. Cambridge, MA: MIT Press.

Braudel, Fernand. 1981–4. *Civilization and Capitalism, 15th–18th Century* (3 vols). New York: Harper & Row.

Cohen, Anthony P. 1985. *The Symbolic Construction of Community*. London: Tavistock.

Cowan, George A., David Pines and David Meltzer (eds). 1994. *Complexity: Metaphors, Models, and Reality*. (Santa Fe Institute studies in the sciences of complexity. Proceedings volume 19.) Reading, MA: Addison-Wesley.

Davidow, William H. and Michael S. Malone. 1992. *The Virtual Corporation: Structuring and Revitalizing the Corporation for the 21st Century*. New York: E. Burlingame Books/Harper Business.

Derrida, Jacques. 1974. *Of Grammatology*, trans. Gayatri Chakravorty Spivak. Baltimore, MD: Johns Hopkins University Press.

Featherstone, Mike and Roger Burrows (eds). 1995. *Cyberspace/Cyberbodies/Cyberpunk: Cultures of Technological Embodiment*. London: Sage.

Giddens, Anthony. 1991. *Modernity and Self-Identity: Self and Society in the Late Modern Age*. Stanford, CA: Stanford University Press.

Granovetter, Mark. 1982. "The Strength of Weak Ties: A Network Theory Revisited," in Peter

Marsden and Nan Lin (eds) *Social Structure and Network Analysis*. Beverly Hills, CA: Sage.

Hannerz, Ulf. 1992. *Cultural Complexity: Studies in the Social Organization of Meaning*. New York: Columbia University Press.

Haraway, Donna. 1989. *Primate Visions: Gender, Race and Nature in the World of Modern Science*. New York: Routledge.

Hiltz, S.R. and M. Turoff. 1978. *The Network Nation: Human Communication via Computer*. Reading, MA: Addison-Wesley.

Huber, Peter W. 1987. *The Geodesic Network: 1987 Report on Competition in the Telephone Industry*. Washington, DC: US Department of Justice, Antitrust Division and US Government Printing Office.

Huber, Peter W., Michael K. Kellogg and John Thorne. 1992. *The Geodesic Network II: 1993 Report on Competition in the Telephone Industry* (2nd edn). Washington, DC: Geodesic Co.

Hudson, Heather E. 1984. *When Telephones Reach the Village: The Role of Telecommunications in Rural Development*. Norwood, NJ: Ablex.

Hughes, Dave. 1987–9. "The Electronic Democracy Debate." Meta-Net BBS, Old Salon, Topics 121, 153, 288, 372; New Salon 3. Also, Chariot BBS, Denver, CO. 1–719–632–3391. Interviews 1987–1989.

Jahrig, Shannon H. 1995. "Have Computer and Fax Modem, Will Travel: NY City Analyst Becomes Montana Lone Eagle." *Montana Business Quarterly* 33(2): 12–16.

Kauffman, Stuart. 1995. *At Home in the Universe: The Search for the Laws of Self-Organization and Complexity*. New York: Oxford University Press.

Kemmis, Daniel. 1990. *Community and the Politics of Place*. Norman, OK: University of Oklahoma Press.

King, Anthony D. 1990. *Urbanism, Colonialism, and the World-Economy: Cultural and Spatial Foundations of the World Urban System*. London: Routledge.

Machlup, Fritz. 1962. *The Production and Distribution of Knowledge in the United States*. Princeton, NJ: Princeton University Press.

Meyrowitz, Joshua. 1985. *No Sense of Place: The Impact of Electronic Media on Social Behavior*. New York: Oxford.

Naisbitt, John. 1982. *Megatrends: Ten New Directions Transforming Our Lives*. New York: Warner.

Nelson, Diane M. 1996. "Maya Hackers and the Cyberspatialized Nation-State: Modernity, Ethnostalgia, and a Lizard Queen in Guatemala." *Cultural Anthropology* 11(3): 287–308.

Nguyen, Dan Thu and Jon Alexander. 1996. "The Coming of Cyberspacetime and the End of Polity," in Rob Shields (ed.) *Cultures of Internet: Virtual Spaces, Real Histories, Living Bodies*. London: Sage.

Parker, Edwin B. and Heather E. Hudson, with Don Dillman, Sharon Strover and Frederick Williams. 1992. *Electronic Byways: State Policies For Rural Development Through Telecommunications*. Boulder, CO: Westview Press.

Pine, B. Joseph. 1993. *Mass Customization: The New Frontier in Business Competition*. Boston, MA: Harvard Business School Press.

Porat, Marc. 1977. *The Information Economy*. Washington, DC: US Government Printing Office.

Robins, Kevin and Webster, F. 1986. *Information Technology: A Luddite Analysis*. Norwood, NJ: Ablex.

Rogers, Everett. 1983. *Diffusion of Innovations* (3rd edn). New York: Free Press.

Rogers, Everett M. and D. Lawrence Kincaid. 1981. *Communication Networks: Toward a New Paradigm for Research*. New York: Free Press.

Sale, Kirkpatrick. 1991. *Dwellers in the Land: The Bioregional Vision*. Philadelphia, PA: New Society.

Sproull, Lee and Sara Kiesler. 1991. *Connections: New Ways of Working in the Networked Organization*. Cambridge, MA: MIT Press.

Stone, Allucquère Rosanne. 1995. *The War of Desire and Technology at the Close of the Mechanical Age*. Cambridge, MA: MIT Press.

Thurman, Robert A.F. 1984. *Tsong Khapa's Speech of Gold in the "Essence of True Eloquence."* Princeton, NJ: Princeton University Press.

Toffler, Alvin. 1981. *The Third Wave*. New York: Bantam.

Turner, Frederik Jackson. 1962 (1894). *The Frontier in American History*. New York: Holt, Rinehart & Winston.

Uncapher, Willard. 1990. "Literacy and Development: An Iranian Example." International Communications Association Annual Meeting, Trinity College, Dublin, Ireland.

Uncapher, Willard. 1995a. "A Geodesic Information Infrastructure: Lessons from Restructuring the Internet." International Communications Association Annual Meeting, Albuquerque, NM.

Uncapher, Willard. 1995b. "Placing the Mediascape in the Transnational Cultural Flow: Learning to Theorize an Emerging Global Grassroots Infrastructure." International Communications Association Annual Meeting, Albuquerque, NM.

Van der Ryn, Sim and Stuart Cowan. 1996. *Ecological Design*. Washington, DC: Island Press.

Varela, Francisco J., Evan Thompson and Eleanor Rosch. 1991. *The Embodied Mind: Cognitive Science and Human Experience*. Cambridge, MA: MIT Press.

Vichorek, Daniel N. 1992. *Montana Farm and Ranch Life*. (Montana geographic series 18.) Helena, MT: American and World Geographic.

Wallerstein, Immanuel. 1990. "Culture is the World System: a Reply to Boyne," in Mike Featherstone (ed.) *Global Culture: Nationalism, Globalization and Modernity*. London: Routledge.

Zuboff, Shoshana. 1988. *In the Age of the Smart Machine: The Future of Work and Power*. New York: Basic Books.

Chapter 12

Cyberspace and disadvantaged communities

The Internet as a tool for collective action

Christopher Mele

Twice monthly on Thursday evenings, officials from the local housing authority and residents of Robert S. Jervay Place do what was a short time earlier unlikely if not unthinkable: they gather together at the local community center to map out the agenda and argue the fine details of the forthcoming demolition and reconstruction of the low-income public housing development that was built near the central business district of Wilmington, North Carolina, in 1951. Each meeting has its predictable elements. First, the setting. The residents, all African-American women, sit unitedly at one side of the metal table; housing authority officials, all white males, sit at the other side, each group equipped with their own microcassette recorders to catch every word. The vicinity outside the cavernous meeting hall is strangely quiet, dark, and ghostly. Only 109 of the original 250 units are occupied, the rest have long been vacated and boarded-up – evidence of contention between the parties over the direction of Jervay's future. Second, convictions. Like other older public housing developments throughout the country, Jervay Place has been stamped obsolete, its architecture of barrack-like rowhomes castigated for encouraging deviant and criminal behavior and holding back the aspirations of its residents. Bringing it down, so the housing authority officials contend, is an important first step to ending blight. Fewer new homes will be erected. Some townhouses will replace rowhomes and single-family homes will be built to encourage family bonds and the future possibility of home ownership. The new Jervay of culs-de-sac, sidewalks, and "defensible space" will fit squarely into the "new thinking" of self-sufficiency and an end to dependency promulgated not only in the post-November 1994 Congress but also by the Department of Housing and Urban Development (HUD).[1]

To the contrary is the resident's understanding. Demolition and new construction are important and worthy of fulfillment. Jervay Place is outmoded and badly in need of reconstruction. Self-sufficiency and independence, however, cannot be built from bricks and mortar, but by removing obstacles to tenant self-respect and self-determination. According to the residents, over 95 percent of whom are African-American women, the emphasis of redevelopment should be placed upon employment training, child and elder care, and educational and recreational activities for young people.

After the meetings, once the housing officials are long gone, the women tend to linger outside the community center. The conversation inevitably turns to a full discussion of the intentions of the housing authority, of trust and broken promises, of the officials' fidgeting whenever new issues were introduced, and of the importance of the women's voice at the meetings. Gaining official representation at planning meetings came only after months of collective action. In between managing child care, working overtime, and maintaining a home, the residents – mostly single mothers – have pored over site drawings, HUD regulations, and hundreds of pages of development documents. They have met informally to compare notes about requirements for playgrounds and to digest the regulations in the most recent *Federal Register*.

As the hour wears on and the evening's significant events are rehashed, questions arise whether the time and effort dedicated to the meeting – indeed the entire struggle – are pointless or worthwhile. On one occasion, the president of the resident organization interceded,

> We can stand around here all night whining and complaining about this and that, how no one around here listens to us, or seems to care. Or, we can do something positive. There may not be many options left around here for us to get our point across – if there ever were any. But on that machine in the center, there are people who are listening and wanting to know what's going on. We don't live in a shell. We tell our stories, the word gets around. All over. They get back to us, we get back to the people around here. The powers that be are going to know that a lot other people besides those who live here know what's going on at Jervay.

The president was referring to a personal computer locked up in the resource center and how access to the Internet, including email and a residents' page on the World Wide Web, had helped transform the resident organization's position in the two year conflict with the housing authority from one of imposed silence and exclusion to a formal seat on the planning committee. Within a span of a few months online, the resident organization's difficulty in accumulating public housing design details and guidelines had been overcome and knowledge of the contention between the two parties had moved beyond the city's limits to seminar rooms at Xerox in Palo Alto, to planning conferences in Toronto, and to architects' studios in Berkeley, Phoenix, and Atlanta. Online networking initiated a series of discussions about low-income housing design and the shelter needs of elderly residents and led to working relationships between the resident council and housing specialists and consultants from around the country. In weekly tenant organization meetings, residents pulled together information and recommendations for site drawings and building design gleaned from dozens of exchanges with housing advocates and volunteer architects conducted via email. Through access and use of the Internet as a resource, the resident organization bypassed conventional and costly means of compiling information and secured an active role in planning the future of Jervay.

Computer-mediated communication and networking is a useful mechanism for disadvantaged groups in their efforts at collective action and empowerment. I recount the story of collective action and the use of online communication by the Jervay resident organization in its struggle against exclusion from participation in the redevelopment of the community. Resident mobilization for inclusion in the planning process and the resistance mounted by the housing authority were particularly embedded in the local customary (paternalist) forms of interaction that have long existed between dis-enfranchised African-Americans and political and social institutions. In order to challenge the unilateral decisions of the housing authority effectively, residents found it necessary to circumvent local obstacles to sources of information that were essential for planning and decision making. Jervay residents made use of local access to the Internet to tap online resources, to network online with supportive individuals and community organizations, and to broaden awareness of the dispute beyond the local community. The flexibility of online communication and networking afforded the women an opportunity to operate as agents outside the local and exclusive pathways of information, discourse, and social action that were either controlled or influenced by the institution of the housing authority. The chapter concludes with a discussion of the possibilities for online communication to mediate historically unequal relations between disadvantaged groups and social institutions.

The local historical context of race and power

At the most basic level of understanding, the conflict between the residents of Jervay and the Wilmington Housing Authority (WHA) was one of resident exclusion from the redevelopment planning process. Immediate issues, like those of housing and residential displacement, rather than abstract notions, such as power and inequality, are often the impetus for collective action (Tilly 1978: 143). Like most controversies, however, the unfolding of the dispute revealed a deeper and more significant meaning to the dis-agreement than is first implied. Collective action, defined as joint action in pursuit of common ends (Tilly 1978: 55), seeks to contest and, in various degrees, overcome inequalities of power that have been reproduced historically and systematically. The efforts of the residents to determine the future disposition of their homes challenge in addition to the housing authority's rulings the expressions of long-standing and local paternalist patterns of interaction that reproduce inequalities of class, race, and gender. To understand the story of the dispute over the development of Jervay and the utility of online communication as a tool for collective action, then, is to first appreciate how deeply it is suffused within the context of gender, race, and power in Wilmington, North Carolina.

Wilmington is a port city located on the southeastern coast of North Carolina with a population of some 56,000 residents, 34 percent of whom are African-American (US Department of Commerce 1990). Part geographical, part state of mind, the area's social life and culture remains somewhat parochial and isolated from the "New South" phenomenon associated with larger southern cities and regions, such as Charlotte and Research Triangle Park. An expansive historic district of grand homes and an overtly cordial hospitality afforded visitors parallel the city's obdurate attachment to the culture and fabled charm of the Old South. Those very attractions have not eluded real estate developers who have capitalized on selling Wilmington's allure to urban-weary migrants and retirees. Since the mid-1980s, the area has experienced unprecedented development in tourism and a significant increase in arrivals of white-collar professionals and elderly people.

What is not advertised to tourists and newcomers, of course, is Wilmington's "other" history. The classic film, *Blue Velvet*, was made in Wilmington. Like the story of the imagined town of Lumberton depicted in the film, there lies beneath the facade of giant magnolias, lazy oaks, and fragrant air, an acerbic and, in the past, violent side to Wilmington. This uncelebrated dimension is governed by the history of relations between whites and African-Americans in Wilmington. Racial discord has dominated the political landscape since the Civil War in degrees unmatched in other southern cities of similar size. More significantly, historical incidents of widespread violence figure notably in the contemporary discourse of race relations in the region.

One of the earliest instances of racial violence occurred after African-Americans established a foothold in the city's late-nineteenth-century political and economic life. Following Reconstruction, urban African-Americans in North Carolina and other southern states had won state and local offices by joining electoral forces with impoverished rural whites in fusion tickets in 1894 and 1896 (Edmonds 1951; Kornegay 1969). In 1897, four of Wilmington's five aldermen were African-Americans (Byrd 1976: 3). On November 10, 1898 white elites killed an undetermined number of African-Americans in a coup to regain political and economic power over the city and the surrounding county. Following the massacre, a diaspora to rural areas and northern industrial cities emptied the city of its African-American middle class (Cripps 1901: 7).

With the coup, white southern Democrats quashed the economic and political influence of the city's African-Americans and ushered in a period of political isolation that has endured well into the 1960s. African-American Wilmingtonians were forced to settle into an uneasy truce in which economic subsistence was ensured in exchange for an acknowledgment of and subservience to the white-privileged power structure.

In the late civil rights era, other occurrences of violence erupted and met harsh reprisal when younger African-Americans in Wilmington (as in other cities across the United States) challenged the local power structure. In 1968, residents responded with street protests to the assassination of Martin Luther King. The assassination was especially senseless for Wilmingtonians as King had been scheduled to appear in Wilmington the day he was killed. In 1971, student protests occurred in reaction to a school desegregation order that led to the closing of the predominantly African-American Williston High School. A group of African-American students required to attend the suburban and predominantly white Hoggard High School staged a sit-in to object to the failure of both the school and the city to recognize and commemorate Dr. King's birthday. In the ensuing protest, high school classes were disrupted and the student demonstrators suspended. Protests and demonstrations became more frequent and violent in the weeks following, leading to a full-scale rebellion of African-American students and their supporters in February. As racial tensions escalated in the crisis, several nights of violence erupted in the mostly minority neighborhoods within the city. The Williston activists and organizers, including Benjamin Chavis, were arrested, tried, and convicted of charges related to the unrest. The Wilmington Ten, as they soon became known, were given lengthy prison sentences decried by supporters worldwide, including Amnesty International, which cited the imprisonment as a human rights violation. A federal investigation eventually revealed that a key witness for the prosecution had been bribed. The conviction of the Wilmington Ten was finally overturned in December 1980 when the Fourth Circuit Court of Appeals in Richmond ruled that the right to a fair trial had been denied.[2]

For the political aspirations of the African-American community, the reaction of the white community to the protests, the harsh sentences received by the Wilmington Ten, and the revelation of a miscarriage of justice were apparent confirmation of an unchanged and unequal power structure and a strong admonition to them not to challenge it. In the late 1990s, the history of the Wilmington Ten and the Massacre of 1898 is barely acknowledged in any public forum; the events remain remarkably time-less and unduly potent. Despite official reluctance, the 1898 massacre has not been forgotten by local residents.[3] With the one-hundred-year anniversary approaches few efforts have been made to recognize the significance of 1898. The event will continue to remain both subversive and contemporary. As local activists currently engaged in collective action contend, all issues that deal with race in Wilmington are filtered through the experiences of 1898 and 1972. Many of the active and vocal African-Americans leaders attribute political lethargy and civic inaction to the silence and fear imposed following 1898 and reproduced since then. Issues of empowerment, such as Jervay, are subjected to a type of political and social time warp, where, as one resident put it, "you have to fight the past all over again."

Although the acute and public malice that once marked racism in the south has for the most part been purged, the demeanor of relations of the white-privileged power structure toward African-Americans remains implanted in paternalism, exclusion, and privilege. The gains of the civil rights era, while important, have not erased institutional antagonism toward organized community mobilization and collective action, especially around interests of education and housing. The predominantly white power elite retains its role as gatekeeper of economic and political resources, meting occasional assistance but excluding participation in decision making. In the case of Jervay, the community *was informed of* the local housing authority's blueprint for the redevelopment of Jervay. The authority had extolled the merits of redevelopment to local and state governments, but the residents, represented by the resident organization, had been excluded from the development process. Several of the women residents of Jervay, using the clinical language of substance abuse, referred to this paternalist dependency as addiction and the need to mobilize against it as recovery. Their identity as African-American women within a local and increasingly national politically hostile environment has made their efforts particularly compelling.

Contention over the future of Jervay

> Jervay Place is only the beginning, the Housing Authority knows that if they can get away with wiping our homes out of existence, they can do the same thing anywhere else in the city.[4]

The issues contested at Jervay – tenant control and empowerment, displacement and community organizing – are germane to low-income housing struggles in general. The changes that have transpired over the history of Jervay Place mirror the varying social and economic conditions that have occurred within Wilmington and many other cities since World War II. The 250 homes of Robert S. Jervay Place were constructed in 1951 by the Wilmington Housing Authority as part of a slum clearance campaign to replace substandard wood-frame housing concentrated on the southside of the city.[5] Following the example of many other public housing developments built after World War II, the architects of Jervay Place designed a complex of military-style barracks of row after row of identical brick two-story multi-family houses. The housing authority chose to name the development in honor of the first publisher of Wilmington's sole remaining African-American newspaper, *The Journal*, which was founded in 1911. Completed during the era of Jim Crow, the complex housed African-American families exclusively. Since the enactment of court orders ending desegregation, the demographic composition of Jervay Place has remained predominantly African-American as has the surrounding neighborhood of Wilmington's predominantly minority southside (Freeman 1995).

Following the unrest of 1971, a sizeable number of white homeowners fled the city's downtown neighborhoods to the suburbs, followed by the flight of commercial and retail establishments. The city's viable blue-collar workforce, which included many Jervay residents,[6] suffered from the closing of light manufacturing industries (garments, box making) located on the city's southside. Currently, the income of 39 percent of the inner city's African-American population is considered below the poverty level.[7] Social problems have escalated, including a shortage of well-paying and secure jobs, rising street crime and inadequate police protection, street corner drug markets, and abandoned and deteriorating homes and storefronts.

Since 1990, business and government concern for elimination of the blight in and around Jervay Place has taken on a new urgency. The city's redevelopment of the downtown waterfront area generated unprecedented growth in housing demand and sales. The effects of incumbent upgrading and gentrification of the historic district began to spill over to predominantly African-American neighborhoods, leading to displacement pressures for fixed-income homeowners and renters. The revitalization of Jervay remains the linchpin of the city-led effort to revive the south side.

Of concern to residents was whether such plans for revitalization would include a commitment to maintain low-income housing at Jervay Place. Charges voiced to the resident organization by tenants of willful neglect of declining living conditions at Jervay fueled conjectures that the city and the housing authority intended to eliminate or down-size the development. Rumors abounded that given its location on a major thoroughfare and its visibility to tourists and others entering the city, that the "eyesore" Jervay was to be done away with and its tenants displaced. The resident organization responded to such concerns by becoming active and vocal in demands to the housing authority to address the social problems and physical decay of Jervay Place.

In the early months of 1992, the housing authority brought news to the residents that Jervay Place would receive federal funds from the US Department of Housing and Urban Development for a total renovation of the site's 250 units. Jervay Place was designated a pilot project for modernization that included renovations to buildings and renewed commitment to addressing and solving social problems. In the initial stages of planning, residents were asked to "please come help plan the future of your neighbor-hood,"[8] as required by HUD guidelines. The resident council responded with enthusiasm laced with skepticism, commenting in the local press that the residents' goal was "to see to it that we are heard, listened to, or at least considered."[9]

At early stages of planning, the president of the resident council insisted on strong participation and saw to it that residents were appointed to a newly formed modern-ization committee.[10] Residents' aspirations of full partnership with the housing authority were partially realized in a three-day planning charette of residents and personnel from the housing authority and the architectural firm hired for renovation. By formally including residents in the planning and strategy session, the authority created an atmosphere of a working and equal partnership that would generate real changes at Jervay. The charette proved to be a landmark in the later conflict between residents and the housing authority over the exclusion of tenant representation. In subsequent months in preparation for renovation, many residents were relocated off-site. According to the relocation plan developed by the housing authority and residents, those relocated would return once their units were renovated.

Fault lines began to develop in the relationship between residents and the authority in July 1993, when demolition, rather than renovation, of a number of housing units was first breached to tenants. Citing poor design that encouraged illegal activities,[11] the authority planned to demolish four buildings within the complex and replace the units lost with Section 8 low-income housing vouchers or certificates.[12] At a meeting in February 1994, the resident organization offered a compromise, requesting the con-version of two of the four buildings to a community center that would provide classroom space, day care, job training, and other services demonstrated as needs in both the planning charette and the architect surveys.[13] Citing expenses, the housing authority opposed the idea unless residents and staff could locate funding for such a conversion. Despite the resistance of the housing authority to the counteroffer, residents signed a memorandum of understanding and approval (as required by HUD)[14] for the demolition of only two of the four buildings. In addition, the resident council questioned the intentions of the authority's efforts to demolish units without replacing the identical number of units. The housing authority denied such intentions.

The relationship completely unraveled in the spring of 1994 when residents learned that the housing authority no longer intended to renovate units but would petition HUD for funds to demolish the entire development and rebuild a smaller Jervay. In place of 250 units, a mix of 125 townhouses and single-family homes would be constructed on the site and 125 additional units would be built as single-family homes on lots scattered throughout the city. Without consultation with the resident council, the architectural firm originally contracted for renovation was removed and replaced by an out-of-town firm hired to put together a demolition–reconstruction concept plan. At the time the housing authority would submit the application, 125 families had temporarily relocated off-site. Under the new plan, only the remaining 125 families would live in the new Jervay; those who had left would no longer be eligible to return.[15]

The announcement was immediately interpreted within the historical framework of power and race relations. Whether the soundness of the authority's revised plan merited consideration or not was shrouded by the heavy-handed delivery of a drastic course change matched by the total disregard of the partnership with the council. As far as most residents were concerned, they were swindled and the turn of events was a betrayal of the working relationship developed between themselves and the housing authority.[16] For those residents incredulous of institutional power in general, their worst fears had been realized.[17] Subsequently, the council questioned whether the housing authority's previous gestures toward collaboration were a smoke screen for a hidden agenda to eliminate Jervay altogether. In a letter written by a resident organization officer to the Secretary of HUD, the sentiments of many were expressed:

> The Housing Authority feels that new buildings will change the situation here. They don't feel that education helps, that hiring some of the tenants and helping out with unemployment on a long-term basis helps, or trying to keep an interest in real maintenance and cosmetics of the complex helps in the morale of the resident – at least not until now. They feel that the place has been neglected for over 10 years and now everyone else is feeling we should jump on the bandwagon and give thanks for letting us go through decades with drugs, crime and some poverty. We are thankful for them [Housing Authority] offering us deliverance now, but I for one, know that this vision of loveliness is an illusion to fool the residents one more time, and the public for the thousandth.[18]

The women residents immediately pressed the authority to return to the former plan and allow a process of full participation in revisions, including the possibility of demolition–reconstruction. By July 1, 1994, however, the housing authority had already secured the necessary approvals from city government and submitted the application for demolition.[19] Letters were written by Jervay residents to the local press, civic associations, HUD officials, and congressmen; hours were spent reading HUD regulations and procedures for possible means of recourse. An opportunity developed for residents in August 1994 when HUD officials discovered the demolition plan was not in compliance with protocol requiring an offer be presented to residents to purchase the development.[20] In situations where a housing authority and a development are in agreement, the regulation is perfunctory. When the Wilmington Housing Authority extended the offer, the resident organization accepted, setting a clock in motion that froze the demolition application in Washington. In October, the residents contacted the Office of Public and Indian Housing to inform HUD that the local housing authority had not solicited resident participation for the demolition plan. Although details of the decision were never made public, HUD sent back the unfunded application for revisions.

The residents temporarily prevailed but were soon stymied by the housing authority's efforts to discredit their opposition and by a lack of local resources to fully develop their own plan. The authority sought to circumvent the council's legitimacy as the representative body of Jervay residents. The authority chose not to focus on the council's objection to resident exclusion in the process but claimed instead that the dissenting women could not adequately present nor explain the revised plan to the residents.[21] In August, the authority sent each resident via certified mail an agreement to be signed that they understood and concurred with the demolition plan. Only seven residents returned signed notices.[22] The housing authority, along with the several other public officials and the city's main press, appeared bewildered by the protestations of the women residents. No word was mentioned about the lack of consultation with the residents or the women's charge of duplicity on the part of the housing authority.[23] Public perception of the validity of the plan based on housing authority information was coupled with the stereotypical image of the dissenting women as ungrateful and unreasonable. Both the residents' reaction and their voiced opposition to demolition and redevelopment were portrayed as illegitimate and even dangerous to the success of an otherwise sound plan for low-income housing. "You may ask why Jervay residents wouldn't want brand new homes to live in," wrote a journalist in the local African-American press in response to the widespread questioning of the residents' motives. "The answer is simple, they are afraid to trust the system."[24] By labeling the resistance to the plan as unwarranted and illegitimate and marginalizing the council as a fringe group, the authority successfully silenced the residents from local avenues for questioning details of the development plans. Throughout the conflict, the resident organization made clear that its singular opposition was to exclusion and not to the merits or drawbacks of the new development plan. Finally, after several months, the president of the resident organization rescinded the buy-out option, allowing the authority to resubmit the demolition plan with resident support. In exchange, the Jervay Place Task Force was formed as the official body to oversee the formation and implementation of demolition and reconstruction at Jervay Place. The Task Force was designed to allow residents to bring their ideas to the physical and social planning of the new Jervay. Although the creation of the Task Force was an important formal mechanism for the residents to make claims to the housing authority, it did not address inequalities in power between the two parties.

Given such obstacles, the council was convinced that they could not rely on the housing authority as a source of credible information and technical assistance. The residents who served on the Task Force had token autonomy as long as they remained beholden to the authority for information needed to make decisions about development. The housing authority remained gatekeeper to the details needed to design the site plan, create model prototypes of the development, and set schedules for demolition and reconstruction.[25] The women officers were well aware that without access to material and the opportunity to assess it independently, the Task Force was a hollow gesture toward empowerment. Options, however, were limited. There were no local coalitions or organizations for housing and tenant assistance available in Wilmington. Although a housing advocacy group from Chapel Hill was contacted, they were short-staffed and the distance between Chapel Hill and Wilmington made consultation unfeasible. The problem of access to information and available technical assistance became acute.

Getting vocal online: collective action through the Internet

It became apparent to the resident organization that new links to assistance and counsel outside the purview and control of the housing authority were required if effective participation on the Task Force was to be realized. In March 1995 the Jervay residents chose to take their story online, transforming their roles from reactive to proactive participants.

The circumstances that brought Jervay residents online and eventually to the creation of their own Web site were a unique coming together of the resident organization's commitment to self-reliance, an urgent demand for independent information, and several propitious factors. Jervay residents' familiarity with computers began long before the idea of collective action through the Internet was first introduced. Several residents were graduates of computer instruction and a variety of software courses at a local community college. In 1994, the resident organization convinced the housing authority to convert an empty apartment into the resident-run Jervay Resource Center. Once funds from a HUD Drug Elimination Grant were used to purchase several computers, the center sponsored on-site computer instruction courses taught by competent residents.

When the dispute with the housing authority occurred in the summer of 1994, resident leaders began to utilize public terminals at the university library to access the Internet for information related to HUD protocol and rulings. The use of public access to the Internet had its shortcomings, however. Visits to terminals and the length of sessions online were restricted by travel and time constraints. Information storage and retrieval were cumbersome and, without an email account, dialogue between residents and online contacts was limited. The resident organization inquired into obtaining Internet access for one of the more powerful (486) computers housed in the Jervay Resource Center through contacts with local supporters in the planning department and the local university. In March 1995, the resident organization requested and received funds from a public service grant administered by the University of North Carolina at Wilmington for the purchase of a 14.4 modem and initial fees for Internet service.[26] The non-profit component of a local Internet service provider, Wilmington Internet Service Enterprises (WISE), furnished Jervay with a SLIP/PPP account (for access to the World Wide Web) and email service (jervayrs@wilmington.net).[27] Residents with advanced knowledge of DOS, word processing, and spreadsheets easily assimilated the fundamentals of Internet access and applications.

Within a time span of a few weeks, Internet access provided the resident organization with a new means of communication, networking, and presence that would transform their efforts to become active participants in the Task Force. Initially, the resident organization leaders conducted online searches and browsed various sites for materials on housing. Using a World Wide Web directory of listserver discussion groups, the resident council soon discovered and subscribed to three Internet discussion groups dedicated to architecture, sustainable community development, and urban planning that reached a total of 426 readers. Each listserver provided residents admittance to a focused community of interested persons with knowledge and experience of housing and design issues. As members, residents posted direct queries for assistance and took part in online discussions. A small working group of residents spent 20 minutes to write and disseminate the initial listserver posting which introduced the resident council, presented the issues surrounding development, and requested technical assistance from knowledgeable readers:

> March 24, 1995. This is an urgent request for assistance in concepts and designs for public housing that integrates households headed by single mothers and the elderly. We are residents of Robert S. Jervay Place, public housing in Wilmington, North Carolina. Currently, we are being challenged by the local housing authority to come up with concrete ideas for the design and development of 125 + units on 14 acres. The housing authority has put forth its own plan based mostly on single family homes. We, the residents, rejected the plan for 2 reasons: 1) the authority did not properly consult with the residents on the design of the plan, and 2) we feel the plan does not represent the needs of the current population who are promised homes in the new development. At present, we are 120 families the majority of whom are female-headed, low-income, African-American. We also have a sizeable elderly population. The local authority's request to demolish the existing site is under review at HUD. A DECISION IS EXPECTED VERY SOON. Once the decision to demolish is approved, our time to develop an alternative plan is very short. If you or someone you know has any suggestions on how to proceed (design of units, layout of units on the acreage, etc.) please respond quickly! Thanks and may god bless. President Jervay Place Residents Organization.

Twenty-three persons and organizations responded within two weeks, including ten architects, two low-income housing lawyers, individuals with various experiences in low-income housing development, and several well-wishers who offered support and advice.

In the following weeks and over a number of email messages, the resident organization developed its own site plan for Jervay online with the help of three architectural firms specializing in housing. First, copies of the housing authority's site plan were sent to the firms as AUTOCADD .dxf files (provided by the housing authority at the request of the Task Force). The residents provided the architects with their concerns and design issues. From the moment the housing authority's plan of single-family homes was first unveiled, the residents detected two major design problems. First, single-family homes on individual lots do not encourage or facilitate cooperation between residents. Many of the single mothers at Jervay had long argued for a design that accommodated the sharing of household and child care duties. In the older development, residents had cooperated in elder care and child care despite structures that were poorly designed to do so. The new design, they contended, should allow such sharing to continue and not penalize it. Second, the residents agreed with the housing authority that the new Jervay should blend into the surrounding community of single-family homes. In the site plan, however, lots for single-family homes were placed willy-nilly along culs-de-sac that ringed the development while townhouses were tightly clustered in the center.

Each of the three architects responded to the residents' concerns and developed rough drafts of a site plan that addressed the issues of communal sharing and site density. Upon the architects' request, the council provided more detailed material, including local zoning codes, a list of design prerequisites such as unit square footage, and the breakdown of units by number of bedrooms. One firm based its design on cohousing, placing a large community center with programs implemented and managed primarily by residents, space for both formal day care facilities and informal child care and elder care sharing as the centerpoint of the community. Another design which showed a new Jervay indistinguishable from the surrounding residential neighborhood generated much enthusiasm among members of the resident organization.[28]

> May 03, 1995. Jervay residents: If one of your goals is generate a greater sense of neighborhood and less that of a "project" you will want to clearly distinguish between spaces that are public and spaces that are private. In the current design, persons easily pass through alleys and front and back yards (what we usually consider private), not being able (or asked) to distinguish what is public from what is private. You may wish to consider creating multiple layers of privacy progressing from the street, to the sidewalk, to the front lawn, the porch and house. This would allow you to promote community between the residents of Jervay and the surrounding Dry Pond neighborhood and, therefore, a sense of community.

The architect argued that it was important to decenter the cluster of multi-family homes in the core of the site, eliminating the focal space that is typically not accessible to the surrounding neighborhood nor vice versa. Residents knew from experience that this area was the least defensible because it was insulated from approach from outside the site. It created an island that was distinct, different, and separate, and violated the idea of blending Jervay into the neighborhood. Over a series of communications online, the resident organization and the firm developed the plan further to include the continuation of streets through the development, mimicking the rest of the city's grid-iron street plan. Doing so, it was argued, would break up the space into quarters that are more defensible by each smaller community. It would also allow all new units to be positioned with street access.[29]

Through the relationships developed online with the architects, the women had introduced a *de facto* third party of volunteer experts to the Task Force negotiations table. The presentation of the technical assistance and ideas dispensed by the online consultant architects was first approved, reworked, articulated, and finally presented to the authority by the women, imparting greater control at the meetings. Armed with graphic information and new design ideas, the Task Force members were often able to dominate the discussion. The efforts of the resident organization to contract assistance through Internet did not go unnoticed by the housing authority. The authority had originally sanctioned the acquisition of the modem and Internet service for the Jervay Resource Center to facilitate electronic communication between its staff and residents. To continue and protect their advantage in soliciting and receiving detailed assistance online, the resident Task Force members did not share important features – the number of consultants, the identities of the architectural firms, the number of transmissions – of their online activities with the authority.[30] Officials of the housing authority rarely objected at meetings, but were troubled when the residents appeared to have overpowered the agenda. An excerpt from housing authority correspondence illustrates their frustrations:

> The Jervay Task Force seems to have lost sight of the fact that it is an advisory committee and is not in charge of day to day operations of this Housing Authority or responsible for development activities of Robert S. Jervay. . . . It will not be managed by outside committee – whether that be residents or resident's consultants – but by WHA staff and Board of Commissioners.[31]

The Jervay Web site

Soon after the original discussion group requests were posted, the residents at Jervay clearly established a presence on the Internet. A substantial number of messages from non-profit organizations and individuals were received seeking detailed information about Jervay, the development plans and about the residents themselves. As the frequency and content of online discussions trebled, the need for an easily accessible site to store and retrieve information became apparent. It soon became unwieldy for the resident organization to respond to individual email requests for information and impossible to send sketch drawings of site plans online. At the request of the resident council, the local non-profit Internet service provider furnished support for the construction and maintenance of a home page on the World Wide Web. Jervay Place became the first public housing development in the country with a resident-managed Web site.

Jervay's Web site was developed through a collaborative division of labor between the resident organization, the non-profit component of the Internet service provider, WISE, and the urban studies curriculum at the Department of Sociology and Anthropology of the University of North Carolina at Wilmington.[32] In addition to mounting plans drawn up in collaboration with online architects, the resident organization selected topics and projects of importance to Jervay resident self-empowerment. Residents controlled the purpose, content, additions, and revisions to each of the site's pages. Technical creation of the Web pages (translating resident-produced text files to html language, scanning photographs for .gif files, etc.) was provided by student interns.

A modest early version of the Web site (http://www.wilmington.net/jervay) went online April 15, 1995. Since then, new pages have been added and updated on a continual basis. The site serves three central purposes: it presents an up-to-date status of residents' efforts to guide the rebuilding of Jervay, it provides historical and cultural information about Jervay Place, and it maintains hyperlinks to related sites and to the HUD Web and gopher servers.

The Jervay Web site, titled "Jervay On-Line," houses the most recent information about the progress toward redevelopment. A series of pages connected to the link, "Work In Progress," eliminates the difficulty of disseminating design information to interested persons. The pages contain text and links to images of Jervay's current site plan and draft plans created by the collaboration of residents and architects. This set of pages also records the status of the redevelopment application being considered by the Department of Housing and Urban Development. Although this particular link is accessible to any browser, it is primarily an archive of design-related material to be used by those providing assistance in the development of the plan.

In addition to pages dedicated to future plans for the development, the Web site also includes a narrative and photographic history of Jervay. The "Jervay History Project" was initiated by residents in the spring of 1995 and developed in response to frustration over Jervay's tarnished image propagated in the media and in everyday public discourse. In a local newspaper article announcing Washington's approval of demolition, for example, the fact that the majority of households are headed by single women raising children was cited as one of the development's "many social problems."[33] Officials from the housing authority, in their enthusiasm to legitimize razing the structure, had also contributed to the demonizing of Jervay, portraying it as unfit and unsalvageable. Many of those who had lived in the development for years were affronted by such harmful characterizations that overlooked both their efforts and those of previous residents. The concerns and resentment prompted the idea of a community scrapbook that would document the positive aspects of Jervay's past and present. Photographs collected by residents from their personal collections were mounted on the Web site in a project with the university and the Internet service provider. The photographs (as .gif files) were linked to a narrative history of the site's earliest years that shows the development of Jervay as a clear accomplishment over the slum conditions that prevailed in Wilmington in the early 1950s. The project also includes a discussion about the original mandate of federal housing assistance and how public perceptions of subsidized housing have changed. For the residents, the Jervay History Project has been instrumental in correcting some of the misinformation about public housing in general and Jervay in particular. The project is used in the African-American history studies series conducted by the resident organization on Thursday evenings at the resource center.

In conjunction with community networking, the Web site also provided a link from Jervay to other Web sites, including civic networking, housing and community development, child care and substance abuse, and economic development and training.

These links allowed regular and easy access to sources of information. The site's link to HUD's home page (http://www.hud.gov) was interactive, allowing residents to download HUD information from the site for their use and to communicate directly to any one of HUD's program offices.

Although the stated purpose of the Jervay Web site was to provide a public ledger of the history of Jervay and the goals and activities of the resident organization, the leaders were quick to make the most of its use as a collective action tool. With institutional resources and political connections at its disposable, the housing authority easily made its view of events at Jervay available to the public. As the electronic voice of the resident organization, the Web site would function as its 24-hour billboard. Through the Jervay home page, an open record of the residents' struggle and agenda and events was established and maintained for audiences beyond Wilmington. By broadening the scope of awareness of Jervay, the resident organization gained collateral against the possibility of intentions by the housing authority to silence their participation or to initiate drastic changes and later legitimize them through an uncontested "rewriting of history." The resident organization aggressively marketed the home page to the network of architects and other subscribers to the planning and urban-community discussion groups. The Jervay Web site was well received by HUD officials in Washington and was listed as well on several community-based and housing-related Web sites, including the Three Rivers Free-Net in Pennsylvania (http://trfn.clpgh.org/), the Community Networks Directory supported by the Boulder, CO Community Network (http://pclab.csied.unisa.it/cdrom/pages/wwwrmsdd.com/comnet/wwwvl_ci.htm), and the Homeless Home Page of Communications for a Sustainable Future (http://csf.colorado.edu/homeless/).

Conclusion: implications of Internet for collective action

The most successful mobilizations of disenfranchised social groups against institutional power require, among other factors, vast commitments of time, resources, and un-flagging dedication, a clear sense of purpose, and a flexible course of action in the face of overwhelming obstacles. The residents of Jervay have shown their resilience. At the time this chapter is written, however, the questions about Jervay's redevelopment remain unanswered. The immediate and long-term future of the community will not be decided in Wilmington but in Washington, where the Department of Housing and Urban Development has rescinded the 1939 Housing Act (leaving the future of public housing an uncertainty) and the federal budget crisis of 1995–6 has shelved all funding for project development. Thus an assessment of the residents' experience on the Internet must focus less on the outcome of their struggle and more on its utility in the process of collective action. Specifically, the case of Jervay raises the question of the potential capacity and limitations of the Internet as a tool for the collective action of small players against institutional power.

A central problem confronting the resident organization was obstacles to infor-mation and collaboration with other organizations and individuals. The struggle unfolded in a setting of historic and systematic repression of African-American attempts at collective mobilization. Key to both repression and the maintenance of institutional power was the deprivation of access to knowledge and information resources. As gatekeepers to knowledge, privileged elites assured the reproduction of a paternalist pattern of meting out political and economic donations in exchange for political acquiescence. When the residents of Jervay sought to challenge this tradition of political discourse, they faced a slew of efforts by the housing authority to squelch their attempts, including the token offer of participation in redevelopment proceedings. When the more vocal tenants were granted a seat at the planning table, the non-existence of a regional network of supportive community organizers left little doubt that the housing authority would prevail in its unilateral control over the future disposition of Jervay. At Task Force meetings, residents arrived with a willingness to explore issues and concerns but lacked the important information and resources to control and implement their agenda. Based on their experiences, the women maintained that the authority could not seriously consider them as agents or subjects involved in the making of their own history. Their negation as participants in decisions about the future of their homes fueled the commitment of the residents and explains their ultimate decision to use the Internet as a viable resource for collective action.

The flexibility of the Internet proved useful in developing a surrogate electronic community and network and breaking down the isolation of Jervay and its residents. Computer-mediated communication was well suited to residents' lifestyles, allowing for variable schedules and multiple layers of commitments and responsibilities to employment and child care. The information culled from interaction on the Internet was timely, cost-effective, and integral to residents' participation on the Task Force. Connections with the world outside Jervay and Wilmington diminished the sense that their efforts were isolated and marginal. Residents learned that people had taken interest in their story and that some had gone so far as to lend technical support. This had a positive transformative effect on the attitude of the resident council. As a result, the resident organization has gained some ownership of the development issue and has since become an active player in the decision making of Jervay's short-term and long-term future.

Although online communication appears as a useful tool to challenge and even subvert differentials of power expressed as control over the access, transfer, and application of knowledge and information, the implications for social change are unclear. Online communication offers disadvantaged or what the ethnographer Terry Williams has called "hard to reach" populations access to sources of detailed information beyond the confines of locale and to bring those resources to bear on real and immediate problems.[34] Yet the potential for putting to work electronic communities and networks to effect change in place-based communities is thwarted by several realities. While online communication may ameliorate negative features of face-to-face interaction between consumers and producers of information and knowledge (e.g. onerous expert–client relationships) and modes of discourse that reproduce and perpetuate social inequalities (Feenberg 1991; Jones 1995), it does not eliminate them. Computer-mediated networks are said to point toward a new kind of civil society that is technologically predisposed toward a more democratic interaction (Frederick 1993; Hamelink 1991), but new patterns of inequality and forms of division are created (as shown in other chapters in this volume).

There are other obstacles to such grassroots application of computer-mediated communication. The fragility of the set of circumstances that led to the residents' access and use of the Internet for collective action – prior training in computers for a core of residents, the support of a local Internet company, and university community outreach – speaks to a missing infrastructure for the inclusion of disempowered social groups in cyberspace. The continued rapid expansion of computerized online information-based services has not been matched by a similar growth in the availability and access to such services for historically disadvantaged social groups. The probability of replicating the Jervay model in similar situations is hindered by a lack of access to the requisite technology. The technological gap exists along lines of social and economic inequalities of class, race, gender (Harasim 1993: 33), and location. Recent surveys of Internet users find the majority to be middle-to-upper class, well-educated white males. Although the gap between male and female users appears to be narrowing, the dearth of minority, low-income users remains unchanged.[35] A survey of computer use by households conducted by the US Census Bureau showed that compared with whites, non-whites were lagging in both ownership and use of computers (*New York Times* 1995). In a recent online survey, the racial composition of respondents was 86.0 percent white, 1.47 percent African-American, 1.84 percent Hispanic, and 3.02 percent Asian.[36] In his study of Los Angeles, Mike Davis argues that a principal characteristic of marginal neighborhoods is their growing isolation from information access. "The ghetto is defined not only by its paucity of parks and public amenities," he writes, "but also by the fact that it is not wired into any of the key information circuits" (Davis 1992: 155). Once wired, it is difficult to predict the effects of online communication for collective action conducted by disempowered groups. For the women activists at Jervay, their connection to the Internet peeled away some of the historic and systematic layers that blanketed access to essential information. Whether it translates to long-term success is perhaps less important than the positive effect upon the activist role of the women themselves.

Notes

1   See US Department of Housing and Urban Development (1995) Program Consolidation [Online]. Available gopher: //gopher.hud.gov:70/ 00/hud.news%7E/15ways.txt%7E.
2   See Thomas (1993).
3   The novel, *Cape Fear Rising*, published by local author Philip Gerard (1994), provided a vivid if unflattering account of the events of 1898 that rankled the nerves of the local power elite, many of whom could trace their ancestral roots to key players. See also Leon Prather's *We Have Taken a City* (1984) and Jack Thorne [pseudonym for David Bryant Fulton], *Hanover: The Persecution of the Lowly. A Story of the Wilmington Massacre* (1901). In interviews I have conducted with African-American residents for a project on migration from the north, the political acquiescence of the African-American community is frequently attributed to the legacy of the 1898 massacre.

4 Quote from a former resident who moved from Jervay Place expecting to return after renovations. "Jervay, A Place to Call Home," *The Journal*, June 30, 1994: 2.

5 For view a photographic exhibition of Jervay Place in the 1950s, see http://www.wilmington.net/jervay.

6 Interview, former residents, February 1995.

7 Wilmington's inner city consists of census tracts 101, 103, 110, 111, 112, 113, and 114. The African-American population for the city in 1990 was 18,815 persons (US Department of Commerce 1990).

8 From a written announcement for a residents' meeting held February 10, 1992 sponsored by the Wilmington Housing Authority.

9 "Jervay Restoration, Unity in the Community," *The Journal*, February 27, 1992: 2.

10 "Jervay Restoration: Unity in the Community," *The Journal*, February 27, 1992: 1 and copies of correspondence from Jervay Place Resident Organization to the architectural firm hired by the Wilmington Housing Authority, 14 February 1992.

11 The buildings were known as four "C" type structures. Unlike the majority of multi-family structures on the site in which tenants had their own separate entrances to their apartments, the "C" buildings had common stairways used to access individual apartments. These stairways were said to act as hide-outs and meeting places for the sale and consumption of drugs. The housing authority insisted on demolition of the buildings to discourage criminal behavior. The residents' organization, concerned about the potential loss of housing units, initially supported redesigning the buildings with private entrances. The housing authority claimed such renovations were cost-prohibitive.

12 Minutes of Resident Relocation Committee Meeting, July 6, 1993.

13 "Renovations Underway at Jervay Place," *The Journal*, August 12, 1993: 1.

14 The housing authority was required by HUD regulations to provide the necessary documentation for the removal of the four buildings as dwelling units. Documentation included signatures from the residents of Jervay and an affidavit from the resident organization officers that they were in agreement with the proposed plan. From a housing authority memo to Jervay residents, January 31, 1994.

15 The authority legitimized its decision to demolish and reconstruct on three factors: the high costs associated with renovation, especially the abatement of asbestos and lead paint, a theory that lower density and units with "defensible space" would decrease crime, and the assumption that a built environment of single-family homes would foster responsibility and self-sufficiency among residents. In the fall, the housing authority once again changed its development plan. Rather than construct 125 new units scattered in sites across the city, the authority would apply for 125 Section 8 certificates and vouchers. The rationale was that such a proposal was more synchronous and, therefore, more amenable to the new ideology and thinking of HUD that promulgated free-market housing choices for low-income residents. Vouchers would allow residents to move into homes of their choice in any neighborhood, provided enough landlords would participate in the Section 8 program.

16 Interviews with officers of the Jervay Place Resident Organization, September 1994.

17 Interviews with tenants, September 1994.

18 Letter composed by resident council officer to the editor of *The Journal*, September 29, 1994.

19 The single exception to gaining approval was the city planning department. The city planning department cited the lack of resident input into the new plan as the reason for denial of approval.

20 Section 116(a) of the Housing and Community Development Act of 1992.
21 In the fall, the authority held meetings outside the resident council's purview with
    15–16 residents who supported demolition (source: Transcript, "Jervay Meeting,"
    December 15, 1994). Efforts to circumvent the residents' organization were in vain,
    however, as HUD regulations clearly maintained that local authorities must deal directly
    with elected officers of the resident council (see Federal Register R46074 Notice PIH
    9317 April 2, 1993, Section 116 (a) HCD Act of 1992) .
22 Transcript from tape, "Jervay Meeting," December 15, 1994.
23 According to the demolition application to HUD, however, the authority was aware of
    the source of resident opposition: "The majority of those [residents] against demolition
    cited the reason that they had been told that renovation was planned and no mention
    was made of demolition in the lengthy planning process of Jervay." Source: Section A.
    General Provisions, Resident Involvement. Demolition Plan submitted to HUD by the
    Wilmington Housing Authority, July 1, 1994.
24 "Jervay Place Update," *The Journal*, October 13, 1994: 1.
25 Given the organizational structure of public housing, it is difficult for resident organiza-
    tions to circumvent the local public housing authority (PHA) and deal directly with the
    Department of Housing and Urban Development. Resident organizations address claims
    to the local PHA, the local PHA addresses the HUD Field Office, the field office com-
    municates with the Office of Public and Indian Housing at HUD.
26 The modem and the monthly Internet service was funded by a grant from the Z. Smith
    Reynolds Foundation awarded to the Department of Public Service and Extended
    Education at the University of North Carolina at Wilmington.
27 In later months, WISE would provide technical assistance for the Jervay site's URL and
    free storage on its server.
28 This site plan is available at Jervay's Web site (http://www.wilmington.net/jervay).
29 Text and drawings from the site plan are available online through Jervay's Web site
    (http://www.wilmington.net/jervay).
30 Because negotiations with the housing authority over final designs of Jervay Place are
    undergoing, the resident organization has requested these details remain unidentified.
31 Letter from Wilmington Housing Authority of May 10, 1995.
32 Student involvement in the development of the Jervay home page is a model of partici-
    patory research which is guided by the principle that both the process and product of
    social research be collaborative and address issues of direct concern to the community.
    Although the community group sets the agenda for research, student interns reap the
    benefits of applied research. The history and current issues involving Jervay Place are a
    mainspring of sociological topics, including those of federal legislation and funding and
    collective action among historically disadvantaged social groups.
33 "Plan for Razing Jervay Wins OK," *Wilmington Star News*, Thursday, April 17, 1995: A4.
34 Williams uses "hard to reach" to describe the difficulty of access both to disadvantaged
    persons demanding political and economic power and to researchers seeking to docu-
    ment and analyze the social worlds of historically marginalized social groups; see
    Williams (1989).
35 See discussions of results from the Information and Directory Services (MIDS) survey,
    conducted in October 1994 (http://www.mids.org/index.html) and the Graphics,
    Visualization, & Usability (GVU) World Wide Web User Survey, Fourth Survey, October
    10–November 10, 1995. Survey of 23,000 Internet users. The GVU Center is a research

center affiliated with Georgia Tech's College of Computing COC (http://www.cc.gatech.edu/gvu/user_surveys/survey-10–1995). In the GVU survey, the estimated median income of Internet users is in the range of $50,000 to $60,000. The national median income is $36,950 according to the 1993 US Census.

36 Graphics, Visualization, & Usability World Wide Web User Survey, Fourth Survey, October 10–November 10, 1995 (http://www.cc.gatech.edu/gvu/user_surveys/survey-10–1995).

References

Byrd, John Timothy. 1976. "The Disenfranchisement of Blacks in New Hanover County, North Carolina," master's thesis, Department of History, University of North Carolina at Chapel Hill.

Cripps, Thomas R. 1901. "Introduction," in Jack Thorne [pseudonym for David Bryant Fulton], *Hanover: The Persecution of the Lowly. A Story of the Wilmington Massacre*. M.C.L. Hill Press. Reprinted 1969. New York: Arno.

Davis, Mike. 1992. "Fortress Los Angeles: The Militarization of Urban Space," in *Variations on a Theme Park*, edited by Michael Sorkin. New York: Noonday Press.

Edmonds, Helen G. 1951. "The Wilmington Race Riot," in her *The Negro and Fusion Politics in North Carolina, 1894–1901*. New York: Russell & Russell.

Feenberg, Andrew. 1991. *Critical Theory of Technology*. New York: Oxford University Press.

Frederick, Howard. 1993. "Computer Networks and the Emergence of Global Civil Society," in *Global Networks: Computers and International Communication*, edited by Linda M. Harasim. Cambridge, MA: MIT Press.

Freeman, Lance. 1995. "Residential Segregation in North Carolina: a Barrier to African American Opportunities," report issued by the North Carolina Institute of Minority Economic Development, April.

Gerard, Philip. 1994. *Cape Fear Rising*. Winston-Salem, NC: J.F. Blair.

Hamelink, C.J. 1991. *Communication: The Most Violated Human Right*. Stockholm: Inter Press Service Dispatch.

Harasim, Linda M. 1993. "Networlds: Networks as Social Space," in *Global Networks: Computers and International Communication*, edited by Linda M. Harasim. Cambridge, MA: MIT Press.

Jones, Steven G. 1995. "Understanding Community in the Information Age," in *Cybersociety: Computer-Mediated Communication and Community*, edited by Steven G. Jones. Thousand Oaks, CA and London: Sage.

Kornegay, Ralph B. 1969 "The Wilmington Riot, November 10, 1898," master's thesis, Appalachian State University.

New York Times. 1995. "Computer Gap Worries Blacks," May 25: B1.

Prather, Leon. 1984. *We Have Taken a City*. Cranbury, NJ: Associated Press.

Thomas, Larry Reni. 1993. *The True Story Behind the Wilmington Ten*. Hampton, VA: U.B. and U.S. Communications Systems.

Thorne, Jack [pseudonym for David Bryant Fulton]. 1901. *Hanover: The Persecution of the Lowly. A Story of the Wilmington Massacre*. M.C.L. Hill Press. Reprinted 1969. New York: Arno.

Tilly, Charles. 1978. *From Mobilization to Revolution*. New York: Random House.

US Department of Commerce. 1990. *Population and Housing Characteristics for Census Tracts and Block Numbering Areas:Wilmington, NC MSA*. Washington, DC: US Government Printing Office.

Williams, Terry. 1989. *The Cocaine Kids*. Reading, MA: Addison-Wesley.

Wilmington Housing Authority. 1995. *Re-Exam Recap Report*, February 9.

Index